BIRTHMARK

To Trudie –

BIRTHMARK

With many best wishes to a lovely lady whom I've 'met' through Sally Ann – Hope you enjoy my journey.

Diana

DIANA O'LEARY

TATE PUBLISHING
AND ENTERPRISES, LLC

June 2015 Florida

Published by Tate Publishing & Enterprises, LLC
127 E. Trade Center Terrace | Mustang, Oklahoma 73064 USA
1.888.361.9473 | www.tatepublishing.com

Tate Publishing is committed to excellence in the publishing industry. The company reflects the philosophy established by the founders, based on Psalm 68:11,
"The Lord gave the word and great was the company of those who published it."

Published in the United States of America

ISBN: 978-1-62510-581-3
1. Biography & Autobiography / Personal Memoirs
13.08.23

PREFACE

As I collected my mail from the post office, I noted with pleasure that I had a letter from my daughter, Tara, who was a student at the University of Miami. She wrote that she was reading her homework for her English class and that it reminded her of a conversation that we had had at home.

Tara continued with an excerpt from 'To My Dear Children' by the seventeenth century American author Anne Bradstreet.

> This book by any yet unread,
> I leave for you when I am dead,
> That being gone, here you may find
> What was your living mother's mind.
> Make use of what I leave in love,
> And God shall bless you from above.

Tara went on to write:

> Dear Mum, as I read this, my thoughts immediately went to you. I never want you to leave me. You are inside me and always will be until I am no more, but at moments of weakness I would like to have something to go to and be near you when I can no longer hear your voice or touch your hand.

Birthmark is dedicated primarily to my daughter, Tara Devon, and I am humbled by her beautiful words, wanting to have something to remind her of me. However, it made me think of mothers in general, and I realised that after a woman becomes a wife and mother, their past lives are like figments of their imagination. They are so involved with babies, toddlers, preteens, and so forth, and the children are so immersed in their own lives, that Mum is just that—it rarely occurs to our children that mothers too were children and had a life before they became Mum—so I wanted to encourage mothers to share their memories with their children.

Thus, with the moving request from my daughter, I have written my memoirs so that she will know the person who was her mother, and I will leave her with the message that no matter what you endure, so long as you have faith, miracles do happen.

Yesterday is but today's memory—tomorrow is today's dream.

—Kahlil Gibran

1

The bedroom was large and painted light blue with white trim. I pretended I was interested in looking out through the top of the windows at the flame flowers of the Poinciana tree and watching the crows flying around. The curtains moved gently, disturbed by the swirling fan, but I couldn't hear the hum of the fan, as all I could hear was the desperate coughing of my mother. Looking up at her as she lay on her large bed propped up by many pillows, I knew she had had another asthma attack, and my three-year-old soul told me to stay and protect her. I watched her as she put the little bottle she called her puffer to her mouth and squeezed the rubber bottom, and eventually the coughing subsided.

Looking down at me, she managed a faint smile, and I said in a serious voice, "you worry me," and left the room.

I was the eldest of the three daughters of Gordon Munro and Patricia Pantin. Gordon and Patricia had met at one of the many dances at the Grand Oriental Hotel, the GOH as it was affectionately known. The fabled old hotel, which was opposite the harbour, was the venue to the start of many love affairs in Colombo, Ceylon. All the young single men and women would attend the GOH in the hope of finding a mate, while they danced under the twirl of the long fans to the romantic music of the live orchestra.

Gordon was the third of four sons of Donald Munro, a Scottish timber merchant and the director and manager of the A & G Paterson's Sawmills at Silverbank, Aberdeenshire. He was also the provost of Banchory in Scotland from 1822 to 1828. Donald Munro received the OBE, from Queen Victoria for the immense charity work he did during the Great War. His wife, Lizzie Glen Munro, was a well-known opera singer in Banchory and an illustrious hostess. Thus,

Gordon came from a wealthy background and grew up with every creature comfort.

The family home, known as Ravenswood, Banchory, was the setting for many a renowned social gathering and often starred the famous Sir Harry Lauder whom Donald Munro had introduced to his affluent world. In his early twenties, Gordon decided to move to London and work for the Bank of Scotland. He was an accountant by profession, and while there, was offered a job by the firm of Harrison and Crossfield & Eastern Produce to work in their offices in Colombo, Ceylon.

My mother, Patricia Pantin, was the middle daughter of Vincent Pantin, an impoverished aristocrat who spoke eight languages, including Sanskrit. Despite his mother's royal lineage, dating back in a direct line to Charlemagne and William the Conqueror, Vincent was disowned and banished by his family in England and sent to Australia. In Melbourne, Vincent met Edith Elton, a beautiful petite lady with a lovely singing voice, who became his wife. The family was very poor. Despite Vincent's brilliant mind and having written several books, including "Britain is Pawned", he thought work was an anathema, so the family lived on charity.

Patricia had to leave the Loretto Convent at twelve years old, as her parents could not afford to pay the fees. She managed to educate herself with the help of her parents' tutelage and by reading; she was a voracious reader. In her late teens, she started modeling to help pay the bills and discovered that she had a talent for writing, so became a journalist. Her real passion, however, was the stage, and she found work acting in small parts of various productions. At the age of twenty-seven, Patricia was disillusioned with her life, and together with one hundred-and-thirty pounds, her talents, her dreams and a one-way ticket, she left Australia for the island of Ceylon, which was once described by Marco Polo as "the finest island in the world."

The island, shaped like a tear drop in the Indian Ocean and situated at the tip of India and just above the equator, was an island of coconut palm-fringed beaches, jungles with exotic animals (especially the revered elephants), rubber crops, magnificent tea plantations, rice paddy-fields, and gems. It held the history of ages past, the temple ruins, the palaces of bygone royalty, and eclectic religions: Hindu and the prominent Buddhist religion. That incandescent island had it all, including intrigue and mysticism.

Patricia was beautiful, erudite, talented and, fascinating and much in demand at the GOH dances. It wasn't long after her arrival in Colombo that she was offered the job as the beauty, health, and etiquette advisor for women on Radio Ceylon, and was asked to write in the women's column of the daily newspapers. Patricia had many admirers, but Gordon was the most persistent beau, and five years after her arrival to Colombo, she became pregnant.

A drawing of Dad by Mother

Years later she made it clear to me that I was not wanted, especially not at that time. I was often told that her pregnancy was an accident and that she was not in love with Gordon; however, despite many a gin bath, I was on the way. She often reminded me that if it hadn't been for me, she would never have married my father and probably would have had a much happier life. Fortunately, I learned very early on, to try not to be offended by her many hurtful remarks. Anyway, for the sake of each of their families they married and to the sound of Beethoven in a humble home in the area known as Slave Island, assisted by a wonderful lady doctor, Mother gave birth to me on January thirteenth, 1942. My mother told me that when I looked at her after my birth, she knew that I disliked her. We obviously were not off to a good start! The area, Slave Island, still exists today. The name dates back to when the African slaves (Kaffirs) were brought to Ceylon by the Portuguese in 1630, and were used by the Dutch to build the Fort in Colombo.

World War II was already in existence in Europe when on December seventh, 1941, Japan attacked the Pacific fleet at Pearl Harbour, and the United States declared war with Japan. About six months after my birth, my parents, fearing for my mother's and my safety, decided we should leave Ceylon, as Trincomalle—a major town in the northeastern part of the island with a fine natural harbour and one of the most important Asian seaports—became the nerve centre of the Allies for southeast Asia and thus attracted the hostile attention of the Japanese. So my young mother and her new baby took the dangerous voyage on the "SS Amsterdam" to Australia to stay with her parents in Melbourne. Apart from all the danger of travelling during the war and coping with her baby, my mother had the added concern of praying I did not die, as I had contracted bacillary dysentery and was very sick. As I look back on my life, that was the first of several near-death encounters. I survived, thanks to the determination of my mother, a great doctor on board ship, and lots of glucose and water.

Mother and I returned to Colombo and to Dad a year later. I was eighteen months old, walking, and gorgeous with big blue eyes, a mass of tight-red curls and an infectious smile. We lived in a beautiful house called "Roath" with a lovely garden and frangipani (Temple) trees, jacaranda and the flame tree, Poinciana. Even at that young age, I loved trees. I had a wonderful nanny, a little dog called Toby, and a handsome Persian cat, Smokey. I was a happy little girl and even happier when my sister, Vanessa, arrived in September of 1944.

My parents, thanks mainly to my father, belonged to all the social clubs, so as little children there were always lots of parties to attend.

The Sinhalese staff at those various clubs took pride in serving their white masters, and in the years of growing up in Ceylon, it seemed natural to have servants. We would spend many afternoons at the beach, and in the mornings I would attend a small nursery school. My young life was busy and fun.

I had just had my fourth birthday, and it was time for my father to take his six-month tri-annual holiday. The four of us travelled to Scotland in the British Isles in order that Dad could introduce his wife and daughters to his family. I have no memory of the visit, but later my mother told me that the family did not like her—as they found her far too flamboyant for the likes of the dour Munro clan—and during the visit, my father behaved so badly, being drunk most of the time and flirting outrageously with the wives of his brothers, that his family disowned him, and there was never any further contact with them after we left. Mother told me that when she married Dad, she did not know that he was an alcoholic, as he was teetotal at the time.

We returned to Colombo and to a different home. Toby and Smokey weren't there, which made me sad. The house was big, and there was a cook and several servants. I started at a new dance school, learning ballet and tap dancing. I wanted to go every day, as I loved the classes. I really liked going in our rickshaw, which was like the family car; though as I grew older, I felt that it was a lot of work for the poor coolie who pulled it. His sinuous arms and thin back hidden by a torn shirt – his skinny legs, and bare feet, which would go pat-pat on the hot road—would make me wonder how such a frail man was able to pull the heavy rickshaw with adult passengers and two children, and go at a steady speed, but it was the usual form of transport for those who couldn't afford a car.

Then things changed for me. After a few months of being back in Colombo, my mother took me to a convent and left me there. I vividly remember sitting on the floor of the large wood-panelled assembly room and sobbing. I felt very alone and didn't understand why I was being sent away from home. The only comfort I had was my thumb, which went into my mouth every night for years and years. That episode in my young life troubled me, and as an adult, I finally asked my mother why she'd abandoned me, she gave a stumbling explanation that she couldn't cope with me, Vanessa, her busy work life and looking after Dad. She really found it a struggle to tell me this and was surprised I had remembered. She said she was sorry. Her apology did little to eradicate the hurtful memories.

Mother also told me she was having a hard time coming to terms with the fact that her husband was an alcoholic and the terrible embarrassment his behaviour had caused her while at the family home in Scotland. In addition, she didn't want me to observe the fights between her and Dad, and thought it best for me to be away. At four years old, it was my first experience of learning how to cope on my own and to come to terms with a stressful situation—and that crying didn't help. Fortunately, I wasn't left in the convent for too long, as I needed to have my tonsils and adenoids removed. I was admitted to the Joseph Fraser Nursing Home in Colombo where I was so spoiled and ate lots of green ice cream!

Upon my recovery, I was happy to be at home again with Dad, Vanessa and Mother, however, my mother had a bad temper. She would find it necessary, in her opinion, to spank me with a strap. I suppose there were times when I was trying to get her attention, as it was obvious to me that Vanessa was her favourite. Once I threw her glasses out of the window. I was being mischievous and it made her very angry, so in a fit of rage, I was beaten with the belt despite the futile remonstrations of my dad. I didn't cry, and made a mental note not to enrage my mother again, no more innocent pranks.

In my younger years, I learnt to do everything possible to try to keep the peace in our family. It was upsetting to see my parents fighting. I never wanted Vanessa to be around if Mother was shouting and hitting Dad. After those episodes he would promise Mother on the Bible that he wouldn't drink, his promise would last until the next upset. Mother usually had to take to her bed to recover from the bad asthma attacks that were caused by the awful rows with Dad.

Mother was offered a job to teach elocution at St. Thomas College out at Mount Lavinia, and for a short time the three of us lived at the Mount Lavinia Hotel. Dad would join us for the weekends. The hotel was a little outside of Colombo and had the most beautiful beach. Our stay at Mt. Lavinia was happy. I loved playing on the beach, collecting shells, watching the catamarans coming and going, and was fascinated by the fishermen and their nets. After building sand castles with Vanessa, I would sometimes lie on the beach looking up at the tall coconut palm trees—swaying in the gentle breeze, giving shade and casting their shadows. Occasionally, I would see a coolie with a rope tied between his feet, skirt up the trunk of a tree to loosen a coconut or two. We would often drink the coconut water directly from the shell and then enjoy the meat.

Although we had a nanny, I was protective of Vanessa, especially as we had to be careful of the jellyfish. I was mesmerised as I looked at them with their translucent bodies and long tentacles, and it was hard for me to imagine that they could be so harmful. It was fun living in that beautiful hotel with its old world charm and enjoying the amenities. I realised early on that I loved my creature comforts! I later learnt that the Mount Lavinia Hotel was once the home of the British Governor, Sir Thomas Maitland, who built it as his official residence around 1806 and named it after his mistress. It didn't become a hotel until 1895.

I celebrated my fifth birthday at the hotel, and Mother arranged for a few children to attend my party. We were in a private room and had fun playing pass the cushion and musical chairs among other games.

During the day Mother would give me lessons, helping me to read and write, and the nanny would play with Vanessa. Mother wanted us to learn the piano from an early age—I think mainly due to the fact that her mother was a brilliant pianist and she hoped that one of us would have been given the gift—Vanessa and I went a couple of times a week to our piano teacher, who lived in a little house within walking distance of the hotel.

The lady had a lovely black-and-white dog, which Vanessa and I would look forward to playing with before our lessons. One day mother received a note saying that Mrs. Perera's dog was suspected to have rabies, and because we had been with the dog we would have to have the rabies injections. Mother was terribly upset when she learned it would mean that her small daughters, ages five and two-and-a-half would have to have seven injections in their stomachs, which would be given over several weeks. The doctor came to Mrs. Perera's house to give us the injections. Mother could not bear to witness our suffering, so it was Dad who was there to console and endure our cries and fears. I would brace myself as I saw the long needle approach my tummy and tried to be brave for my sister. The dog was killed, and later on my parents were told that the dog did not have rabies.

Mother, Diana and Vanessa

2

The time came for us to leave Mount Lavinia Hotel. Mother had been offered several jobs to teach elocution in many of the schools in Colombo. I was happy we were returning home to be with Dad. I started kindergarten at a proper school called Bishop's College. My nanny took me there in our rickshaw. The school was near a lake that didn't have much water in it, but had lots of birds. At school I loved having a little desk and chair and being with other children. Sometimes I would do something wrong and would have to put out my hand to have the teacher hit it with her ruler. Of course, it stung a little. If one of us didn't behave well, the teacher would grab us by our ear and take us up to the blackboard to make sure we concentrated on what she was saying!

After lunch we would have to rest with our arms folded on the desk and our heads on our arms. If it wasn't too hot outside, we would have our lessons under the Poinciana tree. I returned to my dance school, and even at that young age was told that I could never be a ballerina, as I was growing too tall. That, however, didn't deter me from continuing ballet and totally believing that I was destined to be a ballerina.

At school I contracted chicken pox and was ill for a time. When I had recovered, we moved out of Colombo to an estate in the low country. I imagine my father had been sent there for a while. I enjoyed being in a house with a garden and especially visiting the tea factory. I shall never forget the wonderful aroma of the fresh tea. I did miss not attending school. Although my mother was always writing and gave the impression that she was enjoying being with us in the house, I sensed that she was missing her work at the schools. It also worried me that Mother kept a machete near her all the time. She told me it was in case snakes intruded. We didn't stay on that estate very long and returned to Colombo. Mother, who was already established as a teacher of elocution, began teaching at more and more schools. In addition, she was instrumental in producing many of the school plays. She also continued her radio broadcasts, talking to women about health and beauty, and writing in the local newspapers.

I went to several different schools during that time—the American School in Colombo for a term, a term here and a term or two there, never staying at one school for too long. I am not too sure of the reason, but I suppose it had something to do with Mother teaching at those different schools, and if she had a disagreement with the headmaster she would leave and so I would be removed from the school.

Mother always found an acting part in her end-of-term plays for Vanessa and me, and as my wish was to dance, I was usually cast with the other dancers. Mother was so busy she didn't have much time for my father, and thus he took to working late most evenings. He tried hard to be with us during the weekends. I loved being with him and the smell of his pipe tobacco. He was very funny and made me laugh.

Shortly after my sixth birthday, I was enrolled as a day student at St. Bridget's Convent. We had moved to the Galle Face Apartments, opposite the famous Galle Face Hotel. Dad was given a car and driver by his firm. We had a Hillman Minx and a marvelous driver called Silva; it was so exciting. It was a happy time for me as I saw a lot of my parents, and life between them seemed peaceful. It was one of those times when Mother had made Dad swear on the Bible that he would go teetotal, which he did.

Sometimes at the weekends, we would all go to the swimming club, which only allowed white people to be members. I loved going there as I was with other children, not that I made any friends. It was just a retreat from being at home. I would notice the rich white children ordering the servants around and asking to be brought their drinks and sign the little chits that were presented to them. It was a different world, especially not seeing any Tamil or Sinhalese children. As I hadn't had swimming lessons and wasn't able to swim, I would enjoy being in the shallow end of the big pool or in the children's pool. My parents didn't swim and didn't belong to the ex-pat set, though due to my father's job, we were members of the club. Mother was a working lady, and because of her beauty and involvement with the people of Ceylon she was not really accepted by the white ladies of the community. It was difficult for Dad to join the men, as he had to be careful not to drink. I realised we were different and in a strange way was happy with how things were.

Mother tried to make sure that we had a normal life as children; she and Dad took us to visit the beautiful Peradenya Gardens and the Dehiwala Zoo, where I fell in love with the elephants. On Sundays in the cool of the early evenings, Dad, Mother, Vanessa and I would walk on the Galle Face Green, which was a large area of flat land like a park but without trees. The Green wasn't very green as it was dry in Colombo, except during the monsoon periods when the rains came, but to have that wide open space where the breeze from the Indian Ocean enabled us to fly our kites was so much fun. Many Ceylonese families came out on Sunday to enjoy walking and playing on the famous Green.

There were a few cinemas in Colombo, and occasionally Dad would find the time to take me to see the musical films, which he enjoyed, and it was a treat for me to go with him. One day both my father and mother, knowing how passionate I was about ballet, took me to see Moira Shearer in "The Red Shoes", and as I left the cinema, I knew I was going to be a ballerina like her. After all, we both had red hair!

When Mother wanted to shop, she would take Vanessa and me to Cargill's, the Harrods of Colombo. Cargill's was an impressive old building, a nineteenth century department store that sold luxury imported goods for the benefit of the British tea-planters and ex-pats. I loved visiting that shop and was always curious about all the beautiful things I saw there. We didn't have the car as Dad needed it, so we rode in the rickshaw through the Pettah market, which was noisy and colourful with the women in their bright saris, lots of little stalls selling all sorts of bric-a-brac, and many food stalls emitting exotic aromas. There were coolies spitting their chewing beetle or slumped on the pavement, having consumed too much arrack. The intoxicating atmosphere was different to the quiet area where we lived, and I knew that at the end of those visits we would stop at the Sunday tea rooms and have an ice cream sundae, which was a really big treat. The tea rooms, with their potted palms, large fans, quaint tables and chairs, always bustled with lots of people, was my idea of heaven.

I was enjoying attending St. Bridget's Convent in Cinnamon Gardens as a day girl. I continued with my dance lessons and liked living in the Galle Face flat, though I missed not being able to have a cat or dog. Mother was busy with her teaching at the many schools and producing the end-of-term school plays. It was during that time that Mother confided to us that she was pregnant and was expecting our sibling around the time of my seventh birthday. I was excited that the baby would be a birthday gift, but it didn't arrive on that day, so I had a little party, which I celebrated with a few friends and a big chocolate cake.

A few days later, Vanessa and I developed whopping cough. Mother quickly left the apartment and went to live at the nursing home. The Joseph Fraser Nursing Home was comfortable with large rooms, so Mother was happy to live there and receive excellent attention while waiting for her baby to be born. The new governess, Matilda, had already moved into the flat a few days earlier to look after us. Our baby sister arrived five days after my birthday, and was named Sylvan Gail. Vanessa and I were anxious to see her, but as we were contagious, we could only wave to Mother, who was holding Sylvan, across the compound at the nursing home complex.

Before too long Sylvan was with us at the apartment and life with our baby sister was happy; we saw more of Mother than usual. Matilda, our governess, was a mature woman, experienced in looking after small babies. As Mother was able to leave Sylvan with Matilda, she spent more time with Vanessa and me, taking us to the dressmaker to have new clothes made and to shop for shoes and other necessities. I loved pretty dresses and was allowed to take part in the choosing of the materials and the designing of our dresses.

We also had to visit the dentist, something I wasn't too sure about, but when the dentist showed me the mercury that he would use as the filling in my tooth (by placing it in the palm of my hand to play with), I felt sure the procedure wouldn't be too painful, despite the terrible noise of the drill.

It wasn't long before I understood why Matilda was hired rather than the usual nanny. Matilda was a governess and a responsible woman who was experienced in taking care of new babies and small children. I also realised why we were having clothes made, visiting the dentist, and generally spending more time with Mother. It was three years since Dad's last vacation when we visited Scotland, so he was due his six months holiday, and both he and Mother were going to Europe. Arrangements had been made for me to be a boarder at St. Bridget's Convent, and one of the small apartments on the grounds of the convent (kept for foreign teachers) was rented for Matilda, Vanessa, and Sylvan. Sylvan was six months old when our parents left us.

3

I was a boarder at the convent, the youngest at seven-and-a-half years old. My bed was a little high for me, but I was tall for my age, so I'd climb up onto it by stepping on the rung at the end. All the beds looked like hospital beds, and of course, I was taught how to fold hospital corners when making it in the mornings. At first it was a little difficult but I managed eventually. Being near the window in the front row of the line of beds made me happy, as I was able to see the tops of the trees and imagine I was in a tree house!

We were awakened each morning by the Mother on duty who rang a small bell. After falling out of bed onto our knees to say our prayers, we would then make a dash for the washrooms. I had to learn to conform to a different life. My Mother hadn't told me what to expect, though I doubt she knew. I copied the other girls by cleaning my teeth with powdered charcoal in the palm of my left hand and then wetting my right index finger, pressing it into the charcoal and using it to rub my teeth—no toothbrush! I suppose that added to all of the trouble I would have with my teeth and gums later on in my life. Apart from washing one's face, the other ritual was holding one nostril, and with the water in the palm of the other hand, sniffing up the water in alternate nostrils. We didn't have the luxury of tissues, so it seemed that by doing that procedure we could clear our noses. If you did want to blow your nose, you would press your thumb to one nostril and blow out with the other, releasing your snot into the air. Of course, one should be outside to do that. As a well-bred convent girl, I was not encouraged to indulge in that habit!

Going to the toilet was also an experience, as there was no toilet paper, only a large bucket filled with water and a small empty tin, which we would fill and proceed to wash our backsides, and there was some form of paper to dry oneself. Needless to say, the floor was always wet. I couldn't help feeling that those new experiences were good for me, as they made me understand to expect the unexpected and always keep an open mind. I was also learning quickly how to be self-sufficient.

Being the only white girl in the school with my freckled skin and red hair, I was easily recognisable. To me there was never any colour distinction, everyone was the same. The large open dormitory was for all the boarders, half for those who had not started to menstruate and the other half for those who had, and they were given privacy by being able to draw a curtain around their bed. I tried not to think of missing my parents. Living in a school rather than at home, and not being allowed to see my sisters during term time was a little difficult.

I became sick with a high fever and felt very alone as I lay in my dormitory bed. I missed not having any home comforts, as it was all quite austere; my thumb was my only consolation. The nuns were attentive and took care of me, and I looked forward to the school day being over, so that I could see the girls in the evening when they came to the dormitory to sleep.

St. Bridget's Convent was founded by the Irish sisters of the Good Shepherd, and their motto was "Gently and firmly." Every morning I would put on my white uniform, pin on my green tie and run down the stone staircase to Mass, and then to the refectory for breakfast. We sat on benches at long tables, and the Mother in charge would come and prod our backs if we were slouching. We had to sit up very straight. We then proceeded with lessons, learning the piano, going to ballet and doing everything involved in the school curriculum, always under the watchful eyes of the Irish nuns, who were strict when it came to behaviour, manners, respect and courtesy. I learned well, and the harsh discipline at an early age helped me through every phase of my life. Heather Fairweather, a Burgher of Ceylonese/Portuguese descent who had a lighter skin than the Sinhalese children, was my best friend. One evening as we were preparing for bed, we saw the biggest sunset. The sun was enormous and so red it frightened us.

We thought it was the end of the world! When half term arrived, Heather was unable to invite me to her home, which made me sad. At that time there wasn't any room in the apartment with my sisters; I thought I would be alone in the big dormitory for half term. The nuns, however, had arranged for me to spend the four days with a Sinhalese girl from my class. It would be a new adventure for me.

Padma's father came to collect us; he was very friendly and said how happy he was that Padma would have my company over the half-term holiday. I settled back into their car with all the windows open for whatever breeze we could get. There wasn't much conversation, so I tried to observe and absorb everything I saw as we drove out of Colombo through the little villages, waving to the women simply dressed in their sarongs and short blouses and to the children playing by the roadside. I particularly observed the sleeping dogs and wished I had one with me. We passed the rubber trees with the small cups attached to their trunks, the bamboo-roofed huts, and people with buckets on their heads having collected water from the pump.

The long, hot drive seemed endless, and the sun had started to set.

Finally Padma said, "there's our house."

It was a small bungalow on the edge of a paddy field. It looked pretty, nestled in some trees. There was no electricity, only kerosene lamps, and the water was pumped from a well. Although everything was different to what I was accustomed to, I felt right at home, as the Sinhalese family was so welcoming and I was eager for them to know how much I wanted to be with them.

Rice and various delicious aromatic curries were spread out on mats on the floor, and we all ate with our fingers. I learned how to eat curry and rice with my right hand, to roll the rice and curry with the tips of my fingers and push it in my mouth with my thumb; one should never dirty one's palm. I was a little frightened to go to the lavatory, as it was dark outside, but the mother kindly came with me, carrying her oil lantern, which she left by the open door, and stood outside while she waited for me. The outhouse, as it was called, was a hole in the ground, but it did have a wooden seat (many didn't).

However, I didn't like it very much, and hoped I wouldn't fall in the hole. I slept in the same room with Padma on a mat on the floor. I was very tired by that time.

Staying with the family was another new experience. I was grateful to them for their kindness and for giving me much attention and affection. As we drove back to the convent, I thought about the wonderful weekend that I had spent. I had enjoyed the simplicity and the kindness of the family, and living for a few days like the majority of people in Ceylon. As I said my prayers on my knees that night, I prayed for my mother and dad, but sometimes I did wonder if my parents thought or even cared how we were all doing. Little Sylvan was so young, just a baby. Mother should have been with her.

After half-term my greatest excitement was preparing for the day of my first Holy Communion. I could hardly contain my emotions at the thought of Jesus coming to me. I was always a little envious when attending Mass to see the other people receiving communion. Heather, I and two other girls were the first communicants. We had catechism classes every day for weeks, and finally the great day arrived. The nuns had made me a long, white dress, and I was given a beautiful mother-of-pearl rosary, which I carry with me to this day. I felt special despite being much taller than the other three girls.

The chapel was decorated with a mass of white flowers and filled with people. The singing of the nuns was like a heavenly choir. I was so excited to receive Jesus, I was glowing with happiness. Matilda and my sisters were at the Mass. I was sad that my parents weren't present to experience this most important day in my life. After Mass, Mother Superior invited me, Heather, her parents and the other two girls and their parents, to a celebration breakfast in the nun's dining room; it was a special treat. From that day on I felt different. I felt a great peace, knowing that Jesus was now my friend, my protector. He would always be with me, as up until that time when I knelt beside my bed every night to say my prayers, I didn't understand whom I was asking to take care of me, except Matthew, Mark, Luke and John, but on that day, I understood.

Soon it would be the end of the term, and we had to prepare for sports day. The large, dry lawn lay in front of the classrooms, and it was where we had the egg and spoon race, sack race, three-legged race, wheelbarrow race and many other races. The parents joined the children, and despite the heat, everyone seemed to have a grand time enjoying the free soft drinks and food. I was very good at those games and had a lot of fun in participating.

A few days later, it was time for the girls to leave for the holidays. I secretly wished I was going home with Heather, but instead I would be staying at the convent. I felt happy for my friends as I watched the cars come and go and to see the girls excited to be going home for their holidays. I couldn't help wondering where they were all going, what sort of homes they had. I stood next to the nuns, and they made me feel as if I was one of them, saying good-bye to the students; after all that was my home now.

Following the exodus, a strange quiet permeated the air, and I ran quickly to be with Matilda and my sisters in their rented apartment on the property. I moved into an adjoining room, which had become empty while the teacher was on holiday. During the days I would be alone. Matilda, Vanessa, and baby Sylvan had their own agenda, and as much as I loved them, I needed to do my own thing. There was no one my age staying at the convent, so I would wander around the grounds looking at the flowers, the caterpillars and the beautiful butterflies. I would stroll across to the main building of the convent and walk through the empty corridors, through the classrooms where the chairs were stacked on the desks, and go into the assembly room to do a little tap dance on the stage.

I remembered the last end of term performance that Mother had produced, and in my mind I could see the Sinhalese girls doing their exquisite dances and wished I could dance like them. Their hands were so pretty, and they were able to move their necks sideways. I had tried so hard to do that but never did manage the movement. I too had a small part. I was dressed in a beautiful white organdy dress, and in amongst my red curls I wore a headdress of white flowers. I sat on a white cushion, blowing bubbles out to the audience, while the choir behind sang, "I'm forever blowing bubbles." Jumping off the stage I felt that Mother had produced a lovely end-of-term show. As I left the assembly room, everything was so quiet; only the noise of the crows shattered the stillness.

Skipping along the verandahs outside the classrooms, I would think of the girls and how many would faint. At first it was frightening for me to see them faint, but then I became used to it and tried to help by rushing forward to sit them up, push their legs up and put their heads between their knees. I was grateful not to have fainted. Some of the girls found it too hot, though I don't recall being uncomfortable. We just became used to the heat. There was no such thing as air conditioning and I don't really remember ceiling fans. The classrooms had large windows, which were open on either side, taking advantage of whatever cross breeze was around.

I couldn't help thinking sometimes as I wandered the grounds alone, how strange it was that no one knew where I was. I didn't see anyone and felt that I had the whole of the empty convent to myself. I wasn't scared, as I knew Jesus was with me. One day, I decided to go upstairs and walk through the dormitory, curious to see if the beds behind the curtains were the same as mine. As I walked through the senior bathrooms, I heard a noise, and looking up, saw a man high up near the ceiling where the pipes ran. When he looked down at me, he lifted his sarong and exposed himself. He was a man working there, a plumber, I supposed, but he gave me such a fright and made me feel so unclean that I fled down the stairs, tore through the empty corridors, and ran to the chapel, asking Jesus to please forgive me. I thought that I had just witnessed the devil himself, knowing that something very wrong had happened. I was too ashamed to tell a nun. What if she didn't believe me? I decided not to venture towards that part of the convent again, but restrict my movements near the grounds where Matilda and my sisters lived and around the chapel area.

During those long holidays, I never stopped going to my dance classes, which included tap, ballet, Scottish dancing and reels; I was very good and won many certificates. On the important days, Matilda would bring Vanessa and Sylvan to watch me. I loved spending time with my sisters. I also looked forward each day in the hope of receiving postcards from Mother. Mother would write to us from the places she visited in France and Italy, telling us all about her adventures. I was happy that my mother was having a lovely holiday, but I also wanted the time to go quickly, so that she and Dad would be back with us again.

I did wonder why my father never wrote, nor did my mother ever mention anything about him. I prayed that they weren't fighting.

However, years later Mother told me that Dad had stayed for almost all of the six months in the South of France and spent most of his money at the casinos in Beaulieu-sur-Mer and Nice and that he was drinking heavily. After being in France and spending a miserable time with Dad, she left him and travelled to Italy, spending the rest of the holiday by herself.

In the mornings when I attended Mass, I would ask Jesus to please bring my parents back quickly, as I missed them and us not all being together in a proper home. During that time I made friends with an Australian teacher, Mary, who was staying in the convent apartments next door to Matilda and my sisters. She had a beautiful German Shepherd dog, and I delighted in playing with him for hours. We had all the grounds of the convent to play in. Mary was kind to me and became a special friend. I was so pleased to have her company. At dusk we would walk her dog, and when we stopped by the big Bo tree, she would show me the bats hanging on the branches; it was fascinating and I hoped that they would not accidentally dive into our hair.

Although I didn't have anyone of my age to play with, I never felt lonely. I was quite happy being on my own. I realised that I enjoyed my own company, and talked continuously to Jesus. He was my friend. In the middle of those holidays, I became ill with mumps and was taken to a room that was used by the nuns as a guest room for visiting clergy. The room was in a courtyard not too far from the chapel. When I looked out of the window, however, all I could see moving were the crows. I felt isolated and tried not to feel too abandoned. The monsoon rains had also started, so at times I couldn't see anything other than the rain. As I started to feel better, I worked on jigsaw puzzles and read books. I enjoyed painting and colouring, those activities kept me busy. I knew Jesus was with me, and that was a big comfort. The only people I saw and spoke to were the nun who brought me my food and the doctor who checked on me. I realised it was a growing period so that I could learn to know myself, to accept what couldn't be changed. I was, however, happy when I was well again and able to see my sisters.

4

I don't recall Christmas nor celebrating my eighth birthday or Sylvan's first birthday. My parents hadn't returned as yet. When they did at the end of January 1950, we moved out of the protection of the convent to a house that had been rented off Boyd Place. I was excited to see my mother and father and receive the gifts that they had brought for us—especially the dolls Mother brought, as they were dressed in the costumes of the countries she had visited. Mother seemed upset that Sylvan didn't recognise her; after all she had been with Matilda for all of her little life. It was a difficult time for Sylvan, and it didn't help matters that the holiday hadn't brought my parents together. In fact, they were fighting so much, I was scared, especially when Vanessa and Sylvan were able to hear all the shouting.

I had just started the new term at St. Bridget's when Mother and Dad returned to Colombo. As soon as they were settled in the house they had rented, I returned to the convent as a day girl. I knew that Mother was going to have a meeting with Mother Superior, and that afternoon when she returned home as I was doing my homework, she told me that I would not be continuing at St. Bridget's Convent, because she had had a falling out with Mother Aloysius; and from that day she never taught at the convent again.

Mother enrolled me at Bishop's College where I had attended kindergarten, but this time I would be a boarder and in a different part of the school. This prestigious college was founded by the Anglican Church and was one of the earliest mission schools of the Church of England in Ceylon. At first I was unhappy at leaving the convent, as I was used to it and felt settled there. I was really sad when I learned that the new school wasn't Catholic, which meant that I wouldn't be able to go to daily Mass nor receive Holy Communion.

I was learning to become used to disappointments and quickly settled in to my new school. I continued with my piano lessons, "The Blue Danube" was my party piece. I didn't enjoy learning to play the piano, as I had to practice while the other girls were out playing. I liked the physical education class, which we had daily and always started off by us pupils carrying books on our heads while we walked back and forth in the assembly hall. Our PE teacher was determined that we would attain perfect posture and have very straight backs!

Mother taught elocution at the school, and I had to attend her classes. She always seemed to pick on me, which was embarrassing. I did not like going to her classes where I had to call her Miss Pantin. I knew she was my mother, but in her class I was just one of her students. Mother also produced the end-of-term school play. I didn't act in her part of the production, but was in the dancing section. I danced Manuel de Falla's 'Fire Dance' wearing a red-and-orange costume and danced my heart out, so exhilarating and exciting. I loved every frenetic second, and when I finished, received enormous applause. I think Mother was really proud of me.

Sports day was also fun, and I competed in all the races. I was a fast runner, hurdle and long jumper. My parents did not attend. I don't ever remember them attending any school event, unless I was in one of Mother's productions. While I was running in the flat race and almost arriving first at the finish line, the girl running next to me tripped me, and I fell on my wrist, breaking it. After the doctor had set my wrist, I was in the infirmary for a few days.

My doctor was very nice, and I think that as he had met Mother, wanted to be sure that he had taken good care of me. He therefore appeared anxious for me to acknowledge that I had received his best attention, which I knew I had. I liked being in the infirmary as it was cool and peaceful, but after a few days, I wanted to be back at class and have my friends autograph my plaster of Paris, and especially get back to doing my PE exercises. I wasn't going to let my plastered arm keep me from returning to life as normal.

At Bishop's College I wasn't in a large dormitory. Five other girls shared a nice, airy room with me. Every afternoon during our naptime, one of the girls would sit on my bed with her fine-tooth comb and go through my long, red hair, catching lice and nits, and I would have to do the same for her. It wasn't at all pleasant, especially as we had to crush the lice between our thumbnails! But like everything else, I became used to the ritual. I kept my hair in plaits, hoping to keep the lice away, and for the most part I didn't have too many, but I did have them—we all had them.

The boarding life at Bishop's College was nice. I made friends with the day students and would visit their nearby homes at the weekends. Sometimes I would go home, as our house was across the road from the school. I didn't feel happy when I went home, as Mother wasn't pleased to see me, because she and Dad were fighting a lot. Matilda would take my sisters out somewhere, usually to the swimming club or for a walk. I loved my father and yet never saw much of him. It was a daily prayer of mine that one day we would all live together and be happy.

When Sunday mornings came along, I had to attend service in the Anglican Church together with the other boarders, dressed in our Sunday uniform. I tried so hard to think of other things during the service, as I felt that I was being disloyal to Jesus. I so missed not being able to receive Holy Communion, and there was no way that I would in a non-Catholic church. I just prayed harder and knew that Jesus would understand that it wasn't my fault.

Lessons were all right; for some reason I found myself learning Sinhalese rather than French. Thinking that I would never leave Ceylon, I might as well learn the language of the country. I recall sitting in the classroom that was painted green. I loved drawing, so learning Sinhalese suited me, in as much as the script was like art. However, I wasn't at Bishop's College long enough to learn the language, as once again it was time to move.

One thing I realised about Mother was that our lives were constantly changing. I seemed to stay with other families quite often. Sometimes when Mother was teaching at the various schools, I would be left outside wandering off around the premises. Once I found a circus tent that was being erected nearby and ventured in and was able to meet some of the animals. What a joy that was. I couldn't wait to tell Mother of my thrilling experience, and she tried to show an interest but scolded me for not staying at the school.

5

A new adventure was about to begin, so I had to say goodbye to my friends at Bishop's College, which I was sad about, as I really liked that school with the exception of not being able to go to Mass. My father had been transferred to Meddecombra tea estate about six to seven hour's drive by car from Colombo, and we were all moving to a new home upcountry. Matilda decided to leave us, as she didn't want to move out of Colombo, so Mother employed a young Tamil nanny also called Matilda. Poor Sylvan at eighteen months was losing the only permanent person in her little life, and now had to get used to a new nanny and also had to get to know her mother.

While I was at school, Mother had been going back and forth to Meddecombra, driven by our faithful driver, Silva, to prepare the house. Dad had already been living there for a while. The time finally came for us to leave Colombo. I prayed hard to Jesus that the move would be the best thing to make our family united. It was difficult for me to once again leave a school that I had become accustomed to and to leave my dance classes and the friends I had made. However, having taken my seat in the car with the new nanny—Vanessa and Sylvan and Mother in the front next to Silva—I was excited about what was ahead.

Silva drove out of Colombo through the low country and along the winding and bumpy roads while I sat with my nose to the window, observing the different landscapes as we motored by. Vanessa was never very good in the car, so we had to stop a few times as she felt sick, and poor Sylvan—when she wasn't sleeping, she cried. It was a relief to stop at the guesthouses along the route where we were able to stretch our legs and freshen up. Mother always managed to rent a room where we could spend an hour or so where Sylvan was fed and where we too were able to have some food. I loved the guesthouses, which seemed to me to be buried deep in forests.

Although I wanted to keep my eyes open to see everything, I think I must have slept for part of the journey, and as dusk was falling, Silva told us that we were almost at our destination. The unpaved, gravel road circled around and around, and at the top was our new home. Dad was waiting for us at the front door of our bungalow, together with the houseboy and night watchman. The rest of the staff had gone home for the night.

Moving to a home that was to be permanently ours, where we would all be together was a great thrill for me. I was excited and couldn't wait to explore. The next day Vanessa and I went to investigate. We shared a bedroom; the bathroom was between our room and the next bedroom, which was where Matilda slept along with Sylvan in her lovely big wooden cot. That room was also used as the guest room for my grandmother and aunt when they visited from Australia; Matilda then slept on the floor of the playroom, which was at the end of the passage; those three rooms faced east. Mother's study was opposite our playroom, and the main bedroom was opposite our bedroom with the living room farther down the passage. The dining room was at the front of the house, close to the large kitchen. Mother had bought a piano, which was in the dining room, so we could continue with our lessons and especially for our grandmother to use. GM, as we called her, would entertain us by playing the piano and encourage us to sing along with her. I shall never forget her singing Brahms's lullaby while at the piano.

Mother would spend a lot of the early days planting a flower and vegetable garden. It wasn't too long before the garden looked really pretty, and the vegetable garden was filled with beans, peas, tomatoes, and many other vegetables. I would love to walk through it and help myself to the sugar cane and sweet peas. Mother also had a Wendy house built, and it became our school room for a little while, but Mother's interest in teaching us soon waned, and Vanessa and I would be taken to other tea planter's homes to have lessons. We, however, loved the Wendy house, as we could play outside and still be shaded from the hot sun. It was interesting to visit the other homes, but the long car journeys were tiring, and I didn't really take to being taught by the tea planters' wives. Anyway, after a while that too proved to be an unsatisfactory situation.

Most mornings while we were at home, Vanessa and I would be impatient to knock on the door of our parent's bedroom to say good morning. One morning when we went in, Mother was in the bathroom, so I went into Dad's dressing room and found him disheveled; he wasn't getting dressed for work, and I noticed a bottle on his dresser, which said Gordon's. I thought that it belonged to him, as it had his name on it! I was distressed to see my dad like that, and just as I was about to say something, my mother flew into the room and angrily told me to leave. There was a lot of shouting, but in a few days things seemed peaceful and everything was back to normal. I, however, had started wetting my bed often during the nights, and that was upsetting for me. I was embarrassed, and although I was still young, I wanted to always please my mother and not cause anything to upset her. Mother was kind about my situation and didn't scold me. I felt sure she wondered why I was having that problem.

The daily ritual after breakfast was to trot behind Mother, who was dressed in her beautiful flowing housecoat. I used to follow her to the pantry, which she kept locked. Each day she would converse with the cook as to what was on the menu. She would then proceed to measure out the rice, sugar, flour, and whatever else was required. All lettuce, tomatoes and in fact, anything that was to be eaten raw, had to be soaked for at least an hour in a fluid. A couple of tablets would be put in the basin, and the vegetables would soak in the pink water. All our drinking water had to be boiled. I didn't go into the kitchen often, but when I did with Mother, I was intrigued to see the kitchen boy grind the chilies on a plank of wood with a wooden rolling pin, while he sat on the floor.

The grinding of chilies was to become the sambol, which went with the curry. I really don't remember what we ate, but I know that more often than not, I would excuse myself from the dining room table and join Matilda in the playroom, while she ate her supper. Her simple meal of Bombay duck (dried fish), rice, curry and red chilies somehow always tasted better than what I had just had for supper!

In the evenings my parents would go into the drawing room and listen to the radio, which usually played some nice music. It was our time to enjoy our parents. Many an evening I would arrange for theatre time. Vanessa and I would dance and sing; fortunately, Mother had kept a lot of the costumes that we had worn in the school plays, so we had dress-up clothes. I, being the elder, would produce our little plays. If Vanessa didn't feel in the mood, I would dance to any music on the radio. Those were wonderful evenings, spending time with my parents and Vanessa; Sylvan would join us and sit on Mother's lap. I loved the aroma of the St. Bruno's rough-cut tobacco that Dad used in his pipe, which gave me a warm and comforting feeling. Mother, who always suffered from asthma, though it had become much better in recent years, wasn't keen on Dad's pipe, but as she smoked her cigarettes, she was in no position to complain.

We had a little Cocker Spaniel, but for some reason he wasn't very friendly, so Mother gave it away, and instead she arranged for us to have a gorgeous German Shepherd, whom we named Rocky and who became my best friend. Rocky and I had lots of fun playing together.

Diana with Rocky in the garden of the house on Meddecombra Tea Estate

Neither Vanessa nor I were attending any form of school, so we had to make our own amusements. I was nine years old, Vanessa almost seven, and Sylvan was two. Apart from our company, Sylvan had no little friends and was always with Matilda. Vanessa and I both read a lot, as Mother had wonderful books for us. My favourite pastime would be to play with my paper dolls. I would have Rocky sit beside me while I cut out paper clothes. I would spend hours drawing, designing, and then colouring different outfits for them. Our playroom was filled with books, toys, and games and a large rocking horse; we spent a lot of time in there.

When the monsoon came with the heavy rains, lashing at the windows and scaring us with thunder and lightning, I would make a cubbyhole with the armchairs in the play room, turning them on their sides and covering them with sheets. Vanessa, Sylvan, Matilda, Rocky, and I would cram in together, laughing and feeling cosy and safe. We were lucky that our house was on a hill so the rain wouldn't settle but gave the parched land a good soaking. The rains would bring out the snakes and lots of creepy crawlies. I didn't mind the geckos or the millipedes, which I found fascinating. I didn't like the mosquitoes. Although we all slept under mosquito nets, every evening the house boy would go around the house and bedrooms with the flit gun, spraying the rooms with DDT to be sure that we weren't disturbed by mosquitoes. Vanessa and I had a beautiful pink net.

During the day, Mother would be in her study at her typewriter; the servant boy would take her lunch. She was not to be disturbed. Matilda and the three of us and Rocky would look forward to meeting Dad when he walked back home from the office. Dad was the accountant for the whole tea estate, and his office was a few miles from where we would meet him. Rocky and I would run down a path that had been formed through the tea bushes with Vanessa following and Matilda carrying Sylvan. We would try to see who would spot Dad first. As much as we enjoyed running through the tea bushes, it was always our hope that we would make it to the street before any leeches would attach themselves on our legs. It was our greatest fear to have one or possibly more of those revolting leeches sucking our blood; it was so horrible seeing them on our legs, and of course, we screeched and stamped our legs hoping they would fall off, which they never did. We learned to carry salt, so if we did have a leech, we would pour the salt on it, and it would drop off. It was dangerous to try to pull the leech off, as it could leave its head under the skin.

At the weekends Vanessa, Rocky, and I would go for long walks with our parents. We wouldn't see anyone else for miles; we just enjoyed the beautiful scenery, the vistas that stretched beyond the rows and rows of tea bushes, and the valleys and purple hue of the hills in the background.

Mother would say to us, "head up, tummy in, and shoulders back!"

We always sang on those walks. My father had a lovely voice, not unlike Bing Crosby. My mother didn't, which used to keep us in fits of laughter. Sometimes on those walks we would pay a visit to the tea factory on the estate and watch how the tea from the bushes was processed to become the tea that we drank.

It wasn't long after Mother had the house and garden looking nice that GM and my Aunt Vernon, Mother's middle sister, came from Australia to stay with us for a couple of months. Before their arrival both Vanessa and I had to have our hair washed in wood chips and a special shampoo that mother hoped would kill all the lice. Mother knew that her mother would not appreciate seeing her granddaughters constantly scratching their heads! It didn't kill all the lice, but for a time we were both more comfortable. Mother decided to cut my hair. I didn't have any say in the matter, and I didn't look pretty with short, frizzy red hair!

I was happy to have GM and Aunty Vernon stay with us. Their visit made life a little more exciting for me. GM would sit at the piano and encourage us to sing with her. She had the most wonderful voice, and Mother was happy to have their company. To my delight, Aunty Vernon brought me a beautiful doll. She had a lovely porcelain face and a cloth body, magnificently dressed, and I called her Princess Elizabeth. She was very precious to me. During GM and Aunty Vernon's visit, I sensed that Dad wasn't happy. Apart from Rocky, my poor Dad was surrounded by seven females. Normally he would have loved that, but Mother wasn't nice to him. I felt that they didn't love each other anymore. Alas, the time came for GM and Aunty Vernon to leave, so Mother, Vanessa and I drove back with them to Colombo to say good-bye. I was sad to see my Aunty Vernon leave. I liked her a lot and wished that she was my Mother. I never saw her again, as she died of cancer a few years later.

After their departure we returned to Meddecombra. We were isolated in our home on the hill. The nearest tea planter lived at least half-an-hour's drive from us. I became more involved with my paper dolls, designing lots of new clothes and taking an interest in my own clothes. I liked to accompany Mother into Watagoda, about an hour's drive from the house, and followed her around while she did her grocery shopping. It always amazed me that we managed to find everything we needed in those little, overcrowded shops. All the shopkeepers spoke English and were very proud to be able to sell to the white English tea planters.

Often in the evenings if Dad returned early from his work, he and Mother would have a game of badminton; the net was set up in the garden to the east of the house. We all laughed a lot while they played. Unfortunately, it wasn't too long before I began again to sense an atmosphere between my parents. Our idyllic life was about to end, as mother was becoming restless. She didn't want to entertain the tea planters to dinners or to her famous Sunday curry tiffin. Dad was teetotal at the time, and although it was necessary for him to remain so, Mother found life with him boring. She longed for the activity in Colombo and busying herself with producing and acting in plays. She also missed the admiration of her male friends in the city. I knew that she was not happy and made it very clear to all of us that she must return to her work in Colombo. It seemed to me that she couldn't wait to leave Dad.

6

Dad didn't go with us to Colombo as he had to work and neither would my beloved Rocky. Mother, Matilda and the three of us girls all packed into the Hillman for the long six-hour drive to Colombo. I actually loved those drives, through the beautiful tea estates, and the little villages, past the timber collected by the roadside for a delivery by river to somewhere.

We would stop halfway at a picturesque rest house in Kitulgala. The rest house was cool, and we had the use of a bedroom for our stop. It seemed so remote. As I stood on the wooden veranda drinking my lemonade, I looked over to the other side of the Kelani River with its mass of thick trees. It was a jungle to me, and I imagined tigers, snakes, and monkeys all living together. Looking down from the rest house, I saw the murky brown river where the timber logs floated by. It was wondrously picturesque.

The only thing I didn't enjoy on those drives were the waterfalls. There were two, and I always closed my eyes until we drove passed. I was really terrified of the waterfalls. Talking of water, I managed to accept the pools at the swimming club, but I was once pushed in at the deep end while sitting on the edge of the pool watching the people swimming. I grappled with the water and fought hard not to drown. I didn't tell Mother. I didn't tell anyone, but I did thank Jesus, as I knew He had me in the palm of His hand. I asked to have swimming lessons after that incident.

Mother had found a place to stay in Colombo where she had rented a granny flat in the house of Selina Fernando of Pedris Road. Vanessa, Sylvan, Matilda and I would stay in Selina's house on our visits to Mother. Selina was a warm, kind lady, and we all loved her. As there wasn't room for me in Mother's little flat, I would stay with

Selina and spend most of my time with her and her daughter in their part of the house. I loved to listen to Selina play the piano and sing. I observed her graciousness, how her sari was arranged, how gentle she was when she spoke to anyone. There was never any shouting, though Selina's daughter was difficult at times and wasn't nice to her mother, which made me sad, but brought me even closer to Selina.

Some days when I would be with Selina, we would hear tapping outside, and that would announce the arrival of a Buddhist monk who would come with his begging bowl. I would watch with fascination as the young man, wearing only his saffron robe and sandals on his feet, would quietly open the gate and enter the yard. Selina, a Buddhist herself, was always ready to fill his bowl with food and offer him a drink of water. He wasn't allowed to accept money. The monks who visited looked so young, and I watched them with interest as they stood under the breadfruit tree in the small garden while they ate their food. Even at my young age, I sensed such peace while observing that ritual. Most of the time I spent with Selina, I didn't see much of my mother, as she was busy rehearsing her next play and, unlike Vanessa, I really wasn't interested to sit and watch the rehearsals.

The few days I spent with Selina were different to being at home. Selina would offer me an English breakfast, but I would say, "no, I want to eat kiribath with some roti and a small piece of juggery," which was so sweet and so good.

There was plenty of delicious fruit too—papaya, mangos, mangosteins, rambutans, and guavas, among other fruit. I told her that I wanted to live just like she did. That would make her smile; I loved her so much. Although I realised that being a Buddhist was different to being a Catholic, I felt that Jesus was with Selina as much as He was with me; she had an aura about her.

One morning I was in the bathroom under the makeshift shower, and Selina came to see that I had everything I needed. While in there, she said, "Diana, darling, you have a birthmark on your bottom that is very lucky. You will have a good life."

I went with her to her bedroom, and standing in front of her long mirror, I turned my head around and saw my birthmark. It was the first time I had seen it. I smiled at Selina and thanked her for telling me. I wondered what it all meant. After an hour or so, I didn't think about it again and made no mention of it to my mother.

Before Mother left for rehearsals one afternoon, she came and sat with Selina and me, as she wanted Selina to understand about her productions. Mother said that she, together with her friends Arthur Van Landenberg and Winston Serasinghe from her days at Radio Ceylon, had helped form the International Theatre Group, and that she would be producing and acting in many plays in the future. She had just finished "Le Grand Guignol," and her next production would be "A Man About the House," which she would start the following year. I feel sad that my mother, Patricia Pantin Munro, who devoted much time to Radio Ceylon, to teaching elocution at the request of most of the schools in Colombo and eventually producing first-class plays equivalent to London and New York, is not mentioned or thanked by the government for all of her ardent passion for the islanders of her beloved Ceylon. Since her arrival on the island, her whole life seemed to be dedicated to making sure that school children would be educated in etiquette and the English language, and that Ceylon would have an international theatre.

When Mother started rehearsing for "A Man About the House," we returned to Meddecombra and to our lonely Dad and Rocky. I had missed them both and was happy to be home. Rocky and I went to say hello to our pet rabbits and then walked around the garden. I looked at the flowers, the colourful plants and the trees. I especially loved the eucalyptus trees and felt a sense of peace and gratitude.

From our home on the hill, I could see the terraced rice paddy fields, which were built slightly into the hillside and were being ploughed by two water buffalos and one lone coolie walking behind them. All around the paddy fields were the vibrant green hills of the tea bushes, interrupted only by small interjections of the colourful tea pluckers' saris. The tea pluckers were women who carried a wicker basket slung over their shoulders and expertly picked two leaves and a bud from the tea bush and threw them into the basket on their back. They worked together in groups of about twenty.

As dusk approached, the hills turned to mauve, and soon it was night. I wasn't allowed to go outside at night for fear of snakes, but sometimes as a family we would step out into the garden to see the moon and stars, which we felt we could almost touch, as they seemed so close. Everything was quiet except for the crickets. We watched with delight as the fireflies danced around like little lighted fairies and would smell the perfume of the deadly nightshade, which occasionally brought out the snakes. The snakes seldom ventured into the garden, and we knew not to go beyond its boundary. Sometimes Rocky and I would stand alone at the back door looking out into the night, and at those times I knew Jesus was very close. I could hear my own breath, so silent, so beautiful.

Mother had returned to be with us for Christmas. Vanessa and I started making our Christmas cards. Christmas for us, like most children, was very exciting, and we would borrow one of Dad's long socks to put at the bottom of our bed. We woke early in the morning, anxiously taking out the little goodies that Santa had left us, trying to keep quiet for as long as we could, and eating the mandarins and sweets before rushing into our parent's room, which was always such a thrill, as we delighted in showing them the contents of our stockings.

We were really too excited to have a proper breakfast and waited until Matilda and Sylvan joined us, and we all went to the playroom to see and wonder at the beautiful Christmas tree that magically appeared during the night. The tree looked exciting with many gifts hanging from the branches and surrounding the base. Mother had done a very good job. We all had lovely presents, including Rocky. That was the first and last Christmas that was the happiest for many a year to come.

7

My tenth birthday had arrived. I could now boast of being in two figures. Mother sometimes didn't choose the right time to talk to me, especially as I thought it was my special day. Mother, however, being an actress and Australian, very dramatic and direct, called me while she was going into in her bathroom. I sat on the edge of the bath. I knew despite it being my birthday, I wasn't going to like what I was about to hear. Keeping court with Mother while she was on the toilet did not bode well for me. She tried to be gentle, I think, as she told me that I would soon become a woman and proceeded to tell me in detail what that implied. I was terribly upset, but I didn't want Mother to know it. I had no idea at all that I had to face all those horrible things and was totally unprepared, having always believed that I was like Peter Pan and would never grow up; I therefore dismissed the whole conversation.

The next day before Mother went to the bathroom, I found a chili that looked like a scorpion and put it in her empty bath. I heard her scream, which was what I wanted, and then went in and told her that it was only a chili. She told me that I shouldn't frighten her like that. Anyway, we both laughed about it, and I didn't receive her wrath!

I loved going into Mother's cupboards and looking at her dresses, asking if I could try them on and play dress-up, using her lipstick and whatever else I could find on her dressing table. I didn't realise at that time in all my innocence of pretending to be like my beautiful mother that many, many years later, she would recall the incidents and tell me that I had been jealous of her. I still feel a tremendous sadness when I reflect on her words. I was a normal young girl who admired her mother and all her clothes and hoped that one day I would be just as pretty as she was.

Vanessa and I had almost forgotten what school was all about. We hadn't been to school in some time, apart from several weeks of home schooling. Dad was doing well at his job and felt, together with Mother's approval, that Vanessa and I should attend the expensive, most prestigious and all-white co-ed school in Nuwara Eliya. Mother too was doing well with her productions, so it seemed appropriate that we should attend the school as boarders. I really dreaded going to that posh school. I had been used to being at many different schools, but always with Sinhalese, Burgers and Tamil students. That school was for white, rich planters and ex-pat children.

My father, mother, Vanessa and I set out to buy our uniforms. Faithful Silva drove us to Nuwara Eliya, which was about three hours drive north from Meddecombra Estate. On our drive to Nuwara Eliya, if we needed to su-su, (spend a penny) as we called it, Silva would stop by the side of the road where there were many bushes, and Dad would take us to a bush where we couldn't be seen and stand watch until we were finished. He always managed to find a dry spot in the hope that there weren't any leeches.

Nuwara Eliya was a lovely English town with a couple of beautiful hotels and a golf course, and the air was considerably colder than the rest of the country. We went to look around the Hill School, and it was decided that I with three other girls, would share a room called Pavlova—the room was named after the famous Russian ballerina, Anna Pavlova—as ballet was my passion. Vanessa went into a larger dormitory for the younger girls. The school was small and had a cosy atmosphere. The main part was almost like a private home, but the classrooms were pre-fabricated.

After looking around the school, we went to the large department store in town to buy our uniforms. We needed a warm grey suit for church on Sundays, which was also used for all important occasions; a brown cardigan over our brown skirts, and yellow blouses and brown shorts with yellow aertex shirts for our run in the early mornings, gym and sports. It took a whole day to buy all that we needed. I was happy when we stopped at the Hill Club, where Dad was a member.

I knew he missed playing golf and I hoped that once we were at the Hill School, he would frequent his club when visiting us. We had an early supper there and chatted about our shopping and especially my reluctance to leave Dad and Sylvan alone.

As we were driving back to Meddecombra, a heavy fog descended. Silva couldn't see the road. I was so proud of Dad when he got out of the car and walked in front of it for a good while until Silva could see where he was going. It was an intense drive home, but Dad made us all sing, "we'll be coming round the mountain when we come!"

Finally, the day arrived to start at the Hill School. My heart was aching; I didn't want to leave my beloved Rocky nor Dad. Over the years I had learned the discipline of accepting what was expected of me. Mother had already left again for Colombo with Sylvan and Matilda. Silva had to return to be with Dad, who took us to the Hill School. I enjoyed the drive to Nuwara Eliya, going through the tea estates, the villages, watching the terrain change, seeing the enormous hornet nests hanging from the trees, at which time all the windows in the Hillman were tightly closed. As we drove higher into the hills, I was in awe of the jungle, knowing that it was filled with many animals that were still able to roam free in their habitat. Dad made sure that we sang on any car trips. It kept our minds off anxious thoughts and possibility of carsickness.

I was extremely nervous, arriving at the Hill School. The headmaster greeted us, and before I knew it, I was saying hello to the other three girls in my room. One girl, Ann, was taller than I was and lived in Colombo, so as I had spent most of my young life there, we had something in common and became good friends.

As the Hill School was co-ed, it took me a while to get used to being around boys. I was the only girl with crazy red hair and freckles. I wasn't fat, but I wasn't thin either and, therefore, a little self-conscious. I also found learning difficult, having been to eleven different schools in my ten-and-a-half years, due mainly to Mother, who never seemed totally satisfied with the education I was receiving, and also the fact that our lives were constantly changing. However, I hoped the Hill School would be my twelfth and last experience at another school.

About three weeks after my arrival and on one of my visits to the bathroom, I found that I was bleeding. I had totally dismissed everything that Mother had told me and was mortified that I wasn't like Peter Pan after all! What my mother had told me was true. I was terrified. I stuffed almost a whole roll of toilet paper in my pants and kept running to the toilet where I cried and cried. I was embarrassed. I didn't want anyone to know. Somehow it came to the notice of Matron that I was spending a lot of time in the toilet, and she came to me. Matron was extremely kind and gentle and set me up with a belt and sanitary pads. It took me a while to recover from that shock, but I did.

As the days went on, I noticed my body was beginning to change. I was starting to develop breasts and was growing taller, and apart from Ann, I seemed to be big compared to the other girls of my age. I was teased a lot, especially by my Latin teacher, who loved to call me moon face, freckles, and carrot head. Although I tried to take all of it in my stride and not let it upset me, it was difficult at times not to feel like the odd one out. It is amazing how many jokes can be found to embarrass a red head. My friend Jesus was with me at those difficult times, and He always seemed to give me a sense of peace.

I enjoyed learning Latin, and the teacher, who was a big man himself, liked me despite his teasing. I loved art classes and dancing, however, I was now too tall to be in the ballet productions, which was sad. Instead I was given parts in folk dancing and felt grateful to be doing any form of dancing.

Vanessa was going to be eight years old, and we were given a message that our parents would take us out for the day and asked Vanessa to invite a couple of her close friends to join us. Mother had prepared a wonderful picnic lunch, which we enjoyed at the Hakgala Botanical Gardens, where we spent most of the afternoon, and afterwards we were taken to the Grand Hotel for an early supper. It was a beautiful day. I was so happy to see my parents, especially my dad. I really don't remember Sylvan being with us. It was the last happy memory I have as a child of Mother and Dad together giving us a fun school outing.

I settled in at the Hill School, becoming used to being around all-white children and boys too. Nuwara Eliya is six thousand feet above sea level and can be extremely cold. I did not enjoy going for the early morning runs around the lake in the cold air, but by the end of the run I did feel invigorated. On our arrival back to school after our run, about eight girls would go into the bathroom for a shower, all of us naked bodies crammed into one small bathroom in the bathtub. It was at that time that I saw that Ann had pubic hair. I was surprised, but realised it wouldn't be so much longer before I would be in the same position.

In our room Pavlova, we had midnight feasts from time to time, not that it was allowed. Heinz baked beans were always the favourite, together with condensed milk. It was fun to sit on our beds late at night and eat the forbidden food. One day I was dared to steal a pear from the pear tree in the garden. Everyone knew that was not allowed, and I think those who gave me the dare wanted to see what I was made of, as to them I looked different: I was a loner, and was not clever in class, unlike Vanessa, and was not good at sports, so I took the dare and stole a pear. Well, of course, the headmaster was told, and I was sent to his study where on each hand received five strokes of his bamboo cane. I had a sense of achievement, however, proving to those that I could take the dare, and afterwards I was respected.

Every Sunday we attended service at the Anglican Church in our grey suits. I really didn't want to enter the church, and when I did I found the interior so cold, compared to the beautiful Catholic church of St. Bridget's. I kept telling Jesus how sorry I was not to be with Him in His home. I didn't sing the hymns. The Lord's Prayer was different; it was all so strange. While I was in that church, I would look around at all the pupils, and many of them had their parents with them. After the service the students and parents would chat amongst themselves. I stood alone, watching all the children and their well-to-do parents. The atmosphere seemed so snooty to me. I really didn't belong at the Hill School. My parents never attended any church service, parents' day, nor any other special day. It didn't bother me, but I really wished I was with them.

Diana and Vanessa wearing their Hill School Uniform

8

The year had gone by and it was Christmas, and I don't honestly remember the holidays; things between my parents had started to deteriorate. During those holidays I turned eleven years old.

My mother had decided to produce the play, "The Women" written by Clare Boothe Luce, and thought that I would be perfect to play the part of Mary. My passion was dancing. I did not want to act nor complicate my life further by being drawn into the hectic lifestyle of my mother. So it was decided that Vanessa, who was a natural actress, was the perfect choice. Mother took Vanessa out of the Hill School, and she became an overnight success. I returned to school alone and didn't miss Vanessa, as I never saw her when she was there. I settled back into the routine and loved walking through the woods at the back of the school, roaming through the bluebells and enjoying nature.

From time to time we had to watch a football (soccer) match, which was exciting for us girls. I was sitting next to Ann when I noticed Richard on the football field. After the game he walked passed me all muddy and hot.

I smiled at him and said, "well done."

He smiled and said, "thank you."

He had beautiful eyes and a great smile. From that moment I had a big crush on little Richard! I found out that he lived in Colombo, and during the holidays he would go to the swimming club. It was fun to have something different to think about and to feel a flutter. During our midnight feasts I would sing, "after the ball was over, after they'd all gone home, Richard met Diana," etc. Of course, my roommates thought it was all a hoot.

When half-term came around, my mother was in Colombo, busy with her production of "The Women." Silva and the car were with her, so Dad didn't have transport, and anyway, as Dad was working, I would have been alone in the house during the day, so I had nowhere to go for half-term. The headmaster told me that he would find a family who would take me for the long weekend. It was déjà-vu as I watched the parents collect their children. Almost all the children had left except for a young brother and sister.

When their parents arrived, the headmaster asked them if they would have me for the half-term holiday. I didn't know the children, who were younger than I was. I felt it was an imposition, but there was nothing I could do. All I remember about being at that home was that it was comfortable, nothing atmospheric about it, but comfortable. I also sensed that the parents knew that my mother was an actress and had heard derogatory things about her. I remembered to make my bed with hospital corners and made sure that I cleaned the bath after I had used it and always offered to help wherever I could. I didn't feel unhappy, as by now I was used to being planted in unfamiliar surroundings; so it was just another situation, which I accepted as part of my life. I was, however, very grateful to the family for taking me to their home for the short holiday.

I looked forward to seeing Ann after half-term. Early one morning while attempting to get ready for our morning run around the lake, I told Ann that I was in terrible pain and that I just couldn't make it. I returned to my bed. I had my period, but the pain was far worse than the usual period pain. I couldn't go to Matron. I couldn't move. Ann told Matron that I was sick.

When Matron came to my bed, I grunted at her that I had the most awful pain in my left side, which was totally confusing, as I discovered later. Also I had my period, so perhaps it was nothing more than a bad period pain. I was never one to complain, but as I couldn't move and said I was in agony, Matron knew it had to be something serious. I lay there praying to Jesus. I just knew He would take care of me. I vaguely remember the bumps in the road as the ambulance raced from Nuwara Elyia to the Hatton Nursing Home, a two-hour drive.

When I awoke the following morning, I was in a different venue and in a hospital bed, looking out from big French windows to a beautiful garden. I felt I had lost my stomach. The pain was awful, a mixture of period pains and the result of the operation. The doctor came to see me, and brought me a little bottle. In it was my appendix. It looked like a plant with a root and tiny shoots; I declined his offer to keep it. He told me that I was very lucky, as I could have had peritonitis as my appendix was near to bursting, and I had only just made it in time for the operation. He said that he had to operate from the base to the top, which left me with a large four-inch scar.

The nurses were so kind, and later that day I was told that my father would visit me. I was pleased that Dad would be with me, but I didn't really feel in the mood to see anyone. I was in pain, had my period, and the additional terrible embarrassment of having lice in my hair. I managed to stagger into the bathroom, wrap a towel around my head, telling Dad that I'd just washed my hair, and made myself feel in control of the situation, as I didn't want him to look at me as an invalid. For the ten days I was in the nursing home, he visited me every day, the drive taking over an hour each way.

The company had lent Dad a car and driver; neither of my parents knew how to drive. I really looked forward to his visits, especially as he taught me how to play canasta. We had a lot of fun playing cards. Dad was patient and made me feel better. He told me that Vanessa was doing well studying for her part in "The Women," and Mother sent her love and hoped I would be better soon. He told me that Rocky missed us all so much and that he took him on many walks. When I left the nursing home, I didn't recall being bothered again with lice. Perhaps the nurses had helped cure the infestation once and for all. I was very grateful!

As I had to convalesce, I wasn't able to return to the Hill School. In fact, that was the end of my schooling in Nuwara Eliya. I went home with my father to Meddecombra and was happy to see Sylvan and Matilda, who had returned to Meddecombra from Colombo, and darling Rocky. I had to take it easy for a while during which time I made outfits for my paper dolls. If I wasn't to be a ballerina, I thought

I could be a fashion designer. I loved clothes. I also enjoyed reading my wonderful books, including "Veronica at Sadler's Wells."

Sylvan was now four years old, and I felt I had missed so much time of being with her that I cherished us being together, but was unhappy about the way Sylvan cried. She seemed to cry for hours at night. I always remembered her crying since she was a baby, and found it very worrying. It concerned me that Sylvan didn't have any little friends, didn't go to nursery school or start learning at home. I did the best I could, reading to her, trying to teach her the alphabet and playing games, but Sylvan seemed very unhappy. Mother was busy in Colombo with her play. I tried to make things fun at home for Dad, Sylvan, Rocky, and Matilda, but there was a cloud. We knew that Mother's heart was not with us. In a way it wasn't surprising I was still wetting my bed.

While I was convalescing, the doctor living on the estate and in charge of the hospital, who was a friend of Dad's and was checking on me, suggested that I visit his clinic. I wasn't prepared for the experience. For some reason I had imagined the clinic to be a little like the hospital I had just left in Hatton.

The small brick building was spotless, as were the simple operating rooms. I then walked outside to see where the young mothers and their babies lived. The tea coolies lived in lines, tiny little rooms separated by a thin wall. They had outhouses and a pump where they collected their water and did their laundry. When the doctor took me to see the newborn babies, tears rolled down my cheeks. The mothers looked very young as they sat on the floor cradling their tiny, newborn babies; there was nothing in their small space, just a mat on the floor for mother and baby to sleep on. I thought about Sylvan as a baby and how different she looked compared to those little ones. The doctor was such a good man and devoted so much time to the poor mothers and their babies, but apart from giving them his expertise in taking care of them, he couldn't improve on their living conditions, as he needed money.

That was my first realisation that not everyone was as fortunate as I was. It never occurred to me that we were not all the same. I felt enormous sadness after my visit and promised myself that no matter what happened in my life, I would always be grateful for what God gave me, and would try to help the poor and less fortunate. That visit made me aware of what it was to have no money—poverty, such a harsh word, and such a harsh reality. After that visit, whenever I saw the tea coolies, I would wave and smile. I hadn't really thought about wanting for anything. Of course, I wanted my parents to love each other, which was probably my biggest prayer every night, but apart from that, I seemed to have everything I wanted.

I did wonder what it would be like to be poor. When I observed the beautiful tea pluckers with their nose rings and pretty saris, I hadn't thought how those women lived. Seeing the lines, the hospital, the poor quarters, I felt most humble. That night when I said my prayers as I did every night—even at the Hill School when the girls used to make fun of me—"Shoosh," they would say, "Saint Diana is saying her prayers" —I said special prayers for those Tamil mothers and their newborn infants.

I was now completely well from my operation, so it was time to go to Colombo to be at the opening of "The Women." I said good-bye to the servants and gave a big hug to my Rocky and told him it wouldn't be long before I'd be back, but I had lied. Sadly, I never returned to Rocky nor to Meddecombra Estate.

9

Silva had driven up from Colombo to collect us. The servants came to see us off, and I told them to take special care of number one dog! We sang in the car and I wanted Sylvan to learn the songs. Matilda sat in the front, and Dad, Sylvan and I in the back. When we stopped at my favourite guesthouse, I wanted Dad, Matilda, and Sylvan to see my murky river and the dense forest on the opposite bank.

After refreshments, we drove on through the picturesque countryside; everything looked so lush, and then Silva said to me. "Missie, we are coming to the big waterfall."

I thanked Silva and buried my head in my hands. Dad didn't know about my problem. I told him that I couldn't look at the waterfall, that it frightened me and gave me bad dreams.

My father said to me, "If I give you two rupees, will you look at the waterfall?"

Well, I thought about it for a few moments; I knew that I wanted to buy a small gift for Richard for his birthday, and the money would help.

Dad had his arm around my shoulders and said, "It is okay. It's just water."

Anyway, what with the bribe and my father's arm around me as protection, I looked at the waterfall as we passed. It was a traumatic moment, and I took many deep breaths, tightening the grip on my Dad's hand. I did, however, continue to have bad dreams about waterfalls and have always had the greatest respect for the ocean and all water. Many, many years later, I took an excursion to the Niagara Falls by myself, as I was determined to overcome my fear. I stood on the observation deck and braced myself as I watched the falls. Although I did not enjoy the experience, I knew then that my deep fear of waterfalls had finally been overcome.

Arriving in Colombo, we stopped for a while at the new flat that Mother had rented in Horton Place. Dad and I left Matilda and Sylvan there, and we went to the opening of "The Women." My mother was a celebrity. When Dad and I entered the theatre, I was recognised as Mother's daughter and was offered a seat in the front, but chose to sit at the back. Dad made sure I was okay and said he wouldn't stay. Many years later he told me that he was uncomfortable, as too many of Mother's lovers were in the audience. The theatre was packed. The play, like all the rest of Mother's productions was excellent, so professional and Vanessa was brilliant. The show ended with a big ovation. Mother and Vanessa were greatly congratulated and presented with large bouquets of flowers. The show would continue for another week.

I contacted Ann, who was back in Colombo. We managed to see each other, and she asked me to go horseback riding with her. We trotted around an old racecourse; it was most exhilarating. I loved the experience; after all, in Roman mythology Diana was the huntress, the goddess of the hunt and moon, and she had the power to talk to and control animals, so my first experience on a horse was wonderful.

I also enjoyed going to Ann's home. Everything there seemed very normal, but after a while I stopped. I felt I couldn't invite her back, as I never knew how my parents would be behaving. Our lives were erratic, and I didn't want Ann to know, as I didn't think she would understand.

We were in a rented property and it was sparse compared to Ann's home. My parents were fighting a lot, Sylvan was always crying, and Vanessa was never apart from Mother. I sensed that Mother wasn't really pleased that we were back again with her, as she was enjoying being the successful star, and whenever Dad was near her, she wasn't happy. I felt she really hated him.

During that time in Colombo, I was told by my mother that I wouldn't be returning to the Hill School and neither to Meddecombra. I didn't want to show her how sad I was to hear the news. It was only when all was quiet at night that I could let my tears wet my pillow. I thought about Rocky and the house that had come to be my real home. During the day I hoped that my parents wouldn't be together, as they would have the most terrible fights, mainly brought on by mother, who sometimes would take the kitchen knife to attack Dad. I stood there between them, my arms pushing them apart and screaming at them to stop. I was so frightened that my mother would kill my father. I also didn't want my sisters upset by what was going on. Mother had just succeeded with her play, we had a solid home on the tea estate, and Dad had a good job; I was bewildered and confused.

Before Dad left Colombo back for Meddecombra, we had a few happy days, and I didn't want him to leave, but it was the best thing for us all, as Mother really disliked having him living with us. I felt sad that although I didn't love being at the Hill School, I wanted to continue with my lessons and feel a sense of belonging somewhere. What really upset me was not returning to my home in the hills, my safe place. I was devastated, but I kept it all to myself. I had learned that it was best not to say anything that would cause Mother to verbally attack me.

Matilda went back with Dad, as her home was in Meddecombra, and I believe she was his girlfriend. After all, they were alone together for so long. Mother then employed a new nanny called Grace. I was immediately concerned when I saw her. I didn't like Grace. I thought there was something wrong with her, and as time went on, I really didn't like the way she was taking care of Sylvan. As I wasn't going to school, I could have looked after Sylvan, but Mother insisted on having a nanny for her. I found myself keeping as close to Grace and Sylvan as I could.

One day we went to the swimming club, and Grace was supposed to be watching Sylvan in the babies' pool. I was having a lesson in the big pool, and for some reason I rushed to the little pool and saw Sylvan in distress. She could have drowned, but I was there in time. I looked for Grace, but there was no sign of her. I told Mother about that frightening incident, and she said she would talk to Grace. Mother didn't seem concerned that Sylvan had still not attended nursery school or kindergarten, as she seemed too busy with other things.

I was soon aware that mother had a friend, a handsome Italian called Pino, who was the lead in her play, "A Man About the House." I didn't know that he had been a friend of hers for a while. I knew that Mother had many male admirers, but he seemed to be special to her. Pino was charming and good-looking and Mother was always happy when he was around. While with us one day, he said he would like us to have a picnic on the beach, as it was full moon. I was still trying to overcome my fear of water, and the thought of sitting on the beach at night with the vast ocean in front of me was really scary, but I succumbed, as I didn't want a fight with Mother.

It turned out to be enjoyable, as we had a little fire and ate string-hoppers, one of my favourite foods. String-hoppers are like spaghetti made into a pancake, and on top of the string-hopper it was usual to top it with curry and then roll it and eat, so good! To add to the romantic evening, our string-hoppers were served on large banana leaves. It was full moon and the Indian Ocean was calm, the sand shone in the moonlight, and Mother seemed happy. I didn't feel entirely comfortable, despite Pino trying to be attentive towards me, as I really wished that Dad had been with us. That night as I lay in bed, I wondered whether the terrible fights between my parents had been due to Mother's affection for Pino.

10

After Dad had returned to Meddecombra, I had a sense of uncertainty around me. I couldn't help wondering what was happening. I found out soon enough, as Mother said that she had to go to an office near the jetty, and would I like to go to the pettah with her. I asked if she would leave me at the jetty while she went about her business. I loved to visit the jetty, watching all the boats going to and fro from the big liners. Sometimes there were a couple of navy ships and submarines in the harbour. I found it all so colourful and exciting, and wondered whether I would ever go on one of those big liners to faraway places. That evening Mother took Vanessa, Sylvan and me to dinner at a Chinese restaurant.

During dinner Mother proceeded to tell us that she was leaving Dad; in fact, she was running away with us. Dad would not know anything about our departure. Mother went on to explain that she didn't wish to live in Ceylon anymore, and neither could she live with Dad anymore. I also noticed that I had not seen Pino for a few days. Mother had saved enough to buy our tickets for the voyage, which would only take us as far as Italy; she went on to tell us that she had arranged for all of our possessions to be sent to Colombo from Meddecombra, and those things she would have to sell in order to pay for a place to live in Italy. She had told Dad that she and the three of us would be living in Colombo and therefore needed our possessions.

Later I learned that Mother had spent so much on her productions, financed mainly by my father, that he had to tell her that he couldn't continue to do it. He couldn't afford her lavish productions or lifestyle. Of course, it was difficult for me to assimilate all that she was saying, as Mother was verbose and dramatic. I just couldn't understand what was happening, as she had seemed to have enormous success with all her wonderful plays, but in truth, she never made a profit.

I don't recall that Christmas at all, but I do remember Mother arranged a big party for my twelfth birthday. Some close Sinhalese friends of hers offered to give her the party at their home. I remember the colourful merry-go-around in the large garden, which I loved. There were many people, all friends of Mother's, and I really didn't know any of them, except Selina. I felt it was also Sylvan's birthday party. After all, she would be five in five days, so I wanted to make sure she had a fun time and to that end we both had many turns on the merry-go-around. That night as I said my prayers, I recall thinking about the future and hoped that everything would be all right—would I ever see my Dad again? What would happen to Rocky?

Well, Mother had given him away and I found out later that he was badly treated, poor Rocky. My life was just hanging, and what was to become of my sisters, particularly Sylvan, whom I was worried about? Mother had little time for her, and although she would be five in a few days, she had not experienced the life of a normal little girl. I was now twelve years old, but I was still too young to show any disrespect to my mother by asking her if she couldn't make things all right again; she was my mother, and I had to trust her.

In April, Queen Elizabeth II and Prince Philip were visiting Colombo, and there was tremendous excitement. Flags hung from the lampposts, the roads and sidewalks were cleaned, and buildings were repainted. Vanessa and I stood on the pavement outside the swimming club to watch the procession. There weren't too many people, so we were able to see the Queen and Prince Philip clearly, as they rode past in their open car. It was a memorable moment for us, as we stood there waving our Union Jack flags.

Despite our seemingly dire prospects, Mother knew that Gregory Peck was filming the "Purple Plain" in Sigiriya, the archeological site in central Ceylon with the ruins of an ancient palace complex. So she decided that she and I would make an excursion to visit Gregory Peck on location. Gregory Peck was a real favourite of Mother's and I think she hoped that something would develop out of her visit. My mother was beautiful, but like most possible opportunities in her life,

I and my sisters would eventually be blamed for her misfortunes, for if we weren't around she would have been free to succeed with all of her dreams.

Mother and I, and whoever else was with us—I do not recall—had rooms in the same guest house as the film crew, which was exciting, but we didn't see Gregory Peck until the following day when we went out to the area where he was filming; the area had been made like an airfield. There were several large tents, and Mother sent word that she would like to say hello. We didn't wait long before the star walked out of his tent and greeted us. He was totally charming, tall and good-looking. I liked him and knew that my Mother would have loved an invitation to spend more time with him, but with circumstances as they were, it was not possible. Mother looked lovely in a grey flowered halter-neck dress. After chatting for a while, we were invited to watch some of the filming, but Mother declined and told me that if I hadn't been there, she would probably have been invited to dinner.

While in the plains of Sigiriya, we left the film site and went to look at the Lion Rock fortress, which was the cliff-top citadel built around AD 473 to 478. Midway up the stairway of the Lion Rock, which was six-hundred-and-fifty-six-feet high, are the Sigiriya Damsels, also known as the celestial nymphs, the only secular art to have survived the early kingdoms of the Sinhalese, and the art showed skimpily clad females. I, being the prim and sheltered convent girl, was embarrassed by it all and chose not to go on farther to the top. Apart from that, I did not like heights.

We didn't visit the famous ruins of Anurradahpura, but I vaguely recall a visit to the great ruins of Polonnaruwa, the former capital of Ceylon. The car journey was hot and uncomfortable, and I had never spent so much time in such close contact with my mother. I wasn't particularly interested in visiting all the fabulous ruins that Ceylon had to offer, as I was more concerned with what the following months held for our future.

On the way back to Colombo, we stopped at Dambulla, and Mother insisted that I visit the Cave Temple with the murals of scenes of Buddha's life. Much to Mother's surprise and disappointment, I absolutely refused to enter the Buddhist temple. I was a Roman Catholic, and didn't want to offend Jesus by entering a Buddhist place of worship. My mother talked a lot. She always had much to say, although she had left school at the age of twelve and was self-educated, but through voracious reading—and of course, her breeding—she was an erudite and educated lady, just too overpowering for me.

I realised that Mother thought I was a bit of a moron, as I didn't show the same interest that she did in all the things that were mentally stimulating to her. She often forgot how young I was. Leaving Dambulla, we stopped at Negombo overnight. I remember looking out at the lagoon, the water being very low, and felt surrounded by water. The fear was still with me. I was happy to leave.

We drove through the dusty roads, my nose close to the window. I enjoyed the changing scenes and hoped that we would not be trapped behind a bullock-cart making its slow way along the road. There was always much to see, especially the little stalls on the road selling fruit, coconuts, and home-cooked pasties and other mouth-watering food. It amused me to see the dhobi, who, having washed his clothes in the river, would then hit them on the stones before splaying them out in the sun to dry. It was a long time before I learned about washing machines!

We had to leave Horton Place, as there was no money coming from Dad to pay the rent, because he wanted us back home in Meddecombra, so we moved to an old colonial property, which a friend of Mother's had offered her to stay rent free. The house had large rooms, big verandas, and a small garden.

The day of the sale arrived. I helped Mother take out all our china, cutlery, pictures, books and our toys from the packing cases and arrange everything on long tables. It was like a bad dream and I was sad to see that my beautiful antique doll Princess Elizabeth was going to be sold. I asked if I may keep her, but Mother said she would fetch a good price. The only other thing I wanted was a painting of me at about a year old, but that went too. I wasn't really attached to anything, but seeing so much that was part of our young lives vanish in a matter of a few days was really tough. I don't remember us being left anything that we treasured. Fortunately for me at this difficult time, I had my thoughts on Richard and was happy to be able to see him at the swimming club and give him the Parker pen that I'd saved up for. He wrote me a thank you note, and I rushed into the bathroom to have some privacy to read it—my first love letter, except that it wasn't. It was just a nice thank you note! I had a little camera, which I was given for my birthday and was so excited to take a photo of Richard before leaving the island.

While all of this was going on, I became more aware of Grace and was really frightened of her, especially as she was in charge of looking after Sylvan. I told Mother that I felt there was something very wrong with Grace, and she should tell her to go. Well, it just so happened that Mother sensed the urgency in my voice and found out that Grace had been in a mental institution and apart from that, had been prone to epileptic attacks. Mother finally got rid of her, and there was no need to have another nanny, as I was able look after Sylvan.

The few friends who knew we were leaving would come to say good-bye. I shall always remember saying good-bye to Selina. She had tears in her eyes as she hugged me.

She said, "Darling, take care of your Mummy. God will take care of you, and I will see you again. Remember what I told you about your birthmark. You have a lucky birthmark, and everything will be all right for you."

"I love you, Selina," I said. "And I shall remember what you told me about my birthmark."

I did think momentarily there was no sign of luck in me having one.

My emotions were torn. I couldn't understand what my father had done that was so terrible to make my mother run away from him. I knew they had awful fights, but for us to leave everything? From having a good life, we now had nothing except a one-way ticket to Italy. Mother had some new clothes made for us, and I was happy to have designed and chosen the material for a few of the dresses for

Sylvan, but we had very little—no toys, as Mother wanted to keep our possessions to the minimum.

I wondered what adventures were ahead of us, so it was a dichotomy of being sad and excited. The day arrived, and now it was us going in one of the launches to the big liner, the P&O "Sydney." The ship was crowded mainly with Italians. We followed Mother to our cabin; it was at the bottom of the ship, very small with four berths. We were in steerage class, as that was all Mother could afford. I have always had a problem with claustrophobia and felt I couldn't breathe in that cabin; anyway, I told myself that it was only for sleeping. We then found our way up to the top deck as the noise from the chimney signaled our departure, and we slowly started to move, drifting out to sea.

11

I stood at the rails watching all the little boats, the big ships, the launches, the jetty, and farther out to the island of Ceylon, my birthplace until it was just a speck on the horizon. Tears were streaming down my cheeks. It suddenly struck me that we had no home anymore. We had nothing. At that moment all we had was a tiny cabin, which we had to share with each other. Gone was our beautiful home on the hill surrounded by tea bushes—our car, our servants, our signing the chits at the various clubs, our precious Rocky, and most of all, our Daddy. I felt frightened and couldn't help wondering what went so wrong in our lives. Mother had been the toast of the town, beautiful and successful. Dad too was successful, and through his job we had security. I was really too young at that time to understand why it was necessary to leave Ceylon, so as always, when I felt alone and unsure, I would pray to my friend Jesus, asking Him to please take care of us.

The voyage seemed long. I was unhappy being in such close quarters with my mother; I wanted my privacy. After all, despite being only twelve, I was maturing rapidly and was already five-feet-seven inches. I had learned early on to enjoy my own company, as my mother hadn't been there for me as I was growing up, and now she was with me all the time. I found myself flirting with the crew. It was all very innocent, but my life had just been turned upside down, and I needed to think about other things. Vanessa was always with Mother, which was good, as Mother was experiencing the most terrible time with Sylvan, who was so obstreperous and cried a lot, which was embarrassing to the three of us. Mother was unable to control Sylvan, but that wasn't surprising, as Sylvan didn't know her mother. Since Sylvan was born, she had been with different nannies, and I felt she was rebelling. Both Vanessa and I did our best to help Mother. I loved my little sister and wanted her to be happy.

In the evenings the Italian families would make their own entertainment, and whenever I could I would dance, even when the weather was stormy and the sea was rough. Like Isadora Duncan, I would just dance barefoot and interpret the music. The Italians, with their big tummies, sat around in their under vests singing. It was all very jolly. Mother knew that the three of us were safe on board, as the Italians loved children and were only too happy to keep us company. One evening the weather was really bad, and I did feel very sick, I told Mother that I felt sick and had to go to the toilet; we had to share the facilities with the passengers in other cabins. I wasn't used to my mother showing concern for my wellbeing, so when she opened the door of the bathroom, I was surprised, and being such a private person, was mortified, just mortified. Later on I thanked Mother, but asked her to please not enter the bathroom while I was in there, and from then onwards I decided to lock the door.

Our first stop was Djibouti, a tiny country on the East Coast of Africa at the entrance to the Red Sea. I noticed how very hot it was there, and while on deck looking down at what was going on at the port, I was amazed at how black the people were. I had grown up being the only white girl in a few of the schools I had attended but never noticed the skin difference before.

The passage through the Red Sea was rough, so most of the passengers stayed close to their cabins. I was excited for us to sail through the Suez Canal. The land on either side was arid and much of it was desert, but there were a few small homes here and there. The Canal was not very wide, and the ships had to go slowly as they maneuvered through it. Mother had told us much about Egypt. I had hoped to go ashore at Port Said, but she said that she and her Italian friend, Diego, with whom she became friendly while on the ship, had planned to visit the pyramids, and she knew that I would take good care of Vanessa and Sylvan while she was away.

I was only too happy that Mother was having a break from us and taking some time for herself. I took Vanessa and Sylvan to the deck to watch the activity going on at the pier, but was frightened when the vendors started climbing up the ropes attached to the ship, trying to sell souvenirs. I quickly rushed us to the safety of our cabin, but to my surprise they were at the porthole peering in! I was relieved to see Mother, who had loved the experience of her visit to the pyramids and had rewarded us with a few gifts from the excursion.

Shortly after leaving Port Said, Mother told the three of us that Diego had offered us to stay at his family home in a seaside resort called San Benedetto del Tronto on the Adriatic coast of Italy. It was a relief that at last we knew where we were going and that we had somewhere to live. Arriving in Naples was chaotic. Vanessa wasn't well and had to be taken off the ship in a wheelchair. Diego was able to help us with our train journey to his hometown.

I was grateful that the voyage on the SS "Sydney" was over, as it wasn't the greatest trip for me. As far as I was concerned, I was no longer a child, nor was I an adult, and to be suddenly in a different world with hundreds of other people, to be restricted to the poor quarters after only knowing a comfortable life, and also having been so cloistered in convents and boarding schools, I found life on board a little perplexing. I was neither fish nor fowl nor good red herring! We had managed, however, and with the help of Diego found our train and were on our way to San Benedetto del Tronto.

I couldn't help wondering what further adventures awaited us. I felt older than my twelve years, and looking over at Mother, I was suddenly sad for her and promised myself to help her as much as I could. I reflected that Mother was very brave travelling with three young girls with little money, and not knowing what the future held. I was still confused as to why she had given up her life that seemed full and exciting; she was Patricia Pantin Munro, the actress who had produced Broadway productions for Ceylon. Dad had always supported Mother in her work and paid a lot for it, both financially and emotionally. So there was my famous Mother with no money, no possessions, and running away from her husband and the country she loved. I found it all very disturbing.

12

We rented a couple of rooms in Diego's house, which was comfortable and across from the beach. It took me a few days to settle in. I wanted more from Diego; being half child and half adult, I needed love and attention. I was out of my safe place. Diego was kind and managed to console me like a father figure. I really don't know how serious his friendship was with Mother.

Our days were spent mainly on the beach. We had very little money so would eat spaghetti with tomato sauce for lunch every day, together with a salad and drink cheap red wine mixed with water. And for dinner we ate the most wonderful pizzas. That was our daily menu, and Mother never heard us complain. Although Sylvan was still very difficult, we settled into our Italian life. Mother made a few nice female friends. It was September, and the weather was warm and beautiful. I didn't think about the future. I was happy and thought life in that Italian seaside resort was idyllic.

In the evenings after putting Vanessa and Sylvan to bed, Mother, together with a friend or two, would let me accompany them to the open-air bar, which had a small dance floor. It was during our second visit that a tall, good-looking red-headed Italian man approached our table. I think Mother thought he was going to ask her to dance, but instead he came to me and turned to Mother to ask if he could have her permission to dance with me.

From that moment Mario became my best friend. I saw him every day on the beach. He had lots of friends and was certainly loved by everyone. Wherever Mario was, there was always much laughter and happiness. Mario showed me a lot of attention. Despite all the attractive Italian women that surrounded him, I was his "love." I didn't use makeup, and being a redhead, had blonde eyebrows and eyelashes. I was not glamorous. Mario, however, wanted me with him all the time, and enjoyed driving me on the back of his Vespa.

In the evenings we would go 'ballare' (dancing) to the open-air dance floor where we had met. Mother would leave Vanessa and Sylvan in the care of Diego's mother and insist on accompanying me to the outdoor bar. She and her friend would sit there with their glass of wine and watch me dance with Mario. It was not a good time for Mother, as she couldn't believe that at the age of forty-four years old and beautiful, she was now the chaperone of her twelve-year-old daughter who was dancing the night away.

Mario was a gorgeous twenty-nine-year-old and spoke excellent English. One evening he asked Mother if he could take me out alone. She agreed. We had dinner at his favourite pizza restaurant, and then he said he'd like to show me his apartment, which overlooked the sea. In my innocence I went with him. When he drew me to him to kiss me, I was trembling. I told him that I was twelve years old, which surprised him, as all along he had thought I was sixteen. As he kissed me, I pulled away from him with tears running down my cheeks, saying that I didn't want to have a baby.

Despite Mother's talk to me when I was ten years old, I had no idea how babies were made. I was totally innocent of everything. Due to the fact that I had never really wanted to grow up, I hadn't been interested to know about the birds and the bees. Mario was so gentle and sweet. Our kiss was the most beautiful memory that I kept secret in my heart for a long time. He told me that he loved me and told Mother the same thing and that he would wait for me until I was of age for marriage.

Mother confided in me that money was running out and that she had written to her relatives in England to let them know that she was in Italy, and could they send funds to help us out. Well, Mother wasn't exactly prepared for the reply. Mother's cousin Elfrieda Pantin married to Charles Wallis the brother of Barnes Wallis of "bouncing bomb" fame, wrote to her saying that she must leave as soon as possible for London and that the children must be enrolled in school—that she couldn't keep three young girls without schooling. I imagine that as Mother left school when she was twelve and was self-educated, she didn't feel the same urgency for us. Money was sent for our tickets to London. I said good-bye to Mario, and we promised to write to each other, but as time went on, keeping in touch became too difficult, so we lost contact.

13

Once more we were on the move, and were all sad to be leaving our friends and our lovely free life in Italy. Mario and Diego took us to the station where we boarded the train for Milan. It was November, and it was becoming cold. We arrived at the enormous and majestic Milan railway station. I had never seen such a lovely railway station and had to help Mother find the train that took us to the English Channel, where we would travel on the ferry and then connect with another train to London. Mother was amazing, and I knew that she was happy to have my help for the tedious journey. I wanted to and did help with Vanessa and Sylvan, and we were all grateful to settle back on our train out of Milan.

After a long and tiring trip, we finally arrived in London and took a taxi to the little hotel where a room reservation had been made for us. The room was small, and we were cramped together with our suitcases. The weather was cold and dreary. I wondered what had happened to the sun. We had no warm clothing, so were happy to be in the hotel with a small heater in the room. The days spent in the hotel were no fun at all. We were constantly cold, and to add to that, London was very foggy; something we knew nothing about. The air was awful to breathe, and it affected Mother, causing her to have a bad asthmatic reaction. When I was at the Hill School, I told everyone that I had a brother, Michael, who lived in England, a magical place where I would travel to one day and be with my brother. What I had experienced so far was not the England of my imagination! Our relations had kindly arranged for us to go to their home in the country for Christmas, and much to our delight, it snowed before we left London. The three of us girls, together with Mother, had our faces pressed to the window of our room, as we had never seen snow, and were fascinated while we watched the snowflakes fall outside.

As we left the small hotel room and stepped into the cold winter air to catch our train to Dorset, we were miserable. Having arrived from the heat of Ceylon and enjoyed the warmth of our stay in Italy, we were not prepared for the bitterly cold weather. We didn't possess a coat or gloves or any form of warm clothing. How grateful we were that Charles and Elfrieda Wallis had invited us to their home in Gillingham, Dorset, for Christmas.

Auntie Elfrieda had some of her winter clothes ready for Mother and had anticipated that the three of us had nothing appropriate to wear, so she had gone to a jumble sale and bought us clothing, which was adequate for that time. During the holidays Elfrieda's brother, Uncle William, came to stay, and we had the pleasure of meeting our benefactor, Professor William Pantin, an expert and teacher of medieval history at Oriel College, Oxford. Uncle William was a bachelor and an ardent Catholic, a convert. He was exactly as I thought a real professor should be. I liked him, although he didn't say much and seemed shy, but I was most grateful to him, as he was going to look after me financially until I left school, and he offered to do the same for Sylvan. Vanessa would not be parted from Mother, and Mother wanted her with her, so once Mother had found a place to live, it was decided that Vanessa would attend a state school in her area in London.

I was most thankful to Uncle Charles and Auntie Elfrieda for inviting us to stay in their comfortable, warm home. As we celebrated a family Christmas, I thought about Dad and wondered what he was doing and how he had felt when he found out that the four of us were no longer in Colombo and had absolutely no idea where we were; it made me feel sad. I didn't dare let my thoughts go to Rocky. Instead I enjoyed playing with the Wallis's two lovely little dogs. While we were at Wyke House, it had been decided that Sylvan and I would attend a convent in Tring in the county of Berkshire.

Money was given to Mother to buy our uniforms, and she was told that all the bills for our education at the convent would be paid. There was, however, one strong proviso for Mother. She would have to find a job as a secretary and forget any ideas she may have about trying to find work as an actress. Mother had ideas to act on the West End stage, and her hope was that the three of us would be taken care of while she pursued her dream. That wasn't to be. We often heard her say that she should never have had children, that she wasn't cut out to be a mother and that she had sacrificed her life and her talents for the three of us.

We were all rather reluctant to leave the beautiful and comfortable home in Gillingham, but we had to. Mother found a room in a building in Earl's Court, a popular section of London, with one large bed and a small sofa bed. The room had a basin, an electric two-ring stove, and a small electric heater that had to have money inserted before it gave out heat. The bathroom, which was not heated and was on the landing below us, was used by some of the other occupants of the house. We spent my thirteenth birthday in that small room. All we could afford was a meal of mashed carrots and potatoes, which became our daily staple.

Mother managed to make the little money we had been given stretch. She even enjoyed half a bottle of wine at the weekends and five cigarettes to last her the week. There were times that I just couldn't believe what we were experiencing was real, and I hoped that one day I would awaken and we would be back as one happy family in our comfortable house with servants, a garden, Rocky, and surrounded by God's beauty. Alas, the bad dream became more of a nightmare. Thank goodness there was a small heater in the room, as that winter was proving to be viciously cold. Going down a flight of steps to the bathroom and taking a bath was most unpleasant. I was always cold.

It was a few days after my birthday and Sylvan's sixth birthday, that we had to start at the convent in Tring. It was a freezing cold day as we travelled by train and then took a taxi to the convent. Sylvan was in a terrible state when Mother and Vanessa had to leave us. The nuns took Sylvan away from me, and I didn't know where she was being taken. I normally didn't feel scared, but this was an exception. Even at the young age of thirteen, I seemed to have a sixth sense about people and places, and the vibes I received from that place were not good. For the first time in my life I really dreaded being left at the convent. I knew Mother couldn't do anything; we were the poor relations, and I had to be brave for her as she said her good-byes. The thought of not being with Sylvan, not taking care of her under the difficult and strange circumstances was a great worry to me. I was so miserable, and it was so cold. That evening in the refectory I found the food was strange too: big slices of white bread—doorstops, they were called—and lots of potatoes. I wasn't used to that bland food and thought about the delicate curries that I ate with gusto, all the wonderful fruit, mangoes, mangosteens, rambutans and the fresh vegetables. The Italian cuisine was different, but it too was delicious compared to what we had to eat in the convent. As I was so cold, I had no option but to force myself to swallow the horrible food. It wasn't long before I started putting on weight.

I was always such a happy person and accepted almost everything without complaining. Not ever being able to see Sylvan made me very anxious. The most vivid memory of her was watching her screaming and crying at a window. I asked one of the nuns to see her but was told that she had mumps or measles, and we couldn't be together. It broke my heart, but there was nothing I could do. I wanted to be with her and for us to be out of that terrible place.

I had made up my mind we had to leave at the end of the term. Sylvan didn't know that after dinner every night I had to walk with five other girl boarders for half a mile in the freezing cold to our dormitory. I developed chilblains. My toes were very sore, my fingers too. There were times when I couldn't feel my toes nor fingers. I had one friend, Helen, and after we had knelt beside our beds to say our prayers, she and I would sometimes cuddle up on our "hospital" bed in order to radiate warmth and try to sleep. I made up my mind to run away, but always the thought of leaving Sylvan was uppermost. My little sister had suffered a lot. Her young life had been so turbulent. It just didn't seem fair.

At half-term Mother and Vanessa came to Tring, and we met in a little café where I told Mother that there was no way that Sylvan and I would return for the following term. Mother realised how desperately miserable both Sylvan and I were. Especially Sylvan who was only six years old, and mother had agreed to have her sent to a boarding school. Sylvan was a difficult child, which was hardly surprising, considering that her life had been so disrupted. I couldn't help feeling that we were being punished, but for what? Mother kept telling us it was all due to our father; his drinking had ruined her life and ours. She had to run away from him and take us with her.

The only other thing which kept me going for that term at Tring, apart from just knowing that Jesus would release Sylvan and me from that awful place, was my dance class. I could escape into dance and forget the reality of the freezing cold, the awful food, not being allowed to be with my little sister, and every other painful experience I had to endure. I remember learning how to dance the Sailor's Hornpipe. It gave me exercise that I so desperately needed and allowed me a certain freedom. The dancing also helped my circulation.

We had to ride on a bus to church on Sundays, and as I stared out of the window looking at the cold, bare countryside, I saw the sheep trying to find a little grass. I had never seen sheep before and despite their woolly protection wondered how they managed to survive the terrible cold.

At last it was time for the holidays, and due to my pleas to Mother to take us away and Mother seeing our pitiful plight, she managed to talk Aunt Elfrieda into arranging for us to go to a convent in Shaftesbury, Dorset, which was the next town to where she and Uncle Charles lived. Vanessa would continue to live with Mother in the tiny one-room in Earl's Court and go to the day school where she was doing extremely well and was happy.

14

I now weighed one hundred and seventy pounds. I hardly recognized myself! I was excited at the thought of attending the new school, which would be number fourteen. Sylvan and Vanessa would live with Mother and I with my aunt and uncle in their beautiful home where I had my own bedroom and bathroom and a cat and dogs to play with. I felt so happy and was grateful to Jesus as I said my nightly prayers; very happy that my nightmare was over. I helped Uncle Charles feed the chickens and grew to learn about a baby tortoise that was a pet. I went for walks over the fields and breathed in the country air. I wore Auntie Elfrieda's clothes, which made me look much older than my thirteen years, but having gained so much weight at the convent in Tring, it was a blessing that I was able to wear her clothes. I watched Aunt Elfrieda cooking in her lovely, spacious kitchen and enjoyed our dinner time with such tasty food served on blue-and-white cottage china. I was really happy and at peace.

Sylvan would often stay during the holidays, and we had fun playing with the dogs, enjoying the tree house, and discovering the countryside with Auntie and Uncle. We loved to go in the car for drives and especially to Corfu Castle, Swanage, and Studland Bay. The seaside wasn't like that of Colombo, neither of San Benedetto del Tronto, but it didn't matter. Sylvan and I were with two amazing people who loved us and who tried to bring a sense of normalcy and fun into our lives.

Settling into St. Mary's Convent took a few days, but that building was like a palace to me. When I saw the chapel, I walked over to the altar, and as I was on my knees, tears flowed freely as I gave thanks to Jesus. I was overwhelmed with gratitude. I knew I would be happy there. I felt a sense of belonging, a sense of feeling secure. Being a loner by nature, I didn't need to make friends, but I seemed to be popular, despite having a mass of red hair, freckles, and being the heaviest girl in the school.

With prodding from my mother, Auntie Elfrieda managed to have the convent arrange for me to be on a special diet. The school food looked appealing, nothing like the St. Trinians diet of Tring, but it was necessary for my health to lose weight, so I went on a strict diet. While all the girls were served the delicious convent food, I would have to eat salads and fruit. For some strange reason I was put in charge of the tuck shop, not a good idea. There were many times when the temptation was too great, and a Mars bar would disappear!

I was determined to do my utmost to work towards passing my GCE exams in order to show how grateful I was to Uncle Billy, and of course, my wonderful Aunt Elfrieda, whom I loved dearly, and Uncle Charles. As I had attended so many different schools, studying did not come easily to me, I had to work very hard. It wasn't long before I gave up algebra and geometry, but I did enjoy history, geography, Latin, religious teaching, and most of all art. French was rather difficult, as was English grammar, but English literature I found interesting. The nuns were just lovely, and I felt comfortable.

I attended Mass every morning and became a Child of Mary, which meant that there were certain duties we would volunteer to do, and one of them was to help at the Cheshire Homes, which were not too far away. I would spend time with autistic children, talking to them, trying to play games, and helping them with their tea. Those young people with all their disadvantages seemed so brave and happy. I was in deep admiration of them, and although I was often bemused as to why God made those children different to me, I was happy to have had the honour of being of some small assistance. The experience had a profound effect on me, and made me thank Jesus every night for my good health.

Uncle Billy was very generous; he didn't want me to feel in any way inadequate and paid for me to have tennis lessons, and I was able to join a small group of girls to watch the tennis at Wimbledon, which was such an exciting experience. If there were any school outings, I could be part of them. My main sport was hockey. As I was large and had a good eye, I was goalie. I did the best I could but didn't make the top team! I had always enjoyed PE, but now as I was so heavy, I really hated to be asked to climb up ropes and jump over the horse and do other impossible tasks. I usually ended up in tears. Eventually I was excused from gym.

The holidays came, and I spent lovely days with my aunt and uncle. Life with those two gentle people was heaven to me. I shared my holidays between Wyke House and Mother, taking the train from Gillingham to Waterloo where Mother met me. The small room we lived in was bedroom, living room, and kitchen, and somehow the four of us made the most of it. I think my poor mother felt so cramped, but that one room was all we had; it was home to us. Mother would somehow manage to take us to the theatre. We would sit up in the "gods," the cheapest seats, but it was a treat, and we loved the shows. We went to the zoo and enjoyed playing in the parks. Mother did her best to make our holidays as interesting and happy as possible.

I had mixed feelings when it was time to leave to return to school. Although it was good to spend time with Mother and my sisters, it was cold and uncomfortable, and to be constantly subjected to how Mother had sacrificed her life for us and how she regretted her marriage to Dad, which, of course, was my fault, wasn't very nice. She seemed, at times, to be filled with bitterness. However, despite those difficult times, which weren't easy for the three of us, we did have happy moments just being together. I was getting used to packing my own suitcase and being left at the railway station to get the train back to Gillingham. I never felt scared, as I knew that Jesus was with me. I would try to find a window seat so I could enjoy looking at the countryside. My thoughts used to wander back to Ceylon and to Dad, wondering whether I would ever see him again.

15

Mother had been hoping to arrange for Vanessa and Sylvan to join me at St. Mary's Convent, so it was decided that Vanessa should try to win a scholarship to the convent and that Dad's rich brother and his wife be contacted to pay for Sylvan's fees. Dad's brother, Uncle Ian, was contacted by Charles Wallis, and he reluctantly agreed to pay for Sylvan. However, there was one stipulation—that under no circumstances would they wish to have any contact with us as a family. We were nicely surprised when we received one pound sterling and a hamper for Christmas, and as we had so few luxuries, it was a big treat for us. Dr. Munro and his wife, Nancy, were well off, and they definitely didn't want to be associated with their poor relations. They had not forgiven Dad for his sins.

Vanessa won a scholarship to St. Mary's and started there with Sylvan. Vanessa was popular and clever, always coming top of her class. We all had our own schedules. I kept very much to myself, but was around if any of the girls wanted to chat or had a problem to discuss with me. I was possibly the largest girl in the school, though never really considered myself unattractive. I just looked different to the other girls. I have to admit that I did enjoy eating bread spread with yummy fat at break time, during the winter months.

There were times when I really thought I would love to become a nun and devote myself to Jesus. However, it would mean no pretty clothes, no makeup, no boys. I prayed for an answer; Jesus answered me. I didn't have a vocation. My happiest times seemed to be in the beautiful chapel and during the tranquil retreats.

When the holidays came, Mother was invited to stay at Wyke House with Aunt Elfrieda and Uncle Charles. It was wonderful for the four of us to be together in their home, and I knew Mother felt relieved that her three daughters were now in a beautiful convent and having the best possible education. Sometimes David Wallis, Elfrieda and Charles's son would visit. I wasn't sure if he was happy to see another family in his home.

One evening after dinner, Mother, being the consummate actress, waited until we were all gathered in the drawing room and said she had some news for us. Mother told us that when she was walking through Russell Square on her way to a temporary typing job, she noticed a familiar figure coming towards her. She said she blinked, not sure if she was seeing things, but when the familiar figure stopped and said hello, it was Dad. Naturally, we were all stunned. In the whole world, in the whole of London, for Mother and Dad to bump into each other seemed totally incredible.

There was complete silence in the room for a minute as we were trying to digest what Mother had just told us. The last we knew, we had left Dad in Ceylon. I immediately felt that Jesus wanted Dad united with us again and was excited; though Mother, who was so venomous and had tried to fill us with every derogatory notion about him, soon quashed our spirits, especially mine. I was curious to know how he looked, where he was living, and much more, and especially what Mother thought of seeing him again. As it was time for us to go to bed, we didn't hear further news.

After a couple of happy weeks in the country, we returned to London to vacation with Mother. Our Australian mother answered all our eager questions about Dad. Vanessa was Mother's favourite and hadn't spent a lot of time with him, and Sylvan didn't remember much. I was amazed again when Mother told me that in all the places in London to choose, my father was actually living in a small hotel in Earl's Court exactly opposite the building where Mother was living. The little room where Mother lived on the second floor looked right into the hotel. Mother told us that when she met Dad they went for a drink, and he told her that he was a broken man when he heard that Mother had run off with the three of us. He had a terrible nervous breakdown, was drinking heavily, and told his employers what he thought of them and was consequently fired from his job. Once he recovered he decided to travel to London in the hope that maybe he would find us, and amazingly he did. Mother did not say whether she would see Dad again.

I was almost fifteen years old. I found that the short periods I spent with Mother and my sisters in the small room were becoming more and more difficult. I was a teenager, and although so young, looked eighteen. I started wearing a little mascara and lipstick and wanted to meet boys. Around the corner from where we lived was the famous Overseas Club in Earl's Court, and although I was still a child, I really wanted to be a grownup. I hung out with the young men from Australia and South Africa. They were not aware of my youth and fortunately did not take advantage of me. I was so innocent, but I wanted a boyfriend, some young man to be my friend whom I could trust and love.

I did make friends with a South African, who was a member of the club. I treasured the time when we would have a coffee together or when he'd invite me to his room to iron his shirts. One day the secretary of the club said that one of the members was stealing money, and to my dismay the young man I was friendly with was found guilty; purple dye had been put in the pockets, and he was caught with dye on his fingers. I stopped going to the club after that experience and said nothing to my mother about the incident.

I then found the company of a young Thai student who rented the room next to us in the building. He was very sweet and took my mind off the experience I had had with the South African. He became my friend while I was staying with Mother and my sisters, and I looked forward to talking to someone a few years older than me.

Dad lived across the road, and I couldn't really understand why we all hadn't got together. However, I did see him for a cup of coffee a couple of times, but I felt awkward, as the whole situation seemed very strange, and I didn't know whether to be happy or sad. I knew that I really wanted to return to the convent and the innocent life I led there.

The term seemed to go quickly. I learned how to sew and embroider, and most of all I learned ballroom dancing. I was in charge of the music every evening, and any of us girls who wanted to dance were allowed to; it was our evening recreation. Once a week we would have a lovely blonde ballroom dance teacher show us how to tango, waltz, foxtrot, samba, and so forth. It was my dream day; I wished it would never end.

I was busy studying for my General Certificate of Education. I really wanted to show my gratitude to Auntie Elfrieda and Uncle William for their great kindness in taking care of me and giving me the opportunity to be educated at that wonderful convent. It was important that I should pass all my GCE exams. I knew I wasn't as clever as Vanessa, and as I had had a varied upbringing, it would be difficult, but with Jesus taking care of me, I believed I would be all right—so long as I worked very hard.

After being in various dormitories, Mother Gregory, the head mistress, finally gave me a room to myself. I was fifteen and a half and was thrilled to have my own little room, which consisted of my bed, a desk, and a chair and a small cupboard for my clothes. Just as I was settling into the thrill of having my own space, Mother Gregory called me to her office. I felt uneasy, as it was not her normal summons. I didn't think I had done anything to upset her, nor had I abused the rules of the school, so when she asked me to sit down, I was apprehensive. Mother Gregory had small, rather piercing brown eyes, a pointed nose and bucked teeth; all the nuns still wore the habit. I could see she didn't smile as she usually did when she spoke to me.

"Diana" she said. "I have some very sad news for you. Your auntie has died of a brain tumour."

A brain tumour, I hadn't been told how ill she was and my heart was broken. I loved Auntie Elfrieda more than my mother.

Mother Gregory told me that Uncle Charles had thought it best if she broke the news to me; I understood. I sat in Mother Gregory's little study and looking at her face, I knew how hard it was for her to give me the news. I stood up and thanked her for letting me know.

I went straight to the chapel to pray for my aunt's soul and made a promise to her that I would pass my GCEs. Auntie Elfrieda made me feel safe, so once again I felt I was on my own and vulnerable. Apart from the sadness of never seeing Rocky again, that was my first experience with deep sadness, of losing someone I loved so much.

From that day I woke at four in the morning to study then went to morning Mass before lessons. Auntie Elfrieda had had a lot of sadness in her own life, though she never spoke about her two children who were mentally challenged. I had learned much by observing Auntie's inner strength; I never heard her complain or be angry. To me she was a saint.

I thought about Uncle Charles and wondered how he was coping. Just being with those two lovely people and their desire to please me was overwhelming at times. I was very grateful that they treated me like their daughter. Our visits to the windy seaside were always rewarded when Auntie opened the picnic basket! There were delicious cheese and marmite sandwiches and chocolate digestive biscuits, and a little treat for their adorable spaniel, Sonja.

Some weeks after Auntie Elfrieda went to heaven, I received a phone call from Uncle Charles, asking if I would like him to take me out the following weekend. I told him that I would like that very much. When I saw him, I felt sad. I knew how much I was missing Auntie Elfrieda and could imagine how much more he must be missing her. Uncle Charles was an old military man and used to making decisions, so I was surprised when he asked me what I would like to do on our day out together. Despite all the sadness, I told him that I would really like to go into the town of Salisbury and see Elvis Presley in the film "Jail House Rock." I don't think Uncle Charles had any idea what the film was about, but he agreed. Needless to say, I was very excited, as I loved Elvis! Before going to the cinema, we had a visit to the beautiful Salisbury cathedral.

Over lunch at a lovely little restaurant, I had the opportunity to ask him about Auntie Elfrieda's illness and also what he thought I should do when I left the convent. He told me that Uncle William and he had decided that I should attend Langham Secretarial College just off Park Lane in London. He also told me that Mother and Dad had now found a new home in Wimbledon Park, so the journey to and from the college wouldn't be too difficult. Uncle Charles made it clear to me that if I had a certificate from a reputable secretarial school, I would be able to find a job and contribute to paying the bills. I was relieved, as I was now aware of what was expected of me.

We then made our way to the cinema. I knew that Uncle Charles had not heard of Elvis Presley, and for him to see that film would be an education of a sort. At the end of the film, I asked him if he had enjoyed it. He gave me a big smile. I felt that he had never in his life seen anything like Elvis. I think he had many chuckles after he dropped me off at the convent. I was a happy girl, having had a wonderful outing, and Uncle Charles was a really good sport!

Life went on at the school and I was studying hard. Vanessa was always busy with her own friends. Unfortunately, Sylvan just couldn't settle into life at the convent. Her young life had been so disturbed that it was best for her to be with Mother, so she left the convent. I had hoped that despite Auntie Elfrieda not being at Wyke, Uncle Charles would still have me to stay for the holidays, which he did.

During the holidays he suggested I might like to visit his brother, Barnes Wallis and his wife, Molly, in their holiday home in Plymouth. I was used to visiting other people's homes during my holidays—and with my training of etiquette from the Irish nuns and also from my Mother, who made sure that I knew to always leave the bathroom as I found it, and many other indelible pieces of advice, not forgetting to always write the "bread and butter" letter—I was never nervous at being a house guest. My breeding and sense of decorum showed up from an early age.

Uncle Barnes and his wife were just super. I really enjoyed my visit to their lovely cosy home, and Uncle Barnes delighted in teaching me how to play poker dice and showing me around Plymouth and the harbour. He never spoke of his amazing invention, and Uncle Charles had not mentioned it to me either. It was years later when I went to see the film "The Dam Busters," starring Richard Todd and Michael

Redgrave that I understood how important Uncle Barnes had been with his invention of the bouncing bombs during the attack on the dams of the Ruhr Valley in Germany during World War II. He was also well renowned for his other inventions.

My last term at St. Mary's was emotional. I was studying hard, anxious that I should succeed in passing my exams. At least now I knew that Mother and Dad were back together, and when I left for London, I would be in a flat rather than sharing the one room. I was also relieved that Uncle William was still going to take care of me and pay for me to attend secretarial college for a year.

After sitting the GCE exams, we had an end-of-term performance where the seniors either sang or danced for Mother Gregory, the nuns and the rest of the school. I decided to be Debbie Reynolds, and dressed in a nightgown, I sang "Tammy". Mother Gregory didn't look too pleased with my performance, but I received a resounding applause from the girls! It is still remembered to this day. Although thinking back, I suppose I was brave, wearing just a nightdress and being rather plump with long, red frizzy hair. However, I felt like the movie star Debbie Reynolds, but it was obvious that Mother Gregory didn't feel the same!

Finally, the last day had arrived. It was the end of my blissful life at St. Mary's Convent. I had spent four wonderfully happy years with those amazing nuns in beautiful surroundings, and was filled with gratitude. I knew I would miss so much about my alma mater, especially the beautiful chapel where I had spent many peaceful hours. During the holidays I received my certificates, having passed eight subjects. I was elated; all my hard work had paid off, and I was delighted to pass the good news onto Uncle Charles and especially to Uncle William, who had made it all possible. I knew that my dearest auntie would have been very proud; she knew that none of it came easily to me, and would have appreciated my success all the more.

After Auntie Elfrieda's demise, Uncle Charles sold Wyke House and bought a smaller house. Much to my surprise, he informed me that he would be marrying a family friend. We all knew Christine, who was the mother of two sons who were our friends. When term ended, I went to spend a little time with Uncle Charles and Christine. During those few weeks, they had a young cousin, also called Charles, visiting from South Africa. He and I became very close, innocently close. However, our friendship caused concern, so I left for London and for Mother and Dad and a new home.

I never visited Uncle Charles and Christine again. Uncle Charles came to see me in London while I was at the Langham Secretarial College. It was good to see him, and once again I thanked him for everything he did for me. I wrote constantly to Uncle William, the old college professor, who buried himself in his books. I knew I wouldn't see him, but I always wanted him to know how grateful I was for his kindness to me, for giving me an education and in making me feel special. Uncle Charles died a few years later while rescuing a child from drowning in the sea.

16

Travelling in the train to London, I felt excited. I was about to enter a whole new life. No more wearing school uniforms. I wasn't a school girl anymore. I was sixteen and was thrilled at the prospect of living in London. Mother had found us a flat in Wimbledon Park. The flat was in a semi-detached house at the end of a cul-de-sac. An elderly couple had the bottom flat, and we had the upstairs with its own entrance. The flat consisted of two bedrooms, a small single bedroom, kitchen, living room, bathroom and outside steps that led down to a tiny plot of garden.

When I had Mother to myself for a few minutes, I asked her how it had happened. Mother told me that Dad, while staying in the hotel opposite her building, had spent all his pension money on alcohol and prostitutes; she presumed I knew about prostitutes, and when she saw my blank face, went on to explain. Mother was living in poverty with the exception of what she was earning as a temporary secretary. When Dad had spent all his money, he went to her and asked if she would help find him a job. Mother, who really had no feelings whatsoever for Dad and always regretted the day she ever met him, felt that if he was employed and she working too, then there was a possibility that we could all live together under more pleasant circumstances. After all, he was our father, and she, at times, was a fairly practical woman.

At least it would release her from living in one room. Mother had Dad apply for a job, which she found for him with an important firm in the city of London as an accountant, and his application was accepted. So Mother and Dad moved in together. For a few days I shared the double bed with Mother in the main bedroom, but soon decided that I would prefer to sleep on a bunk bed in the living room. Vanessa and Sylvan shared the other bedroom, and Dad had the little single room.

I travelled from Wimbledon Park to Park Lane during the week to attend Langham Secretarial College. I realised that the girls were all well off. I was again on a mission, as I had to make Uncle William proud of me, so I learned typing, shorthand, bookkeeping and English grammar, which I had not passed in my exams at the convent. I honestly found all of that very difficult; bookkeeping was especially hard for me—and, well, English grammar, I had to take that exam eight times before I finally succeeded. Attending that smart college was not the easiest time for me, but Uncle William gave me weekly pocket money, which I liked to share with my family. I knew I had to pass the exams, as my family was dependent on me working and helping with the household expenses.

The best thing about being at the college was making a friend. Louise was my saviour; she was warm and friendly, and encouraged me at every point. Her friendship and patience were the reasons for me passing my exams. Apart from her being wonderful in the classroom, Louise was a real friend. My last real friend was Heather when I was seven years old. I never had a real girlfriend after that, so I was slightly overwhelmed by all of Louise's kindness.

At the lunch break, I decided to stay in class and eat the sandwich that I had brought from home, but Louise insisted I should go to her home for lunch. Louise's parents' flat was just around the corner from Park Lane. She lived in one of the beautiful buildings in Mayfair, and the butler would greet us at the door. We would go to the dining room where a buffet lunch was prepared. I felt as if I was in some ancient Roman palace surrounded by gorgeous paintings and a feast laid out for us to enjoy. Louise didn't mind that I was poor and that Uncle William was paying the fees. Although I didn't have expensive clothes, I always looked good in the few clothes I had. Going to secretarial college wasn't so bad; I had a special friend.

It didn't take long to get used to living in our new home. I was particularly grateful that at the end of the street was the Catholic Church, and I made friends with a few teenagers, meeting them in the church hall on a Saturday night. That was something new to me, but I tried to fit in for a while. I especially enjoyed the weekends in the summer when Mother, Dad, Vanessa, Sylvan and I would visit Wimbledon Park; it was just so nice to be able to walk through the gardens and enjoy an ice cream and be a family again. I soon discovered that in the town of Wimbledon, the next stop to us by tube, every Friday night the Victor Sylvester ballroom held dance lessons in ballroom dancing. Fortunately the train station was just up the road from where we lived, and I was grateful for that, as coming home between ten and ten thirty at night, I was a little nervous to walk down the quiet, dimly lit street.

For the most part life was normal. Mother did not enjoy any form of housework; even cooking our supper was not pleasurable for her, as she was an artist, a writer, and actress. She often used to remind us that she should never have had children and certainly should never have married Dad. To enjoy some freedom from the boredom of being a housewife, she joined an art school. The art lessons were a welcome release for her, and she was extremely talented.

Dad took the laundry to the launderette on Saturdays, and I spent most of Sunday after Mass listening to records and doing the ironing and cleaning the flat. At Christmas we would go into Wimbledon to window shop. Mother had bought seats to the theatre for us to see the Christmas pantomime; it was always a happy evening especially enjoyed by Sylvan.

Dad was going to his first office Christmas party and asked me if I would like to accompany him, as Mother certainly had no intention of going. At almost seventeen, I still carried some puppy fat, but the ugly duckling was beginning to turn into a swan. I was so excited when Mother and I went shopping to buy the dress that I was to wear for Dad's office party, which was being held at the Waldorf Hotel. Dad was very proud of me, and it was a lovely evening; I received many compliments.

Fortunately there were not too many fights, but Mother did shout at us often; sometimes she seemed out of control. I was used to her outbursts and tried to be as quiet as possible. Every night on my knees

I would pray that Dad kept his word and wouldn't drink, as I knew that would cause a major upset.

After my first term at the college, Mother suggested that she and I go to Paris for the weekend as a treat for my seventeenth birthday. I knew Mother desperately wanted a change of scenery; she needed a holiday. Unfortunately, the weekend was miserable. January was not the time to travel. The ferry crossing was so rough and I felt really sick. Everything about our visit to Paris was a disaster, especially as we had such little money, frankly I was happy to return home, however, I did feel sorry for Mother, as whatever she was hoping for in Paris didn't materialise.

I loved going to Sunday Mass. When the time came for the collections, I would put my shilling into the basket and was not really aware who took the collection, until one Sunday I did notice a very attractive, older man. The Sundays came and went, and gradually we started to smile at one another. After Mass one day as we were leaving the church, he was walking beside me, and said hello. I blushed as he pressed a piece of paper in my hand and said to telephone him. My heart was pounding; I had a feeling that he had to be married, but seeing him every Sunday from downcast eyes, I realised I really liked him. I couldn't wait to tell Louise the next day. In the lunch break she made me call him; his name was Peter. He told me to meet him at his office after lessons. Louise told me to call Mother to say I would be late home, as I would be spending a little time with her.

Peter took me for a coffee; we had a big attraction for one another. He told me that he was married and had two children, but he found me beautiful. No one had ever told me that before. I knew I wanted to be with him, especially as the previous weekend Dad had broken his promise to Mother and had returned to drinking. They had had the most awful fight, and as usual, I thought Mother would kill him. I called the police, who came together with an ambulance, and Dad was taken away. It was always terribly painful for me to watch him, as he looked so pitiful. He told the police that Mother had provoked him and that he had done nothing to hurt her. My heart cried out. I had seen that scene many times before.

Feeling comfortable and safe with Peter, I told him about the anxious home life I had with Mother and Dad. Peter arranged for me to miss school one day. I was to meet him at a pre-arranged place, and he drove me to his sister's home. My innocence was broken. I felt I was in love with Peter, but I didn't expect it to be so painful!

Of course, Louise couldn't wait to hear my news and had similar news of her own. My meetings with Peter would continue. I would arrange to see him once a week at his office for a while after work. As much as I liked Peter, I did feel uncomfortable, knowing he was married, and we were both committing sin, and I had to keep going to confession. I was also becoming bored; the initial excitement was waning.

At that time too, my year at Langham's was coming to an end. I managed to pass all my subjects except English grammar, but with the help of Louise, I eventually passed on my eighth attempt. I will always remember Peter; he was my first real love. I liked being in love and decided that I should always be in love! Having finished at Langham Secretarial College, Louise and I drifted apart. Sadly, I never saw her again.

I was now in a position to find work and to help with paying the bills at home. I was pleased to pass on the news to Uncle Charles and Uncle Billy. I wasn't looking forward to temporary work, especially as I didn't feel at all confident with my shorthand, but typing was easier. I started working in horrible, smoky offices and was miserable. I was young and nervous and most of the time overwhelmed by the work. The best thing about that experience was receiving my pay at the end of the week. After giving Mother what I could afford and keeping enough for fares, I made sure that I had one pound left to buy one or two items of clothing from a catalogue where I could pay on the "never, never" system, as it was called.

17

When I arrived home in the evenings, I was never sure what to expect, as I could sense tension was always around us. Mother appeared to become more and more dissatisfied with her situation, and her bitterness caused an atmosphere. Her continuous fault finding with Dad made him drop his promise again. We knew Mother would make Dad swear on the Bible that he would stop drinking, but in some ways I could understand him starting to drink again, as Mother treated him so badly; she didn't like him eating with us or even being with us. I felt really sorry for him. When Dad started to drink, we knew that he wouldn't be able to go to work, and his drinking made Mother shout at him even more. The fights were terrible.

The screaming would start and Mother's rage was frightening. I would tell my sisters to go into another room while I had to stand between Mother and Dad for fear that she would kill him. Poor Dad, he looked so helpless, so weak. His biggest sin was that he just could not drink alcohol, and once he started, he couldn't stop. He was an alcoholic, but he denied it to the day he died. I feared for his life and would call the police, who were around almost immediately. Once again the ambulance would take Dad away, as invariably Mother had hit him, so he was bruised and bloody. Mother would tell the police that Dad had got in a drunken rage and attacked her, and a fight ensued. Nothing had changed in those awful fights, having experienced them from an early age. I seemed to know how to handle the situation—though they left me trembling, and of course, I would cry myself to sleep. The police department was well aware of the trouble at our house.

Despite finding my mother difficult, I did love her, and I loved my dad too. Mother would say how unfair it was that she had such a difficult childhood, and here she was living again in similar circumstances having to go out to work. I felt sorry for her but sometimes wondered why she had given up so much, as she really had a good life in Ceylon, but she wanted to be free of Dad. How strange that he found his way back to us and to her.

I had a couple of boyfriends of my own age who lived nearby. One boyfriend, whom Mother thought beneath me, was actually a lot of fun. He was a lover of football and would invite me to go with him to watch his club, Fulham. We travelled on the tube with all the other football enthusiasts and sat through the rain watching his team. After the match we would either end up in a pub playing darts or eating fish and chips wrapped in newspaper. Our friendship ended when we moved out of the area, but recalling it was very pleasant. I enjoyed the innocence of our friendship.

In the meantime I was becoming more stressed with going from one job to another. I was usually sent to small, smoky law offices and the work was hard for me. I was really unhappy, which was not usual, so I asked Mother if she could help me find a job that would interest me. She knew only too well that I was not one to complain and was concerned that I wasn't happy with the temporary jobs. One evening after I had returned home from work, she told me that she had been looking at the advertisements in the newspapers and had seen an agency called Manpower, who found jobs for people, and that she had called them to make an appointment for me for the following day. I didn't have a job to go to the next day, so with many prayers and Jesus in my heart, I took the tube to Green Park.

The Manpower Agency was in Jermyn Street, and as I sat with my interviewer going through various possible jobs that might be of interest, she suddenly said, "Perhaps I do have something for you. I just received a call from a Russian lady working in Milbanke Travel Agency, informing me that her assistant had left and she needed someone immediately."

I loved the idea of working in a travel agency, as geography was always one of my favourite subjects. I was asked if I was free to go over for an interview right away. Milbanke Travel Agency was just around the corner in Piccadilly. I was very nervous, but I liked the Russian woman who was in charge of arranging travel for international clients to the United Kingdom, especially Americans. I started work the next day, and although I heard little remarks that my lady boss was difficult to work for and had fired many of her assistants, I felt comfortable with her and was soon totally involved with all the work she put my way. I was thrilled and told Mother how grateful I was for her help. That Sunday at Mass I gave big thanks to Jesus.

18

I don't really remember the details of how we celebrated New Year's Eve, but in the far distant recesses of my mind, I believe the five of us had a happy evening at home welcoming in the 1960s. Thirteen days later, I would celebrate my eighteenth birthday with the news that I could officially be part of the staff of Milbanke Travel. I was elated and thanked Jesus for such a wonderful birthday present. I was completely dedicated to my job and very popular. With all the excitement of the new job and working in Piccadilly, I realised that my puppy fat was almost gone, and I was receiving wolf whistles! I had only been there a few months when my Russian boss berated me for something that wasn't my fault. I knew she liked me but was jealous of my popularity. One Monday shortly thereafter, I arrived at the office and was told I was now in charge of the all-inclusive travel department for Americans travelling to the UK—as Miss Sonja had left.

David Brice, the managing director, knew he not only had a hard, eager, and competent worker in me; he also had a young and attractive redhead. He transferred me, together with all my files to work at the counter near the entrance to the agency. He later told me he knew people from the street would see me through the window, and would want to enter the office! Every day brought new challenges, and I was quickly learning so much about the travel business. I was also meeting many different people.

It was the '60s, age of the miniskirt, the heavy eye makeup and beehives. I fitted into all of that, and in order to make some extra money I would travel to the airport in chauffeur-driven cars to meet my clients off their transatlantic flights and check them in to their hotels. If I received a tip of one pound, I was happy, and then I would travel home by tube. I found I had so much work that I was entrusted with the key to the door of the office and would work until about nine o'clock many a night. I looked forward to the overtime pay.

I tried to be home most weekends, as I took it on myself to clean the flat and do the washing and ironing, as Dad needed his shirts for work. Mother and Vanessa would prefer to be in the kitchen cooking. I also wanted to spend happy times with my family, and with the extra cash I was now contributing we would be able to have little treats like going to the cinema. Life at home was all right, so long as nothing upset Mother. I never knew exactly what would ignite her temper; I had to be careful. When Dad wasn't drinking, he kept to himself, knowing just his presence would sometimes create a storm.

My first year at Milbanke was flying by. I was happy at work and overwhelmed by all the attention I received from my clients. I was given gifts of perfume, flowers and chocolates, in addition to receiving many invitations to dinner, which I didn't accept, as I was far too busy and my work came first.

That was also the year when many Arab tourists were discovering London. Milbanke Travel had an arrangement with a car hire firm, several car hire firms in fact, which I used for transferring my clients from the airport to the hotels and vice versa, and for their sightseeing trips out of London. One day one of the owners of a car hire firm asked me if I would do him a favour and accompany some important Arabs to a nightclub. I was told I just had to sit with them for the evening. I was concerned that I really didn't have any suitable clothes to wear and mentioned it. I felt it was necessary that I was appropriately dressed for an evening out at a nightclub. I was told to go to a certain shop and buy a few dresses and that the bill would be taken care of.

The chauffeur collected me from the office. I was curious as we drove to the Carlton Tower Hotel and was introduced to a smallish man with a strong countenance and expressive eyes and eyebrows. I liked him immediately, though we had little conversation to start with. I knew he approved of me and was happy for my company. We became good friends. I made myself accessible to taking his wife's lady friends shopping, to meeting him at the airport on his arrivals into London and generally being there as his companion. He was in charge of taking care of the young Prince Mucktum of Dubai. There was always a large party of many attractive girls, and we all enjoyed visiting the nightclubs, which we did almost nightly. We were made welcome at the clubs, as lots of money was being spent. I would let Mother know that I wouldn't be home, as invariably we would be at the nightclubs for breakfast, so I would go straight to work.

My Arab friend realised I was working hard to help pay the bills at home and that we lived paycheck to paycheck. He was interested in my family life and knew that I came from an educated family who had fallen on bad luck, mainly due to Dad's drinking and Mother's volatile temperament. As Christmas was approaching, he was returning to his home, and he gave me a gift of cash so that my family and I could have a Christmas. We spent some of the money on a pantomime at the Wimbledon Theatre and Christmas dinner at a restaurant afterwards; it was such a wonderful family outing for us.

At the beginning of 1961, the landlords informed Mother that we must vacate the flat. The neighbours had complained about all the noise and the police arriving during the night and sometimes with an ambulance—all due to Mother's fights with Dad while he was drinking. So once again, Mother was flat hunting. It wasn't long before she found a four-bedroom flat in Richmond Bridge Mansions. We were all very excited, as the flat, although it didn't have a lift and was on the third floor, overlooked the river and had a communal garden. Mother had to go back to work, as she felt that with three of us working—and Vanessa would soon be finished at secretarial college—we could manage to pay the rent and buy some furniture.

There were two large reception rooms overlooking the river and a kitchen with a coal stove, which gave out the only heat in the flat. There was a small room off the kitchen, which was Vanessa's bedroom. Along the passage was a toilet, and at the end of it was the main bedroom, which Mother insisted that I had, as she preferred one of the smaller rooms near the bathroom. Dad had a small room in the middle between my room and Mother's. Sylvan had a camp bed in the living room, which probably accounts for her having a bad back most of her life.

Richmond was a lovely little town, and I would value being home at the weekends. My social life during the week was busy that I looked forward to being with the family and doing the chores. Often on a Saturday or Sunday afternoon, we would go to the cinema, which was just across Richmond Bridge. Other times we would just walk through the town and window shop. Everything was within walking distance, even the church, which made me happy. I would run up Richmond Hill on Sunday morning and seemed to fly back down, so happy to have Jesus in my soul.

Dad would love to walk with us to Richmond Park. It was like

Diana, Mother, Dad, Vanessa and Sylvan in the
gardens of Richmond Bridge Mansions

being in the country. We all felt much happier for the move. The bus stop was just at the bottom of our lane, so I didn't have far to go as

I rushed to work in the mornings, most days with Vanessa. The bus would drop us off at the station to connect with the train to Green Park tube station.

The biggest problem I had was going out after work and taking the tube back late at night or having to stay in town, sometimes ending up sleeping in a hotel. That almost always upset my Mother, who seemed jealous of all the attention I was receiving. There were many rows, mainly Mother shouting at me while I stayed silent, receiving all her abuse and blue language. Mother seemed to release her anger and then apologize the following day. In the meantime, the terrible verbiage that she threw at me remained with me for some time. I often wondered whether she loved me and if so, why I had the impression that she hated me.

Dad was never encouraged to eat with us, though I really wanted him to. He would take his plate of food to his little room and listen to the radio and read his newspaper or book. Now that we had the luxury of a small rented black and white television, I had hoped Dad would join us, but he knew that he wasn't welcome by Mother; all of this was a strain on me. Dad was only with us to have somewhere to sleep and give his salary to help with the rent and bills. He kept enough money for his tobacco and his fares to and from work. I loved my dad and felt sorry for him.

I had my own life growing up, being busy at work and becoming engrossed in my social life. It was difficult to find a balance. At night when I was on my knees talking to Jesus, I would pray for peace in the home and that I could make things more comfortable for the family and earn enough money so Mother would be able to stop working. When Vanessa started to work and make a contribution to the household expenses, this meant that Mother could stay home and write her screenplays and, hopefully, prepare dinner for us.

I was always finding the opportunity to work overtime to be able to contribute more to the home. Everyone I met was very kind to me. After all, I was just a working girl, and I suppose it was obvious to most of my clients that to give me a gift, to buy a dress or take the family to dinner, would be appropriate and much appreciated.

I was constantly invited out to dinner; many of the clients were my mother's age.

Mother used to chide me, saying, "what conversation do you have to offer? You have no knowledge of the world, and you are not articulate."

At times she suggested I should include her. I did ask some of my clients from America if Mother could join us; sometimes it worked out, and I was always happy to see my mother enjoy herself. She never went out to any fancy restaurants or had the opportunity to dress for the evening, so whenever it was possible, I had her join us. Those clients I would probably never see again; they just loved having me in their company and were very gracious to Mother.

Diana, Vanessa and Sylvan laughing

19

Mother wanted me to enter a competition for a beauty pageant, as the first prize would be a welcome cheque. I was reluctant but in order to please her, I did, and came fourth; my picture was in the local newspaper. Mother then wanted me to audition for a part in an Otto Preminger film. I wasn't the least bit interested in acting; however, I went to meet Mr. Preminger in his offices in Soho, and I liked him and his deep voice. He came over to me and put his hands on my head, parting my hair. He wanted to make sure I was a real Titian red head! I wasn't offered the part, thank goodness, but I enjoyed meeting such a famous film director.

I was still seeing my wonderful Arab friend when he visited London. I would make sure to drop all other engagements and be at his beck and call when he was in town. One evening at dinner, he told me that he would like me to have a holiday. He said that he had a couple of friends in Beirut who would look after me. I really wasn't aware of all that he was saying. The next thing I knew, I was travelling first class on Middle East Airlines to Beirut, Lebanon. It was my first experience to travel on an aeroplane and I felt such incredible excitement. I sat next to a little old lady who was so nervous about flying, and despite it being my first flight, I managed to make her feel relaxed.

Also on the flight was a journalist called Rex North. He was with "The News of the World" newspaper, and during the trip he came over to me and asked if I was a participant in the Miss Universe competition. I had no idea about such a competition. He gave me his card and wanted to know where I was staying in Beirut. I told him I would be at the Carlton Hotel, but that I was being taken care of by friends. He wrote his phone number on his card and asked me to call him if I had any free time and that he would enjoy seeing me and introducing me to the Miss Universe contestants.

Rex North was a lot of fun, and I did have some super evenings with him and his friends. My family in London knew of my arrival in Beirut before I had a chance to let them know—Rex North had written about me in "The News of the World," which had included a photograph heading it: "Why isn't this beautiful nineteen-year-old redhead, Diana Munro, a contestant in Miss Universe?" I was most flattered!

From the moment my feet touched the soil, I was in love with Beirut. My room in the Carlton Hotel, which overlooked the sea, was very comfortable, I had never experienced such luxury. Every thing, every place, every person was totally magical. I was treated like Miss Universe wherever I went and inundated with invitations. The kind Armenian couple took such good care of me. I wanted for nothing. I did have the evenings to myself, which was great.

My special Arab friend had arranged for the Armenian couple to drive me to Bethlehem, as he knew my love of Jesus, and he wanted me to see His birthplace. The three of us drove out of Beirut past the famous temple ruins of Baalbek and observed the beautiful cedar trees. We crossed the border into Syria and stopped in Damascus, which seemed to me such an intriguing and exciting city. I was bought Damascus brocade and chose the most beautiful green and silver material, which was made into a fabulous dress on my return to Beirut. At the Syrian border into Jordan the guards were objectionable; I think they made it especially difficult for me, as I was young and different.

The drive to Amman, Jordan, was hot and barren, but when I saw Amman, I was amazed, especially seeing the beautiful royal palace. While we were there, my friends thought I might like to go to the races. I had never been to the horse races, and to be attending one in Amman was mind-boggling. I was constantly pinching myself to make sure that at nineteen years of age I was having such an incredible travel experience, and I was not dreaming!

We stopped in Nazareth to visit the home of Jesus, Mary and Joseph, and then drove on to look out over the tranquil Sea of Galilee, where I tried to picture Jesus and His disciples with their fishing boats. Our next stop was the Dead Sea, where I had so much fun floating around in the salty water and found it amusing to see a few people reading the newspapers while they floated. It was certainly a phenomenal experience. When we finally arrived in Jerusalem, I was speechless; I was in such awe. That night when I went out on the balcony of my room and looked out at the city, I felt a stillness that was so spiritual, and the silence was breathtaking. I was sure I could have heard a pin drop. I looked at the star-filled sky and felt choked with emotion, as my heart was over flowing with love. How lucky I was to be seeing and feeling all of that. We visited Bethlehem the next day, and the little Church of the Nativity where I knew Jesus was my guide. What an incredible trip. I just wish I could recall more of the details. At nineteen years old, I was the luckiest girl in the world.

On our return to Beirut, it occurred to me that the husband was paying me too much attention, which I didn't want, as I knew his wife would be jealous. Although I was used to having men fall for me, married and single men, and was popular and in demand, I was, however, really innocent about it all and took it in my stride.

Two young men and another girl, who were introduced to me by Rex North, invited me to join them for an evening at the famous Casino du Liban. I wore my beautiful new dress made out of Damascus brocade, my hair was up in a chignon and I looked rather good. We drove to the Lido. The show was fabulous, and we had a super evening with lots of champagne. It was around two in the morning when we left the Casino in the Opel Kapitan, a German-made car that one of the men was driving and he was going rather fast. I kept quiet as the two men and the girl chattered; I was scared as the road from the Casino had a steep drop on one side down the cliff and to my horror as we drove around a corner the car went off the road, we were tumbling down, the car rolled over once, fortunately something prevented it from going all the way down and it stopped upside down.

Amazingly the four of us managed to crawl out of the upturned car, very shaken and disheveled, but without a scratch. I knew we had been protected by Jesus as we scrambled up to the road in search of assistance. It was a close call and very frightening.

I was kept busy during my wonderful visit to Beirut, falling in love with that luminous city and having everyone fall in love with me. I was a very happy girl! Each night I was dancing at a different nightclub. I was never alone, except when I thanked Jesus before going to sleep at night. A couple of days before my holiday came to an end, I received a phone call, it was my Arab friend. He was in the hotel and invited me to his suite. I didn't know he was arriving, so it was a lovely surprise and I told him how grateful I was to him for giving me such an amazing holiday. It was many years later that he was told by the wife of the couple who was taking care of me in Beirut, that her husband was smitten by me. My friend was not happy. My special friend was just that; he asked nothing of me. We were not sexually involved and he was faithful to his wife and five children. He just liked me a lot. He hadn't made any stipulation as to me not having any men friends, but subsequently I realised he had wanted me for himself, without being physically unfaithful to his wife.

The evening before I was due to leave Beirut, Rex North had arranged a party for me. I had to return to the hotel to pack and change my clothes. As I ran to the reception to grab my key, there were several men standing at the desk.

I was given my key, and the receptionist said, "Oh, Miss Munro, I'd like to introduce you to—"

And I said, "I am so sorry. I'm late, must run."

The telephone was ringing as I entered my room. The receptionist said that Mr. Sam Spiegel would like to speak to me. Sam Spiegel, his voice deep and gravely, said that he had just seen me downstairs at the reception and would like to invite me to travel with him the following morning on his private plane to Amman to see the filming of "Lawrence of Arabia".

Wow, really? Oh, that was Mr. Spiegel of "Lawrence of Arabia"?

My heart stopped for a moment, such a big temptation, but I refused, as I had to return to work. My holidays were over. I told Mr. Spiegel that I had to leave for London the next day. He asked where I worked and said he would call me when he was in London. He kept his word and took me to the theatre, where we had the best seats in the house and dined afterwards in an elegant and expensive restaurant.

I looked very much the starlet, as I wore my beautiful Chinese evening coat for the first time. It was all rather exciting. My mother was dumbfounded that I would be spending the evening with the famous film director, Sam Spiegel. We kept in touch for a while and he did arrange for me to have a part in a television show, as Mother had requested I should ask him, but I was not interested to pursue it. I was not an actress and had no interest in becoming one. Sam Spiegel was an interesting man, and I am pleased I met him.

I continued seeing my special Arab friend when he came into town, and he was now a good friend of the family, visiting us at Richmond Bridge Mansions. When he wasn't in London, I would make sure to visit his brothers who were studying there. My gratitude to my friend for his kindness to me and my family will never be forgotten. To this day I often think of him. I know he lives in the United Kingdom and is listed as one of the hundred richest men in the country. I am delighted he made such a big success of his life and strangely enough, never asked anything of me except my friendship. We both had the utmost respect for one another. I don't think he ever really understood my desire to be loved or to give love, nor the enormous responsibility I felt towards helping my family and growing up to be the peacemaker.

I longed for tranquility, security and love. That was my prayer, not only for me, but also for my family. Every night I would fall asleep knowing that I was surrounded by Jesus' love, and one day I would be given the security I needed to take care of my family.

There were good times, but I constantly felt I had to tread carefully. I often asked myself if I loved my mother, as for most of my life I didn't really feel any love from her towards me. I did feel a duty to look after her and do the best for my family. During one of our many rows with her shouting and me listening, I told her that I felt it was my duty to do whatever made her happy. It wasn't until the last years of her life, and especially after her death, that I suppose I began to understand her, and to this day, I knew I always loved her.

Mother in Richmond Park

20

My life at Milbanke Travel was so hectic. Not only was I working long hours, I was also being invited by the hoteliers and airlines on inaugural trips to Europe. When the directors were unable to accept the many invitations that came their way, they were passed on to me. Naturally, I accepted every trip I was offered and was treated like a princess wherever I went. Olympic Airways and Greek hoteliers invited me many times to Greece. I was usually the only female travel agent on most of those European visits. Hoteliers in Switzerland and Italy invited me to visit their hotels. Alitalia became a favourite airline of mine, and I often travelled on the jump seat in the cockpit with the captain and his crew. I went over to Rome on numerous occasions, as I had a gorgeous Italian boyfriend for a while who worked as a co-pilot for Alitalia. It was through Bruno that I discovered real romance, and what could be more fabulous than driving along the dramatic and stunning Amalfi coast being in love with a deliciously handsome and romantic Italian?

In between my busy life, Vanessa and I managed to spend a weekend together in Paris, which was a lot of fun. We met two nice young men from extremely good and wealthy families who gave us a happy time. While in Paris I stayed with Pierre in his lovely apartment on the Avenue Foch and made the mistake of inviting him to spend a weekend with us at the flat in Richmond. Poor chap! His uncomfortable visit only lasted two days—the flat was freezing, and he eventually ended up sleeping in the kitchen next to the coal stove. Such a disaster. I was very embarrassed, especially as he had brought me an Hermes scarf!

I was bringing in many new clients to Milbanke, and the directors knew that despite my popularity, I was a hard worker and totally loyal to the firm. I was often invited to lunch, but most days I would go next door to buy an apple and carton of buttermilk.

If I wasn't invited out to lunch, which I tried not to do, I would take the opportunity to run down to Leicester Square to the French Catholic church to confession. Those were the swinging sixties, and this convent girl was having too good a time, so going to confession was a must!

Despite my busy social life, I was experiencing a strange phenomenon. I had become rather shy, especially while travelling in the tube back and forth to work. I would stand in the corner with my back to everyone and my head usually in a newspaper, as I knew that at some point I would start blushing if someone caught my eye; my face would become very red. It was awful. My hands too became red. The strange occurrence lasted a while and was most distressing. However, no one seemed to notice, and I didn't mention it to anyone.

One day one of the chauffeur's who worked for Milbanke, whom I knew due to travelling with him to meet my clients at London airport, asked me if I would like to meet Cary Grant, as he was going to meet him at London airport in a few days. Goodness me, wow, Cary Grant. I think if my mother had been made that offer she would have been over the moon. I hadn't seen many of Cary Grant's films at that time in my life and didn't really know much about him. If the chauffeur had said Elvis Presley, then my heart would have taken on an extra beat! When I returned home from work that evening and told Mother that I had been invited to meet Cary Grant, she was incredulous. Once again, she wondered how it was that I was meeting all those famous people. I chose a plain black-and-brown dress with short sleeves and a high-neck collar. I didn't have much to choose from, but that dress made me look fairly slim. I put my hair in a chignon.

The chauffeur arrived to collect me in his Daimler. We drove to the Hyde Park Hotel, which is now the Mandarin Oriental Hotel. I hadn't really given much thought to the invitation to have lunch with Cary Grant. I was often meeting wealthy and important people in my job, so I wasn't overly excited to meet the famous film star, just a little nervous. When I arrived at the hotel, the manager was waiting for me and escorted me to a private dining room, and the gentlemen stood while I was seated. Lowering my eyes, I took a deep breath and made an invisible sign of the cross.

When I opened my eyes fully, I looked into the beautiful brown eyes of Cary's. He was on my right, and across the table was the attractive Roderick Mann of the "Sunday Express" newspaper, and as I shyly smiled at the next gentleman, it was Peter Sellers. I knew I was in awesome company and wondered what I was doing there! I didn't think I would have much to offer those three gentlemen when it came to conversation. I really didn't have to worry. They were good friends and the conversation flowed with much laughter. Peter Sellers kept us all laughing. I liked Roderick Mann. Cary was totally charming, taking an interest in me and asking questions.

Halfway through lunch, he noticed my red hands and became concerned. Earnestly looking into my eyes, he told me, in that inimitable voice of his, to put my elbows on the table so that the blood would run down from my hands into my arms! That caused much laughter, but I knew it was all meant with affection. Although I was out of my element with the three erudite and sophisticated men, I really enjoyed their company and began to feel at ease. The conversation never stopped, except when Cary talked about my hands, which was rather embarrassing and caused me to blush profusely. I never thought to ask for their autographs, as I felt I was Cary's guest for lunch and not an autograph hunter.

After lunch Cary invited me to his suite, and I was happy to be alone in his company. We talked for a while, and then he said he wanted to run his bath. While the bath was running, we were becoming intimate and had totally forgotten the bath. Our romantic moments were interrupted by the ringing of the telephone. Cary answered it, and his head turned towards the bathroom. Replacing the receiver, he was off the bed in a flash, paddling through the water, which had seeped into the bedroom. We were both a little concerned about what damage it may have caused, as it had obviously run into the next room. However, we were soon laughing at the hysterically funny situation, right out of a Cary Grant comedy. When I returned home, Mother wanted to know everything, and I told her that our luncheon was a lot of fun.

Cary would call me regularly when he came to London, and it was always exciting to hear his familiar voice. I would meet him at his accommodations in South Kensington. We were both Capricorns, and although we felt comfortable in each other's company, I was only nineteen years old, thirty-eight years his junior. He didn't want to take me out, as he didn't want any publicity, and he didn't spoil me like all my other suitors. I had heard that he was stingy, and as he never gave me anything, I knew it had to be true. I was busy with my life, so although Cary was good looking and charming, and I loved the cleft in his chin, he wasn't exciting for me, and I began to feel bored just seeing him in his home in London for afternoon tea; so we drifted apart.

Years later I realised the chauffeur who had told Cary about me, knew he was looking for a companion at that time after his separation and imminent divorce from Betsy Drake. Four years later he married Dyan Cannon, who was five years older than I was, and strangely enough, also a Capricorn. Naturally my mother couldn't understand why I hadn't been more interested in Cary, the most desirable man on earth. I had destroyed her dreams, I think! Anyway, I told her that it wasn't meant to be. Being with Cary Grant will always remain an unforgettable memory and has a special place in my heart, as I recall his motto: "Never explain, never complain!"

21

One of my favourite clients was the Lebanese owner of a large travel agency in Beirut and Rome. I would enjoy his visits to London, as he took me to expensive restaurants and made me feel special. He knew of my circumstances at home and suggested I work in his office in Rome for a couple of weeks for my summer holiday. That way I would be earning a salary and enjoying the eternal city. It was a wonderful experience. I loved Rome, and living in a different environment was good for me. I stayed in a small family hotel and had a room and bathroom on the top floor. I called it my nest, as I felt like a bird with only the treetops to surround me.

That kind and dear friend made it possible for Mother to go on vacation to Beirut. I tried to do as much as I could to give Mother whatever she desired; that was one of the many trips I was able to arrange for her. Mother always told me how life had been so unfair for her, which saddened me, and now as I was working in a travel agency, I was able to make some of her dreams come true.

I tried to spend my weekends at home with Dad, Mother and my sisters. We would manage to have fun together, going to the cinema, walking through Richmond Park and visiting Kew Gardens. We all liked to walk; just walking by the river in Richmond was gratifying. I wished that life was always so serene. I bought a radiogram by paying it off weekly and was happy to listen to Elvis while ironing and cleaning the flat. As long as Dad wasn't drinking and I was home, Mother seemed content. Dad did start visiting the local pub at the weekends, and somehow he managed to keep sober enough to attend his job on Mondays. Everyone at the pub loved him, his visits were good for his morale. Of course, the fact that he was drinking scared me, and I would go and bring him back home. I really didn't want any fights, and it was imperative he kept his job.

All would be calm with Mother if I came home straight after work. If I was going for a drink or to dinner, I would let Mother know. That, however, was never enough, as more often than not I was put through the third degree. Mother wanted to know whom I was with and where I went and why I was late home. Sometimes Mother was so angry with me that I couldn't help wondering what the other people in the flats below thought of all the screaming. I was brought up by the nuns, and whatever happened, even when Mother used to grab a knife in her rage, I would say nothing. I had to respect my mother; I think that by keeping quiet it seemed to enrage her more. Despite my red hair, I did not have a temper, thank goodness. The awful things she said to me were hurtful, and usually the next day treated me as if nothing had happened. I couldn't help feeling sorry those incidents occurred, as it just made me want to find peace and affection elsewhere.

Christmas arrived and I was spoiled by my clients; I was able to take home lots of goodies for the family. We decided to go to a restaurant for Christmas dinner, and although I had to hold my breath at times, for the most part we had a good celebration, no major rows. Dad only had to take a sip of wine, and it was like putting a red rag to a bull as far as Mother was concerned. I suppose all the past memories of Dad starting his day off with a bottle of gin and eventually losing his job were never far from her mind; plus the fact that she really didn't like him.

In the New Year Milbanke Travel moved their offices to New Bond Street. New Bond Street was an interesting street and still in the centre of everything, especially the shops. I turned twenty in January of 1962. My life continued to be busy both with work and socially. Money at home remained short, and as I contributed most of my salary to the house, there were times when I would have liked a little more pocket money for myself. I decided to spend some of the money I had saved on a short modeling course at the Lancôme offices in Upper Brook Street. When the Playboy Club opened in Park Lane and was looking for "bunnies," I knew I fit the criteria, but after I read the rules and realised what the work would entail, I decided I was not cut out to be a Playboy bunny. I was often invited to the Club for drinks after work and was pleased that I was a guest and not a bunny. I continued to have many admirers, many invitations to dinners, to the theatre, movies, and so on, and at times I found it all overwhelming. However, I continued to try to keep the weekends for my family.

22

Milbanke's new offices were larger than those in Piccadilly, and I was pleased that all my clients came with me. One afternoon sitting at the counter together with my friend and colleague, Norma, I happened to look out of the large picture window onto New Bond Street, and among the people walking by, one gentleman caught my eye. To me he looked like a film star, a mature film star with his long overcoat, rolled umbrella, and wearing a fedora. I was really mesmerised by the way he walked and the way he was dressed, so different to the normal type of men that walked passed. I told Norma to look out too, and then realised he was coming into the office.

He came straight to the counter and put an airline ticket in front of me. He said he had been recommended to see the managing director. I told him that David Brice was out for lunch but that his secretary could help him. I was enthralled by his beautiful voice as he told me that he felt sure I could assist him. He said he needed to attend the Derby horse races in Dublin and wished to travel on a certain flight and on a certain day. I was only too well aware that all flights to Dublin for the days he required were completely booked, and I felt that as he already had a paid ticket, he was asking a bit much. Nevertheless, something stirred in me when he told me he was sure I could arrange the impossible and that he was staying at the Connaught Hotel. I told him to leave his ticket, and I would see what I could do.

The Irish gentleman with a slight American accent, mixed with beautiful English, was impeccably dressed and had thrown the gauntlet, I was determined not to let him down. I called up one of my friends in Aer Lingus and laughingly said to him that he owed me a favour. "No problem," he said. "You have your seat."

Before the office closed, I asked the office messenger to take the ticket round to Mr. O'Leary at the Connaught Hotel.

The following day I received a phone call from Mr. O'Leary. He told me he had had to speak to several women before reaching me. I later learned that my colleagues in the office all wanted to hear his voice! Mr. O'Leary gently rebuked me for not taking the ticket around to the hotel and giving it to him personally. He made me promise that on his return to London I would dine with him. I said I would. In the meantime, my life was not only busy at work, but very busy socially. I had to make time to attend my yoga classes, where I learned how to revive myself. There were times when I was so exhausted that the meditation was a blessing. I lay on the floor on my back for ten minutes and thought only of a lighted candle. It worked every time and gave me renewed energy.

With all that was going on, I had forgotten about Mr. O'Leary and really hadn't expected him to call.

However, one day the operator called me and said, "that the client of yours with 'the voice' is on the phone for you."

He told me he was in London only for a short visit but would like it very much if I would dine with him at the Connaught Hotel the following evening, and I said I would, though I did have to cancel a previous dinner date.

I phoned my mother and said that the interesting Irishman had invited me to dinner, and she told me to call him back and tell him to send a car for me. I did call back, as I didn't often go against my mother's wishes. The following evening the chauffeur-driven car arrived at Richmond Bridge Mansions. I looked attractive in a simple black cocktail dress, one of my choices from my book of dresses, which I could pay off little by little. I had my hair in a chignon and felt like a princess arriving at the ball! Mr. O'Leary, I could now call him Patrick, was totally charming and engaging.

We had a delicious dinner and enjoyed each other's company. I really liked the gentleman, whom I found extremely interesting and excellent company. He was thirty-six years my senior. I did give a thought to Cary, but I was now almost three years older than when I had met him. I found out that Patrick's zodiac sign was Pisces, and I being a Capricorn, knew it was one of the best astrological combinations. The chauffeur-driven car returned me home. My Mother was waiting up, all excited to know about my evening. In a strange way I felt that it was just the beginning of a deep friendship. Despite our ages, we were attracted to one another.

At home we were still having financial troubles, so I decided to become an escort. I heard that the money would be good and I would only have to go out to dinner, to the theatre and look beautiful, no strings attached. I really needed the extra money, as Mother had some problems that required attention, and generally the extra pounds would come in handy. My job as an escort didn't last long as I was propositioned by each of my clients, none of whom I fancied. Also, I began to think about leaving my lovely Milbanke, as despite my excellent work, I, like every other employee, would not be receiving a raise in salary.

While I was thinking about all of this, I received a letter from Patrick, who was in the Bahamas. I had mentioned to him that I had applied to Kuwait Airways for a job, as the salary I would receive there would be considerably more than at Milbanke. I was accepted by Kuwait Airways and gave a month's notice to Milbanke Travel.

Patrick, in his letter, said that I should have a holiday in view of the fact I was going to join Kuwait Airways and would only be entitled to a holiday after working with them for a year. As I was in the travel business, I arranged the flights with British Overseas Airways Corporation, BOAC, and reserved my room at the Emerald Beach Hotel, Nassau. All expenses and pocket money Patrick would give me on my arrival. I loved to travel and was excited to be going to the Bahamas, especially as the weather in London was cold and dreary. The flight stopped briefly in Bermuda before arriving at the little airport in Nassau, where Patrick was waiting for me on the tarmac. The air was warm and welcoming, and the sultry breezes were exotic.

Before leaving London, I had a couple of outfits made from some dress material left over from my dressmaking class at St. Mary's Convent. Fortunately, there was an inexpensive dressmaker just on the corner of the lane where I lived. It was fun to have her make clothes from my designs. My friend Norma lent me a couple of items of clothing and a client of mine had given me a suitcase, so I was all set; and I did have my gorgeous Damascus brocade dress with me. Mother was not happy about my forthcoming journey, and although I was now twenty-two, she wrote a letter to Patrick, which I hadn't seen until he read it to me. It basically asked him to take care of me and to be a gentleman. That was my mother.

My room at the Emerald Beach Hotel was wonderful, overlooking the white beach and aquamarine sea. I couldn't be happier. Patrick wasn't staying in the hotel and told me he wouldn't be able to be with me all the time, but made sure I had enough money to enjoy myself while he was otherwise occupied. There was no problem for me to be on my own. I was living in a beautiful hotel with a glorious beach and had met a super Bahamian who loved to dance; so in the evenings when Patrick wasn't with me, I was with my Bahamian friend. He took me on his motorcycle to all sorts of native clubs over the hill, and as dancing was my passion, I danced a lot. I told Patrick that I had made a friend, and he was happy I had the company.

I was pleased that Patrick was able to spend his birthday with me. We went to Blackbeard's Tavern on Bay Street and then to the Big Bamboo nightclub. Too soon my holiday was at an end, and it was time to return to London. I was looking forward to seeing my family and telling them all about my adventures in little Nassau. I would see Patrick back in London in April.

I returned to my hectic life, and despite feeling sad at leaving my friends at Milbanke Travel, I was looking forward to the change and to working at Kuwait Airways. Amazingly, Kuwait Airways offices were at 164 Piccadilly, so I was back at my old address and in familiar territory behind the counter. Our manager was from the Sudan, and the small staff was a mixture of English- and Arab-speaking people.

I realised that joining that Arab airline, I was in a different world to Milbanke Travel.

Once again my social life seemed in a spin. I met a lovely red-headed Greek Adonis who was studying for his PhD in economics at Cambridge University. We had a beautiful interlude, which included punting on the river in Cambridge and attending the May Ball—an experience I shall always remember. I was really fond of Yannis and started thinking about him seriously, as I didn't think that my Irishman would be anything more than a dear friend.

Just before I left Milbanke, I was invited by a travel agency in Cairo to join them for the opening of a new hotel. I shall always recall my arrival at Cairo airport. I was told I would be met at the airport by a representative of the agency and taken to the hotel; what I didn't expect was to be met by four male representatives. I was ushered into the car with two men in the front and one on either side of me in the back. While I sat in the car, it did cross my mind that my mother's words might actually come true, and I was scheduled for the white slave traffic! Fortunately for me, I had just received a rather over-the-top welcome. I loved Cairo and was invited a few more times, both by the hotel and United Arab Airlines. One of the captains of my flights became a friend—a beautiful Egyptian pharaoh!

23

I heard from Patrick from time to time; he was busy travelling, and as he was divorced, he was the number one bachelor in London and popular with the ladies. When he was in town, he would invite me to lunch, and one weekend asked whether I would like to go to lunch in the country. He told me he and the Earl of Carnavon, whom he called Porchy, owned a couple of race horses together and that Porchy had invited him to lunch at his home at High Clere. We had a lovely drive out to Newbury and were impressed with the grounds and more so when we entered the Castle; although it seemed to me more like a museum. We had a good lunch in the opulent surroundings, but I was relieved when we left, as every time Patrick's back was turned, Porchy was being over flirtatious. Driving back to London, I mentioned it to Patrick, and he laughed saying he wasn't surprised.

Diana and colleague behind the counter at Kuwait Airways, Piccadilly, London

The Sudanese manager of Kuwait Airways was an interesting young man who gradually introduced me to members of his family, and I was invited to visit Khartoum after Christmas. On December twenty-seventh, I arrived in a hot, dusty, and seemingly deserted city. My friends, who had much energy in London, appeared lethargic, as the heat really was a problem, though it didn't bother me. One of the highlights of my visit was attending the horse races. I was fortunate to be with the members of a well-known and respected family. When I think back, not only was I a western woman, I felt I was the only woman at the racetrack. I was a white, red-headed woman mingling with hundreds of Sudanese men in their djellabahs and turbans, all excited at placing their bets—betting is no longer allowed. I felt like some sort of a freak! The white-robed men were not sure whether to look at me or the horses; it was an experience and a little frightening too.

Another adventure I had during my visit was to be driven to see where the Blue Nile met the White Nile. Although my memory is a little blurry, I felt the significance of what I was witnessing. The water was powerful to me. Eventually I could see the faint distinction between the Niles. The White Nile was a muddy grey, and the Blue Nile more of a greenish brown. The meeting is known as the "longest kiss in the world," and most astonishing was that the waters did not mix.

The following days went by slowly and gave me time to think about the ghosts of Gordon of Khartoum and the Mahdi, as I reflected on the turbulent history of that vast country. I was grateful to be finally leaving Khartoum—it was not one of my favourite cities—but seeing my friends in their home environment was interesting, as they behaved differently in London. My recollection of the head of that family will always remain a joy; he was a remarkable man, very wise, fascinating to talk to, and a prominent judge at the International Court of Justice at The Hague. He, like my Arab friend, will be remembered by me with great affection.

I stopped in Cairo on my way home to see my friends. Cairo was one of my favourite cities and different to Khartoum. I returned back in time to celebrate my twenty-third birthday with my family. Life at home remained turbulent. There were constant fights between my mother and father, and now I had become the brunt of many of Mother's outbursts. I didn't fully understand why Mother became angry with me. She really didn't like me travelling so much and would shout at me, and when my father tried to intervene, she would almost kill him. I made sure that any extra money I made, I gave to Mother so that she could also go on the occasional trip or spend it on whatever she wanted. I realised that things became much worse after my sister Vanessa decided to go and live in Majorca. Vanessa was Mother's love, but Mother gave Vanessa her blessing to go abroad; despite the fact that now we didn't have Vanessa's salary to help with the living expenses.

I let it be known at work that I would be prepared to clean the flats of the rich Kuwaitis who lived in London. I would do that after I finished work in the evenings. I was used to cleaning the flat at home, as no other member of my family took an interest; though later on Sylvan helped out a lot. Frankly, I did not mind, as long as I had music in the background. The money was good, and I was happy to take the strain off my parents.

Somehow I managed to have ten days off from work during August of 1965 and joined Vanessa in Gibraltar. We had such a happy time together and travelled on to Tangier in Morocco. When I was at Milbanke Travel, the manager of the Rif Hotel had invited me on numerous occasions to visit his hotel, gratis, so I took the opportunity to accept; it was my twenty-first birthday gift to my sister. We were excited to be at the famous Rif Hotel and enjoyed the amenities until the manager wanted more from me. I was totally unprepared, and at dinner, after being in the hotel for a couple of nights, I confided to Vanessa what was expected. I was not going to capitulate to the manager, but we also didn't have enough money to pay for our room for the following night. As we were in the hotel restaurant mulling over our situation, our conversation was overheard, and the gentleman at the next table came over to us. We were two attractive, well-educated and well-spoken young ladies, both having careers in the travel business.

The gentleman told us that he had heard our sad plight and, if we would trust him, he would take care of us until it was time for us to return from our holiday. It transpired that he was the minister of the railways in Morocco. He was a family man with three or four children. We packed our few belongings, I left a note for the manager, thanking him for his hospitality, and we were off on another adventure. It was a long car journey to his villa in Rabat, but for Vanessa and me it was a dream. We were welcomed by his family and treated as such until it was time to return to Gibraltar and then on home.

Kuwait Airways was becoming rather boring, and once again I was thinking of moving to another job that was more interesting and paid more money. One day a gorgeous Kuwaiti gentleman walked into the office. He looked like an Arab Clark Gable. I was attending to his ticket, and while chatting to him, he told me that he was on his way to Paris and that he was also in the middle of a divorce from his English wife. He invited me to join him in Paris, which I did on numerous weekends. He was the agent for all of the Lancôme beauty products, which were sold in Kuwait. Needless to say, I was never short of supplies.

Our weekends in Paris were totally magical and so much fun. He was very romantic and introduced me to another aspect of the city for lovers. He took me to the famous Lido, where I saw the beautiful Bluebell girls; and one of the special places that I loved was an amazing Russian restaurant, which was totally seductive. Nevertheless I was a realist, and although I really wanted to be with him, it just wouldn't have worked out.

I was surprised at Christmas when Patrick called and asked how I was doing. I told him that things at home were becoming worse with my mother, and despite everything I did to pacify her—arranging for her to have holidays and taking her out for dinners—it was just miserable for me. I also felt that my poor dad was being unfairly attacked due to me, and that I was especially concerned for Sylvan.

Patrick gave me a big cheque so I was able to arrange for all of us, including Vanessa, who came home, to enjoy the festivities and have a lovely Christmas dinner in a hotel. I had given in my notice to Kuwait Airways, and on January twentieth 1966, I was on my way to Patrick in Nassau.

That time I stayed in a room in a building on Cable Beach that belonged to the Nassau Beach Hotel. I saw a little more of Patrick during that visit, though I was also entertained by his good friends, the head of the police force and his wife, and spent a lot of time with them in their apartment at the police barracks. Patrick took me to the Lyford Cay Club, where he was now a member, and for the last days of my holiday, I stayed with him at the luxurious club. I felt like a fish out of water, as the women there were all much older than I and dressed in their designer clothes. I was happier when Patrick didn't spend too much time at the club and took me to restaurants downtown for dinner.

Having enjoyed every minute of my beautiful holiday in Nassau, I now had to face starting a new job in the travel section of a large bank on Bruton Street. Although Mother was happy with my friendship with Patrick, she seemed to resent it too. She would ask me what we would talk about and often asked how he could find me interesting and said that he would find her company far more stimulating. I think Mother loved me, but she did have a strange way of showing it. It is true that I didn't talk much in Mother's company, not that I was given much of a chance, as she was most verbose. If I did try to make conversation, she would often correct my grammar or become impatient if I had something of interest to say; so it was easiest for me to listen and say nothing.

Although I was considered beautiful by many, I never gave it much thought. I concentrated on my work and tried to make money to help my family. My family really came first, but when life at home became intolerable, I looked for companionship elsewhere. It is true, I was still young, and a very young twenty-four year old at that. Despite being in love all the time and having many men attracted to me, I was quite innocent. My main desire was to take care of my family, and there wasn't a night that I didn't say my prayers kneeling beside my bed, with one special prayer that one day I would be able to look after them. I used to fall asleep imagining a big house and enough money for everybody; though Vanessa seemed to be doing very well on her own.

24

Patrick's housekeeper called me at work one day and said that Patrick had been admitted to the hospital. I was very concerned and immediately called the nursing home and was allowed to speak to him. He told me he was suffering from diverticulitis. I went to visit him every evening after work. During that time he suggested I move from Richmond and that he would pay the rent for me to stay in a small flat. I really didn't want to leave my parents and Sylvan, but life was difficult, especially when Mother took a kitchen knife to me. I felt at that moment she hated me so much and was so full of bitterness.

When Patrick was better, he invited me around to his beautiful small apartment in Upper Grosvenor Street. I had told Mother I would be dining with him. I went over after work and felt very comfortable in the serene surroundings. Patrick's Italian housekeeper was a fantastic cook, and I always looked forward to having a delicious dinner. Irma soon discovered my proclivity for her chocolate mousse, so that was permanently on the menu when I was invited for dinner. My initiation into the world of wine started at those intimate dinners. Patrick loved his wines and had the best. He bought a lot of them through his friend, Michael Broadbent at Christie's; also many wines came from the resplendent cellars of Berry Bros. & Rudd.

I was beginning to feel relaxed with Patrick and found him fascinating and so knowledgeable. I felt safe and secure in his friendship. He was interested to know about me and my family. He never made me feel ignorant nor talked down to me. After dinner he would play music. I was delighted to have the opportunity to express myself through my impromptu dancing. When it was time for me to leave, Patrick would give me money for the taxi fare back to Richmond. I was most grateful for his thoughtfulness, but as I was just a few minutes away from Park Lane, I went to the bus stop and caught the bus to Richmond. The taxi money was a lot, and I could use it on other things. I never told Patrick about this until years later.

We had made a date to dine together sometime during the following weeks, and I mentioned it to my mother. When the day arrived, Mother handed me a thick envelope and told me to give it to Patrick when I saw him that evening. I was hesitant about doing so but I felt Patrick, being the person I was getting to know, could handle whatever was contained in the envelope. After all, my mother couldn't hurt him. On my arrival at his flat that evening, I gave Patrick the envelope, and we had dinner, enjoying our time together and Irma's wonderful food. At the office the following day, before I could call to thank him for the evening, I received a call from him. He told me he was going out for dinner, but would I stop by for a drink on my way home. I sensed something was wrong when I observed his face as he greeted me.

He poured us a drink and then asked me if I knew what was contained in the envelope from my mother. I told him that I had no idea. He proceeded to show me about seven typed-written pages. He said Mother had written about her life and was asking him to take care of her and my sisters and her mother and aunt in Australia. I was mortified; my mother had interfered with all my previous friendships, and it occurred to me that it would now be the end of my friendship with Patrick. Fortunately, Patrick believed me. We had been friends for a while now, and in that time he knew of my integrity. Patrick was also aware of how grateful I was with whatever little surprises I received from him. He also knew that I wasn't with him for anything other than himself. He told me that under the circumstances, he would not ever wish to meet my mother, and that the letter would be given to his lawyer. He said he would never mention the subject again, and that nothing had changed between us.

After leaving Patrick I walked over to Park Lane, where I waited for my bus. I went upstairs and took a seat in the front row, trying to choke back my tears. I didn't know much about Patrick; to me he was just another rich client and a friend. I felt sad that Mother had to resort to sending a begging letter to a man I had known for a comparatively short time, and was grateful that the letter hadn't spoiled our friendship. I realised Mother came from poor and humble beginnings, despite her aristocratic lineage. I admired the courage it took for her to do all that she did in Ceylon, and her battle with dad and his drinking. I also knew that it was through her sacrifice and tenacity that the three of us had had a good education. I was beginning to think that Mother wasn't happy about my friendship with Patrick, and sensed she was jealous.

It was all too complicated and confusing for me, so I told her I was accepting Patrick's offer to move to a flat off Edgware Road. I was weary of the constant interrogation, the tempers and tears. I really didn't want to leave Sylvan nor my dad, and in a strange way, neither my mother. I felt it was my duty to be with her, but I had to maintain my sanity. Her explanation to me about the letter was "that a man like that should be happy to help a poor family." I was only aware that Patrick was my friend, and I had not been overawed nor saw any big signs of wealth.

It was strange to leave Richmond Bridge Mansions. My father was most understanding, and I told Sylvan that I would see her often. I had been in the rented flat just over a week and was miserable. The flat was cold and uncomfortable, despite its proximity to work. For some reason, and I suppose it had a lot to do with my home life, I just couldn't settle into my new job either. I told Patrick I would return home rather than live in those digs, and he invited me to dine with him at one of my favourite restaurants, the White Elephant on Curzon Street.

Through the course of the evening, he told me that if I would like to, I could give two weeks notice to the bank and move in to live with him. There was one stipulation, however, that I must stop smoking. I wasn't a heavy smoker, but like most girls of my age, I smoked socially. He was going to Europe, and if I stopped smoking, I could meet him in Nice in a couple of weeks. Irma would look after me in the meantime.

I found it difficult to believe what Patrick had just told me. I wasn't going to have to go to work again after giving in my notice, and I would move into his beautiful small apartment in Upper Grosvenor Street.

I was twenty-four years old, and believed that Jesus had heard my prayers. On Sunday I went to Mass as usual, and while giving thanks, was emotionally overcome with gratitude. I knew Patrick was the man with whom I wanted to spend the rest of my life. I went back to Richmond Bridge Mansions to collect some of my belongings and to break the news to my parents that I would be going to live with Patrick.

Sylvan was hurt that I hadn't confided in her, telling her more of my friendship with Patrick, but I just didn't want her to suffer further by constantly being questioned by Mother. I was close to Sylvan and felt protective of her. I didn't like the way she was insistent Sylvan would become an actress; and to that end was sent to the Corona acting school and to the Arts Educational at Hyde Park. Sylvan hadn't really had any formal education, so she was a little out of her depth in those schools. I knew Vanessa would organise for Mother and Sylvan to visit her in Spain, but even so I felt anxious at leaving the family. I told Mother and Dad that Patrick would arrange to have a monthly allowance sent to them, which would make up for not receiving my share for the household expenses. I would always keep in touch with Mother, Dad and my sisters.

When I moved into Patrick's flat, he suggested it would be easier for me if I had my hair cut short. Patrick was very diplomatic. There was a wonderful hair salon just opposite the apartment in Upper Grosvenor Street. I was nervous to be in such a plush establishment, not to mention to have all my hair cut. I shouldn't have worried, as my naturally curly hair looked wonderful, and Patrick called me his "proud beauty," referring to my looks as being similar to Queen Alexandra. As time went on, I understood that to be a big compliment.

I had much to think about during the few weeks before leaving London. I would look at the little three-diamond ring that Patrick gave me which meant I love you, and to me that was my engagement ring.

During the few weeks Patrick was away, I received a couple of beautiful letters from him, professing his love for me. Each day I would smoke less and less, until I finally stopped smoking three days before my departure to Nice.

I felt very fortunate as I walked back to Patrick's apartment after work, knowing Irma would have my supper ready. I had to tell her no more chocolate mousse, as giving up smoking, I was bound to gain weight, which I really didn't want to do. Patrick called me every evening, and I realised I was falling in love with him. Our friendship had survived three years and now I was to begin my life as his girlfriend. I did think about "Pygmalion", but that wasn't my story. I was well bred and educated. Mother always reminded us that despite our poverty, we had breeding and that blue blood ran through our veins. My friendship with Patrick seemed normal despite the difference in age. I knew he was proud to have me on his arm. I also knew that I had much to learn from him; the world with Patrick O'Leary would be most exciting.

Patrick O'Leary

25

July the sixteenth, 1966, arrived. I had given up smoking and was on my way to meet Patrick at Nice Airport. Although by now I was a seasoned traveller, that journey was special. Patrick met me at the airport with his beautiful custom-built Silver Shadow Rolls Royce. I was aware there would be some gossip at the hotel that day, as the manager and desk staff all knew Patrick well. When we checked in to the Hotel de Paris in Monte Carlo, I was embarrassed to hand in my passport, as everyone would know I was just another of Patrick's many girlfriends. However, that was the situation, and I would just have to live with it. Up until that time, I had only been introduced to one couple, who were Patrick's closest friends. I was his secret, due mainly to the fact of the difference in our ages.

We had arrived for the Grand Prix, an exhilarating and noisy time in Monte Carlo, especially in the early mornings. Our days were tranquil, enjoying long lunches in beautiful surroundings, relaxing in our cabana by the swimming pool at the hotel—where we often saw Princess Grace and her young children—and generally exploring Monte Carlo. Patrick introduced me to his dearest and oldest friend, Prince Youka Troubetzkoy and Princess Marcia, who held a magnificent party for him at their villa in Èze-sur-Mer, and I was certainly the surprise to everyone that evening.

The parties at their home were fabulous; all the jet-setters who were in town were at the Villa. As usual, I felt nervous at the thought of mixing with the rich and famous, especially as Patrick was well known as a desirable bachelor. At twenty-four and rather shy, always conscious of my mother's words telling me I never had anything of interest to say, I asked Patrick if he had any tips for me. He told me there may be the possibility of certain women asking what he saw in me, and he told me to say, "youth!" I was treated with much affection and interest; I never again had to worry about being accepted.

I loved Monte Carlo, the beautiful little restaurants, the palace, the casino, and generally the luxury and comfort was fabulous. We would drive into San Remo and I was wonderfully spoiled with beautiful new clothes, my first Puccis! One super couple, who were Patrick's friends, spent a lot of time with us, and fortunately for me, the husband loved to dance. Patrick would say good night while I went off to the fancy discos and danced until the wee hours. I was so grateful that he understood I needed to do that.

Every day with Patrick was like opening a gift. I never knew what he had planned. I just knew I was in a dream world and loving every minute of it. Patrick was also happy, and we were enjoying discovering our new life together. After being in Monte Carlo for three weeks, it was time to move on. The Rolls was waiting for us as we exited the Hotel de Paris, and at that time I didn't realise we were to have an awesome summer driving through Europe.

Departing Monte Carlo, we drove along the coast to San Tropez, where we took the ferry across to the nudist beach on the Isle de Levant. I absolutely refused to go naked, so we didn't stay long, as the people who were dressed were not appreciated as voyeurs. Driving in the luxury of the Rolls, which Patrick loved, was just wonderful, and although it was August and hot outside, we had the comfort of air conditioning. Many times as we drove through the villages, people would come out on the sidewalk or just stop and salute us. The Silver Shadow was a star, and our destination was Barcelona.

The Ritz Hotel in Barcelona was like a palace. Patrick was amused by my reaction to the marble bath in our suite, which to me was more like a miniature pool; as I lay back soaking in the suds, I imagined myself to be Cleopatra! We ate a delicious dinner and Patrick requested the chef to make us a picnic for the following day and handed him the picnic basket that he'd had made at Asprey's of Bond Street. We were now en route to Valencia and found a delightful oasis in the countryside under the olive trees to enjoy our five-star picnic. I felt I was on honeymoon, so romantic.

Patrick loved to drive, and I loved to be driven. We didn't talk much during our travels but listened to an assortment of great music and just enjoyed absorbing the views and vistas, the villages and people.

After stopping briefly in Valencia, we were on our way to Granada. What a magical drive. The proud Rolls performed stupendously. It was funny to see people with their legs hanging out of the windows of their cars, and we were fortunate enough to sit in the car with our windows closed. I didn't know anything about Granada apart from the lovely song, so arriving at the magnificent Moorish citadel and palace, the Alhambra, was fantastic. The architecture was graceful with the beautiful columns and mosaics. The garden was equally lovely, and the views from the top of the hill of Assabica were breathtaking. We spent the night at the old and famous Alhambra Palace Hotel. I was in another world and would have happily stayed longer.

Our final destination for that part of the trip was the famous Marbella Club on the Costa del Sol. Patrick was acquainted with Prince Alfonso Hohenlohe, who owned the club. We had a comfortable cottage on the attractive property, which reminded me a little of the cottages at the Lyford Cay Club, but the atmosphere there was quite different. I felt self-conscious—as I had put on some weight since I stopped smoking, not to mention enjoying all the appetising meals on the trip—so I didn't exactly feel like one of the beautiful people. However, Patrick reassured me I was.

Shortly after our arrival, we went to the big buffet dinner on the property, and I wore one of my new Pucci ensembles. I did feel like one of the beautiful people that evening! During the course of the night and into the early morning, I became very sick and had to have a doctor visit me. I had eaten crab at the buffet. I had no idea I was allergic to crab. Patrick took good care of me, and after two days of being in bed, I was resurrected and able to be myself again. There wasn't much to do at the resort—the beach wasn't like the one in

Nassau, and neither of us liked to spend too much time in the sun– I was happy to be on the move again.

After making the long drive to Madrid, we arrived at the Ritz and stayed for a couple of nights. Our days were filled with sightseeing around the proud city, and I especially enjoyed a visit to the fabulous Prada museum. We then left for San Sebastian and back into France and on to Geneva in Switzerland, where we stayed for a week. I had been to Switzerland before, at the invitation of an hotelier when I was a travel agent, but I had not visited Geneva. The lovely city spread out around Lake Geneva with Jet d'Eau, the water fountain, being the focal point. Walking through the city was exciting, especially looking at the expensive shops and all the incredible watches and jewellery. I felt comfortable there and revisited Geneva many times afterwards.

We drove on to Montreux, which is situated at the foot of the Alps on the northeast shore of Lake Geneva. It was serenely beautiful, and staying at the Palace Hotel with its blissful views over the lake and environs was a dream. Patrick visited the famous Clinic La Prairie, which offered revitalisation and other beneficial health treatments. While he was there, I walked through the parks around the lake, visited Chateau de Chillon, and generally enjoyed the peace and relaxation. My heart was so full of gratitude for all the exciting experiences.

About ten days later, we left Montreux and were on our way to Vienna, the capital and largest city in Austria. I was thrilled to be visiting Vienna, a city full of beauty and romance—the city of the Viennese waltz, and the Vienna Boys Choir. I knew Vienna was also the home of Sigmund Freud, the neurologist known for his interpretation of dreams.

We had a large suite at the Imperial Hotel, the Italian Neo Renaissance Palace, and I felt like an Austrian princess! The hotel was gorgeous, our enormous suite was immaculate and regal, and I could have stayed forever! There was so much to see in Vienna, especially the Spanish riding school where I was entranced by the famous Lipizzaner horses. We were fortunate to have ringside seats at a special anniversary show for those magnificent horses, and I shall never forget their eyes and long eyelashes, not to mention the amazing concentration as they performed the Dressage. If it wasn't for General Patton saving those horses during World War II, we would never have had the privilege of seeing them.

I loved Vienna. Patrick spoiled me with some beautiful petit point handbags, and although we tried to keep away, we had to visit the Café Sacher and sample the Sacher torte! I was also pleased when Patrick surprised me, saying that thanks to the concierge at the hotel, we had the best seats for a performance at the exquisite Vienna State Opera House. We spent a week in Vienna soaking up the history of that magnificent city. While there, I told Patrick about me practicing the "Blue Danube" by Johann Strauss when I was at school in Colombo, and I really wanted to see the river. So on our way out of the city, Patrick stopped the car for me to take a look at the murky brown river, and I have to admit, I was a little disappointed.

Our visit to beautiful Vienna was now at an end, and our next stop was the home of Mozart-Salzburg. We booked into the charming little hotel called the Goldener Hirsch. The hotel, just down the street from Mozart's house in the Old Town, was a short walk from the boutiques and the Salzach River. On the hill above stood the imposing Salzburg Castle, the Salt Castle, and everywhere, we heard the magic music of the Maestro. We said good-bye to Salzburg and to awesome Austria and were headed for Cologne, Germany.

Patrick wanted to see an old friend who lived there. After checking into our hotel opposite the Grand Cathedral, we went over to Heinz's love nest, where I was introduced to his mistress, Margit, who was my age. Heinz's business, among other things, was the importation of Mikimoto pearls from Japan to Germany. At breakfast the following morning, Patrick gave me a beautiful green jade and pearl necklace, the Irish colors! I was overcome and immediately put it on; it was so beautiful.

We made a visit to the Grand Cathedral, which was imposing, as it was enormous and had the most beautiful stained-glass windows. Our sightseeing took us for a walk along the Rhine, and we ended up at the pedestrian shopping street where we did a little shopping, which included a large bottle of 4711 Eau de Cologne! That night before going to bed, I thought about my birthmark and hoped it would never fade away. I didn't forgot where all my good fortune was coming from and thanked Jesus every day.

After our lovely days in Cologne, we drove on to the city of Hamburg. I was enthralled by the autobahns where there was no speed limit for cars, so the Rolls seemed to fly along the fast-moving motorways. Once we had settled in to our suite at the Atlantic Kempiniski Hotel, we decided to have dinner at a local restaurant where Patrick ordered pig trotters and other German delicacies—none of which I had tasted before and didn't particularly like too much. Feeling replete, we headed to the red light district. We went from one erotic show to another. I wasn't enthusiastic about the shows, which were graphic and crude, though the audience found them amusing. I told Patrick I could have done without the experience.

Our final destination, before returning to London, was a visit to Denmark to meet more of Patrick's friends. Preben was a Danish film producer, and together with his lovely wife, Ellie, lived in an old Castle, Nakkabolle, on the island of Fyn. The rooms were huge and comfortable. It was indeed different and fun to be staying in a real castle; the only problem we faced was all the tempting food! While in Fyn we visited Hans Christian Andersen's home in Odense, which was delightful and interesting. Sometimes in the afternoons we would go for walks along the lanes, and one afternoon Ellie suggested she and I go for a bicycle ride. Well, I had to tell her that I had never ridden a bicycle. Ellie found that hard to believe and immediately said she would teach me. Fortunately there was no one on the lanes of the estate, so if I fell off, it only caused me embarrassment and gave much mirth to Ellie. In fact we laughed so much I found it hard to concentrate. However, I did manage to ride in the end but not successfully.

After a relaxed and lovely stay with our friends, Patrick and I drove to Copenhagen. We made our home at the historic Hotel D'Angleterre.

It was fun to visit the Tivoli Gardens and eat at the various restaurants. One day we drove out to Helsingor to see Hamlet's Castle; it looked foreboding, and I must say that the moat was of much interest to me, never having seen one before. The "walking street" in Copenhagen came as a shock. I couldn't believe there were so many places showing pornographic shows. The Danes seemed to take it all in their stride, which I found astounding.

The food in the many delightful restaurants was most appetising. One restaurant I liked overlooked the statue of the famous Little Mermaid. The smorgasbord was tantalising, and on that day I became a big fan of the herring! While we were in Copenhagen, Patrick told me one of his main reasons for being there was to take me to the exclusive leading furriers, Birger Christensen, where he bought me a beautiful silver mink stole, a black Persian lamb coat, several mink hats and a white mink-lined raincoat. In addition to which, I was fitted for the Saga ranch mink coat, which was to follow. Needless to say, I was more than a little overwhelmed by his generosity. I had never dreamed of having any fur coats or hats, for that matter, but even if I say so myself, I looked rather good in all those luxurious purchases!

26

We headed for the ferry at The Hague, as the time had come to return to London. It had certainly been a summer to remember. Patrick and I had had a wonderful time getting to know each other and discovering that travelling in the Rolls in close quarters was a way to bond.

I was happy to be back in London and especially to visit my dad, mother, and Sylvan, who were eager to hear about my trip. It was at that time Patrick introduced me to one of his closest friends, the Reverend Canon Gordon Albion, who was the parish priest of St. Edward's Catholic Church in Sutton Park where Patrick was an acolyte as a boy, and where his parents and siblings were buried. We drove to Sutton Park frequently at the weekends to see Father Gordon and to lunch together. I did enjoy the intellectual conversations between those two erudite gentlemen. I also loved visiting the little church and looking at the gravestones of most of Patrick's immediate family. Just up the road from the church and presbytery was the main home of Paul Getty, Sutton Place, which was impressive, overlooking his many acres of beautiful parkland.

My life with Patrick was different to what I was used to when I was working, not nearly so hectic, but certainly never boring. I couldn't help wishing my family was enjoying the same good fortune. Patrick offered to buy a building in London, which could be converted into flats—one of which my parents could live in. They would be in charge of the property.

Mother retorted, "what your father and I live like Darby and Joan? Never!"

Darby and Joan were mentioned in an eighteenth century song depicting a devoted elderly couple living happily together—so that offer fell by the wayside!

While we were in London, Patrick said I should learn how to drive. I signed up with the British School of Motoring, and although I liked the challenge of learning something new, I was fearful of not doing well. Driving didn't come easily to me. The day of my test arrived, and much to my surprise, Patrick asked for my keys to the apartment. He told me that if I didn't pass, not to return. I hoped he was joking. When I returned to the flat, I had to ring the doorbell. I knew Irma would be nervous, and through the door, Patrick asked whether I had passed. I told him I had, and he asked me to put the proof, which was in writing, under the door. I did. Why I had to go through that game with him, I really didn't know, but he seemed surprised I had passed my test, as apparently not too many people in London pass their driving test on the first go. I was not offended by his strange behaviour. Patrick was a tough guy, and my quiet, gentle reaction, not to mention how excited I really was having passed the test, won me a super dinner at Les Ambassadeurs Club that evening.

I came to realise that Patrick, although I was his live-in girlfriend, really liked women and knew many. I did approach him on the subject, asking him if I wasn't good enough for him, and he told me that men are really not meant to be monogamous, and so long as I was in his home and woke up in his bed in the morning, then I was his number one lady and should not worry if he philandered. Being young and believing in being in love, it was difficult to accept. Despite quietly crying myself to sleep on many occasions, I came to grips with the situation. If you love your man and he is good to you, you make the most of all the happy times and bury your hurts. I had to accept Patrick's life, and it was a great deal better than what I had experienced in the past. I didn't have to worry about money or work to all hours, or think of various ways to make extra cash. Patrick was great in every way, except for his proclivity for women. I couldn't help thinking he had the best woman for him. I also knew that in time my love for him would make him really love me, and I would be all he would ever want.

Patrick frequently played patience or solitaire, and it was during those times that he formed his plans. It intrigued me to watch him, and after he had stacked away his cards on that particular day, he turned to me and said we would be moving to an apartment in Grosvenor Square. He had had his name on the list for a special flat and was thrilled that it had now become available. When he worked in London as a young man before immigrating to America, his dream was to live in Grosvenor Square. We walked over to see the flat; it was completely empty but perfect.

Life would soon become very busy—talking to the interior decorators, choosing carpets and curtain material, wallpaper, having furniture made to specification, and then there was the shopping. We shopped for Waterford crystal chandeliers and glassware. Many trips were made into the country to antique shops to find beautiful old furniture, and of course, we made numerous visits to Harrods. I always loved the thought of decorating a home and was totally fascinated by Patrick's amazing taste; everything he did had my greatest admiration. I knew I had good taste and a great appreciation of beauty, and sometimes thought that if life had been different for me, I may have ended up as a dress designer or interior decorator, but now my biggest dream was to be Patrick's wife.

Finally it was time to leave the flat in Upper Grosvenor Street, and as the work in the new flat in Grosvenor Square would take about eight to nine months until completion, Patrick had made plans. We took up residence in the Connaught Hotel for a month while he finalised the details. Over dinner in the Grille Room at the Connaught Hotel, Patrick told me he was planning a trip around the world. We had to have various visas and shots before leaving London.

When Patrick told me our trip around the world would take about nine months, the period of gestation, he laughed and said it would be like our honeymoon, and he then gave me the wedding ring of his previous wife. I wasn't at all offended; in fact, I was so happy and loved the simple platinum ring, which fit my finger as if it were made for me. Now that I wore a wedding band, I felt more confident being his mistress, but to all and sundry, we were married and on honeymoon. I did learn many years later he had told his close friends that if we both survived the nine months, he would marry me.

Before leaving on our world tour, Patrick decided we should spend Christmas and the New Year in Monte Carlo, and we departed from London on December twenty-third 1967.

Christmas and New Year's Eve festivities in Monte Carlo were amazingly happy—many scintillating parties, beautiful women in magnificent couture dresses. Patrick seemed to know everyone, and Prince and Princess Troubetzkoy being his closest friends, made sure we were included in all the main events. One party I recall was hosted by Dino de Laurentis and his wife, Silvana Mangano. I was thrilled to meet the actress and always recall her perfume, having had the opportunity to shake her hand, which lingered on my skin all evening. There were also quiet evenings when Patrick and I were alone and walked through the streets of Monte Carlo, to eat at Rampoldi's Italian restaurant, which we did many times, and to visit the Café de Paris, which was so much fun. Naturally, we went into the legendary Casino of Monte Carlo, where I watched Patrick play blackjack—that was his game, and I don't ever recall him leaving empty-handed.

27

We returned to London, to the Connaught Hotel, and on January fourteenth 1968, Patrick and I left for Nassau, Bahamas. That time I stayed as Patrick's wife at the Lyford Cay Club. It was super to be back there again, and our month flew by. I watched Patrick play golf and tried to play the game myself, but was very nervous, so decided to walk the course and watch him play. During the day after sunning, swimming and sometimes while Patrick was playing golf, he suggested I take the hired car and practice my driving, especially parking.

After our beautiful visit to Nassau, we were on our way to the famous Sandy Lane Hotel in Barbados. I was enamoured with the lovely island and the hotel. The Sandy Lane was a little less overpowering than Lyford Cay Club and was very romantic. We spent leisurely days walking the beaches talking about our lives, and in the evenings having dinner and dancing while being caressed by the gentle breeze. I was thrilled to find a Catholic church close to the hotel, which made me very happy. Our days at the Sandy Lane Hotel were blissful, and I was sad to leave such an idyllic retreat where life was clement and relaxed.

The next stop was the jet-set resort of Acapulco, where the pace of life was so different. There were large, modern hotels along the beach and many tourists, mainly from America. It wasn't long before we met lots of people and were invited to many parties, which included a big party at the home of Debbie Reynolds, who was such a gracious and entertaining hostess. Life in Acapulco was like a merry-go-round; it was a little overwhelming for me, as the friends we made seemed to do nothing but have a good time.

We visited the Las Brisas estate, but although Patrick said we could have stayed in one of the cottages, he preferred to be on the beach. One evening we went to dinner at a restaurant where we had a great view of the famous rock divers, which was most exciting to watch. During the day we shared a cabana near the pool with some Americans from New York. Patrick said he had to leave me at the cabana and would be back in time for lunch. As I was in the cabana, I couldn't help but overhear the conversation of our new friends, though I was more interested in the music that was being played near the pool. In a mild sort of way, I heard the men talking about the stock market. I knew it was a subject always of much interest to Patrick, so I listened. When I met Patrick for lunch, I related to him what I had heard. I guess I did well, as Patrick told me later that the information I had given him in Acapulco about the stock market had paid for our whole nine months around the world. I smiled and thought to myself that I wasn't just a pretty face after all! I was thrilled to be able to repay Patrick for some of his kindness to me.

Our next exciting destination was Hollywood, California, and the Beverly Hills Hotel located on Sunset Boulevard. We had a beautiful bungalow in the manicured gardens, and I was able to wear my pretty cotton Pucci dress! I was actually in America and staying at The Pink Palace, as the hotel was affectionately known. I felt a little like Alice in Wonderland as we walked through the hotel, dined in the Polo Lounge, lunched alfresco, watched the bathing beauties by the pool, and generally soaked in the atmosphere of the luxury hotel. Not only that, I was in Hollywood and wondered if I would see any film stars. I marveled at the different architecture of the large homes and how pristine the lawns looked. Patrick and I dined at some of the illustrious restaurants, which brought back many memories for him, as he recalled the years he spent living in Los Angeles in the 1930s. We only stayed a few days, as we were on our way to Honolulu, but Patrick promised we would return.

Aloha, Honolulu, Hawaii. Arriving at the airport, we were presented with sweet perfumed frangipani leis. Our suite at the Kahala Hilton was spacious and gorgeous, overlooking the eight hundred feet of secluded beach and ocean. The hotel was breathtakingly unforgettable with the grounds displaying heavenly orchids and other glorious vegetation, which was almost mystical to behold. In the evenings we were wrapped in the lullaby of tropical breezes, as we watched the hula dancing while dining under the stars. We stayed for six weeks, as during that time we were required to have inoculations for the rest of our trip. Every day we did something different, and, of course, we visited the Royal Hawaiian Hotel, walked the Waikkii Beach, attended many lovely luaus and watched the beautiful girls dancing the sacred hula, which I tried so hard to learn. Patrick played many rounds of golf at the Waialae Country Club, and I would breathe in the beauty of the greens and surrounding areas. We were always aware of the crater Diamond Head– one of Hawaii's famous landmarks, which was also visible from our hotel. It was a total joy to explore the island, and I believe we saw most of Honolulu.

One morning Patrick said he had a surprise for me and that we would be lunching at a restaurant near Waikiki Beach. It was indeed a surprise when Heinz and Margit came to join us. I was happy to see them, as the last time we had met was in Cologne. I was delighted that they intended to stay for a few days and help celebrate Patrick's sixty-second birthday. The four of us had a lot of fun together, and I felt close to Margit, knowing she too was a mistress, but at least for me, Patrick was not married to someone else.

Patrick bought me a couple of muu-muus and an elegant Chinese evening gown. We also made a visit to Pearl Harbour, which was so interesting. I had to admit to Patrick I didn't know anything about the history, but by the time I left, he had educated me as to what had happened at Pearl Harbor, and it left a big impression. Our six weeks in Honolulu was finally coming to an end, and as I was in the lobby waiting to depart, I saw Shirley MacLaine standing in a corner, trying not be noticed. I did notice her and wanted to go up and say hello and that I had read most of her books and thought she was amazing, but I didn't. After six weeks I was ready to bid good-bye to beautiful Honolulu and say Konnichiwa to Japan.

Our home in Tokyo was the Imperial Hotel, which was most impressive and where once again we had a large suite. From the moment I arrived at Narita Airport, I fell in love with Japan. I loved the courtesy, the beauty and gentleness of the women, the politeness of the men, the food, the flower arrangements, and so much more. The country was different to any other country I had visited thus far. The owner of the travel agency through whom we had booked—Kunio, a most wonderful man, who became a close friend—had arranged for a lovely English-speaking girl, Yumiko, to be our guide. She too became our friend and was with us most of the time. Patrick had made sure our arrival and stay in Japan would coincide with cherry blossom time, the rows and rows of flowering trees were breathtaking.

We visited the beautiful Japanese gardens, ate delicious delicacies, visited Sony, went to watch sumo wrestling, paid our respects at the Shinto temples, and in the evenings, Kunio took us to the nightclubs in the Ginza, where invariably I was the only woman guest. Patrick wanted me to be with him when he went to the nightclubs. It was amusing, really, as many of the girls in the show were fascinated by me, and I received some delightful little billet-doux, much to Patrick's chagrin!

Kunio had planned for us to visit his hotel in Hakone, so we left Tokyo on the bullet train. What a thrilling experience it was to watch the campestral landscape fly by. Patrick had chosen a plain, rather boring-looking sandwich for his lunch. I was far more adventurous and chose a Japanese lunch, which was delicious. The train arrived at Hakone, and there was a member of the staff from the hotel to meet us, waiting exactly where the door of the train to our apartment would open. I was most impressed, having been a travel agent, to note how every detail had been attended to so perfectly since our arrival in Japan.

When we arrived at our sweet little hotel, we found kimonos spread out on the bed of our bedroom. It was required that we wore those to dinner. Our Japanese maid was there to help us unpack and dress us in our kimonos. Patrick and I were happily surprised that Kunio was waiting for us in the dining room and would join us for dinner, and he too was wearing his kimono. We had a perfect evening. Hakone was gorgeous. The cherry blossoms were fantastic. I loved wearing the kimono and eating Japanese food. I was falling more in love with Japan. The next day we were taken to visit the "shy mountain," the majestic Mount Fuji. It was a lovely sunny day but very cold. Anyway, we managed to find our way to the halfway station and then decided to return to the hotel, as we hadn't been prepared for the snow and bitter cold. I didn't want to leave Hakone and the hot springs and all the beautiful foliage, but it was time to travel on to Toba.

The hotel where we stayed was remote and the landscape was powerful, as it was not too far from the volcano. We made a visit to Mt. Usu and looked into the crater, which was daunting and the smell of sulfur was most unpleasant. Toba was a beautiful town, lots of verdant vegetation. We walked down the spacious streets, and it just happened there was an outing for schoolgirls who were visiting the town. I don't think they had ever seen anyone with red hair, as they couldn't take their eyes off me. We had stopped in Toba, as it was en route to the Mikimoto Island.

Patrick told me that the pearls on the pearl and jade necklace, which he had given me in Cologne, were Mikimoto pearls, so visiting the island was fascinating for me. I learned that only six species of oyster out of a hundred thousand are used for cultured pearls. It was also a memorable spectacle to watch the girls diving for the oysters. I marveled at the statue of Mr. Mikimoto and a copy of the Liberty Bell both made out of Mikimoto pearls. Visiting the Mikimoto Island was like being in another world, a world of pearls, really spectacular. Patrick bought me a few small souvenirs and told me he had some bigger surprises, which he would give me at a later time.

Our next stop was the city of the Golden Pavilion—temples and shrines, the amazing and captivating city of Kyoto. Kunio had booked us into a ryokan. The little inn was just delightful and proved to be an adventure for us. Our room was perfect, although I did wonder where we were to sleep. However, after a delicious Japanese dinner, we returned to our room, and there were our beds on the floor— tatami mats all laid out for us—and on top were our happy coats and slippers. I don't think Patrick was quite prepared for the tatami mat, but it felt familiar to me, having slept on a mat on the floor many times as a child. There were no closets to hang our clothes, so having folded them, we laid them on the floor.

Although we had a toilet and basin adjoining our room, we had to use a communal bathroom to bathe. In the bathroom was a large stone bathtub of clear, clean water. I understood from the Japanese maid that I was to soap myself outside the tub and then use the hand bucket to dip into the water and rinse off the soap; so when all the soap was washed away, I was then permitted to climb into the tub to soak.

Having completed my ablutions, I arrived back to our room and explained the ritual to Patrick, who had finished his breakfast and eagerly told me to enjoy the cold dead fish, sticky rice, miso soup and a small fruit that looked like a cherry; it was a pickled cherry. He was watching me as I toyed with my fish and rice, and then he told to me to try the cherry. Well, he had a good laugh when I spat the horrid thing right out. Patrick had already tried it, but I wasn't there to watch his reaction. It was then my turn to laugh when I saw him trying to shave as he sat on the lid of the toilet, bending down to see into the mirror, which was set at the height for the average Japanese man—hilarious!

The day was beautiful, clear, and cool as we visited the serene gardens and palaces of Kyoto. The flowers, the ornamental shrubs, and of course, the cherry blossoms were magical. We were introduced to the Tanuki statue, the little raccoon and dog-like figure who carried a bottle of saki and his credit cards. What more did he need! We walked in the old town and generally loved everything about the city. In the evening of the second night, Kunio arranged for us to enjoy a special dinner.

We had been invited to join him at a Geisha house. Normally women are not permitted, but I was warmly welcomed. As we sat on cushions ingesting a delicious assortment of divine delicacies served by the Geisha girls, I truly felt I was Japanese that night. The girls were beautiful, and although they had such decorum, they were playful and proved to be enchanting company. After dinner we played some innocent and rather childish games and laughed a lot. It was such a wonderful, happy evening shared with incredible, educated, and fine young ladies.

The following day we were invited to be part of a tea ceremony and in the evening attended a Kabuki Theatre. The explanation of Kabuki is, 'Ka' meaning songs, 'bu' meaning dance, and 'ki' meaning skill. I was mesmerised. The energy of the performers and the spectacular colours, makeup and movements were different to anything I had ever seen, and I loved it all. Leaving Kyoto was difficult for me, as I had embraced the romantic city, which also hid deep passion. Patrick bought me the most beautiful kimono and accessories so that I would always be reminded I was his Geisha!

After leaving the mystical Kyoto, we spent a night in Kobe, where we were told that the bulls were given beer to drink and were massaged daily; hence the palatable and tender Kobe beef. The following day we boarded the ferry to travel on the Inland Sea to Beppu on the island of Kyushu. The voyage on the Inland Sea was refreshing, and the day was perfect, as the ferry gently sailed through the dark-blue waters, making a contrast to the paler blue skies above. Beppu is renowned for the hot springs. Patrick wouldn't allow me to bathe in the communal baths, not that I really wanted to, as he could already see how all the school children were totally awestruck by me and imagined how the older men in the baths would ogle. I watched Patrick enjoy himself as he drove a go-cart; he was like a happy child riding the track in his suit and tie.

Patrick riding a go-cart in Beppu

Kunio invited us to visit his charming home in Beppu, which was surrounded by an exquisite traditional garden with abundant bonsai. I was interested to notice that Kunio and his wife's clothes were not hung, but laid flat in elaborate boxes. The home was simple yet refined. Our last visit was to a natural zoo noted for its Takasaki, tamed monkeys; once again the school children were around, so I wasn't only followed by the children, but the monkeys too. I knew it had to be my red hair!

We returned to Tokyo to meet up with other friends and especially to enjoy an elegant farewell dinner, hosted by Kunio and his gracious wife, Hiroko. I wore the Chinese cheongsam that Patrick had bought for me in Honolulu and used my silver mink stole for the first time; I felt rather special. Thanks to Kunio we had had the most incredible and memorable visit to that intriguing country, and I was really sad to leave as I bid sayonara to my friends and to Japan. While we were seated comfortably on the plane headed to Hong Kong, Patrick said he hoped that after living in Japan for six weeks I had learned from the Japanese women how to take care of him. I knew he was joking, but he also knew that taking care of him was innate to me.

Diana with school children in Beppu, Kyushu, Japan

28

I was conscious of letting Patrick know how grateful I was to be experiencing such an incredible life with him. I knew he was rather aware of our age difference, more so than I was. Having felt older than my years since I was a little girl, I was able to respect him and make no demands, as I eagerly accepted the life he was offering me. I had my pride and decorum and never felt subservient to him. It was more difficult for him to share his life with me, as he could be quite controlling. I suppose that being in the Coldstream Guards had helped make him a man of great discipline. Patrick had been in California when the war in Europe started and had the awesome responsibility of training many a young man sent over to America from Britain to become pilots. Later on he was based in Washington DC and worked for the Air Transport Command during World War II as a captain, and was in charge of critical missions. I respected that he liked order in his life, and I tried hard not to upset him.

I did, however, dread his drinking, which at times in the beginning of our relationship ignited his Irish spirit, and whatever frustrations he had were at my expense. The vodka sometimes brought out his volatile temper, which fortunately didn't last long. Those incidents weren't too frequent, thank goodness, as they also brought back vivid memories of my dad and his drinking; though my father didn't have a temper. Anyway, I was Patrick's companion, he had taken me into his life, and I loved him. I always carried his precious letters with me, which was my reminder that he loved me, because he didn't say those words often.

Hong Kong was to become my favourite place in the world. Hong Kong was completely different to beautiful Japan. I was so excited arriving at the airport and was whisked off to the Mandarin Hotel. The lovely hotel had only been opened five years, and many an evening we would close the Captain's Bar as we mingled with other visitors from abroad. Our suite overlooked Victoria Harbour, and at night it was such a wonderful spectacle to look out over the glittering lights of that vibrant city. Everything about that exotic little haven thrilled me.

Patrick had some influential friends living there, and one of his close friends was connected to the Hong Kong Shanghai Bank, so we were well taken care of. We visited most of the sights that Hong Kong had to offer, and of course, we had to see Victoria Park and pay a visit to the fishing port of Aberdeen. Patrick wanted to have dinner on the famed floating Sea Palace restaurant, and to get there we had to take a ride in a sampan, which was such a thrill. It was all so colourful—many sampans going back and forth, and the restaurant in the middle of all of the activity was brightly lit and inviting. I found it totally intoxicating. I was still in a bit of a dream when Patrick showed me a tub of live lobsters and asked me to choose which one I wanted to eat; inside I felt sick, but I let the thought of those poor lobsters dissolve quickly and chose one. I hadn't eaten lobster before and decided it wasn't one of my favourite foods.

A few days later, we met Kai-Bong and Brenda, the son and daughter-in-law of Patrick's friend. They took us to their country club for lunch, and while Patrick went to the races at Happy Fields after lunch, Brenda took me to a fortune teller at my request. The fortune teller could only speak Mandarin, so Brenda had to be my translator. The little old man looked at me and asked me to show him my hands, which I did. I was wearing the wedding ring Patrick had given me. The fortune teller told me that unless I took off the ring, he couldn't read my hands, as I was not married.

Brenda was so surprised. "Diana, you are not married?"

I told her it was our secret. I wasn't married and removed the ring. The old Chinaman went on to tell me I would marry a man who was much older than I was and went on to describe Patrick, that I would always be taken care of, and that I would have a baby girl. He went on to say that life would be difficult and sad for me, and thus the meeting ended. I thanked him and replaced my ring. I told Brenda that Patrick had said he would never marry me and that he was unable to have children, so it was difficult for me to believe anything the old Mandarin had said. I nevertheless did dwell on our meeting and the fact he knew I wasn't married had me thinking.

Patrick wanted to do a lot of shopping in Hong Kong for the new apartment in Grosvenor Square. I was most interested in watching him make his choices and was looking forward to seeing all the beautiful purchases back in London.

Although Hong Kong was busy and bustling, there was a form of order, and it was British, which I suppose made me feel at home. The city not only vibrated, but was also very romantic. I loved going on the Star Ferry back and forth across Victoria Harbour, and during our two-week visit, when Patrick wanted time to remain in the hotel, I was allowed to venture out. I felt so safe, as if I belonged.

Two weeks in Hong Kong just flew by. I didn't want to leave. So with all the shopping accomplished, we were now headed for Manila in the Philippine Islands. We had an introduction to meet Hans Kasten, who became a close friend of ours. We were introduced to him through friends we met in London and an ex-girlfriend of his, whom we met in Tokyo. Everyone who is anyone and has visited Manila knew of Hans Kasten. He was especially well known for his famous luncheon parties where he entertained heads of states, film stars, and all persons of importance. He was an attractive and interesting American/German, who had lived in the Philippines for many years, and we both liked him immediately.

Entering his home was like being in a miniature museum. Hans was a collector of beautiful and original artifacts from all around the Far East, especially India. He had many magnificent statues of the Buddha, rugs, furniture, and so much more. Being with Hans and seeing the well-to-do community where he lived was different to other parts of Manila, which were not that salubrious: the open sewers, the flimsy huts and poor little children wondering around half naked. Apart from meeting Hans, I have to admit I was happy to be leaving Manila after being there for a week.

On June the second, we arrived at Jakarta, Indonesia. My first impression reminded me a little of Colombo. We only stayed one night, as we were travelling on to Denpasar, Bali. I had not heard of the island of Bali so was not only happily surprised when we arrived, but knew I was going to love the tropical island, as it was my sort of place. The Bali Beach Hotel overlooked the tops of coconut trees, and from our suite I could see the pristine beach, which seemed endless, and the beautiful, clear waters beyond. The beach reminded me of the beaches in Nassau, and I also felt that I could have been back in Ceylon. Bali was heavenly, a real tropical paradise.

As we were walking through the lovely gardens of the hotel, we met an Indian Guru, and Patrick asked his permission to take a photograph of him together with me, and he said he would be delighted. I felt like the island girl. My Sinhalese upbringing would always be in my heart. I realised I wanted to wear the sarongs, carry rice on my head and wear flowers in my hair—I did wear flowers in my hair! During our visit to the island, we were invited to have lunch at the charming home on stilts of Jimi Pandi. His Balinese home was surrounded by an awesome tropical garden near the breathtaking beach. Jimi was well known for his collection of Balinese art and furniture.

Patrick and I seemed to be the only tourists around. We walked to most of the villages, and wherever we went I was followed by school children. They were so sweet and so curious and so well behaved. We walked along the unpaved road, passed the rice paddy fields and saw the girls with parcels of rice on their heads and carrying other food to the temple; that was their routine, as the food had to be blessed by the local priest before they took it home. Apart from the hotel, there was no electricity or running water in the villages. There were numerous little streams where the bare-bosom girls would bathe. That was stopped once Bali became known as a tourist destination.

Patrick and I joined the procession of women accompanied by their children carrying their offerings of rice and parcels of food to the nearest temple. The veneration and blessing of the food was most interesting to watch. All the beautiful young women who carried so much food on their heads, none of which fell off, came to the priest and laid it out in front of him. When he had blessed the food, he was left with enough to eat, and the remainder was returned for the villagers to consume. It seemed to us that the women did all the work. The men were priests or teachers or worked in the two or three new hotels.

Diana surrounded by children while walking on a road in Bali

As dusk gently embraced the land, the entertainment arrived in the villages in the form of barongs. They were men dressed in costumes and wearing masks usually of animals, and walking on stilts. The barongs would walk from village to village entertaining the villagers, who sat outside their little homes and listened to their imaginative stories. They were so popular, especially with the children, as I suppose they were like fairy tales read to us as children. We were fortunate to experience the normal life of the Balinese families.

The various and many rituals were strange but fascinating. We were invited to join a family in a burial ritual, or watch a witch doctor or the medicine man perform their magic; and at times it all felt rather ethereal as we stood under the banyan tree in semi-darkness surrounded only by candlelight. We were the only two foreigners at some of those events and felt honoured to have been invited. The Balinese people we met were gentle and kind. They were also very pious; their gods and priests came before all else.

One of our excursions was to drive to Sukarno's summer palace, which at the time of our visit belonged to President Suharto. The palace was guarded, but we were allowed on the premises. Our guide pointed out the public baths in the gardens below. He told us Sukarno liked to watch the women take their baths, and if he fancied a woman bather, he would have her brought up to him. The baths were still used by the villagers. We met one mother with her three children on their way to bathe; they were grateful they could use the baths, as there were no other bathing amenities for them.

That evening after having returned to our hotel, we joined the villagers and were privileged to be in the audience to see the famous show of Rama and Sita. It seemed to us as if the whole village had turned out. The garden was filled with an audience of many families, and the stage was the entrance to one of the temples. The orchestra sat on either side. We were interested to see backstage and were invited to watch the performers get ready, paint their faces and regale themselves in their appropriate costumes. The evening was magical, soft and balmy.

Suddenly it became alive with the clash of cymbals, the metallic sounds of the gamelan, and sounds from the gongs, flutes, drums and chimes. The instruments helped tell the story. It was a story of mystery and adventure, the struggle of good against evil. Prince Rama had been unjustly banished to the forest, and with the help of his brother and a monkey, he was rescued. He then freed the beautiful Sita from a giant ogre and they both returned victorious. The dancing was wonderful and the whole show was so appealing and captivating. The entire audience was silent until the thunderous applause at the end. Patrick bought me a set of the long nails that were used in the dance, which can be used as brooches today. The show was a memorable farewell to our visit to the incredibly magical and mystical island of beautiful Bali.

We had really enjoyed our visit to Bali and felt relaxed and thankful to have shared so many different experiences together. I think at times, Patrick was happy to see how easily I fit in with every diverse situation. Mainly due to my early life, I had learned to accept whatever came my way and to be grateful for everything. I loved all the eclectic food, ate with the correct utensils or my hands, if that was what was called for, and had no complaints. I felt blessed to be seeing the world in all its beauty. My big regret was not being able to attend Sunday Mass during the trip. However, every night as I knelt beside whatever bed was mine, I gave thanks to Jesus. I knew He understood. I also thanked Patrick daily for being with him and sharing the wonderful journey.

29

After eight unforgettable days, we were now on our way to Singapore. Leaving the simple island life of Bali, we found Singapore to be rather sophisticated. The famous colonial style Raffles Hotel was sensational, and our luxurious suite was enormous. We were reminded that Noel Coward had stayed at the fabled hotel in the 1930s and that Ernest Hemingway and Somerset Maugham had enjoyed the Singapore Sling cocktail in the Stone Long Bar, which Patrick and I frequented during our stay. Interestingly the Raffles Hotel, which was named after the founder of Singapore, Sir Stamford Raffles, was the first building to have electricity in that city. The interior of the hotel with its ceiling fans and the general façade was very impressive.

I was amazed by the cleanliness of the city, but on one of our tours was surprised to see houses on stilts near the harbour. The area was known as Old Clarke Quay and it seemed incongruous with the rest of the city. We dined at the popular Omar Khayyam restaurant, which Patrick arranged especially knowing how much I loved his poetry. We strolled through the hotel arcade with all the tempting shops and couldn't resist a beautiful chess set. After a wonderful week in Singapore, experiencing the colonial days of a time gone by, it was on to Bangkok, Thailand.

Our home in Bangkok was the eminent and gorgeous Oriental Hotel. Before I could even think about what I wanted, a maid was ready to be of service. We had a romantic suite overlooking the Chao Phraya River. As we did a lot of sightseeing during the day, we usually ended up dining in the hotel.

Patrick arranged for us to pay a visit to the dazzling and architecturally spectacular Grand Palace and hired a car and guide to show us around. We also visited the temple of the Emerald

Buddha, whose robes are changed according to the different seasons. That temple was most fascinating. I felt such a sense of peace and connection to Buddha. How much I had grown up since my first negation of Buddha in Ceylon! I had become more aware of his teachings as I grew older, and whenever I was in a Buddhist temple, I felt a great serenity, just as I had done when the Buddhist monk came begging at Selina's home in Colombo.

The hotel arranged for us to take a long tail boat on the Klong tour. We embarked from our hotel and it was fun that we had it to ourselves. It was such a beautiful adventure travelling on the smaller canals of the Chao Phraya River, the Venice of the East. We were curious to see how the boat people lived on the river. Their tiny homes on stilts made us realise how terribly poor they were, but they appeared happy. We saw the floating markets selling fruit and vegetables to the people in their homes. At one point, all the boats selling produce congregated together and soon were surrounded by smaller boats buying their supplies; it was an unforgettable scene. The children were adorable as they waved to us, but we were concerned when we saw them swimming in the dirty river water. The backdrop to the tour was the iridescent temple, Wat Arun, the Temple of the Dawn, which was breathtaking in its beauty.

Patrick wanted to have a few Thai silk shirts made and a few dresses for me. I particularly liked the batik, so we went to the famous Jim Thompson House. Jim Thompson, the founder of the Thai silk company, had built himself a wonderful home, which was located in beautiful gardens. He had disappeared the previous year, and it is still a mystery today as to what happened to him, but his home is now a museum filled with stunning Southeast Asian art.

We paid a visit to see the Royal Barge museum, which was located on the banks of the Noi Canal, off the Chao Phraya River across from the Grand Palace. The six beautiful barges used to be viewed on New Year's Day by the Royal family in the great parade on the river. I believe that on important days (such as the king's birthday) there are now fifty barges that sail down the Chao Phraya River in a regal flotilla. The barges were very majestic; so much intricate work was involved in their assembly. I wasn't too impressed, however, with the city of Bangkok. The traffic was chaotic and noisy, and the air smelt of diesel fumes.

There were many poor people begging and especially young girls who were actually offering themselves to the tourists. One house in particular accommodated the girls in a large cage from which men would choose a girl, and she would be taken to a room on the premises. It was all disturbing to me, but prostitution was the only way for some families to live.

As Patrick was a former welterweight champion with the Coldstream Guards, he wanted to see a Thai boxing fight. The event was very entertaining, starting with prayers, and then it was anything goes, knees and all. The fights had no resemblance to those of the Coldstream Guards!

On June twenty-third we departed Bangkok for Istanbul—a city of mosques and minarets built beside the ever-moving Bosphorus and the Sea of Marmara. Our accommodations overlooked the Bosphorus. The Hilton, which was one of the first luxury hotels to be built in Istanbul, was convenient for us to be able to explore the immediate area on foot, being within walking distance of Taksim Square and the heart of Istanbul.

What an exciting city, a mixture of the East and the West. Patrick hired a guide to take us to the main places of interest. I was amazed and enraptured by the St. Sophia Church, the Hagia Sophia, which is the Shrine of the Holy Wisdom of God, and was the largest cathedral until the Seville Cathedral was completed in 1520. It remains an important religious monument—one of the greatest works of Byzantine architecture that had been converted into a mosque in 1453—but it was still possible to see some of the Christian frescoes on the walls from when it was a Roman Catholic Cathedral under the Latin Empire from 1204 to 1261.

From the magnificent Aya Sofya, we visited the Topkapi Palace, a home to all the Sultans for many centuries. The fascinating palace overlooking the Bosphorus and the Sea of Marmara spiked my imagination with all its many stories of the Sultans, their concubines and eunuchs. Patrick and I were enthralled by what our guide told us as we visited the harem section of the palace, which in bygone days was kept separate from the rest of the palace. It was private and used only by the family and was called a Place of Felicity. The Sultan's Mother, Valide Sultan Dairesi, was in charge of the girls, and she chose the girls whom she thought were special enough to entertain her son, the Sultan. The girls were from poor families and usually picked for their looks or talents. Many families who needed money offered their daughters as slaves to the Sultan. The girls were guarded by black eunuchs and were taught how to read and write; eventually after a certain number of years being of service to the Sultan, they were allowed to leave with a husband who had been chosen for them. They also left with many gifts and were never known to reveal any of the intimate details about life with the royal family.

Our next visit was to the Sultan Ahmed Mosque, commonly known as the Blue Mosque, which radiated majesty and splendour; its name came from the blue ceramic tiles that adorned the walls. The interior of the mosque was just beautiful—the intricate mosaics on the walls, the numerous little windows, the simple chandeliers with many lighted bulbs, and the floors covered with rather worn carpets, which, when totally threadbare, are replaced by donations from the faithful. Worshippers still attended the mosque and were there while we were visiting.

I was happy to be sharing so many new experiences with Patrick. We decided we should take a boat ride on the Bosphorus and saw the Florence Nightingale Hospital from a distance. I loved looking at the architecture of the numerous riverside homes, some of which were very old. Patrick and I enjoyed our leisurely boat trip, and on our return to land were shown the dancing bears. At that time I had no idea how much those poor bears suffered, and I am pleased that the practice has been stopped.

We both appreciated all the stimulating city of Istanbul had to offer and found the cosmopolitan atmosphere exhilarating. Our last and most exciting visit was to the Grand Bazaar, so many temptations! It was a maze of winding lanes with hundreds of different shops. At one point I was scared that I might lose Patrick. There was so much to see and buy that it was overwhelming. However, I did manage to leave with some delightful mementos.

After exploring the intrigues of Istanbul, Patrick wanted us to see the ancient archaeological site of Ephesus. We boarded a small aeroplane and flew to Izmir where our guide met us and drove us to Ephesus. We did not go into the town of Izmir but delighted in seeing the houses along the route—especially those that had storks making their homes in the chimneys.

Ephesus is an ancient city dating back to the tenth century BC. Patrick and I, together with our guide, were the only visitors on that day, and we felt that the ancient site belonged to us as we walked the old cobbled road marked by chariot wheels, visited the ruins of the homes of noblemen, saw how the drainage system had worked and marveled at the fabulous remains of the Library of Celsus. Apart from the many other wonders, we could not miss the large amphitheatre nestled in the hills. It was so interesting to think that St. Paul lived there, wrote many of his epistles, and was jailed there too.

In the fields not far from the centre of the city were the ruins of the famous temple of the pagan goddess, Diana, daughter of Jupiter and twin sister of Apollo. As we shared a name, I was always fascinated to hear about the goddess Diana. The temple of Diana was considered one of the seven wonders of the ancient world. When St. Paul went to Ephesus to bring Christianity to the people, he made many converts, and Diana was no longer considered the mother of God (as the pagan followers had thought of her), but the converts believed the Virgin Mary was the mother of God. Eventually, St Paul's christianity triumphed, and Diana's temple was destroyed.

Farther along from the ancient city was a little stone house almost hidden by olive trees, and that simple little house was where the Virgin Mary lived; it is now a small chapel. I couldn't help but feel a great sense of serenity and humility to think I was in the home where the Mother of Jesus had lived. As we left the house, we noticed all the crutches, and our guide told us that they were left by those who were cured by the Virgin Mary; she had performed so many miracles. By the end of the excursion, I too felt I understood a little of what it was like to have lived thousands of years ago. I just wish that I had taken my hat, as it was very hot!

We drove back to the airport, and the little plane that flew us back to Istanbul was not pressurised. I wasn't aware of it until my ears became so painful I was in tears. It was a blessing the flight wasn't too long. Patrick was attentive and concerned, but after landing and as the evening wore on, the pain subsided, thank goodness.

July started off with a visit to Athens. The last time I had visited Athens was while I was working for Milbanke Travel. This time I was a little older and happy to be able to show Patrick around one or two special places. We visited the Acropolis and the Parthenon, and once again we had those famous ruins all to ourselves.

As Patrick was a member of the Royal Thames Yacht Club in London, he had no difficulty in being invited to the Yacht Club in Pireaus. We had a delightful lunch overlooking the colourful port, and I didn't have to choose a lobster. We were glad to leave Athens. Despite the ancient ruins, we didn't really enjoy the city.

Arriving in Rome was a thrill for me. I had been there many times before, and it brought back happy romantic memories; and although I had worked in my friend's travel agency for one of my summer holidays, the visit with Patrick was different. I saw a more elaborate side to Rome than I had before. Patrick had a close friend, Count Ermanno Franquinet, who was delighted to show us around. We visited the beautiful Villa D'Este, where I had my photo taken in front of the sixteenth century fountain of the goddess Artemis, who was the Greek equivalent to the Roman goddess Diana.

Count Ermanno was a great guide and introduced us to many interesting places in Rome, which I think was mainly for my benefit, as Patrick had previously lived in Rome for a while. Despite my past frequent visits, I had never been to the Vatican, and needless to say, I was enraptured by the beauty and sanctity of that magnificent holy place. During our sightseeing of St. Peter's, Ermanno took us to a secret bar in the Basilica. It was very small, and not too many people knew it was there. However, we did see a few Swiss Guards enter for a light libation. It was a special moment to be enjoying a glass of wine in a bar in St. Peter's Basilica!

While in Rome we stayed at the Excelsior Hotel on the Via Veneto. Rome was sensational, especially as Patrick knew it so well. We had an exhilarating time enjoying all that the eternal city had to offer. It was fashionable and naughty and the "in city" at that time.

After spending ten glorious days, we were headed south to Sicily. One of Patrick's Italian friends from New York, who lived in Florence, had told him that if he ever had the opportunity to visit Taormina, Sicily, he should, as it was one of the most beautiful places on earth. We said good-bye to Ermanno and to Rome and headed for the country of La Cosa Nostra.

Taormina was indeed beautiful, and we had rooms reserved at the San Domenico Hotel, which was once an old monastery. The hotel was set in gorgeous gardens and situated high above the Ionian Sea with the volatile volcano Mount Etna in the distance. We had only planned to be in Taormina for less than a week, so we made sure that we would enjoy all that that little piece of paradise had to offer. On our second day, we explored the charming town, and while walking along the main corso, noticed an antique shop. The owners, Carlo and Mirella, introduced themselves to us, and having talked to them for a while and accepted an espresso coffee, they invited us to their beach house for dinner.

Much to my delight, Gayelord Hauser, the famous American nutritionist and great friend of Greta Garbo, was also a dinner guest. I was so excited to meet him, as I had read his book "Look Younger, Live Longer", and although the book belonged to my mother, it was precious to me, and for years while I was a working girl, my breakfast consisted of brewer's yeast, wheat germ, plain yogurt and blackstrap molasses—a Gayelord Hauser special!

During the course of dinner, Patrick asked if there were any houses for sale, and they all agreed there was one house that had been uninhabited for fifteen years. The following day we visited the villa, together with Gayelord, his partner Brownie, and Carlo, and everyone thought that the potential for that villa to be made into a livable abode was stupendous. It was in a superb location and being sold for a very reasonable price.

The location was indeed fantastic-the villa overlooked the Ionian Sea with a clear view of Mt. Etna. The grounds were almost two acres with an additional cottage on the property and a beautiful wishing well at the entrance.

Patrick visualised how magnificent the house could be but there was so much work that needed to be done to make it livable, comfortable and up to date. Patrick hadn't confided in me that he wanted to buy a house, and I was not totally sure if he knew it himself until he saw the property. Two days later at the airport before boarding our flight to Monte Carlo, Patrick signed the contract to buy our home in sunny Sicily.

We left Taormina to spend time with Patrick's friends in Monte Carlo, and tell them of the many adventures of our world tour and of our exciting news regarding the purchase of a house in Taormina, before returning to London at the beginning of September.

What an incredible journey it had been, a trip of a lifetime. I felt blessed. Everything had gone according to plan, and we were still together! I was anxious to put all the photographs in albums in order to look back and recall all the fantastic countries we had visited. Patrick had only allowed me one large suitcase for the months we were away, so I was eager to unpack and wear some different clothes.

As we left Heathrow airport on our way home at 37 Grosvenor Square, our thoughts were on our new apartment. Walking through the front door of the flat was so exciting, though there were still a few things that had to be attended to, but on the whole it was a dream. The decorator and all her people had done a great job. Patrick and I were very pleased with the result. I don't think I was fully aware that I was going to live at one of the most revered addresses in London, and it took me a few years to fully comprehend the fact. To me, the beautiful apartment, which I called home, was just that, and it was perfect. Patrick had hired a cook-housekeeper who was not only a Cordon Bleu cook, but also loved to clean silver, so it was an excuse for several visits to the silver vaults.

While we were discussing the villa in Taormina, Patrick again wanted to make it clear to me that he was unable to give me children, and although he would take care of me, he would not marry me. I knew in my soul that Jesus might have other plans, but in the meantime I loved Patrick and just wanted to spend my life with him. There was one problem for me, so I decided to do something about it—I had my name legally changed by deed poll to O'Leary. If I couldn't have Patrick's name through marriage, then that was the next best thing, and my passport would now be issued in the name of Diana Vernon O'Leary, not Diana Vernon Glen Helena Mary Elizabeth Munro. I wanted to be known in Taormina as La Signora Diana O'Leary. I did not want people to think of me as Patrick's mistress, but I was going to be his chatelaine. I didn't tell Patrick until it was all done. He didn't mind at all. In fact, he was amused by my ingenuity. I told him that since he had no intention to marry me and for me to take his name, I had to do it my way. It made all the difference to me, and everyone believed we were married.

30

Patrick, being a man who liked everything done yesterday, decided that we should go back to Sicily the following month to start things rolling for the rebirth of our new home, which was going to be called "Ionia House", as it overlooked the Ionian Sea. He hired a lawyer and an assistant to start employing electricians, plumbers, workmen to excavate the ground for the swimming pool, and arranged for the local artisans to work on upholstering the furniture, wall-papering and a hundred and one other things. We were fortunate enough to meet a lovely young girl, Pina, who was my age, and her brother, Franco, who both spoke English and helped us find our major-domo and his wife, the cook. Yano and Angelina were hired immediately and moved into the staff flat. Franco and Pina became close friends, and Patrick invited them to spend Christmas with us in London.

We returned back to London in late November and had a lot of catching up to do, seeing friends and inviting them to dinner parties in our new apartment. It was at that time that Patrick decided he should learn Italian. I had to admire his determination. I gave him his school bag, which contained a small flask of coffee, and he walked down the street to the Berlitz School of Languages in South Audley Street. When he returned home, he would tell me that he had homework, so we would sit in bed, and I would quiz him on how much he had learned. Well, it just so happened that when we returned to Ionia House in January of 1969, I had managed to learn a lot of Italian by helping Patrick with his homework. Fortunately, Yano spoke excellent English, so he was always at Patrick's side. I, on the other hand, had to talk to Angelina, who didn't speak any English, and neither did the two housemaids, who were in her charge. It wasn't long before I was making myself understood and understanding Italian. My friend

Pina was a tremendous help to me, not only when it came to the language, but also in many other ways.

Back in London the first Christmas at our new flat was busy and exciting. Pina and Franco arrived, Pina stayed in our guest room, while Patrick accommodated Franco at the Britannia Hotel, two doors down from us. At the same time, our new friend Basil, whom we had met on our return to London, joined us and my sister, Sylvan, for some of the celebrations. We all had a wonderful Christmas and New Year, and it was a joy to show Pina and Franco the sights of London Town.

Before we returned to Taormina, Patrick wanted us to have two Golden Retrievers at Ionia House. We found two adorable puppies and reluctantly had to leave them with the breeder until we were ready to have them sent to Sicily. In keeping with our new adopted country, we would call them Romulus and Remus. I couldn't wait for them to be part of our lives, and we were there to welcome them on their arrival. Poor babies, it was quite a trip, but they survived, and I was so happy to have those gorgeous puppies to look after. Once we were back in the house, it suddenly occurred to me what a massive undertaking Patrick had ahead of him to create the most beautiful villa in Taormina.

Patrick had much of the furniture made to measure in Florence, together with a whole set of crockery and cutlery. The attractive furniture for the large terrace that he'd had built by the local artisans, was imported from Hammacher Schlemmer in the States. The seven-foot square bed for the main bedroom and the green leather chesterfields came from Harrods, together with most of the linen, dinner services, silver canteens and crystal glassware. Patrick attended auctions to buy porcelain, carpets, mirrors, and antiques.

Together with our three gardeners, he created a wonderful vegetable garden, and all the main gardens were replanted with over three hundred ornamental shrubs and fruit trees. The kidney-shaped swimming pool, hewn out of the rock on the property, took over a year to build, as did the sun terrace with classical style his and hers changing rooms, bathrooms and a poolside kitchen and bar.

The marble artisan from across the street made the final touches to the changing rooms with marble heads of "male" and "female," which were attached to the doors. The wrought iron artists made all the ornamental lamps for the terrace and throughout the garden. Patrick had the window of the little room at the top of the house made into a fabulous large window so that we could see the full panorama of the Ionian Sea and Mount Etna, and had a sauna installed in the room; it was my hideaway where, after my sauna, I would relax with a book and listen to music with Romulus and Remus by my side.

Patrick's friend in Florence was a collector of long playing records, so Patrick bought over two thousand records from him, and we had music everywhere in the house and throughout the gardens. Once Ionia House was ready to receive guests, friends visited us from all over the world. I enjoyed preparing and arranging wonderful parties, luncheons, and dinners. When an American Naval carrier anchored off Giardini, a small fishing village a mile or so from us, Patrick invited the Captain and senior officers to a lavish luncheon at Ionia House with about thirty-six men attending. Everyone enjoyed themselves so much, that we were invited back to their ship and were given many lovely gifts, which included large cans of coffee. Onassis would often anchor his yacht "Christina" in the Ionian Sea within clear view of our property.

We entertained many of the top echelon in Taormina and environs, and the Catholic Monsignor was a frequent visitor. Although we were not aware of it, Ionia House was becoming very well known.

Every so often Patrick left me to go back to London; he needed a break to recoup. Patrick had faith in me to look after everything. I had learned a great deal from watching him. I also had an innate talent for knowing what to do and how to do it. I felt I was born a chatelaine in my previous life. I was responsible to make sure the house always had beautiful flower arrangements and potted plants. I planned all the menus and was the perfect hostess to everyone, whether I knew them or not. I was twenty-seven years old, taking care of a magnificent home in Sicily, making myself understood with the staff of eight, and

it all came naturally. I was, of course, happy to have my good friend
Pina with me.

Diana with friend Pina in the garden of Ionia House

I was fond of the people who worked for us. I loved Taormina, its
beauty, and of course, I especially loved Romulus and Remus. They
were my children. I bathed them, played with them, and they were
always with me. The Sicilians would see them in the garden when
they looked over the wall and called them the lions. I loved it all.
I wanted Patrick to feel proud of me and to know I was capable of
attending to everything in our beautiful Ionia House.

When purchasing our home in Taormina, no one had told him
that the Mafia was in charge of the workers, and as we had eight in
staff, there were constant problems as to how much we had to pay
them. We soon learned that every Saint's day was a paid holiday, and
there were so many of them! There were other laws that protected the
staff. We had to hire a local lawyer just to keep abreast of doing the
right thing by the Mafia. Patrick would joke that we were the Irish
Mafia, but when it came to hiring staff, it was another matter. We
thought we were looking after the staff in accordance with the laws,
but the Mafia did not agree.

Luckily, we had made some good Sicilian friends, and Peppino just happened to be acquainted with the Mafia. So when I had to go to court in Palermo with regard to the demands made by the local Mafia union member in charge of our workers, who said that our employees had not been paid the required amount for holidays and holy days, I asked Peppino to help me. Yano drove me to Palermo, where I met Peppino, who accompanied me to the courthouse, where I had to appear, and in my Sicilian patois said that our staff had been paid everything that was required. Thanks to Peppino, our case was concluded quickly and easily. It was good to have an influential friend.

During our visits to Taormina, we would enjoy the town and visit the nearby villages. There were so many places to see, and little by little we were learning about the Sicilian people. We were well known and never happier than when mingling with our friends. Patrick bought a small open car called the Schelette. Romulus would sit in the front with Patrick and Remus in the back with me. It was the perfect car to navigate the narrow roads of Taormina, and the four of us loved it. Despite all the work, we were both happy and delighted to learn and see so much of that intriguing and historic island.

Romulus and Remus in the Schelette in the driveway of Ionia House

Sometimes in the evenings we would walk up to the magical and ancient open air Greek theatre, usually stopping to say hello to friends, who owned the glamourous Hotel Timeo, which was located in front of the Greek theatre. We tried to attend all the wonderful concerts and other events, such as the film festivals which were held in Taormina. The year we were in residence at Ionia House was the year of Franco Zefferelli's "Romeo and Juliet." Nothing was more romantic than sitting in the Greek theatre with the moon and stars above, and Mount Etna, the largest volcano in Europe, spewing forth her red and gold lava, while we watched "Romeo and Juliet". Well, sitting on the terrace of Ionia House was almost as good.

Patrick and I also made many trips over to Malta. We had a good friend who was Maltese, and through him it had been recommended to the Knights of Malta that Patrick should be installed as a knight. That necessitated several visits, and during one of them we were introduced to Bishop Gonzi and other important people connected with the knights. It was suggested to Patrick that he make a large donation to the blood bank, which he did, but none of it meant anything when it was discovered that we were not married and Patrick had been divorced—so Patrick was not made a Knight of Malta.

We returned to London for the summer. I was really sad to leave Romulus and Remus and gave strict instructions as to how they were to be taken care of. Our local butcher would supply the fresh meat for Angelina to cook for them. I did trust Yano and Angelina to be their surrogate parents. However, on returning to Ionia House, we saw how thin they were and realised that their meat was being enjoyed by the staff, and Romulus and Remus had been eating spaghetti. When we left the following time, I made sure that there were boxes of tinned dog food and Pina would visit them as often as she could, and even stay in the house to be sure they were all right and fed properly.

We would spend the winter in Taormina. I especially loved my life there. The beautiful heated swimming pool that seemed to blend in with the Ionian Sea was such a luxury, which I enjoyed with Romulus and Remus. We adopted a tiny Siamese kitten and called it Mongibello, the Italian name for Mount Etna. Romulus and Remus, who normally attacked any cat that came on the property, were mesmerised by

Mongibello, who had them both right where he wanted them. There was much laughter in the house as we watched how the little cat caused so much exasperation for our two big Golden Retrievers.

Patrick was happy to a point, but after he had created his masterpiece, he was exhausted and not so enthusiastic about living at Ionia House. He would return to London often and leave me to take care of everything, which I could do, but I missed him. I had Romulus and Remus, whom I adored, and I had my good friends nearby. I loved to go dancing to the local nightclub, La Giarra. The owner was a fantastic dancer, so I was in my element. Needless to say, even when Patrick was in England, there were friends who wanted to visit, so life was always busy. Gayelord Hauser and Brownie often dropped by and I enjoyed going to their home on the beach in Letojanni. They were so pleased that they, together with Carlo from the antique shop, introduced us to what was now the showcase villa in Taormina.

Though I relished being in Taormina (especially due to Romulus and Remus), it was lovely to return to London. I also loved our beautiful apartment and London itself. Since arriving from Ceylon, I had always considered myself a Londoner. We were busy in London, where we had many friends, and frequent dinner parties.

On May nineteenth, 1970, we hadn't been back in London very long and were having breakfast in our bedroom and reading the morning newspapers, when Patrick rested his newspaper, looked at me and said that we were going to be married at Caxton Hall, a London registry office, the next day. I had not received any previous warnings and had not suspected anything at all. Wow, really! Oh, I was so excited. My first thoughts were to thank Jesus. I was beside myself with happiness, but being a woman, I wondered what I was to wear. I decided to wear the green leather mini skirt and jacket that Patrick had bought for me recently in Palma, Majorca, with a white lace blouse. I could hardly sleep that night. It didn't bother me that Patrick told me he was marrying me to make sure I would be looked after, if anything were to happen to him, as I knew he was marrying me because he loved me. He was just too scared to tell me.

31

May twentieth was such a beautiful day. We arrived at Caxton Hall, the Register Office for civil marriages. The only people with us were Patrick's lawyer and his wife, our witnesses. I cried all the way through the brief ceremony. I was so happy! After lunch at Les Ambassadeurs Club, Patrick sent me to the passport office to apply for a new passport as a married woman. That evening I wore a smart white trouser suit to enjoy our celebration dinner at the home of Patrick's lawyer. I loved my second-hand wedding band more than ever. I was twenty-eight and married to my Patrick. I had everything I could ever need materially, my parents were being taken care of, and I had a fabulous home in Taormina, an apartment in Grosvenor Square, two beautiful dogs and security. My prayers had been heard, and the little Chinaman in Hong Kong had been right after all.

The following day Patrick gave me my wedding gift, which was a total surprise, for as far as I was concerned, the marriage certificate was my gift. I was speechless with tears rolling down my face as I looked at the most beautiful single pearl necklace, a three-row pearl necklace, a three-row pearl bracelet and two pairs of pearl earrings—wow! I remembered what Patrick had told me at the Mikimoto Island, that a surprise would be coming later, and there were my precious Mikimoto pearls. Of course, I had to try them all on right away, and Patrick told me that I looked "trés recherché!" That night as I was on my knees talking to Jesus, I thanked him for all of my good fortune and hoped that my birthmark would never disappear.

Our summer months in London were spent visiting friends and enjoying London and each other. After Christmas we returned to Ionia House. It seemed so long to be away from Romulus and Remus. Life continued to be busy in Taormina, and I was spending more and more time doing the paperwork, together with the help of Pina. It got to the point that Patrick wouldn't see much of me during the day, which made him decide he was going to sell Ionia House.

Patrick left for a few weeks to visit our lawyer in Rome during which time Mount Etna erupted, and Carlo asked me if I would like to go up Mongibello and see the molten lava. I wouldn't have missed the experience for the world. Angelina had brought my dinner on a tray and left it on the coffee table in the bedroom while I was in the shower. Just as I was entering the bedroom, I saw my adorable Remus gently scoffing the steak that Angelina had made for me. How could I scold him? He did it so gently and left no mess! Carlo collected me, and we drove up to the slopes of Mount Etna. It was strange being on the barren land with rivers of red-hot lava running through it. I felt I was on a different planet as I jumped over the burning cinders and observed Mount Etna's wrath first hand. I was grateful the eruption hadn't caused any major damage. Living in Taormina also meant we had sirocco, the hot, dry desert winds from North Africa, which made everything very dusty.

When Patrick returned from Europe, he said he would like to visit Tunis, and I said how much I would like for him to see Beirut and that I would make the necessary arrangements with my dear friend Yousef. My memory of Tunis is a little hazy. I believe we stayed at the new Hilton and, of course, visited Carthage. I do recall that we seemed to be the only tourists, and there was much poverty. The people were warm and friendly, and so proud to show us their humble wares as we strolled through the medina. One thing that interested both of us were the attractive security bars on the windows of the houses, which were installed for the safety of the women.

I was really excited to be visiting Beirut again and especially with Patrick. I had such wonderful memories of the Pearl of the Middle East. Yousef had reserved our accommodations at the majestic St. Georges Hotel. Patrick celebrated his sixty-fifth birthday at the Casino du Liban where we had dinner and watched the flamboyant floorshow. I recounted to Patrick my first visit there and the car accident and how lucky I was to be alive.

The following day was St. Patrick's Day, and Yousef invited us to a splendid buffet dinner where we met some of his close friends, who, during the following days, kindly showed us around the city and introduced us to the nightlife. Of course, we did some shopping, and I left with three gorgeous caftans among other souvenirs. Our week in Beirut was perfect, and it made me happy to spend time in the city that I loved so much and which held many fun memories.

On our return to Ionia House, we found an invitation from a well known gentleman from Reggio di Calabria, asking us to join him and some friends on his three-sail, eight-berth yacht the "Taitu", to Malta. Amedeo was a very interesting and charismatic man, and we both enjoyed his ebullient company. Our trip was relaxed and a lot of fun with good food and lovely wines. It was a nice way to end our last days cruising in the Ionian Sea, before we said goodbye to the little piece of paradise called Taormina.

I had our carpenter make two large and comfy cages for Romulus and Remus for their trip back to London, but my heart was broken when I learned that they would have to be in quarantine kennels for six months. I was also very sad to leave our beautiful Ionia House, where we had imparted so much love and thought, not to mention money. Patrick said he would leave the property as it was, with all the furniture, bed linens, kitchen utensils, cutlery, crockery, a fully stocked wine cellar, the bar filled with every alcoholic beverage one would ever want, two thousand long playing records and so much more. Each bathroom had new toothbrushes. The new owners had only to walk into the house; everything was there to accommodate them.

I felt sick and sad. I told Patrick that I really wanted him to take our lovely carpets, our porcelain animals, a thousand long playing records and few other things, which he agreed to do. Although we had Ionia House listed with Americans Abroad Estate Offices and Hampton and Sons, both of London, Patrick asked the gardener to stick a 'se vende' (for sale) sign outside the property. Once Patrick had made up his mind to do something, it had to be done then and there, so we packed up, and it was time to say good-bye. I was in tears as I hugged Angelina, Yano and the rest of the staff. I shall never forget our three years in Taormina. It had taken that time to restore the neglected villa and garden, and transform it into a magnificent dream house with new plumbing, new electricity, new everything, and all of it was attained in a different country where we didn't speak the language and where we had the Mafia looking over our shoulders. I was so proud of Patrick, but I knew that for the sake of his health, it was time to say addio.

32

We left Sicily in September 1971, and were concerned about Romulus and Remus, who had made the journey safely and were now in their kennels in the English countryside. We went to visit them to make sure that they had every comfort the kennels could provide; six months was a long time, and I knew they wondered why they had to live in such strange quarters without our love and affection. It was difficult for us, but Patrick promised we would start searching for a house in the country, so once the six months were over our boys would be back with us. He informed the estate agents as to what we wanted and that on our return to London we would view the houses.

In the meantime, to help ease the pain of having our beloved dogs in kennels, Patrick decided we should take a cruise around the Seychelles Islands on the Lindblad Explorer, and that our housekeeper would visit the kennels every week with treats.

It just so happened we were travelling with BOAC on their first passenger flight out of London to Mahe in the Seychelles, which in itself was exciting. As we approached Mahe airport, it seemed as though we were going to land in a field. When we exited the airport, we realised the runway was very close to a large field, and standing there, it looked as if all the islanders, dressed in their Sunday best, were waiting to welcome us. It was the first time the people had ever seen an aeroplane, which they thought was a big white bird.

Standing outside the little airport, we were wondering how we would get to our hotel, as there appeared to be no taxis. Within moments a colourful bus appeared and our baggage, together with that of the other passengers, was thrown onto the roof. We found a couple of seats. Fortunately, all the windows were open in order for us to receive what little air was around, and then we were off, waving to the onlookers, who were fascinated by what was going on.

As we bumped along the unpaved roads, missing some potholes and not so lucky with others, I couldn't help thinking about the cartoons one sees with buses filled so full of people that the sides are almost bursting, and the luggage on the roof seemed most precarious. The bus continued on its merry way, inhaling and exhaling along the circuitous route.

We were all quiet on the trip to the hotel; no one knew what to expect, and already us Londoners weren't too sure what we had signed up for. The drive, although rather uncomfortable, was interesting, as we saw no houses, only lots of coconut trees and tropical vegetation. Finally we came to a clearing that was a mass of colour with bougainvillea, hibiscus, lovely frangipani trees and the driveway lined with coconut trees. Goats and chickens wandered freely around the small settlement, which had about twenty little huts with corrugated iron roofs.

One Londoner in the bus said jokingly. "Ah, here we are. This is our hotel."

We all laughed and then fell silent as the bus drew up in front of the main hut. We had arrived at the best hotel in Mahe, the Hotel des Seychelles on the Beau Vallon Beach. It was not a five-star hotel, but we were there to enjoy everything, and I knew that after four days, Patrick and I would move to the luxury of our cruise on the Lindblad Explorer.

We didn't spend much time in our hut, as it was simple and only had the barest of furniture (including two single beds), plus we hardly ever had any water in our bathroom, and the little we had was cold, so bathing was not one of our favourite past times. The second night as I sat on my bed in the dim candlelight, I said to Patrick, who was sitting on his bed, that the floor was moving, and he started to laugh and told me that they were only palmetto bugs. I grew up in Ceylon where we had all sorts of poochies, as we called them, and cockroaches were a familiar sight, but the size of those palmetto bugs all over the floor was scary and horrid. They didn't seem to bother Patrick so much. However, I think he was being brave for me.

The following day we moved to another hut and were fortunate not to see those bugs again. We had our evening meal in a big grass, thatched, open-air refectory. The food was most edible with lots of fish, goat and vegetables. When we left the refectory, we would walk through the perfumed yard and have a nightcap at the beach bar while we watched the irradiant sunsets, or paid homage to the luminous moon. The mornings were spent on the fabulous Beau Vallon beach. The beach made up for everything, and the placid ocean was most inviting. In the afternoons we took one of the rare taxis to explore the island, which was seventeen miles by four. It was a British crown colony, and we made a point to visit the lovely home of the governor.

During the four days Patrick and I spent in Mahe, we grew to love the unspoiled virgin island. The main town of Victoria was like something out of a movie. It had a wonderful clock tower in the middle of town, the Victoria Big Ben! It was fun to wander around and talk to the natives, who were friendly and predominately Creole, with a few Indian and Chinese merchants and some British administrators. There were a number of small fishing boats and the yacht club was situated in the middle of the picturesque harbour, though we didn't see any yachts. The beaches around the island were all heavenly. Mahe reminded me in many ways of Ceylon, especially when I saw the washing lying out on the grass to dry.

In the few days we spent in another of God's paradises, we seemed to have forgotten there was a big world out there, as we felt sublimely isolated on our own private island in the middle of the Indian Ocean. I loved it. I thought Patrick did well despite the lack of sophistication, and we had plenty of laughs, but after four days, we were ready to enjoy hot and cold running water and a comfortable bed.

Our days at the Beau Vallon Beach came to an end, but before we boarded the Lindblad Explorer, we heard from our lawyer in Rome that Ionia House was sold to a pharmacist from Catania, the next large town to Taormina. So with that good news, we found our way on board.

It felt great to move to our comfy cabin with adjoining bathroom and shower. We discovered there was a Chinese laundry on board, which we were ready to use. The atmosphere on the compact and delightful ship was friendly with about eighty passengers mainly from Scandinavia. Our tour guide was a young Englishman called Malcolm. He knew the Islands and accompanied the guests on all the excursions. Cousin Island, owned by the Council for Bird Preservation was our first stop. At that time there were about ten inhabitants who were the wardens of the island, which had several species of birds and twenty-two ancient giant tortoises. Apart from the birds and tortoises, there was nothing much else to see.

The next island was the exotic island of Praslin, seven by two miles. The island offered the famous Garden of Eden. The name was given by General Charles Gordon when he visited it in 1881, declaring it was the birthplace of Adam and Eve. To add to his declaration, a green boa lived in the undergrowth, so Praslin had its own serpent, and I am pleased to say we did not see it. The island is known for the erotic coco-de-mer nuts. They are the largest coconuts in the world and take about seven years to mature and can weigh up to sixty pounds. The coconuts are beautiful and the meat is considered to be an aphrodisiac. Of course, we had to buy a coconut as a souvenir, sans meat, alas!

In between visiting the different islands, we enjoyed the amenities on board, especially eating a variety of delicious food. The third island had houses, which were reminiscent of the poorer homes in the suburbs of Colombo. La Digue was a small tropical island, only three miles by two with about two thousand inhabitants. Life amongst the coconut trees for those people was simple, and the few we met seemed happy. I made friends with a young girl, who offered me a drink of coconut water, which I drank from the shell.

Our next stop was at the Desroaches atoll, owned by the British Indian Ocean Territory, six miles by half a mile. Desroaches was part of the rim of a submerged coral atoll, only a few feet above sea level and once part of the Amirantes group discovered by Vasco de Gama, and almost totally devoted to the production of copra from the coconut trees. Copra is the dried kernel of the coconut from which coconut oil is extracted. It is also an important agricultural commodity, which

Diana enjoying coconut water in La Digue, Seychelles

is mainly used as feed for livestock. I enjoyed "goggling" for the first time in about a foot of translucent water; after that adventurous achievement, I joined Patrick and our guides at the barbeque, which we shared with the children and a hungry dog.

The visit to the Aldabra atoll was exciting, as we had to make it to the beach through the reef in the zodiacs before the tide went out, and all of us had to wear life jackets. Due to the urgency of leaving the ship in time, I forgot to apply sunscreen and on my return found myself with serious sunburn. The doctor said I would need bed rest for at least twenty-four hours. Fortunately, I was well enough to join the group to Glorioso Island. Patrick had had enough of zodiacs and atolls, so he chose to stay on board, while I set off to explore. The atoll really had nothing of interest on it with the exception of the most enormous spider's webs, which hung from rather thin Casuarina trees. Malcolm had warned us about the webs, but I couldn't see them until I had my face almost in them. The red spiders were as big as my face, and their webs were like elastic—ugh, really horrid. The only exciting thing for me as I walked along the virgin beach was to find an old conch shell; it was my treasure.

As we were returning to the ship, I was walking a little behind the other passengers, carrying my shoes and my conch shell, my feet caressed by the gentle lapping water, when suddenly I found myself drifting out to sea, still clutching my shoes and shell. I was sitting on top of the Indian Ocean as if in an arm chair, and I was drifting further and further out. Although I was completely cured of my phobia of water, I didn't dare look around, as I knew the vast expanse of the ocean would frighten me. I looked at the ship, which was anchored fairly close by, and wondered whether Patrick could see me if he was looking out at us with his binoculars. I glided along in the rippling waves and watched the group as they headed towards the ship.

There was nothing I could do except talk to Jesus and focus on Malcolm. I shouted out his name, but he seemed engrossed in conversation. Finally, I don't know if he heard my cry, but he looked back at the ocean and saw me. I was praying to Jesus to please help me—though if He wanted me, I was ready to go to Him. Oddly enough, I didn't feel afraid. In fact, I was very calm, and my thoughts returned to the time when I was buoyant in the Dead Sea. I couldn't understand how I was where I was, and hoped and prayed that the wave—though I have no recollection of any wave—that took me out would take me back, which it did, and Malcolm helped me from the water. It was the strangest experience sitting on top of the water; I didn't move and didn't panic, as I had complete faith in Jesus. I was told later that a rip current had caught me, but the whole episode remains a mystery. I was dry from my waist up with my hat still on my head and clutching my conch shell in one hand and my shoes in the other.

When I returned to the ship, I was a little emotional as I told Patrick he nearly lost me, and I was hoping he was watching me from the ship. Patrick said he had been with the crew who had caught an enormous shark and that he was busy taking gory photographs of its disembowelment. I could see he was upset about my strange incident with the mighty ocean and decided not to let me go alone on any further excursions.

Our cruise continued to Grand Comoro, where we walked through the capital Moroni. There wasn't too much to see, but the market place was busy and colourful. The inhabitants were very poor, and there was an air of despondency. The nationals were mostly Sunni Muslims who spoke French and Arabic. It was strange to see the steep mountains and low hills, which were different to the terrain of the islands that we had recently visited. Grand Comoro was also home to La Kartala, a volcano that seemed to dominate the island.

As the Lindblad Explorer made its way towards the port of Mombasa, our final destination, the Captain informed us we had permission to visit the island of Unguja (before sailing into Mobassa), informally referred to as Zanzibar, which was part of the archipelago of numerous small islands along the coast. That came as a big surprise, as no one thought there would be the slightest chance of a visit to the island, so the information was exciting. However, before leaving the ship, we were told cameras were not allowed, no photographs.

Our visit to Zanzibar was anything but exciting. In fact, it was dismal. As we disembarked we were aware of the Chinese military everywhere. Earlier that year President Karume had been assassinated. He had succeeded the Sultan of Zanzibar in the 1964 revolution, and now the island was under Chinese control. Zanzibar, otherwise known as the Spice Island, was also fabled for its fortunes and exotic mysteries. What we saw were decaying structures, the eerily forsaken buildings of the Old Fort, and the iconic Sultan's Palace. Even the beaches looked neglected and abandoned. As we walked through the winding streets and the maze of shuttered shops of Stone Town, we realised no one was there; it was a ghost town. We did manage to see small plantations of various spices, especially pepper, cloves and cinnamon. Since our visit, I believe Zanzibar, Tanzania, has returned to being the beautiful and exotic island people want to visit.

That evening back on board, we attended the Captain's farewell dinner, and there was much interesting conversation about our time in Zanzibar. The following day we said good-bye to the Captain and the friends we had made and left with our memories of a fabulous cruise, and I am alive to say how much Patrick and I enjoyed every second of it; it was truly perfect.

We found a taxi to take us to the Mombasa Beach Hotel where we stayed for a few days, relaxing in the super hotel and enjoying another wonderful beach. We were introduced to the resident monkey with whom we became friends; he was obviously happy in his lovely surroundings. Our flight for London was out of Nairobi, where we spent the day before our departure, in order to explore the bustling city and do some shopping.

33

Back in London our mission was to find our house in the country, so when Romulus and Remus were out of quarantine, they would have a home. We would try to visit our beloved dogs every week. It was heart breaking to say good-bye to them, as they couldn't understand why we had to leave—such punishment for our two babies. Apart from travelling almost every week to see houses, we enjoyed the autumn in London, going to the theatre, ballets and operas. On Christmas Day Patrick and I spent a quiet Christmas together.

Our cook-housekeeper made a festive dinner and we invited a couple of friends whom we knew would be on their own. Earlier in the day, I told Patrick that I must go to Mass. Patrick was a lapsed Catholic and not interested in going. When I returned from Mass, it was time for gift giving from our tree. I had plenty of small gifts for my husband, and he surprised me with a beautiful set of leather luggage engraved with my initials. I could finally dispense with my big green suitcase; though I still have it today as a memento. He then told me to take something else off the tree. The only other thing I could find was a green dinky toy car. I loved it and was delighted to add it to my collection of small souvenirs.

Patrick smiled and said. "Put on your coat. We are going out."

We left the apartment and walked over to the garage, where Patrick kept the Rolls, and there she was, my very own car. Patrick had ordered a custom-built Vanden Plas Princess, especially for me. It was gorgeous. The interior work was perfect. I couldn't restrain my tears of happiness, as I never expected to have my own car, and it was such a little beauty. My car was useful when it came to going to the theatre and driving to restaurants in the West End, as it was much easier to secure a parking place than with the Rolls. Patrick conceded I could drive my car when we went to look at houses in the country.

That winter we decided to stay in London. Patrick had a new project, which he had been working on for a while, unbeknownst to me. He had lost all contact with his family in England when he left for America in 1930, and was now anxious to find out if any members were still alive. He had hired a private detective. In the New Year of 1972, Patrick was informed that his sister Dorothy was alive and married with children and grandchildren. Patrick broke the news to me and was extremely excited. I was so happy for him. After forty years he was going to see his older sister, who was very close to him before he'd left England.

After Patrick's initial visit to meet Dorothy—Dolly was the name she was known by—and her husband, George, he was to learn that his stepsister, Clodagh, was also alive. Patrick's mother had died when he was four years old, and his stepmother caused Patrick so much unhappiness as a little boy, but he was looking forward to seeing Clodagh and meeting her family. Suddenly from just being Patrick and myself, there was an Irish Clan, and on St. Patrick's Day, Patrick arranged for a big reunion party at the Mayflower restaurant in the country. Patrick's dear friend Canon Gordon Albion was there, as was Patrick's cousin, Canon Maurice O'Leary. It was a joyous occasion. The previous day Dolly, George, and I had celebrated Patrick's sixty-sixth birthday, and they had stayed with us in the flat before meeting the relations, which included Dolly and George's daughter, her husband and three small children the next day.

We continued to see much of Dolly, George and their family. Patrick was close to his sister, and it was wonderful for me to hear stories of his early days in London, especially when Dolly would go to see Patrick in the boxing ring when he was with the Coldstream Guards. There were so many years of catching up.

While we were in London, Patrick and I would walk for miles, just enjoying the city. Sometimes he would take me to the East End, and we would visit quaint old pubs, see the Pearly Queen, eat cockles and mussels, and have fish and chips wrapped in newspaper. Wherever Patrick went he was always greeted as "Guv." I felt so proud to be his wife, and each day opened a new chapter of excitement. One of our memorable occasions while in London was attending the Trouping of the Colour on the Queen's official birthday. Patrick would point out the Coldstream Guards who stood second to none, their motto being, "Nulli secundus," and the motto of the Order of the Garter, "Honi soit qui mal y pense"—"Shame to those who evil think it." He was always proud to have been a Coldstreamer, and I was a very proud Mrs. Patrick O'Leary.

Patrick had good friends who were American, Bud and Gwynne Ornstein. They lived in London but had recently bought a hacienda in Benalmádena on the Costa del Sol, Spain. So Patrick thought it would be nice for us to drive down to visit them with a stop en route in Seville for Holy Week. Our accommodations were at the resplendent and historic Alfonso XIII hotel. Semana Santa was an emotional experience for me. It commenced on Palm Sunday and continued through Holy Week.

As dusk approached we would mingle with thousands of other spectators and watch as the fifty-seven brotherhoods carried one hundred and sixteen floats from their churches to the Cathedral in Seville. The floats were so beautiful, works of art, with some dating back to the seventeenth century. The floats, which showed the suffering of Jesus Christ, the Stations of the Cross and the crucifixion, were carried by the penitents, the sinners who wore hoods over their heads and dressed like monks. It was difficult not to be moved by the chanting of those in the procession, the hundreds of lighted candles, and the scourging of some of those taking part.

There were many floats of Our Lady, the Virgin Mother suffering at what she had to endure and displaying real tears flowing down her cheeks. The beautiful Cathedral, the third largest in the world after St. Peter's Basilica in Rome and St. Paul's Cathedral in London, was the centre of all of the activity. I was very emotional seeing the processions and knowing that Jesus had suffered so much. On Easter

Sunday morning we both went to the big Mass at the Cathedral where it appeared that all of the Catholics of Seville were in attendance. What an incredible Cathedral—so large, so impressive and so beautiful. I felt blessed to have been part of the amazing Holy Week and to rejoice in the resurrection of Jesus Christ in such a magnificent manner.

In the afternoon of Easter Sunday, I was to attend my first bullfight. It was also the first bullfight of the season. I was anxious about the event and told Patrick I really didn't want to go, as I had heard it was a cruel sport. As usual, Patrick convinced me I should experience everything in life at least once, and that it was something I should see. He also said the meat from the bull was donated to the very poor in the city. I can't say I really enjoyed the event, though it was a colourful spectacle. The arena was filled to capacity and I managed to sit through the various fights, as it wasn't as cruel as I had imagined; though seeing the bulls suffer was not pleasant to watch. I was mainly concerned for the horses and hoped that they wouldn't be hurt by the bull. It did occur to me that I was more anxious for the animals than the Matador and Picador! In retrospect, I had observed one of the best bullfights ever. It was exciting and the bulls were killed quickly without too much suffering. However, it was not one of my favourite spectator sports.

We left the beautiful city of Seville and drove to Benalmádena to stay with Bud and Gwynne in their attractive hacienda. It was good to see them and relax in their company. Bud was involved with the James Bond films, together with his friend Cubby Broccoli. Gwynne was the niece of Mary Pickford, so the conversations were always interesting and focused a lot on the world of film. During our stay Vanessa joined us for a few days. I hadn't seen her in a while and was happy to catch up with what was going on in her life; her Spanish was now fluent. Patrick took some good photographs of all of us and some of me in the fabulous flamenco dress and accessories he had bought for me in Seville.

After we left our friends, we headed back to Monte Carlo and drove on to Cannes, where we were to meet our Danish friends at the Carlton Hotel. We were all there for the film festival. My life with

Diana in her Flamenco dress

Patrick was never dull, another first for me being at the famous Carlton Hotel in Cannes, so electric! I would see many of the stars on the beach, and together with Preben and Ellie, we attended a few of the receptions. Preben and Ellie were cruising around the Mediterranean on their yacht, but rather than join them, we decided to stay in Cannes a little longer and explore the hills above the town. Patrick would introduce me to picturesque restaurants, and at times, the roads were so narrow I was afraid that the Rolls wouldn't make it, but I had the best driver with me. Patrick made me feel so wanted;

despite him being a disciplinarian in some ways, I understood him, and we had a lot of fun together. He was giving me the world, and I was learning from him all the time. I loved him so much.

34

We spent the rest of the summer back in London ardently looking at houses. The six months of prison service was over for Romulus and Remus, so we decided to see how it would work to have them in the apartment in London. I took them out to Hyde Park at six every morning and during the day into Grosvenor Square, but sadly, our two beautiful, large Golden Retrievers were not really comfortable. Admittedly, they were better off with us than at the kennels, as they had our love and affection, but it was difficult, and at the beginning of September, as we still hadn't found a suitable house, we returned them to the kennels, requesting more and more of the best that the kennel owner could offer for the comfort of our dogs. The owner was a kind man and understood our disappointment in not being able to have our dogs with us. He made sure that the kennels were heated in the winter months and that they had comfortable beds and large runs. I was very sad to leave them. When we were out of London, our housekeeper Rhoda visited our babies every week with lots of treats and special steaks from the butcher. We were listed with most of the Estate Agents in London, but there wasn't a house we had seen that we liked.

For some time Patrick had wanted to visit an old friend of his in Stockholm, so once again the Rolls was on duty. When we had returned Romulus and Remus to the kennels in September, we enjoyed a lovely drive over to Sweden and the city of Stockholm. On the second day of our arrival, as Patrick had been to Stockholm on numerous occasions, he told me to go on a sightseeing tour, so I took advantage of the tour buses and water taxis to explore the city, which I found very interesting.

That evening in the restaurant of the prestigious Grand Hotel where we stayed, which looked out over the city's waterfront, I told Patrick how I had spent my day. He started to look rather serious and proceeded to tell me he was concerned that when he died I would be alone and asked me whether I would consider his good friend in Stockholm, a member of the Swedish Royal family, a bachelor I had met the previous day and found totally charming, being the father of our child.

For myself I would not think of being with someone else, as I knew if Jesus wanted me to have a child, it would be with Patrick. I believe that all things are possible with God. I always prayed to have Patrick's child—even though he told me it was not possible—but if that was in God's plan, then it would happen. With tears in my eyes, I took hold of Patrick's hand and thanked my dear husband for his extraordinary thoughtfulness; what an amazing man I had married. Before our departure from Stockholm, the three of us would enjoy a couple of evenings together in the Prince's modest home, but I will never know whether he knew of Patrick's intention; though I have a feeling he did.

We drove back to Monte Carlo, where we had arranged to meet Aenna and Franz Burda, the German magazine mogul, and Mirella, our friends from Taormina before returning to London.

Back in London, I knew Mother and Sylvan had left to live in Majorca to be near Vanessa. Mother hadn't really said anything to my father about her plans, so it came as shock to him. All of a sudden he was told that he had to find somewhere to live, and Mother told him she never wanted to see him again. I was concerned for my dad, and it didn't take long for him to start drinking. He left Richmond and found himself a small bed-sitting room in Earl's Court, the area that was familiar to him. It always worried me when the police called and told me that they had found Dad wandering around in his pajamas or he'd be found lying in the gutter. He was unable to take care of himself, and anyway, he thought that no one cared about him. He had tried on numerous occasions to commit suicide, but it never worked.

Of course, Patrick knew about his problems, and many times I would drive out in my little princess to Earl's Court and do what I could to help him, which wasn't easy, especially when he was so intoxicated. Every time he tried to stand, he would fall to the floor. I knew at those times it was impossible for him to change his ways; he needed help. I would call the ambulance to take him to the nearest hospital, where I would visit him. I felt it was unfair of Mother to just decide to leave him. After all, he had proved himself by keeping a good job and contributing to his family. Mother really didn't like him, and it was her opportunity to escape to Palma. She didn't care what happened to dad, so once again she left. Dad was pathetic when he was inebriated. It broke my heart to see him like that, despite having seen him drunk many, many times since I was a little girl. I knew he felt alone and unloved. I loved my dad, and that he wasn't a bad man. In fact, he was very popular and loved by everyone, but he was allergic to alcohol. When he wasn't drinking, he was just the warmest and most wonderful human being with a great sense of humour.

Patrick and I did everything we could to help Dad and succeeded in having him admitted to a home for alcoholics. He was much better due to the treatment. We found accommodation for him where there was staff and where he had the security of a nice clean room, good food, and company in the house, which was extremely important for Dad, as he loved people. His pleasures in life were frugal, his pipe and his pint. When Patrick and I were in London, we would see him as much as possible. Fortunately, he didn't lose his job, as he was much admired in the firm. Whenever I could, I would go into the city and have lunch or stop by after he had finished work to say hello. He only had to make a phone call if he had any problems.

As Patrick had found his older sister, Dolly, he wanted to see her and her husband, George, as often as possible when we were in England. It was a busy time for us, as we continued almost every day to search for our home in the country. We were so determined that our poor dogs would be with us, but sometimes we were in such despair. How was it possible that we had not seen one house that we thought would suit us? If we weren't looking at houses, we would visit Romulus and Remus, who were in kennels about an hour and a half out of London by train.

One day on our way back from viewing a few houses unsuccessfully, I was driving my princess and reached about seventy miles an hour in the fast lane, when I started to drive parallel with a juggernaut. I felt the car being drawn into the immense vehicle and bumped against it, then went back and bumped against the intersection and once again back and forth. All the time I was braking and kept calm, as was Patrick, who was sitting beside me. I stopped the car as it hit the intersection for the third time and, of course, despite my exterior demeanour, I was shaking inside. What did I do to my beautiful car? Well, I had to say good-bye to her, as she was a write-off, according to the insurance company and I was fined when I appeared in court. I was devastated. Patrick was so kind and wonderfully supportive, and I was just grateful that he was unharmed. Losing my little princess was a big loss and punishment to me.

35

We still hadn't found our home in the country, so in February of 1973, to escape some of the winter, we were once again with BOAC travelling to Ceylon, which is now Sri Lanka. The trip was a big surprise to me; although I often spoke to Patrick about my early days growing up in Ceylon and told him how much I would love for him to see where I was born, I had no idea he was secretly planning for us to travel there.

As I sat in the plane, I thought about our imminent visit and remembered Colombo, imagining it to be the same as when I left. I really was quite naïve. A car and driver had been reserved to meet us from our flight and take us to the hotel in Colombo. It was dark when we arrived, and eventually we found our small car and driver. We had been driving for about twenty minutes, and the car broke down. We had just travelled from London, and despite all the comforts of first class, we were nevertheless tired and anxious to reach our destination. Instead we stood on the roadside in the middle of nowhere in the dark, waiting for assistance. Not a good first impression for my Patrick!

We eventually arrived at the charming old Galle Face Hotel, built in 1864 during the British colonial era. Our top floor suite was furnished with English furniture and was very large. In the morning we had breakfast, with our personal butler attending to our every need. I was thrilled to be looking out over the Indian Ocean and the Galle Face Green, where as a child, together with Vanessa and my parents, we would join the rest of the Sinhalese and Tamil families to fly our kites.

I mentioned to the concierge that we must have a reliable car and driver to take us around Colombo. I told our driver I was born there and that I wanted to show my husband various points of interest—where I lived and went to school. The memories came flooding back, but my heart was weeping. Everything was so sad. There were many beggars on the streets, many dilapidated buildings and lots of starving dogs. The red London buses were all knocked about. The driver told us that Mrs. Sirimavo Bandaranaike, the first woman prime minister in the world, was a socialist, though I believe he said, she was a communist. So much had changed in Sri Lanka due to the nationalising of all sectors of the economy—even the schools owned by the Catholic Church.

We drove to St. Bridget's Convent, and I asked Patrick to take a photograph of me at the spot where I stood for my photograph at seven years old, having just received my First Communion. Mrs. Bandaranaike's government had moved more towards China and Russia, away from the United Kingdom and United States of America, and with her socialistic policies, she stifled economic activity. During that time, the problems between the Tamils and Sinhalese gradually started. I remembered Colombo with much affection. After all, it was the city of my birth, but the reality of what I was experiencing made me sad, and I was sorry my husband was not seeing the city as I remembered it.

I was really upset to see how neglected and impoverished Colombo had become. I wanted to go to the swimming club, but it was closed. Our drive out to Mount Lavinia Hotel, although not as I remembered, was where we had arranged to have lunch and meet Selina. My excitement at seeing her again was evident, and she looked exactly as I remembered her. The Mount Lavinia Hotel and the beach brought back many happy memories. I told Patrick about the cowrie shells that Vanessa and I would find and put to our ears and listen to the sea. Sitting out on the terrace overlooking the Indian Ocean, the coconut palm-lined beach, still with the occasional fishermen's boat going out or coming in with its catch, was thrilling to me, and I was especially glad to introduce Selina to Patrick.

During our conversation I reminded Selina of when she saw me at nine years old at her home and commented on my birthmark, telling me that I would be very lucky in my life. Selina had forgotten, but I hadn't, and I told her how right she had been. Nothing had changed.

Diana with Selina at the Mount Lavinia Hotel

I loved her as much then as I did when I was a child. I talked to her about how my parents had met accidentally in a park in London and that we had all lived together, but now Mother had left again and was trying to get a divorce. So many memories came rushing back as we spoke of days gone by at Pedris Road. As we said good-bye, I was happy that Patrick invited Selina and all her immediate family to join us for dinner at the hotel the following evening. He knew what a positive affect Selina had had on my life.

Returning to our hotel, we decided to stay and dine there. While dressing for dinner, a rat came out to say hello—not good! We had the best suite in the hotel, but times were tough, and at the appearance of the rat, I knew Patrick was pleased we only had two more nights at the Galle Face Hotel.

The staff made a great effort in trying to make everything hunky dory for us. We did enjoy the politeness of the gentle staff, who spoke such "pucker" English. Before our delicious curry dinner, we sat with our cocktails and watched the radiant sunset as it disappeared behind the Indian Ocean. I was happy to be eating curry and rice for dinner and was fascinated by the spectacular show, especially of a man walking barefoot over hot coals. I loved the warm and slightly humid weather; it was like a welcome embrace.

The next day we went into the pettah and generally spent the day sightseeing. Although I recalled some parts of the city, much of it I didn't recognise, and I sensed that Patrick was not really enjoying the sights. In the evening Selina arrived with her daughter, Suhini, her husband, and various members of her family. We had such an entertaining evening; though it was with compassion that we listened to Selina's family recount what had happened to their country, as we sat on the veranda of the hotel restaurant with ceiling fans swirling above us, while feasting on at least twenty curries.

Naturally, I thought of my mother and knew how much she would have loved to have been with us. We talked a lot about Mother's wonderful theatrical performances and direction of her incredible and professional shows. Mother gave of herself to Colombo, instigating the International Theatre Group, which she started together with a couple of well-known Sinhalese gentlemen—but Ceylon never gave her credit for all the hard work and dedication she gave to the island that she loved so much. We chattered on and ate of the many, many curries, savouring their tastes and aromas. It was indeed such a feast; to me there are no better curries in the world than those of Ceylon. As we said goodnight, we thanked our white clad waiters dressed in their sarongs and turbans. There were still some segments left of the old English Raj, mainly their impeccable manners. I was transported back again to my childhood. What a dream evening.

We left the Galle Face Hotel the next day for the Bentota Beach Hotel, which came highly recommended. Our almost fifty-mile journey by car was not the most comfortable, especially for Patrick. I think he really missed the Rolls. It was, however, an interesting drive to see the rubber trees, the little villages, and observe what life was like outside of Colombo. The hotel was modern with many bright lights. We had an attractive corner room, which overlooked the Indian Ocean on one side and the lagoon on the other. For all that Patrick was a worldly man, he had never slept under a mosquito net. Of course, to me it took me back to my childhood, where mosquito nets were part of going to bed. I always remembered the beautiful pink net that covered Vanessa and me in our home in Meddecombra.

Our days at Bentota were most serene. None of the grounds were manicured, but the beach was wonderful, and watching the magnificent sunsets every night was overwhelming—just so beautiful. Each day I would go over to the lagoon of the Bentota River when it was bath time for two young elephants. One elephant was Raja, who was four years old, and Mathalie was ten months. I love elephants. I was in heaven to be with those adorable babies and watch them have so much fun in the water. They were looked after by two young men, who obviously loved them. That was the highlight of my stay at the resort.

Diana with ten week old Mathalie in the grounds of the Bentota Beach Hotel

On one of the days I introduced Patrick to the gully-gully man, the snake charmer, but instead of a man, there were a couple of small boys about nine years old. One little boy had an enormous Cobra draped around him, and the other played a tune on his pipe. The Cobra in the basket started to rear and spread its hood. I love animals, even snakes—from a distance! It upset me that those large and splendid snakes were kept in such small baskets. However, I knew the people were very poor, so if they were able to make money by entertaining the tourists in that way, then they had to.

The gulley-gulley boys with their Cobras outside the Bentota Beach Hotel

Unfortunately, the hotel, which catered to many European tourists, didn't have the flavour of being Ceylonese. They tried to please their guests by providing rather inferior European food. Personally, I could have eaten curry every day. I think Patrick dropped a few pounds on our travels! After about five days we had had enough of our visit to Bentota and left for the hills of Nuwara Eliya. Having shown Patrick the places that were important to me as a child in Colombo, I now wanted him to see the Hill School, the Hill Club, Hakgala Botanical Gardens, where Vanessa had her birthday picnic, and of course, stay at the famous Grand Hotel, which was always special to us as children.

On the day of our departure from the Bentota Beach Hotel, our driver arrived in the biggest car available, which was really small and didn't have air conditioning. The car ride to Nuwara Eliya was probably one of the most uncomfortable car trips poor Patrick had ever made. The roads were appalling, and we were grateful to stop at a few rest houses en route. The journey was about two hundred miles, and despite the spectacular scenery, the tea estates carpeting the hills, the picturesque waterfalls and all the lush vegetation, the drive was very tedious. I tried to make the most of it by drawing Patrick's attention to different scenes as we drove along, but was glad when I saw the mist in the distance covering the hills of Nuwara Eliya, which meant we were nearing our destination.

As we were driving through the heavy mist, I told Patrick about Dad showing Silva the way, as he walked on the road in front of our car. The car journey had taken us the better part of a day, and we were truly happy to finally arrive at the Grand Hotel, which, alas, was not grand at all. Patrick never complained about anything, but I knew he wasn't enjoying his visit to Ceylon.

The Grand Hotel had originally been built by Sir Edward Barnes as his home. He was governor from 1830 to 1850. My memories were having tea at the hotel, which was considered the best in Nuwera Eliya. It was late when we arrived and, as usual, we had the largest suite available. It was so cold, however, that we were both miserable. The hotel, like everything else at that time, was really rundown. There was no central heating, and I felt we were in a ghost-like ambiance. The polite and friendly staff tried very hard to make us feel welcome.

The following day I wanted to show Patrick the Hill School but was told it wasn't there anymore, and being so cold, Patrick wasn't interested in doing any sightseeing. We managed to spend one more night, and at dinner Patrick said we were leaving in the morning and would be on the BOAC flight out of Colombo in the evening. I totally understood, as the experience was not what I had intended for Patrick. My memories of Ceylon were very different. I was really grateful that he had tolerated so much discomfort on my behalf. I had no idea how we would travel to the airport in Colombo; the thought of doing that terrible drive again would be agony for Patrick.

The next morning as we walked out of the hotel, a small helicopter was resting on the lawn. That was our transport to the international airport. How exciting, but at the same time, as I had never been in a helicopter and was not good with heights, I was also a little scared at the prospect. I soon overcame any fears and enjoyed the experience.

My one request to Patrick was that we fly over Meddecombra Estate so I could see our home from above. The pilot was fantastic, and he did just that. We hovered over the house, which I recognised immediately. It was still there on the hill surrounded by the green velvet of the tea bushes and the paddy field to the left. It was an emotional moment for me, and as I was wiping the tears away, I told Patrick how happy I was that he could see the little house, which I loved and called home for a while.

Arriving at the international airport in good time for our flight to London, we decided to look at the few shops. Patrick, knowing my love of elephants and having photographed me with Raja and Mathalie, saw an ebony elephant decorated with a silver cover embossed with semi-precious stones. He bought it and gave it to me, saying he was sorry that our trip was so disappointing, but wanted me to have it as a memento of our visit and the elephants.

A few weeks after we returned home, he presented me with a little box, and inside was the most beautiful aquamarine ring. He had bought the stone in Colombo and had it mounted for me in London. How lucky I was to have such a wonderful husband. I checked on my birthmark; it was still there! Although the trip was not how I imagined it would be, and it was a shame that we had visited during that unfortunate period for the country, I felt at least that Patrick was able to comprehend a little of the country where I was born and lived for the first part of my life. I was happy for that, and that he had the opportunity to meet Selina.

36

Back in London, we continued with our quest to find a home in the country. We had already viewed over one hundred houses and were appalled at some of those we saw. One house had over forty cats, and I told Patrick I couldn't enter, as the stench that wafted out when he opened the front door made me feel so nauseous I sat outside during his visit, but I did feel sorry for those poor cats. As we still hadn't found a house, we decided to have Romulus and Remus with us in the flat, however, about a month later, Patrick wanted to take Dolly, George and Clodagh on a vacation, just so we could all spend quality time together. We found comfortable kennels not too far from London to board our dogs.

Patrick discovered that Clodagh had never been out of the country, so the invitation was an enormous thrill for her. Clodagh came up to London to stay with us before we left for the continent, and I was in charge to take her shopping to make sure she had some pretty dresses for the trip. Patrick drove the Rolls to Paris, where we would spend three days at the Ritz Hotel. Clodagh was overwhelmed by it all and loved every minute of her adventure. Patrick suggested I take her on a tour bus so that she and I would see as much of the city as possible, and in the evenings we would join him for dinner.

I had been to Paris so many times and cherished many beautiful memories, but each visit was always like the first. I could never tire of that magnificent city. This visit was different to the first time that Patrick took me to Paris when we'd stay at the Plaza Athénée, dined at Maxim's and the Tour D'Argent, and lunched in a beautiful restaurant in the Bois de Boulogne. I was spoiled!

From Paris we drove to Baden Baden, situated in the foothills of the Black Forest in Germany. We were booked to stay at the distinguished and most luxurious Brenner's Park Hotel. Patrick and I had been there on an earlier occasion to attend the seventy-fifth birthday party of Franz Burda, and I had fallen in love with the hotel. I have slept in some wonderful beds in great hotels, but the bed in that hotel was a total dream, luxury personified.

For this visit Patrick had reserved one of the elegant three-bedroom suites so we could all be together. George and Dolly had flown from London and joined us at the hotel, where we had such a happy, relaxing time. Patrick, with his proclivity towards having a little flutter at the tables, suggested that we try our luck at the exquisite small casino, which we did with much amusement.

We spent our days walking in the ethereal and historic park, and strolling through the village. Patrick and I liked to spend a few hours each day at the famous spa. We both enjoyed bathing in the hot curative mineral waters and especially having the massages afterwards. In the evenings we would indulge in sumptuous dinners enhanced by superb wines. The weather was warm and sunny, and the five of us had a memorable time together.

After a week at glorious Brenner's Park, Patrick decided we should drive to Strasburg, capital of the Alsace region of Eastern France. The city is a fusion of German/French culture and the bridge of unity between France and Germany. We walked around the picturesque city and paid a visit to the beautiful medieval Cathedral with its fourteenth century astronomical clock. After our sightseeing we were ready to savour the famous foie gras, the livers of geese and ducks. There are two delicacies that are considered kings of the kitchen— the Russian black beluga caviar and foie gras. I do have to agree. We relished the sensational tastes in a lovely old restaurant, and I think we all gained a pound or two in one afternoon.

Clodagh flew back to England with Dolly and George and Patrick and I continued on to Avignon on the left bank of the river Rhone. The old city with its ramparts built by the popes in the fourteenth century still encircle Avignon and remain one of the finest examples of medieval fortifications. We walked around the Palais des Papes, which was the residence of several of the popes, and on the famous bridge of Avignon, Sur le Pont d'Avignon, I amused Patrick by doing a wee jig.

We then drove back to Monte Carlo and arrived in time for Patrick to use the tickets he'd had the concierge of the Hotel de Paris reserve for him earlier in the year; so we had seats to see the boxing fight of the middleweight champion Carlos Monzon. It was an interesting experience for me. As Patrick had told me he was once the welterweight champion for the Coldstream Guards, I always took a great interest in watching any boxing matches on the television, especially Mohamed Ali's fights. It is one thing to watch a fight on television, but sitting in the front row of a boxing ring and watching a fight close up was a trifle unnerving for me! I couldn't help but look up at the sky and think what a beautiful night it was, sitting in the open air arena under the stars in Monte Carlo (watching Carlos Monzon beat Emile Griffith) and secretly wishing I had been watching Mohamed Ali instead.

Once again we were in Monte Carlo for the Grand Prix, which was the third one I was about to see. As usual, it was rather noisy for a few days, as the Hotel de Paris was on the course. The day of the big race finally arrived, and we were invited to friends who owned an apartment overlooking the yacht harbour. It had a perfect view of the cars racing by, and we saw Jackie Stewart win the race—so exciting.

Monte Carlo was now familiar to me. We spent the rest of June there exploring all the divine villages outside of Monaco—such special times, and of course, we spent many happy occasions with the Troubetzkoys in their amazing home, "MAYOU". Our stay was soon over, and it was time to say good-bye to the Hotel de Paris, to our lovely friends, and to all the wonderful people we had met. The Rolls Royce was headed for Amsterdam, Holland.

I had told Patrick about my visit to Amsterdam when I was a young travel agent and asked him to take a photo of the Grand Hotel Krasnapolsky, where I stayed with all the other travel agents. This time we stayed at the luxury Hotel De L'Europe on the Amstel River. We loved walking around Amsterdam, visiting the floating flower market, the Bloemenmarkt, lots of little street markets and the open-air markets in the Jewish quarter were fascinating; I could have spent all day just wandering through them. Of course, we saw Anne Frank's home and remembered her incredible and tragic short life.

It was fun going through the canals in our water taxi and taking a tour around a diamond factory, observing the process of diamond cutting and polishing. After the tour Patrick asked if I would like a diamond ring, and I chose a beautiful little ring with twelve small diamonds and a slightly larger one in the middle. Diamonds are not my favourite stone, but this ring is precious to me. After dinner we walked through the red-light district. I wasn't really prepared for what I saw and thought it very sad that those lovely women were exhibiting themselves in the windows for sale. The area was legalised for prostitution. Patrick and I were the only people walking through it that evening, so we were not at all popular. The women were shouting at us. Patrick realised I shouldn't have been there, although it was quiet. The following day we were on our way to take the ferry across the English Channel back to London.

37

For the rest of the summer and autumn we continued with our search for our house in the country and to release our poor dogs from prison. As always we visited them and had them stay with us during our searches, taking them with us in the car to view the potential properties. We also spent a lot of time with Dolly and George and visited Clodagh and her family. Clodagh didn't live far from Canon Gordon Albion. I especially enjoyed the company of the Canon and his wonderful cousin Agnes Beckhausen, who took such good care of him and the rectory.

I would also see a lot of Dad, as he would frequent our apartment. One day he suggested I join him for lunch in the city of London. I wasn't familiar with the city and happy he'd show me around the places of interest. I chose a day when Patrick had a luncheon appointment. Dad had spent so many early years of his life working in the city before leaving for Ceylon, and worked there for the last twelve years before his retirement. As we wandered through the deserted streets on a beautiful Saturday afternoon, he said he was sorry he had caused so much trouble in our lives and that he had always loved Mother, but realised soon after they met, that she didn't love him, and no matter how hard he tried to please her, nothing was ever good enough. He found it difficult when she so often belittled him, but was grateful she made him swear on the Bible to stop drinking for the sake of keeping the family together.

I felt sad when he told me that Mother generally made him feel worthless. He also wanted to assure me that I was very much wanted by him, and it was my mother who tried hard to abort me. For years he knew that Mother was taking money from the joint account and sending it to her mother and aunt in Australia, and generally living far beyond their means. Mother's many affairs drove him further into alcohol, and he admitted that as he was left alone for months on end in Meddecombra, he did take advantage of the nanny Matilda and one or two other young women on the tea estate.

It was a little difficult for me to hear my dad talk so openly, but I knew he wanted me to know. My father was always such a gentleman, coming from one of the most revered families in Scotland. Alas, he had a problem with alcohol, which proved to be the bane of his life and was usually brought on by situations he was unable to control. I couldn't help thinking that my father would have made a wonderful husband for the right sort of woman, and equally my mother would have been so happy with the right man. It pleased me that he was able to talk to me, and thanks to Patrick, he was living a fairly comfortable life, albeit a humble one.

The winter was approaching and Patrick did not want us to spend it in London. So once again our "babies" were returned to their original kennels where they were very well taken care of. If we had had an alternative home for them, we would have been happy not to have them back in kennels, but there was none.

On December twentieth, 1973, we were on our way back to the Sandy Lane Hotel in Barbados to spend Christmas and the New Year. During our visit the hotel staff went on strike for a few days, so I was in charge of room service for breakfast and generally helping out. Those were gloriously happy days for us, enjoying the white sandy beach and tranquil ocean, while staying at such an idyllic location. The hotel was so romantic, and I wasn't surprised to see Harry Bellefonte sunning himself on the beach. I celebrated my thirty-second birthday and told Patrick I didn't want a party, though we knew several people. I just wanted to have a quiet dinner with my husband and tell him that every day I was with him was a celebration.

Having spent a memorable month in Barbados, we decided to visit Antigua for a few days. After it was discovered by Admiral Horatio Nelson in 1784, Antigua in the British Leeward Islands became Great Britain's most important Caribbean base. We stayed at the St. James

Beach Hotel. It was a comfortable hotel, but while we were there, it was extremely windy. The atmosphere was different to Barbados. However, we made a point of seeing as much as possible of the island, but it wasn't a favourite of mine.

Patrick had wanted us to visit Acapulco again, and en route stopped in Mexico City. Having just travelled from the islands, I was looking forward to being in a big city. I knew that the altitude was high, but I wasn't really prepared for the big difference in the air, which was much thinner and such poor quality. I found it difficult to breathe at first, but gradually became used to it and to the awful pollution. We stayed at the Hilton Hotel on the famous Reforma Avenue and did lots of sightseeing. Patrick and I were very interested in visiting the Chapultepec Castle, the former home of Maximilian, and walking through the beautiful gardens. Before leaving Mexico City, we indulged in purchasing some fun silver jewellery, which we found by exploring the silver shops in the hotel area, instead of wandering out into the polluted air. Mexico City was not one of my favourite destinations either.

I was looking forward to being in Acapulco again. Now that I was Patrick's wife, and having just turned thirty-two years and looking good, I was excited and hoped to meet some of the people we had met when we were there in 1968. We were booked in at the Hyatt hotel on the beach and met a lovely crowd of people. Our friend Basil had told us to contact Oscar Obregon. What a marvelous individual. We were both under the spell of that charming man. Oscar was with us a lot during our visit, taking us to the new Princess Hotel, introducing us to fun people and generally giving us a wonderful time. He took us to his newly completed villa, "Nirvana," in Las Brisas, and showed us around the property. Las Brisas was so romantic with charming little bungalows in lush, tropical vegetation. Oscar, the great-grandson of the President of Mexico, was a lovable character, a fun playboy, and he did everything to give us an awesome visit.

While on the beach one day, Patrick decided to go up in a parasail, which really bothered me, as I was noticing that, despite him looking good and full of energy, I instinctively felt he shouldn't have had that experience. Fortunately, it all went well and Patrick was elated, but no matter how much he tried to make me do the same, there was no way I would.

Normally, we would join Oscar and his friends for dinner at various restaurants or parties, but one night we decided to have dinner, just the two of us. We went to a romantic restaurant and had a great meal.

On the way back to the hotel in the taxi, I noticed that Patrick was quiet and didn't say much. My intuition has always been effective, and when we reached our suite, I asked what was troubling him. He reluctantly told me that our dinner had cost double the amount that it should have, and he felt that the waiter had added the extra amount. Patrick hadn't wanted to make a scene.

I never liked any one to take advantage of my husband. I told Patrick that I would return to the restaurant and speak to the manager, but I needed the taxi fare. It was fairly late, but I had to fight for my man! I sat at the bar with a glass of wine while the manager spoke to the waiter. It wasn't too long before he returned, apologised, and gave me the cash he had found in the waiter's pockets.

After two happy weeks in Acapulco, we were airborne to Los Angeles with my sombrero taking up the seat beside me. Patrick had promised we would return to Los Angeles, so I was looking forward to spending more time there and looked forward to seeing our friend Basil. Basil and his new wife invited us to stay in their home at Benedict Canyon in Beverly Hills. We had fun eating at well-known restaurants and being shown the important movie sights.

Valentine's Day occurred during our stay, and Patrick suggested that I might like to have a beauty day at Elizabeth Arden's, to which I said, "Yes, please!"

Before returning to the house, I stopped at a few shops to buy a card and a couple of fun things for Patrick for Valentine's Day. I awoke early on the fourteenth and was quietly arranging my little gifts and card on Patrick's bedside table, but he heard me and asked what I was doing.

I said. "Happy Valentine's Day! I was just going to surprise you with a few small gifts."

He said. "Darling, I am sorry. I totally forgot, and I have nothing for you but my love."

Our stay at Basil's home was just delightful, and one day he said we should visit Disneyland, which was lots of fun. I was a kid again and loved every minute of the experience. Both Patrick and I had such a magical visit with Basil and his wife, and I knew that Patrick's love for me had grown stronger.

I was sad to leave our good friends, who had made us feel so welcome, but I was excited, as we were travelling on to the decadent city of Las Vegas, Nevada. When we arrived at the airport, my eyes nearly popped out of my head. There were slot machines everywhere. As we were checking in at the MGM hotel, I felt I was in a dream. The hotel had only opened in December 1973 and was the largest hotel in the world at that time. Lining the walls of the corridors to our suite were enormous photographs of movie stars. I imagined I was one too, as everything was so lavish, so luxurious.

Our elaborate suite was out of a Hollywood film. The large mirror above our bed took me by surprise, wow! The thing that flummoxed me was that we didn't seem to sign any chits. Didn't we have to pay? Las Vegas was unbelievable. We went to many of the shows and the casinos. Patrick had booked to see Frank Sinatra at Caesar's Palace, but Sinatra cancelled at the last minute, so Paul Anka was the star that night, which was great, as he sang, "Diana." We saw several other shows, one at the Sands and other famous nightspots. The whole night scene was thrilling; we lived at night and slept during the day.

Patrick wanted me to see the Hoover Dam. I didn't really know anything about the dam, so he explained what an important structure it was. When we arrived we joined a sightseeing tour. As I was sensitive to heights and water, it was not one of my most favourite sights, but I did realise I was looking at an amazing invention. The Hoover Dam was the world's largest dam situated in the black canyon of the Colorado River. Such an important dam, but it did make my palms sweaty!

It was time to leave the intoxicating city of Las Vegas and head to New York. Our plane flew over the Grand Canyon, the steep-sided gorge of red, gold and brown carved by the Colorado River, was an inspiring sight, but soon my thoughts were on arriving in New York. I was excited to see the "Big Apple". I had my nose to the window of the taxi that took us from the airport to our hotel. I had seen high-rise buildings, but to me those buildings went up to heaven. We had a cosy little suite at the St. Regis Hotel and that evening had arranged to meet some old friends of Patrick's in the bar. After a few cocktails, we went to their magnificent apartment overlooking Central Park for dinner.

The following day Patrick took me up the Empire State Building, such a breathtaking view, and I stood well back from the edge, not liking heights. I wasn't, however, prepared for the weather. Walking around each corner was painful, as the wind went through me. I hadn't the appropriate clothes to keep me warm and my hands were like ice, so we went into the famous store Saks Fifth Avenue, where my husband bought me a pair of gloves. How grateful I was for those gloves.

My first impression of New York was one of feeling totally insignificant, like an ant, such tall buildings everywhere. We stopped to say prayers at St. Patrick's Cathedral and ate at fine restaurants. I realised Patrick still had a great affinity for New York. It was his first home in 1930 on arriving to America and held many memories. I did enjoy my visit to the stimulating city, but had I had a few warm clothes to wear, I would have been happier.

The day prior to our departure, while eating a breakfast of corned beef hash and eggs, a special treat for Patrick and something new for me, I asked him if there was a possibility that despite everything he had told me and that the doctors had told him, that he could give me a baby. I was now late for my period, which never happened.

"Absolutely not," he answered and laughingly said, "If you are pregnant, you know I'm not the culprit, and I shall disown you!" We agreed that all of the travelling might be the cause.

Our plane left New York for London on February twenty-eighth, 1974. I had had another fascinating introduction to new places and realised every time we travelled, we bonded more and more, and this time we were especially close. I had never been happier. I knew my Patrick really loved me, and I loved him so much. We had an excellent flight back to London on British Airways, as the company was now known. The name may have changed, but the service, as always, was impeccable. Relaxing in my seat and recollecting this last trip, I just had a strong feeling that apart from Patrick, I wasn't alone—and perhaps I had the embryo of a new life stirring in me, my Valentine's gift.

38

It didn't take long for us to settle back into our beautiful apartment. We checked immediately with the kennels to find out how our Romulus and Remus were keeping. We knew the owner was doing everything he could to make our "babies" as comfortable as possible. I thought now was the time we had to find a home. We had seen over a hundred houses, and none of them were what we wanted. It had been such an experience for me to see how people lived, rather depressing really.

Patrick had wanted to be back in London for the elections, and we watched the results with interest. After the possibility of a coalition with Edward Heath and Jeremy Thorpe didn't pan out, Harold Wilson was declared the winner, and on March fourth, Britain had a Labour government.

The night of March sixth, a week after our return to London, Patrick and I were in bed reading. I was reading Mika Waltari's book, "The Secret of the Kingdom," and Patrick was reading the "Evening Standard" newspaper. I became so engrossed in my book that I didn't realise how late it was, but I did eventually look at the clock and was surprised that it was twelve forty in the early morning of March seventh.

Normally Patrick would have said to me, "Well, it's time to say goodnight," I glanced over at him, realising he hadn't said anything. He looked rather strange, so I moved closer, and then I noticed that the newspaper he was holding was upside down and the article in the paper was on wines written by his friend Michael Broadbent. I shivered. I knew something was wrong. I immediately took the paper away and straddled Patrick's body, looking at his face, and I saw the left side of his face slide down. I dialed the number of our doctor. Patrick mumbled, asking what I was doing. I said I was calling the doctor, and he told me not to be such an alarmist. I apologised to Cecil for calling him so late, but I believed that Patrick had just had a stroke. I don't know where the word stroke came from, as I had no idea what a stroke was, but I knew I'd witnessed my husband having one.

Cecil Eppel, who lived in Lees Place on the other side of Grosvenor Square, said he would be with us immediately. In the meantime Patrick tried to sit up and flopped over onto his left side. I laid him back against the pillows and told him he was having a stroke and that whatever happened he must not die, as he was going to be a daddy. I just had the premonition that God had given me Patrick's child, but I prayed that He was not going to take my husband in return.

Cecil arrived and confirmed to me that Patrick had had a severe stroke and arranged for a nurse to come over and stay until the morning when the ambulance would take him to the London Clinic. At dawn the ambulance arrived, and together with Cecil, I accompanied Patrick to the clinic. After leaving him with the doctors, there was nothing more I could do, so I returned to the flat, after first making a visit to the Church of the Immaculate Conception to pray for Patrick. I then spent the rest of the day back at the clinic sitting with him in his room. I saw Cecil later and he said if Patrick survived four days, he would be out of danger. I told him I would like him to confirm my pregnancy, which came as a total bafflement to him. A few days later he congratulated me. I was pregnant.

After early morning Mass at the Church of the Immaculate Conception, I would go and sit with Patrick, praying that he would live. I constantly whispered to him that he was going to be a daddy. After the fourth day, Dr. Eppel said Patrick would live, but he would be paralyzed down his left side and his speech would be impaired, though it would improve with time. I just knew how terribly sad and frustrated Patrick would feel once he understood the consequence of what had happened.

During those many hours that I was with him, I wondered how he was going to accept his immobility. He was such a strong, active man. As I watched his quiet body, I couldn't help but remember what he told me about his early life—how he managed to join the Coldstream Guards at nineteen years old and of his success as a welterweight boxer. He then moved on to work as a secretary to a minister in parliament and at the age of twenty-four felt his destiny was in America and with very little money arrived in New York during the Great Depression. His first job was selling apples on the streets. Eventually he made his way to California. He was a terrific tennis player and was soon asked to join the tennis club in Los Angeles, where he became good friends with Errol Flynn and his buddies. With his beautiful voice and hands, he found work using both for advertisements.

Patrick told me that at the beginning of the war, Britain didn't have enough trained pilots, so many of the young potential pilots were flown out to California, where Patrick was one of the advanced pilots who trained them. During the war Patrick himself worked out of Washington National Airport for the Air Transport Command and was sent all over Europe to bring members of the Royal families to America for their safety, and to fly the American soldiers who were hurt in the war, back home. His missions to Africa were to bring the gold bullion to the United States. My captain had many adventures during those trips and so many near-death experiences.

Patrick was a man of immense integrity and discipline. Although not quite six foot tall, he was a giant of a man. When he walked into a room, one had to notice him. How proud I was to be the wife of such an amazing man, and I was determined to do everything in my power to make him better or at least help him enjoy his life the best he could under the circumstances.

As I gently kissed him, I knew he knew I was there and that he would do whatever he could to fight to live. God moves in mysterious ways, His wonders to perform. I was carrying a new life that Patrick never thought possible. Now that I had heard from the doctors that Patrick wasn't going to die, I brought stationery from home, and while in the hospital room, wrote to everyone we knew, telling them of the sad news and then the joy of my pregnancy. I have to admit each letter brought tears of sadness and tears of happiness. During those days while Patrick was being taken care of in the clinic, I never gave much thought to the fact that he wasn't going to be able to lead as normal a life as he led before, nor that he wouldn't be able to cuddle his child in his arms. I was just grateful he was going to live and that I had been chosen to be the mother of his child.

Patrick was finally allowed to return home. We had day nurses and night nurses, physiotherapists and doctors coming and going all the time, and little by little there was improvement. His face almost returned to normal, as did his speech. On the morning of Patrick's sixty-eighth birthday, March sixteenth, I decided I didn't want nurses around anymore. I could take care of my husband; there was just too much movement for me. I needed peace and tranquility. I didn't need the housekeeper. I could manage to cook small meals and run over to Marks and Spencer in Oxford Street to supply the rest. I seemed to have so much energy that I wanted to look after my husband and the apartment by myself. I didn't want the cleaner, as I had the time while Patrick rested, to clean the apartment, change the net curtains and generally attend to the flat while being close to Patrick. The only person I needed was the chauffeur, as we seemed constantly to be visiting doctors, and he was useful to have around.

I was too busy with Patrick to even think about carrying our child, though I did go to meet my obstetrician, whom I liked very much. He confirmed I was healthy and told me to stop all vitamins and just take folic acid. He said my baby would be due around the middle of November. In my mind I thought I had time to get Patrick as well as possible before the birth. I made sure he always felt clean and fresh. I gently administered his daily shaves, became barber and manicurist, and learned to tie his tie and do all the other daily requirements. I didn't want him ever to feel like an invalid. I tried to make light of my newfound talents and we laughed a lot.

Most unfortunately, however, when I was removing Patrick's pyjama top one morning, I saw that his left shoulder looked strange. Dr. Eppel diagnosed that Patrick's rotator cuff was torn and that possibly one of the nurses had inadvertently pulled his arm too hard trying to help him stand up. Once again we were in another hospital to have it put right. The operation was successful, and from then on I would help Patrick to stand by holding on to the clothes on his back and pull him to his feet. Needless to say, I was conscious of not having anyone hold or help him to stand or move from one place to another.

39

There was no doubt that our GP made sure Patrick would have the best medical care available, and I was glad I had included him on my health insurance policy, which meant that almost all of the expenses were paid for by the insurance company.

On a visit to one of Patrick's many doctors, we were told about a clinic in Switzerland that was famous for its treatment of stroke patients.

I said, "Right, we are going."

I made the arrangements, and we were met at Zurich airport by a car and driver from the "Klinik". Patrick was exhausted when we arrived. It was the middle of June and the weather was pleasant, though a trifle cool for us.

Arriving at the rehabilitation hospital in Valens, we were shown to our room, which had a large picture window; so during the day we could look out at the serene view overlooking the gardens and to the mountains. The room was sparse—two hospital beds and no private bathroom—but it did have a basin.

Every morning I would push Patrick in his wheelchair to the exercise room. Sometimes I found it hard to watch the effort he had to make to do the exercises, but I knew it was important. The ice bath was exceedingly difficult, though the physiotherapist assured us it would help his limbs to gain mobility, but Patrick couldn't take it for long.

In the afternoons after lunch, which was brought to our room, as were the rest of the meals, I pushed Patrick around the grounds of the clinic; I felt that the Swiss mountain air was good for both our baby and us. My heart was filled with gratitude to Jesus that despite Patrick's suffering he was able to benefit from the facilities in a professional and attractive venue. I enjoyed the exercise walking around the gardens and knew it was necessary for us to leave our room to have a change of scene.

Sometimes it was hard for me to believe I was carrying a baby, as my stomach was still flat, and I had had no problems whatsoever with my pregnancy.

The evenings after supper were really bleak. We asked to have a television in our room, which was provided, a small black-and-white. I tried hard to find an English programme, but to no avail. As luck would have it, the World Cup football was showing every night. Patrick and I both liked to watch football, but the commentary was in Deutsche/Suisse. The language was totally impossible for either of us to understand and found the whole thing exasperating. However, we persevered and as the evenings progressed, we began to look forward to our entertainment and somehow managed to work out who was playing whom and eventually saw West Germany win the cup. I shall always be grateful to the World Cup, as heaven knows how we would have endured those long evenings otherwise.

Although after two weeks we had both had enough of the Valens Clinic, there is no doubt that the time spent there helped enormously. Shortly before the end of our stay, it was suggested that we might like to visit Bad Ragaz where Patrick could enjoy the thermal swimming pools, which would be beneficial to him. We took the suggestion, and as we settled into our suite at the Quellenhof Hotel, I remember a wonderful feeling of luxury—back to civilization! I didn't have to go across the landing to the cold public showers. I had a beautiful shower, and we could eat delicious food and feel terribly spoiled—heaven!

We stayed for about ten days and Patrick did well in the pool, not that he was keen on any of the exercises, but he knew that it was all towards him being able to experience a more mobile form of life. Sitting in the plane travelling back to London, we both felt so grateful for the benefits of the excellent clinic at Valens and that we were able to enjoy the beauty and amazing amenities for the disabled at the Quellenhof Hotel in Bad Ragaz.

Back home in the flat, I was anxious to have Patrick fitted for a caliper for his leg. The physiotherapist came every day to work with him, and soon he was able to take a few steps with the help of the caliper. I gripped his clothes at his back with my right hand and held his left arm with my left hand, while he used his right hand to steady himself with his stick.

Patrick now felt that his life could return to a slightly more normal routine. So in the mornings I would help him to his chair, bring in the newspapers and prepare breakfast, which we had on the table in our bedroom. After breakfast it was time for the ablutions, and as Patrick was now able to maintain his balance, he could sit on a stool at the basin to shave by himself. We had a wonderful walk-in shower and I had a hand rung installed so he was able to pull on it while I helped him into the shower, and he could hold onto it while I washed him; the seat in the shower was useful too. Patrick spent most of the day in bed reading, but at teatime I would dress him, and we would sit in the drawing room and remain there through the evening, having dinner and watching television.

I was so proud of my husband. I knew the enormous effort it took for him to do the smallest things. Not having any feeling at all on his left side and having to carry the dead weight of his left arm was a big strain. It helped to have his arm in a sling, but that was a pull on his neck. Patrick never complained about anything. Sometimes he would become sad and tell me how sorry he was to be such a burden. He wasn't a burden to me; he was my most loved husband, whom I married for better or worse. He had given me so much. Now I had the opportunity to reciprocate, not that I had ever imagined it would be in that way.

Due to everything that was going on in my life, I didn't have much time to see how my mother and Sylvan were doing in Majorca. I was delighted when I heard the news that Sylvan had given birth to a beautiful daughter in June and that she and her husband were overjoyed. Dad seemed to be doing well, and I saw him quite often. He was good company for Patrick. Patrick's sister Dolly and husband, George, came to visit, but I was surprised that out of all the people we knew, only a handful of friends kept in touch. It seemed to me that once Patrick was out of the social scene, no more fabulous dinner parties at home or in restaurants, people didn't want to know us anymore.

Every night on my knees I thanked Jesus for all of our blessings. I prayed that Patrick would be totally well again, but I knew from the doctors' prognosis that would not be possible. I also prayed that as long as he could enjoy a way of life despite his paralysis, I would do everything to make his life as comfortable and normal as possible. I prayed too that our baby would be healthy, as there were so many old wives tales about children born to an older father, but somehow through the grace of God, I knew our baby would be perfect.

Since Patrick's stroke, I had become a light sleeper and awoke about every two hours to check on him and help him turn over, as his comfort was paramount to me. I was fortunate to have the most amazing man who tried to make life as easy for me as possible under difficult circumstances. I was also so grateful that the little baby growing inside me was so good. I felt an enormous peace; I knew Jesus was protecting both my baby and its fabulous father.

During all that time, poor Romulus and Remus were still in kennels, which made me very sad. Our house hunting had now come to a halt. I tried not to worry about our dogs, but they were always in my prayers and thoughts.

As we had the flat to ourselves, I would go to the front door each morning and collect the newspapers left outside on the landing, together with whatever magazines were there. We were still on the market for a house and had the "Country Life" magazine delivered. I didn't look at it straight away, but when I relaxed with Patrick in the afternoon, I saw my dream house. My heart started racing; it was the most beautiful, romantic house I had seen, and I knew Jesus had sent it to us. I was so excited and prayed Patrick would agree.

I showed him the photographs of the house and said: "If you still want us to have a home in the country, then this is the house I would like."

That's all it took. He was on the phone to the agent and made plans for us to go to the country the next day.

40

It was a beautiful day in late July. The countryside looked lovely as we drove the hour and fifteen minutes out of London into the county of Hampshire and the tiny village of Borden. "The Old Farm House," a sixteenth century farmhouse, was protected by a large wall and subsequently not noticeable from the road. We turned off into a lane and drove through the gate into a gorgeous garden of a little over two acres. I helped Patrick into his wheelchair and we entered the courtyard, which had a wishing well, just like the one we had at Ionia House, so to me it was a good omen!

I felt the house embrace me as we entered through the front door. It was divine! One side of the house had the master bedroom upstairs, and it was a little difficult for me to help Patrick up the old wooden staircase, but I thought it was important for him to see the bedroom where he would spend a lot of time. The bedroom was large and had many windows overlooking the lovely garden. He trusted me on the rest of the house, which had a bedroom and sitting room for the nanny we would employ, and across from her would be our baby's room, and they would have their own bathroom. The layout of the house was perfect for our requirements, and apart from the most fabulous inglenook fireplace, a guest room with bathroom en suite, the pièce de résistance was a heated swimming pool and sauna in the room that used to be the original barn. The swimming pool would be ideal for Patrick to have water therapy and for our child to learn to swim. I could dream about relaxing in the sauna and then float under the old timbers.

There was a two-car garage large enough for the Rolls and a two-bedroom staff flat above. In the verdant garden were many large rhododendrons, clumps of ornamental and flowering shrubs, and a stream that flowed from the River Wey. There was also a large pond surrounded by graceful weeping willows. It was our home; it had to be. I couldn't wait to tell Romulus and Remus that we had a home for them, which they would love.

The owner and his wife, told us they were moving in order to be near a special hospital so that their six-year-old son could receive treatment. Their little angel son, Rupert, was suffering from leukemia. When I heard that, Patrick's paralysis seemed insignificant to me compared to the suffering and heartache of the young couple. A year later on Rupert's seventh birthday, he went to heaven.

Returning to London, we immediately called Dolly and George and told them that we had found our haven, our dream home in Hampshire. I realised there was a certain amount of work to be done, but before we started doing any work on the house, buying furniture, or attending to many other things, I had a big nag in my head and heart. I told Patrick I did not want to bring our child into the world without us being married in church. I was a Catholic, and in the eyes of the church being married in a civil ceremony didn't count; our child had to baptised in the Catholic Church. I was thrilled when he telephoned his good friend Canon Gordon Albion and said: "The wife wants another wedding, this time at St. Edward's."

The next phone call came from Father Peter Blake, a Jesuit of the Immaculate Conception Church in Farm Street, asking when he could come over to meet us. Canon Albion had spoken to Father Peter about our situation and that Patrick was a lapsed Catholic. We were rather nervous to receive him. We needn't have been, however, as Father Peter was a lovely, jolly man. He made us feel comfortable immediately. He heard our confessions, which was a little emotional for Patrick, but Father Peter made it very easy. We called Canon Albion and thanked him and decided that we would be married at St. Edward's on August twenty-fourth, 1974.

Patrick was anxious to let Dolly know, and of course, she and George would attend; they would drive down with us to Sutton Park near Guildford, Surrey, as would Dad. I wanted to look good for my wedding day and decided to wear the beautiful white and gold caftan Patrick had bought for me in Beirut. Canon Albion had arranged for the children's choir to be in attendance, and Dolly's daughter, Maureen, gave us the gift of the missal of our wedding nuptial Mass. It was an extremely emotional ceremony, Patrick in his wheelchair and I seven months pregnant. The singing of the children was fantastic; it was all so beautiful, and despite my tears, my heart felt it would burst. Now we were really married, and I was over the moon with happiness.

We made another trip to The Old Farm House and arranged to have a walk-in shower built in the master bathroom to make it as easy and comfortable as possible for Patrick. We also knew that we needed to install a home lift, which would be built outside the guest room downstairs and go straight up to our bedroom; nothing else in the house needed changing. We just had to shop! Harrods was the answer, as the famous store sold everything that we would require. Each afternoon our chauffeur, Robert, would take us to Harrods, and I would wheel Patrick around, clutching our list. After about three days, we had furnished our new home.

We ordered the usual seven-foot square bed that we had in the London and Ionia House, the green leather chesterfields, and other beautiful pieces of furniture, also choosing what was required for the nanny's rooms and our baby's room. It was so much fun. The owners of the house decided to leave their attractive dining room suite. In the meantime we had arranged for a couple we had known for a while to be the gardener/caretaker, and his wife the cook. They would have the flat above the garage. We decided to continue employing the woman who worked for the previous owners to clean the house.

Everything was going along smoothly with the purchase of The Old Farm House, and our days in London were busy preparing for our baby and making sure our home in the country would be ready for Christmas. I wasn't prepared, however, for the result of a phone call that Patrick answered.

Patrick beckoned to me and pulled me to him. He said, "I am so sorry, darling, but that call was to tell us Remus has died. The vet said there was nothing physically wrong with him and his conclusion was that Remus had died of a broken heart."

My poor little baby. He didn't know how close he was to being liberated. He just couldn't hold on any more and gave up. The sadness I felt then I feel now as I write. We had spent such a short time together. After receiving that news, it was imperative to have Romulus with us as soon as possible.

I arranged for a day nurse to be with Patrick, while I went to shop for our baby's crib and other requirements for the flat in London. I had to keep to the colours yellow and white, though Patrick was absolutely sure we would have a daughter. Earlier that day I was driven to Queen Mary's Hospital in Roehampton where I had an ultrasound of our baby. It was an exciting experience, and I was filled with wonder as I saw a picture of the fetus and was really happy to be told that my baby was perfect, but the gender was not disclosed.

Another afternoon shortly thereafter, I went to see my obstetrician, who was very pleased with me. He told me to make contact with a lady called Crystal Bruell, who would be of much assistance. Crystal Bruell would come to the apartment and in Patrick's presence would take out her life-size doll and proceed to show me how to feed and bathe the baby and how to change the nappy and everything else I needed to know. She also arranged to have the first baby clothes handmade, together with the sheets and blankets. Our baby was to have the best. What a lucky mummy I was going to be. Even the nappies would be muslin cloth, absolutely no disposable nappies!

I did attend the breathing classes on a couple of occasions, but by the time I had come to the end of my day with attending to Patrick and everything else I had to do, I was tired. I read the baby book, that my obstetrician gave me, from cover to cover, and did all the exercises that were recommended, so I felt fairly prepared.

At the beginning of October, we decided, with the help of Miss Bruell, to interview prospective nannies. We had interviewed a few Norland nannies who were young and demanding. Miss Bruell then called and said she thought she had the perfect nanny and Josephine

Featherstone arrived. Patrick and I took a liking to her immediately. She was a friendly, slightly plump woman in her late forties, and came with excellent references. We knew that lady was for us and agreed that she would start in the New Year.

Next on our agenda was to think of names. Patrick, in his usual prophetic way, said. "We are having a daughter, and her name will be Tara Devon. Devon to rhyme with heaven."

I loved the name. I had just been reading a book about Buddhism and the various Buddhist goddesses, and one of them was the goddess of purity, the White Tara, and that was the name I had wanted too. When I tried to talk about boy's names, the subject fell on deaf ears.

41

I only had a month to go, but I was told first babies sometimes arrive early, so I wanted to make sure that everything was ready in good time. Miss Bruell came with a maternity nurse, a Greek girl whom I liked a lot, she would look after my husband while I was in the hospital and remain with me for the first three months. That was such a relief as I knew that nurse Androulla had the perfect personality for Patrick, and spent a couple of days going through our routine together. It was most important for my peace of mind to know that Patrick would be well cared for and comfortable. I made sure the fridge was filled with food, and told Androulla, she only had to call on Robert the chauffeur or call the local grocers, who would deliver, as would the famous butcher Allens of Mount Street, if she needed their services. I informed her the laundry service came once a week. I hoped I had attended to everything and then went to see my doctor, Mr. Roger de Vere.

While I was with him, tears were wetting my cheeks. I wasn't really sure why. He told me that it was time for my baby to enter the world. Mr. de Vere asked me when I would like to have it. The following day would be October thirtieth or if I would prefer the thirty-first. I preferred the odd number so chose the thirty-first. He also told me that I would be having a caesarean birth. He really didn't think I had any energy left and didn't want to put me to the test. He was well aware that all during my pregnancy I was on the go and waking every two hours during the night to turn Patrick over or attend to whatever he might require.

Amazingly, despite everything, I didn't really feel too tired during the day and therefore seldom rested. However, sitting in Mr. de Vere's office, I suddenly felt exhausted, so was grateful to him when he said that he wanted me to remain in the hospital for thirteen days. He assured me that Androulla would take good care of Patrick and that I had nothing to worry about. I mentioned that Patrick wanted to be present at the birth, but he felt that under the circumstances it wasn't a good idea. I thought the same.

The following day as I was getting Patrick ready, I couldn't help thinking why Jesus had prevented him from being a father until now—semi-paralyzed and sixty-eight years old—he was going to be a dad. Well, one should never ask the Lord why. I felt that our miracle baby would help Patrick live for many, many years, as undoubtedly his health would improve.

Robert and the Rolls were waiting for us. Just a block down the road Patrick asked Robert to stop the car and to go into Constance Spry flower shop and buy a dozen red American beauties and also go next door to the liquor shop and buy a case of half bottles of Moet & Chandon champagne. Patrick had credit accounts at both the shops. That gesture was such a surprise to me, but it was typical of my husband, always so thoughtful and caring.

I checked into my room at the Westminster hospital with my beautiful red roses and champagne and gave my man a big, big hug, saying to him that the next time I saw him, we would be parents, and he would have to learn to sign his name Daddy! Androulla told me not to worry about anything and would be back the next afternoon to see the new baby. After they left I arranged the roses in a vase, which was provided, placed a few bottles of the champagne in the small fridge and unpacked my belongings. I wanted everything to be neat and tidy. After a light supper I showered and washed my hair.

Early the next morning I was wheeled out of my room and felt I was in a dream while being pushed along the corridors and into the operating room. All the time I was praying to Jesus, and knew He was with me and would be close while my child was being brought into the world. I didn't imagine, however, that I would experience His presence so closely. I was wrapped in His overpowering love and saw Him shrouded by a magnificent bright light and heard His voice, which was very beautiful. I was surrounded by so much love that I thought I would explode, and I begged Him to take me with Him.

I pleaded, "Please, please." I said, "I just want to be with you."

And He said to me: "No, Diana, it is not the time. Patrick needs you, and your new baby needs you. I am with you always," and He was gone.

I awoke back in my room with Mr. de Vere smiling down at me and saying, "you have a beautiful little witch."

I didn't understand. He said it was Halloween Day! I was thinking it was the day before All Saint's Day! I tried to be grateful and am sure I thanked him, but the memory of my encounter with Jesus was still vivid, and I sort of resented being back in the world. Whenever I was alone, I would re-live the memory and felt so blessed that He was right there with me. As I looked at my baby daughter, I saw a tiny Patrick. I knew I had to get my emotions under control. It was difficult, but I hoped as the day went on I would show more joy.

Patrick walked into the room with Androulla, while I held our baby girl. I was very proud of him, as he wasn't in the wheelchair and had walked the corridor from the lift with the help of his caliper and Androulla. He told me he didn't wish his daughter to see him for the first time in a wheelchair. I knew his daughter would appreciate the tremendous effort. It was a little difficult at first to bond with my little girl, due to my visit from Jesus, but when it happened, it was glorious. My baby was truly gorgeous—perfect. In fact, when I visited the nursery with all the newborn babies, the other mothers were so complimentary about my little angel. My prayers over the years had been answered, despite Patrick telling me he couldn't father a child. He didn't reckon with Jesus.

Soon my room was like a flower shop, and I began to relax and enjoy my stay in the hospital, learning all the time from the wonderful nurses how to take care of my baby. It was one thing learning how to hold a doll, but quite different to having the real doll. Despite it being such an effort, Patrick and Androulla visited every afternoon, which made me so happy, and little by little, together with other close friends and Dolly and George, we managed to enjoy the champagne.

The day came to take our baby home, and as we drove back home in the Rolls, I felt sure our daughter knew she was in a rather special car. She lay upright in her little soft carry bed, totally content. I whispered to Patrick that he didn't have to worry any more about me being alone when he went to heaven.

Androulla was a real blessing and would bring Tara for her feed every three hours during the night. Patrick was learning how to drag his left arm and leg over to his right side in order to turn, trying not to disturb me, but as I had to wake to feed our baby, I was only too happy to help him. After a few days I realised I had to decide upon the date of the baptism, write the invitations, arrange the venue for the reception and make sure that Canon Albion, Father Peter Blake and Canon O'Leary were available. I also wanted to have a photographer take professional pictures of the three of us. I had to design a special cake and hire a Scottish piper.

Patrick with Tara on the morning of her Baptism

Diana with Tara on the morning of her Baptism
photographed in the Grosvenor Square apartment

The reception would be held at the Britannia Hotel, a few doors from us on our block and within walking distance of the Church of the Immaculate Conception, which was just off Mount Street. Patrick and I decided the baptism ceremony would be on December fourteenth, when Tara was six weeks old, which would give us a little over a week to move into The Old Farm House and prepare for Tara's first Christmas.

Everything was working out beautifully, until there was some dispute as to the name, Tara, not being accepted by the Catholic Church. Canon Albion, who was also very knowledgeable about church history, informed us that St. Taraghta, Tara being the abbreviated version of her name, was a fifth century Irish Saint. Her feast day was August eleventh, and she was a contemporary of St. Patrick's and devoted herself to looking after the poor. It was therefore decided that the name Tara was accepted by the church.

Saturday, December fourteenth was a clear, sunny day, and Tara was just perfect, no tears during the rather long ceremony. Canon

Albion looked regal in his robes, and Father Peter was in his Knight of the Holy Sepulchre robes. Canon O'Leary was abroad and unable to attend. The Church of the Immaculate Conception was so beautiful, and I felt blessed that our daughter was being baptised in that special church. After the moving ceremony, the piper piped us out as he had piped us in, and about forty-five of our guests and family walked over to the Britannia Hotel. Tara slept like angel in her crib, while our friends cooed over her until it was time for her to partake in the cutting of her cake.

42

At eight weeks old, Tara celebrated her first Christmas in her new home in Borden, Hampshire, and our beloved Romulus was finally free from living in the kennels and now had a beautiful home with a large garden. We spent a happy first Christmas in The Old Farm House. Shortly after Christmas Androulla had to leave us. Patrick and I were sad to see her go; she had been such a tremendous help, and what a perfect nurse she was to us all.

We had another nice nurse to fill in and on my thirty-third birthday, Nanny Josephine Featherstone arrived and Tara took to her immediately. The two of them were to become best buddies; they were both Scorpios! It was such a relief for me to know that my precious baby would be loved and well looked after so I wouldn't have to worry while I took care of her daddy.

I was anxious not to miss out on taking photographs of my beautiful baby. My first priority was always to my man; when I knew he was comfortable or when he was with his physiotherapist, I would slip away, usually accompanied by Romulus, to embrace the amazing miracle of Tara Devon. When we were in London, it was easier for Tara to spend quality time with Patrick. I could see the sadness in his demeanour, not being able to hold his child with both arms, but as much as possible, he was always there—the three of us, our Nan, and of course, Romulus. We were a close and loving little family.

I knew Patrick always derived enormous pleasure when he was able to be close to Tara and hold her in his right arm. He found it difficult to believe that bundle of true joy was his baby. How did he manage to make a baby at the age of sixty-eight, after being told all his life that he would never be able to have children? I reminded him our baby was a miracle and God's gift to us and His answer to my prayers.

254 | Diana O'Leary

Wetravelled back and forth between the country house and London, as Patrick needed to see doctors in London, as did Tara for her shots. Both homes were lovely, but The Old Farm House had Romulus and a heavenly garden. It was the perfect oasis for us. At the beginning of May, Patrick received a letter from Canon Albion saying he had sent in an application for Patrick to be considered as a Knight of the Holy Sepulchre. Canon Albion was aware of Patrick's disappointment over the rejection to be a Knight of Malta. It wasn't long after that when confirmation came from the Grand Magisterium in Rome that he had been accepted, and would be invested at Southwark Cathedral on December fourteenth, 1975, giving us something exciting to look forward to.

In June of 1975 at the invitation of our friends Youka and Marcia Troubetzkoy, we flew to the South of France to stay at their villa in Eze-sur-Mer. It was rather strange to stay in their guesthouse rather than the Hotel de Paris, but it was more convenient, especially as Tara and Nan were with us, and they were given the Chinese guesthouse to themselves. Tara, at eight months, loved the flight to Nice. Our friends and the staff were very attentive, so kind, and the change of venue in such blissful surroundings was therapeutic for both Patrick and me.

The chauffeur Alfred took the four of us into Monte Carlo to see all the old haunts that were so familiar. We had to introduce Tara to the casino and finished our visit to the principality at the bar in the Hotel de Paris, which seemed appropriate. While we were at the home of the Troubetzkoys, Tara's godmother came to visit and also our good friend Basil, who was in the area. It was a happy occasion.

After a week with Youka and Marcia, we flew down to Marbella on the Costa del Sol in Spain and a health resort called Incosol. I wanted Patrick to experience every possibility that would help him exercise his muscles and regain more mobility. Patrick was in the pool daily with his physiotherapist, and the whole atmosphere at Incosol was undoubtedly extremely good for him. I could see an improvement in his movements each day and also with his speech. We hired a chauffeur-driven car to visit Bud and Gwynne in Benalmádena, and they had the great pleasure of meeting Patrick's baby. Bud and Gwynne were sad to see their good friend so disabled.

While we were at Incosol, we met a lovely couple who became close friends, Tania and Owen. Our new friendship gave Patrick an incentive to talk and socialise a little and have a meal in the restaurant rather than in our suite. After two relaxed weeks in the warm sunshine of the Costa del Sol, we headed home.

The rest of the summer was spent in the country enjoying our home and garden, and the balmy summer weather. Our friend from Manila, Hans, came to visit and stayed with us for a week. He was so good with Tara and excellent company for Patrick. We had visits from Tara's godparents, and in fact, we had friends either to stay for a few days or just pop in to spend the day with us. I was happy for that, as I felt it was important for Patrick to lead as normal a life as possible and to make conversation.

We returned to London a few weeks before Tara's first birthday, as I wanted her to have a party, and Nan knew a couple of other nannies with children the same age as Tara. We weren't prepared for the IRA (Irish Republican Army) riots in Grosvenor Square, and on the day before Tara's first birthday, the Tratoria Fiore Restaurant on Mount Street was bombed. Our apartment overlooked the American Embassy and South Audley Street, so we were right on top of all the activity. Despite the bombings the previous day, the nannies and their charges were able to make the birthday tea the following afternoon.

The babies dressed in their party frocks looked adorable. I didn't know any of the nannies, as they had met in Hyde Park on their walks. Tara's godparents showed up for her birthday and we sat in the living room, while the babies enjoyed the dining room and played in the hall on the carpeted floor. Grandpa couldn't make her birthday but came to see her the next day.

Soon it was December fourteenth, and I had arranged for the photographer Tom Hustler, who photographed Tara's baptism, to be with us at Southwark Cathedral where he photographed Patrick at his Investiture of the Knights of the Holy Sepulchre. This order was founded around the year 1099 by the knights who participated in the first crusade. Canon Gordon Albion and his cousin Agnes were in attendance, as were Tara's Godfather, Paul, Patrick's stepsister, Clodagh, and Patrick's cousin, Canon Maurice O'Leary. The ceremony was very interesting and Patrick, seated in his wheelchair, was able to

Patrick having been invested as a Knight of the Holy Sepulchre standing with Diana outside Southwark Cathedral

follow the whole procedure. As always, I was so proud of my husband. Patrick wanted to walk out of the cathedral rather than sitting in his wheelchair, and we did that, giving Tom the chance of taking a few photographs of the new Knight of the Holy Sepulchre standing up. All the new knights, together with the Grand Lieutenant of the Equestrian Order of the Knights of the Holy Sepulchre, were invited to the Middle Temple for lunch. Arriving at the historic building, which was erected between 1562 and 1573, was most exciting. We entered the impressive hall and were told that it was where Shakespeare recited his first plays for Queen Elizabeth I.

As we partook of the delicious luncheon and imbibed a few glasses of excellent wine, I noticed Patrick was happy and obviously proud to be a member of the ancient Order of Knights. Canon Albion was also happy that everything had gone so well and his good friend Patrick was deserving of such a prestigious honour. The only thing that made us sad, was that Dolly and George were unable to attend, as Dolly was gravely sick.

Christmas at The Old Farm House was just magical. Tara, now a year old, was cognisant that it was a special and exciting time. Owen and Tania came to stay and Canon Albion and Agnes were with us for our Christmas feast. My heart was bursting with gratitude for all of the many blessings that the birthday of Jesus had brought us. The Old Farm House lent itself to giving everyone a joyous Christmas.

Not too long into the New Year, my mother was visiting London from Palma, Majorca, and my niece Tania was with her. I thought how nice it would be for Mother and little Tania to stay with us and for her to enjoy her granddaughters. I really wanted Patrick to forgive Mother for that letter she had written to him. I spoke to Patrick and asked him to allow her to come and stay with us and meet our Tara, her other granddaughter. It didn't take long for my wonderful husband to capitulate and say Mother could come to stay. I was happy that Tara had the company of her cousin, but the two little tigers were not always peaceful! Both Tania and Tara were born in 1974, the Chinese year of the tiger. My little Scorpio/tiger was not pleased to share her beloved Nan with her cousin!

It was a relief for me that everything went well and Mother's conversations with Patrick were amicable and interesting. Mother enjoyed being with her two granddaughters, not to mention seeing her eldest daughter. Fortunately, Mother's visit was without incident. She really had a good time, and I made sure she kept the conversation light. Patrick was unable and unwilling to converse in depth, much to Mother's chagrin at times.

During our visits to London, we would see Dolly and George, who lived in Hertfordshire. Both Patrick and Dolly made such an effort to be strong for one another. After four wonderful years of being reunited, Patrick was a hemiplegic, and Dolly was suffering with cancer of the esophagus. It was tremendously sad to see brother and sister come to terms with the fact that their time together was now so short. Dolly died in March 1976. Patrick didn't say much, but I knew he was happy that he had found his beloved sister again and able to spend those short and special times together.

After Dolly's death, Patrick said he would like us to go away for the Easter holidays and decided we should go to the Beau-Rivage Hotel in Lausanne, Switzerland. Owen and Tania decided to join us. Patrick and I were very fond of Tania and Owen and enjoyed their company, so we were delighted when they said they would be with us. While we were there, we all thought it would be fun to have a day trip to Evian and travel over on the ferry. When we arrived at Evian, Tania wanted to push Patrick's wheelchair from the ferry to the dock, and by accident it caught on the drawbridge, and Patrick was almost tipped into the lake. I was shaking, but Patrick's composure was amazing. I decided I would take charge of the wheelchair from then on!

We all had a good appetite for the gastronomic luncheon at La Verniez restaurant, and happy just being together. I attended as many church services as I could during Holy Week and was at Mass on Easter Sunday. The services were no longer in Latin, and it was difficult to follow the Swiss language, but no matter. To receive communion was my greatest joy. I tried to go to Mass wherever I was in the world, and if I couldn't, I knew I was forgiven, as Jesus knew He was always my first love.

We were back at The Old Farm House for the summer and I felt confident enough to take care of Patrick and Tara while Nan went off for the day. As it was the weekend, Edie and Charles were either in their apartment or off the property. I had the luxury of having my husband, daughter and faithful Romulus all to myself. We were in the living room playing a game of snakes and ladders with Tara, and I heard Romulus growl, which was unusual. The door to the garden was open, as it was a beautiful, hot summer's day; I went to the door where Romulus was standing, and to my horror, I saw a large snake approaching. I didn't know whether the snake was dangerous or not, but I had my disabled husband, my little girl and my dog, all three were dependent on me.

I quietly went over to the fireplace, picked the shovel off the wall, and went back out. The snake was almost at the door. I love all animals and really didn't want to hurt the snake, but I knew I had to kill it. With a pounding heart, I dug the shovel, severing its neck. Needless to say I felt really sick and was trembling, but thanked Jesus for helping me. I left the shovel on the ground and closed the door resuming my place to continue playing with Tara and Patrick, who were so engrossed that they weren't alarmed by my movements. I gave Romulus a big hug. When Nan arrived back, I asked her to tell Charles to please remove the dead snake from outside the living room door.

43

Patrick and I would have to leave Nanny and Tara in the country while we travelled to London, as there were still appointments that had to be kept. Patrick spent hours reading, and I would make sure that he had a good supply of interesting books. One afternoon I was on my way to Hatchards, the bookshop on Piccadilly, when Patrick asked me to buy him the Bible. I found a nice Bible with easy-to-read print. When I returned to the flat, I realised I had accidentally left my keys inside. Patrick by now was used to being left alone, while I ran out to do my errands; he was safely in bed, his pee bottle within easy reach of his right arm, with the telephone next to him and lots of books to read.

As I stood in front of the door to our flat, I said a prayer, and as I believed in miracles, took the cross from the chain around my neck, which Patrick had given to me in Monte Carlo on our first visit. I truly believed that it would open our front door, so I pushed it into the keyhole, but nothing happened. I went to the head porter and told him of my predicament, and his suggestion was for me to try to squeeze myself through the narrow garbage opening at the back of the flat, which amazingly I managed to do. I felt it was a miracle after all, that I was able to enter the flat through the back without having to cause a commotion or having the locksmiths over to open the door. Patrick had no idea of what I had just been through and was delighted with the Bible, spending many hours reading it each day.

We lived as normal a life as possible and tried to spend a lot of our days in the country, especially as the summer months were so beautiful. Many nights after settling Patrick in bed and waiting until I knew he was asleep, I would go into the bathroom with all the photographs I had taken and, sitting on the floor, I would paste them into large scrapbooks, sometimes until two in the morning. I was determined I would record as much as I could of our baby's life, in order that she would know her father and mother were so much part of her growing up, and how much she was loved.

Living at The Old Farm House not only gave our precious Romulus a beautiful garden to run around, but also each day I would make Patrick walk in the garden. I had a sandpit built and a little splashing pool that Tara could use outside; life was idyllic for us. I would manage to use the sauna and the heated indoor swimming pool, which was also an exercise pool, as one could swim against the current. I loved the pool, swimming under the old beams was truly a dream, and found it very relaxing. I tried to coax Patrick to use the pool, but it was too much of an effort for him. I hired a swimming coach to teach Tara how to swim; fortunately, she loved the water, and from six months onwards was quite a water baby.

It was approaching Tara's second birthday, which we spent in London. As always Tara had a few friends, as Nan was so sociable, and Tara was never at a loss for little people. Life was busy for us back and forth between London and The Old Farm House.

For Christmas we invited Owen and Tania to stay again, and Agnes and Canon Albion came to spend the day. I have to say, our Christmases were wonderful. I loved decorating the tree and the house, but our main joy was watching Tara's excitement leading up to Christmas. We did not enjoy going to the local Catholic Church, as the priest was full of fire and brimstone. We went instead to the sisters of Mount Alvernia to celebrate a Christmas Mass in their little chapel. We became close to those wonderful nuns and would attend weekly Mass with them.

On Patrick's seventieth birthday, Canon Gordon Albion suggested he would come to our house to celebrate Mass, and we had the pleasure of inviting a few of the nuns to join us. Patrick and I were very appreciative of that great honour. For Patrick's birthday I had a photograph taken of Tara and myself. It was more like a portrait, and he loved it. My Mother, Vanessa, and Sylvan joined us in the evening, and together with Canon Albion and Agnes, we all had a happy birthday dinner for Patrick.

The pleasure and happiness that our little girl brought to us was incredibly gratifying, and I saw Patrick becoming stronger. His health was improving all the time. I knew it was Tara's influence on him. The realisation that our gorgeous little girl was his daughter, would bring tears to his eyes at times. He was very interested in everything she did and was always ready to play whatever game she produced. I had considered Patrick to be the boss, but watching our daughter, I wasn't sure anymore.

We spent a beautiful summer in the country, and our trips to London became less and less, as Patrick had a marvelous physiotherapist who visited him every day and a great country doctor, so we didn't feel the necessity to spend much time in London.

As the winter months were approaching, Patrick said he would like us to be in the sunshine and thought a visit to the Lyford Cay Club in Nassau would be the perfect place. I knew how important it was for Patrick to be in a warm climate, as his lack of mobility and disinterest in food had caused him to lose a lot of weight, and thus he felt the cold much more. I also knew our membership at the Lyford Cay Club had lapsed, I, therefore, proceeded to write to the managing director and explain the situation. We were both thrilled to receive the most wonderful letter from the then managing director, saying he would renew our membership. He said he had reserved cottage eighty-seven for us and he would make the master bathroom easier for Patrick to maneuver and would arrange for a ramp to be built at the entrance of the cottage for the wheelchair. In addition to which he would have an extra bedroom built so Tara and Nan would have their own rooms.

44

We left The Old Farm House in the good hands of Charles and Edie, knowing they would love and take care of Romulus. On December fourth, 1977, with fourteen pieces of luggage, we boarded British Airways to fly to Nassau, where we would live for four months. On arrival at Nassau Airport, the warm air embraced us, and as we entered the small airport, my thoughts went back to my first visit. I was really happy to be returning, and I knew that Patrick was looking forward to being in Nassau again.

Although it was fairly late when we arrived at the club, Peter Rickard, the managing director, was waiting and showed us to our cottage. He was lovely with a pronounced North Country accent. I thanked him for making our visit possible, finding it difficult to restrain the tears welling in my eyes. I was not about to unpack until the next day, and after the four of us enjoyed club sandwiches, we settled down for the night.

Cottage eighty-seven was the perfect location. We could see the ocean from the living room window, and the beach was a few minutes down the path. The masseuse, Charlie, was within walking distance for Patrick, and I would walk over with him every day in order that he could have his daily massage. The Little Club, where we would have dinner from time to time, was close by. The cottage was a comfortable size and had a small kitchenette, so more often than not we ate "at home." Patrick was really happy to be at the club and would sit in our little garden, chatting and playing with Tara while enjoying the warmth of the sun. Nan together with Tara, would spend hours on the beautiful beach and soon they became known to everyone, making many friends. There were several children of Tara's age who lived at Lyford Cay, and therefore, many tea parties to attend and host.

Tania and Owen came as our guests to spend Christmas, which was lovely for both Patrick and me. We all joined in the Christmas celebrations at the club, and Tara, at three years old, was the star! During the Christmas holidays, many activities were arranged for the children. Nan and Tara were always busy, which made me very happy. Patrick and I had our routine and had friends visit us in the cottage. Peter and his beautiful wife, Jan, became close friends, and they tried to visit us as much as they could.

On Sundays we would have the club car take us to St. Paul's Catholic Church, which was situated just outside the gates of Lyford Cay. We made good friends with the priest, Father Peter Le Vierge, who often came to our cottage to chat with Patrick. It was always emotional for me to attend Mass in that little island church where Tara and I sat in the front pew with Patrick near us in his wheelchair. I gave thanks to Jesus that attending Mass was now so important to Patrick; he would insist on going with us every Sunday.

In February, Canon Albion and Agnes came to stay for a month, and it was wonderful seeing them each day, especially as their company for Patrick was very therapeutic. We invited Vanessa to visit, and she had a really fun time with some friends that Nan had made. We heard the weather in England was cold and snowing, so were most grateful to be enjoying the sun and warmth of Nassau.

Patrick and I were delighted that Nan and Tara were kept busy attending barbecues, going downtown, and having lots of fun by the pool and on the beach, and we looked forward to hearing all about their adventures at dinner time. The four of us went to dinner at the Little Club to celebrate Patrick's seventy-first birthday, and watched the fire-eating limbo dancer and the rest of the lively show. Nan always made a point to dance with Tara at those events.

Alas, our four months were soon over, and we told Peter that as we had had such a happy and comfortable time, we would like him to reserve our cottage for three months from January fifth, 1979. We had decided to spend Christmas at The Old Farm House.

Romulus was happy to have us home, and I really wanted to spend more time in our beautiful home in the country. Tara kept us entertained; she was growing fast and took such an interest in everything. I was especially delighted to see how much time she and Patrick would spend together. She would introduce him to her various games and would insist he played with her. Grandpa used to come and stay, and it was fun for me to see our three-year-old holding the attention of her two favourite gentlemen fans.

On April twenty-fourth, at three and a half years old, Tara started at Pinewood Nursery School and was happily making new friends. Some of her little friends would come to tea and would enjoy swimming in our pool. Catherine Ashford, a couple of weeks older than Tara, became her best friend. I was really happy that Tara was attending such a great nursery school, and every day she would bring me her little drawings.

We were fortunate to have the most marvelous physiotherapist working with Patrick. He and Joanna became good friends, and it was through her that we were introduced to our doctor, Richard Hardwick, and his wife, who was a teacher at Tara's nursery school. Dr. Hardwick was brilliant and was always on call for us. It made me feel so secure to have a terrific doctor close by, as I never knew what the day would bring for Patrick or, in fact, our little girl.

One afternoon at about teatime, Nanny, Patrick, Tara and I were in the living room. Tara was showing us a new game when Patrick suddenly started to shake. I had never seen an epileptic attack. Watching my poor husband was very frightening. Fortunately, Nan had seen one of those attacks before and brought a wet cloth to apply to Patrick's neck and turn his head so that his tongue would fall to the side. I called Dr. Hardwick immediately, and he was with us within about ten minutes. Tara had been so engrossed in her game that she hadn't seen the actual attack.

When the doctor arrived, he helped me take Patrick up to bed and prescribed treatment in the form of pills, which he later brought over. I was very worried and was assured that as long as Patrick took his medication, it was unlikely he would have another one. After a few days, Patrick was better, and the doctor told us of a well-renowned doctor in Berne, Switzerland, who was reputed to be of great help to stroke patients. We both felt we had to try everything to continue to help Patrick's health improve, so we flew to Berne, staying for a couple of weeks to consult with the doctor. The visit proved most interesting, and Patrick was given some new pills, which seemed to help a lot.

When we returned to London, our friend Basil from California visited, together with his wife and their young daughter, who was about seven months younger than Tara. The two little girls had lots of fun playing together, and it was good to see our friends. We recalled the last time we had seen them in their lovely home in Benedict Canyon, and the magic that happened that early Valentine's morning. Of course, they were both most sad to see Patrick's demeanour. Although Patrick was able to converse and was mentally alert, he did find making conversation an effort. Basil found it especially difficult to see Patrick, recalling what a strong presence he had always emanated.

45

While we were in London, Patrick decided we should go to Harrods and have Tara choose the bicycle she wanted for her birthday. It was a lovely outing and very much between daddy and daughter as to who made the decision. The following day, Nan had her day off, and Patrick suggested we take Tara to the zoo. Our new chauffeur Michael, who came to us when we moved to the country, drove us, and we had the most glorious afternoon. I felt that if Patrick had been able to get up out of his wheelchair, he would have. His enthusiasm was fantastic as he directed Tara to the various animal attractions. It was an unforgettable afternoon.

We returned to the country to enjoy the changing colours of autumn. Prince Troubetzkoy visited us with his girlfriend. His adored wife, Marcia, had died the previous year by falling on the marble floor of their home in Eze. I was happy that Youka had made the trip to the country to see his old friend. Patrick and Youka had known each other in New York. They had both emigrated at about the same time and had been friends for over forty years. Tara insisted that Youka help her start blowing up balloons for her fourth birthday party the following day, which he did with much laughter. He and Marcia did not have children, so he was not accustomed to little people. However, he seemed captivated by Tara.

I had arranged for Mr. Magic to entertain Tara's twelve friends, and what a success that was. The children were mesmerised by Mr. Magic and afterwards went to feast in the dining room with lots of sandwiches, cakes and ice cream. Tara's large birthday cake was shaped as the number four. The tea party was filled with excited chatter, and each little friend received a small gift as they departed. Daddy gave

Tara, a shop with make-pretend vegetables, fruit and money, and the following day Patrick was obliged to play shop all day long!

The weather was cooler, and when we weren't in our beautiful warm flat in London, we were in The Old Farm House; despite the efficient central heating and enormous wood fire, Patrick found it difficult to feel really warm. There seemed to be droughts everywhere. After all, it was an old house and Patrick wasn't able to move around freely. However, we wanted to spend Christmas and the New Year in the country and invited Tania, Owen and their German friend Minchin to stay. As always, I did a good job decorating the tree and generally preparing the house for Christmas. The Old Farm House lent itself to being truly fabulous at yuletide, and that year we were fortunate to have a white Christmas, so the garden looked magical. It was a memorable Christmas, and Patrick, being in good health, enjoyed every minute of the festive season.

We had told Peter Rickard that we would be returning to Nassau after Christmas. As usual, the most difficult time for me was to say good-bye to Romulus. On January fifth, 1979, the four of us were once again on a British Airways flight and headed to the sunshine in Nassau. It didn't take Nan and Tara long to meet up with old friends and hold court on the beach. Our good friends Peter and Jan invited us to spend the day with them on another gorgeous beach, called Old Fort Beach, and they introduced us to their two little children. We spent a happy afternoon with our friends and the three little ones.

I wanted Tara to continue her schooling while we were away, so I signed her up to attend the Lyford Cay School, which she started on January ninth. She made lots of new friends and was inundated with invitations to birthday parties and social events, which we had the pleasure in reciprocating in the small garden of cottage eighty-seven. Life was busy for our four-year-old. Tara also met her first boyfriend, a gorgeous little four-year-old named Todd, who adored Tara. It was a joy to see those two tots together. Both Patrick and I took a great interest in that adorable friendship.

A week after our arrival to Nassau, I had my thirty-seventh birthday, and we all had a lovely evening at the Little Club. When Tara wasn't at school, she and Nan were always busy doing fun things. There was so much to keep the children occupied, and Nan loved all the socialising with the other nannies and privileged children.

The days went by quickly. We had friends visit, Patrick continued with his massages and walks, we went to Mass every Sunday, and somehow Patrick and I filled in the days. March sixteenth was Patrick's seventy-second birthday, and we celebrated in style. The following day Patrick insisted he attend Tara's sport's day at the Lyford Cay School and seemed oblivious that he was in his wheelchair. He took such an interest in everything going on at the school, watching all the children, and especially his beloved little daughter, competing in the races. I was so proud of him, and of course, of Tara.

I sensed it was time for me to take Patrick to the Lyford Cay hospital to see his doctor just to have a check up and make sure he was all right. His doctor confirmed Patrick was in good health, for which I was most relieved. The next few days my antenna was acute. Patrick didn't appear to be himself and was unusually quiet, but he assured me he was okay. I didn't leave his side during the days following, and on March twenty-fifth, I noticed that Patrick seemed a little agitated.

At teatime Tara came into the living room and said: "Mummy, Mummy, please come and play with me. I want you."

I told her I was not able to join her at that time, as I had to be with Daddy. My intuition was telling me to be close to Patrick.

When Tara and Nan had left the cottage, he said: "Come and sit beside me," which I did, and holding my hand, Patrick continued. "Our princess needs you. You must start to spend time with her. You have devoted so much of your life to me, and the time has come for me to go. I want you to know you have given me the happiest years of my life, and I thank you for your love and for our daughter."

Of course, the tears were flowing as he spoke. Everything he said made me feel very happy. At the same time I had a sense of foreboding. I tried to hush him by saying there would be lots of time to play with

Tara, and before she and Nan arrived back to the cottage, I had to pull myself together to prepare dinner.

I just made a bolognaise sauce with mashed potatoes and vegetables. Patrick wasn't himself, being uncharacteristically grumpy at dinner, and I wondered whether the doctor was correct when he said that Patrick was all right.

It was time for Tara to go to bed, and Patrick gave her a big hug with his right arm and said: "Goodnight my little princess. I love you."

She then left for bed, together with Nan. We sat close to each other for a while, trying to watch television on the small black-and-white set, but soon decided to head for bed ourselves.

Before I helped Patrick to his feet to move to the bedroom, he took my hand and kissed it. "Thank you, darling," he said, looking into my eyes. "I love you."

46

I had a strange feeling in my heart as I helped my husband to the bathroom. Then I settled him comfortably in bed, saying that I'd be with him in a minute, as I just had to brush my teeth. It had hardly been three minutes, and as I came out of the bathroom, I looked at Patrick and knew that Jesus was taking him. I almost felt I saw his soul leave his body. As much as I wanted to cry out, "no, no, no," I didn't, and I understood Patrick had decided it was time for him to go, and that's why he was saying good-bye; he was very fey. I felt a calm come over me, knowing that this wonderful, incredible human being was at last at peace. It was ten thirty at night on March twenty-fifth, and I was so grateful that Tara and Nan were fast asleep.

I called the doctor and told him Patrick had died. He said he would be there with the ambulance in half an hour. I sat on the bed and put my arms around his still body, laying my face on his chest, and then I gently kissed his face. I had no tears. I couldn't help but wonder how he had managed to orchestrate his departure, causing as little upset as he could. He just made it to bed before leaving us, amazing. I felt an enormous amount of strength and grace, and I knew my husband would be with me forever. However, I just never imagined that Patrick would die.

The doctor and ambulance came and quietly removed his body. I went back into the bedroom and prayed. Strangely enough, I didn't feel he had left me and remained awake all night. However, not having him beside me was surreal. The only person I needed to be with was Jesus, and I walked up to St. Paul's Catholic Church in order to be there when Father Peter said Mass at seven in the morning.

When I returned to the cottage, Nan and Tara were having breakfast. As the bedroom door was closed, they had no idea what had happened and thought we were still asleep. I had to be strong for my daughter and said that Daddy had gone to a beautiful place called heaven, and he would not have to suffer anymore. I wanted Tara to continue at Lyford Cay School and finish the term. I also felt that I needed time to be by myself and converse with Jesus, and generally come to terms that my mentor, my husband, my lover, my best friend was no longer with me.

I would walk the white sands and spend hours sitting on a rock at the end of the beach, looking out at the ocean while meditating and praying. I was pleased Tara was at school during the day. The news of Patrick's death filtered out, and the few days afterwards it seemed like every member of the staff at the Lyford Cay Club came to say how sad they were at my loss. It was the most incredible revelation to me and made me feel humble that the staff of the Lyford Cay Club—men and women, some I knew, some I didn't—took the time to come to the cottage to give me their condolences, mostly with a warm hug of compassion or tears of sadness for Tara and me.

After the Doctor had signed the death certificate confirming Patrick had died of a massive cerebral hemorrhage, his body was taken to Butler's Funeral Chapel. Peter Rickard said he and Jan would take me to witness Patrick's cremation. It was Patrick's wish to be cremated. I chose to wear a flowery dress. I knew Patrick was in heaven, and I associated heaven with lots and lots of beautiful flowers. It was peaceful in the chapel as I once again said good-bye to my man, reminiscing that it was just over five years when Patrick had had his first stroke and how determined he was to be around for me and our baby. He had fought so hard against many painful indignities. I was proud of him and knew it was his innate control, discipline and love for us that had kept him going, until he decided it was time for him to leave. I also felt he had made a pact with God! As we left the chapel, Peter said he would collect the ashes the next day. I was grateful to have the friendship of that kind and compassionate couple.

Tania flew out to be with me, and together with Nan, attended Tara's last day at the Lyford Cay School. I wanted everything to be totally normal for Tara. Naturally, it was strange and sad for all of us not to have Patrick's presence, and every so often Tara would cry a little, but I would console her, saying that her daddy had a lot of pain, and he was happy in heaven, but that he always loved her and would be looking after her. The friends we had made, especially Tara and Nan's friends, came to give their condolences. Peter brought me my precious ashes and made me laugh when he recounted his conversation with Patrick while Patrick's urn sat beside him on the front seat of his car; and to this day he talks about the memory. I was grateful that Patrick had died so peacefully and as near to paradise as possible.

47

It was time for us to leave Nassau. I had kept the airline reservations for April eighth, two days after Tara finished at Lyford Cay School. Tara, Nan and I boarded British Airways. There were just a couple of passengers in first class, for which I was immensely grateful. As the plane took off and I sipped my champagne, I felt a sense of physical relaxation and a vivid realisation that I was carrying the ashes of my Patrick. I went upstairs to the empty bar, and whether it was the altitude or the relief of being on my own, I dissolved in tears and cried and cried. My heart felt it would break as the sadness enveloped me with the knowledge that my man would never be with me again. I hadn't cried since Patrick's death, and although my heart was heavy, I guess I didn't really accept that he was no longer with me.

I couldn't help but wonder why he felt the urgency to show me as much of the world as he could, to thrust me into situations where I would learn. So many things went through my mind; perhaps he knew our time together would be short. He had taught me so much. Now I had to carry on without him and bring up our daughter the way he would want. I regained my composure, though I was grateful to be able to let go, and returned to Nan and Tara. There was much to be done, and Patrick's funeral was paramount on my mind.

I had talked to Canon Albion from Nassau and wanted Patrick to be buried at St. Edward's with the rest of his family. I also wanted Canon Maurice O'Leary to officiate at the funeral, and of course, our lovely Father Peter Blake. Canon Albion said he would organise everything, and we agreed for the funeral to take place on April sixteenth. On our arrival back at London airport, I had Michael meet us and take us to The Old Farm House from where I sent out invitations to friends and booked the restaurant at a local hotel for the wake.

On April sixteenth, the three priests concelebrated a moving requiem Mass for Patrick, and it was the first time I had heard the poignant hymn "Panis Angelicus." I did not want to show any tears, especially in front of Tara, as I wanted her to believe her daddy was safe and happy, which I knew he was. I made sure that Romulus was with us in the church, as Patrick loved him so much, as did we all; he was very much family. Patrick was buried near his mother, father and siblings, and I had a pink Portuguese marble gravestone made in the shape of a large heart as his tombstone. I put my beloved husband's ashes to rest in the churchyard of St. Edward's church, where he had been an acolyte as a boy and where we had a loving and emotional wedding five years earlier. He had donated the baptismal area to St. Edward's Church in gratitude for his memories and long association.

Patrick had worried that I would be alone when he died, but I had my Tara. However, my other half had gone, and I had to rebuild myself into a whole again. Life had to go on. I noticed the right side of my fringe had turned white and later on was told that it was due to the shock of Patrick's demise. I was lucky that my whole head of hair hadn't turned white.

In May my family came to visit us at The Old Farm House. Sylvan now had her second little girl, Kenia. It was good to see everyone enjoying themselves. Nan, as always, was wonderful, and Romulus liked all the attention. Nan then went on holiday with her sister, and I had the pleasure of taking care of Tara and Romulus by myself. Tara had to continue at the Pinewood Nursery School. I was anxious my daughter would not have to suffer the changes I went through as a child. I wanted her life to be consistent and secure. So for that reason we stayed on at The Old Farm House.

One day I was delighted to receive a phone call from Peter and Jan, saying they could visit for the night. When we had put Stephanie, Michael and Tara to bed, the three of us spent the evening laughing, crying and remembering.

For Tara's fifth birthday, I decided to have Mr. Magic perform again. He was such a success the first time, and now that the children were a year older, I felt they would appreciate him even more. I was right; he was magical again. I invited a couple of the sisters from Mount Alvernia to the party, and of course, Grandpa. My staff was now a local couple, Bill and Ivy, who didn't live on the property, except if we were away, and then stayed to take care of Romulus. They too enjoyed Tara's party.

After Patrick's emotionally moving funeral, Canon Albion broke the news to me he had lung cancer and only six months before he would join Patrick. I invited him to stay at The Old Farm House for as long as he wanted. He needed to have quiet and rest and not be available to his parishioners. His wonderful cousin Agnes was with him most of the time, especially towards the end. Canon Albion died in September, six months after Patrick, and the church gave him an enormous funeral. Gordon Albion was well known for his broadcasts and books. To me he was just a marvelous friend, especially to Patrick.

Christmas 1979 would soon be with us, and I attended the end-of-school nativity play at Pinewood Nursery School, which was so precious. Nan, Tara and I then went up to London for a few days to Christmas shop and to see "Sooty" at the Mayfair Theatre. I invited our chauffeur's wife and young daughter to join us, the two little girls were totally engrossed in watching the cute show and loved their first visit to the theatre.

I was determined to keep life as normal as possible for Tara. Christmas is always such a magical and exciting time for children, and I wanted us to be at The Old Farm House. I decorated a large tree and arranged everything as I had always done while Patrick was alive. Grandpa came to stay and Agnes joined us, together with her little King Charles spaniel, Gwenie. She was still so sad that her beloved cousin Gordon was no longer around. I was really pleased she was with us for Christmas. We both understood our painful emptiness.

48

In the New Year of 1980, I wondered what I would do with myself, as Tara was at school, and I felt restless. I was also missing Patrick, so I arranged to visit Peter and Jan, who were now in Kuala Lumpur, and from there I would travel on to see Hans in Manila. I needed to be away. I had many things on my mind to think about, and I felt a change of scenery and being with close friends would help me.

At the beginning of January we went up to London, and I took Tara, Nan and Tara's godfather to a happy Christmas show, "Holiday on Ice" at Wembley Stadium. It was such a super evening and an extravaganza. A few days later, I left on my trip. Tara and Nan would stay in London for another couple of weeks and then return to The Old Farm House for Tara to attend school. I had made all the arrangements for Nan and Tara to be well taken care of during my absence, including Romulus. I was very fortunate to have a marvelous doctor in the country and a wonderful chauffeur who would ferry Tara back and forth to school and be available to do any errands for Nan. Bill and Ivy were very reliable, and Romulus had an excellent vet who would make house calls any time day or night.

As I boarded Concorde, I knew my family would be all right and in God's protection. Robert Lancaster, the special agent for British Airways, greeted me and showed me to my seat. I told him how much I appreciated all of the kind assistance that British Airways had shown the O'Leary family over the years. Robert, his wife, Carmen, and their three children later became close friends. I was excited as I sat in the cabin of the Concorde, thinking how lucky I was to be a passenger on that supersonic aircraft. I wished that my Patrick was with me— though I knew he was—he would always be with me.

Taking off on Concorde was exhilarating, and I was spoiled by the cabin staff, who made sure that I had copious amounts of their delicious champagne. Robert had told them to take good care of me, which they did, and even gave me a bottle of champagne as I deplaned. I was pleased that the seat next to me was empty, as I wanted to be on my own. I had a lot to think about—what would be beneficial for Tara and what Patrick would want me to do. We had never discussed how he would have liked our future to be without him. Once I did ask him if there was anything special he wanted me to do when he left me. He just said that he knew I would do whatever was best for myself and for Tara. Being away from everything familiar would, I hoped, ease the pain in my heart and help me make the right decisions.

My flight on Concorde was fabulous and came to an end in Bahrain, where I connected with Singapore Airlines on to Singapore. I was immensely impressed with the fantastic in-flight service of Singapore Airlines, possibly the best I had ever experienced. It was strange being in Singapore alone, and the memories of our visit in 1968 came rushing back. I stayed overnight at the Shangri-La Hotel. I just didn't feel like staying at Raffles, though our stay there was such a lovely memory. After roaming around the hotel in awe of the magnificent orchids I decided to stay in my room for dinner. I felt too nervous to sit in a restaurant on my own.

The next day I was on my way to Kuala Lumpur to see my friends Jan and Peter Rickard. They were both at the airport to meet me, and I was excited to see them again. Peter was the managing director of the Regent Hotel. Kuala Lumpur was a mélange of many ethnic groups, Malays, Chinese, Indian, and Eurasians, and therefore, many mosques and temples. Peter and Jan made sure I went to Petaling Street lined with interesting stalls selling everything, and the aromas that flowed out of the tiny restaurants were deliciously overpowering. We also went to Dataram Merdeka (formerly the Selangor Club Padang), which was once the focal point and cricket green of the British Colonial presence in Malaysia. It was the social centre for the Brits, and it was there that the Union Jack was lowered at one minute past twelve on August thirty-first in 1957, and Malaysia became independent.

On one of the days of my stay, Peter and Jan wanted us to drive out of KL to Malacca. The ninety-minute drive was interesting and Malacca was full of Dutch history with beautiful old ruins. The Chinese temples, shops and houses were of great interest, and Jebat Street was intriguing with so many antiques and handicrafts. On our way back, Peter realised we were running a little late, so he instructed our driver to try to get back to KL in time for him to make a meeting he had scheduled. Our little driver was excellent and was driving along at a fair speed, so we were sure Peter would arrive in time. As we were approaching a corner, however, two enormous juggernauts were passing each other. Our driver had no choice but to drive in between the two with inches to spare on either side.

I was sitting in the front next to the driver and kept very quiet, repeating in my mind, Jesus, help! Our guardian angels were with us. After we made it through, I looked back to Peter and Jan, and their faces were ashen. Arriving back at the hotel, we had a bottle of wine to settle our frayed nerves. It was definitely a close call.

The time arrived for me to leave my friends, and we spent the last evening together reminiscing between tears and laughter. Peter took me to the airport and was with me while I boarded Philippine Airlines for Manila. I was the only passenger in first class and therefore had the full attention of the cabin staff. Alighting at Manila airport, I was anxious to see Hans, as the airport was in bedlam, everyone everywhere! Once I saw Hans all was well, and with his contacts, I was able to make a hasty departure into his large convertible. I was soon checking in at the Manila Intercontinental Hotel and then went with Hans to dinner at his amazing home, which he shared with his son and two gorgeous little granddaughters.

The following day was my thirty-eighth birthday. Nan had managed to post my birthday cards from Tara in time so they were waiting for me. What a treat to open those adorable cards and see a beautiful photo of my girl. The evening of my birthday, Hans had invited many of his friends to celebrate the occasion. He threw a fabulous party for me in his tropical garden. Hans, despite being an atheist, was an interesting and good friend and made me feel like family. He even took me to Mass on Sunday where Cardinal Sin officiated. I spent much time with his little granddaughters in his home, which seemed more like a museum, filled with antiques from India, Thailand and Hong Kong.

During my stay I was thrilled that Peter and Jan had to visit Manila. I introduced them to Hans, and I know they have never forgotten him. It was soon time for Hans to be on his shopping expedition. So I accompanied him to Hong Kong. Being with Hans in Hong Kong was different to being with my Patrick! Anyway, I love Hong Kong, and it was interesting to spend a couple of days there with Hans. I was used to staying at the Mandarin Hotel, and soon realised that Hans, although well off, was also very careful about spending his money on hotel accommodations. He would rather spend it on an antique Buddha. Anyway, I didn't suffer too much and enjoyed our trips back and forth on the Star Ferry.

I had kept in touch with Kai Bong and Brenda and wrote to them that Hans and I would be in Hong Kong and would be happy to see them. They kindly invited us to dinner and told us to meet them at a particular restaurant. Hans was impressed when the gold Rolls Royce drew-up and out jumped the chauffeur in his white sharkskin uniform to help Kai-Bong and Brenda from the car. We had a marvelous dinner; the restaurant was jumping, and Hans was immersed in conversation with my flamboyant friends. Brenda reminded me of our meeting with the fortuneteller who had foretold everything correctly.

The following day we were invited to visit their home, Villa D'Oro, and indeed it was. Everything in the house was gold. All the window trimmings were draped in gold, as well as all the bathroom fittings, including an imposing gold toilet. The gold dinner service glittered; even Hans, whose home was filled with beautiful antiques, was speechless. I think he wished he had all that. Brenda and Kai-Bong were so charming, and despite their wealth, made us feel like old friends.

Tara was always uppermost in my mind, I sent her lots of postcards, and we spoke every Sunday, which was wonderful, as I missed her, but I knew this journey was important for me.

Leaving Hong Kong, we travelled to Bangkok to meet Hans's friends and for him to do more buying. I saw a part of Bangkok that I hadn't seen with Patrick, and I was not impressed with all the noise, the traffic and the polluted air, but it was in fact the real Bangkok, so I made the most of it, but was happy to only spend a couple of days there and was grateful I had visited in 1968 and seen much more of the cultural scene.

While we were at Bangkok airport to check in at the Air India desk, I was surprised Hans had bought us economy tickets to Bombay. Patrick had spoiled me and had told me that I should only travel first class. Anyway, I couldn't accept travelling economy on Air India and informed Hans that we were travelling first class and upgraded our tickets. The plane was very delayed, so how happy I was, and Hans too, to relax in the luxury of the first class accommodations where the service and meals were just splendid. That incident became a joke with us, but Hans was Hans, and economy was good enough for him, but not for me.

We stayed at the famous Taj Hotel in Bombay, now Mumbai. Hans had some wealthy friends who invited us to a soiree in their opulent home. What a magnificent evening. The ladies looked resplendent in their gorgeous saris and gold accessories, and the handsome men were beautifully attired. The food was copious and delicious, and I felt I was in another world.

As I was in Bombay, I called the Mother Superior and asked if I could visit the convent. The day following the sumptuous evening with Hans's friends, I came down to earth and saw the real Bombay. I went to visit the Catholic convent where the wonderful nuns would go out each day looking for babies that had been left in the gutters and took them into their care. Patrick had donated to that charity for years, and I continued after his death. I was so impressed with what I saw. The dormitories were immaculately clean, and the children were happy and intelligent. There were many tiny babies that had been rescued in the last few days. I left the convent feeling humble and happy that we had made our contributions to the nuns over the years.

Hans and I walked for a bit in the streets and in no time were surrounded by little children who were begging, children who could hardly walk, children who didn't have all their fingers, as they had purposely been amputated in order to attract more sympathy when they begged—such poor, neglected children. The poverty was terrible. I thought about the previous evening with all the luxury and wealth as I witnessed the awful other side of humanity. I was very sad and thought it was terribly unfair that the rich were so rich and the poor were so very poor. Hans told me that it was the life in India and there was no one who could make everything right, least of all me.

Hans wanted us to go on to Hydrabad and Goa, but I had had enough. I wanted to return to my little Tara. Hans asked me to move to Manila with Tara and live with him, but I declined. There was no way that I would live in Manila. Hans was a good guy, very charming, handsome and an interesting man, born in Hawaii of American/German parents. He was a confirmed atheist and a religious rebel, who during World War II was transported to Berga, a concentration camp in Eastern Germany, and ended up cheating death in Stalag 9-C at Bad Stulza, part of the Buchenwald complex. His terrible ordeals and memoirs are found in "Soldiers and Slaves" by Roger Cohen and "Forever a Soldier" by Tom Wiener. Both books I can highly recommend, though the content is deeply horrendous.

Hans had lived in Manila for many years and was well known in Manila society. He was especially known for his luncheon parties. He would entertain a myriad of fascinating individuals, the cream of Manila society, and any VIPs who were visiting. I was flattered he wanted me to live with him, but a Catholic living with an atheist was impossible. I loved Hans as a dear friend, but there was no way I could make a life with him.

I told him I wanted to return to London. After doing some more shopping and having bought a small silver statue of the White Tara, I packed my suitcase and said good-bye to Hans. My wobbly taxi drove from the hotel to the airport through the empty streets of Bombay in the wee hours of the morning, where I noticed all the tents by the side of the road where the poor people lived, and I was just sickened by such awful poverty. Growing up in Ceylon, I never saw any beggars or any real signs of extreme poverty, except when I saw the coolies in the lines on Meddecombra tea estate, but to see that much terrible poverty everywhere was unsettling to me.

I was relieved to arrive at the airport, and going through customs and immigration, I couldn't help but think of Patrick, who told me a story of his departure from Bombay many years before. He said he was interrogated as to why he was carrying so much money in different currencies; he finally told the curious Indian officer that he was a collector of money, like a stamp collector, so with a laugh and wag of the head, he was allowed to go.

I managed to get through the customs and immigration all right and was on the verge of a body search when the woman said: "Oh, my goodness me. You smell so good."

I beamed at her and told her it had to be my eau de toilette Opium, and I gave her my small bottle. I never did have the body search. I was very happy to board British Airways for my flight home and in time to hug my darling Tara for Valentine's Day!

49

Tara had been busy colouring cards, not only for Valentine's Day, but also to welcome me home; I had lots to look at on my return. How lucky I was to have the love of my precious little daughter, to have my loyal Romulus, and such a gift in Nanny Josephine Featherstone. That night as I was on my knees beside my bed, my heart was filled with gratitude to both Jesus and my Patrick. I felt so blessed. I was safely home after an interesting trip and was grateful to have such good friends.

In early March I received confirmation from St. Mary's Convent, Hampstead in London that Tara had been accepted to the school for the September term. Tara was doing well at Pinewood Nursery School, and I later learned that the school would be closing for good after the summer term. The little school was run by the head mistress, Miss Duggan, and was an excellent start for Tara, as the degree of teaching was exceptional.

I had promised Tara I would take her to Nassau and then to Disney World for her three-week Easter holidays. Nan was going to spend the holidays with her sister, and Bill and Ivy would look after Romulus and stay at The Old Farm House.

On March thirtieth, Tara and I were once again on British Airways headed for Nassau and for the Lyford Cay Club. That time we stayed in one of the club bedrooms. I felt Patrick's presence with me and knew it is what he would have wanted for us. It was the first time I had the opportunity to have Tara alone, just the two of us, and it was wonderful. Tara was a vivacious five-year-old, full of fun and energy. Naturally, we felt comfortable at the club and were warmly welcomed by the staff. The management was new; it was strange not to have Peter and Jan around.

290 | Diana O'Leary

We stayed in Nassau for the two weeks over Easter and attended the Easter ball together, generally enjoying all the many activities arranged for the children and spending much time on the glorious beach. Tara made new friends and saw her old ones, meeting Todd again. Todd was in awe of Tara, and Tara enjoyed all the attention from that adorable little boy. It was delightful to see them together and for Tara to confess coyly to me that Todd was her boyfriend, but it was Todd who was completely smitten with Tara. As our two weeks were coming to an end, I mentioned to Todd's mother that when they visit London Todd must come to stay, so the two little people were happy knowing they would see each other again.

On April thirteenth a very excited Tara said good-bye to Todd and now focused on her flight to Orlando. We were on our way to the Magic Kingdom and Tara's first visit to America, which was also exciting. I had reserved a room at the Travel Lodge Tower, as I thought it would be the most amusing place for a five-year-old to stay, and it was the home of Sleepy Bear. Sleepy Bear would make several appearances a day talking to the children, mainly in the early evening, and the children, including Tara, were all in love with him.

During the day and for four days running we were experiencing the Magic Kingdom—every ride and many ice cream cones. Nothing was left undone. It seemed that the magic was never ending. In the evenings we had dinner in the hotel and then went to watch the Sleepy Bear show, which we saw three times. Our visit to Disney World and the Magic Kingdom had been an enormous success, and I loved every minute of our precious time together, despite going to sleep early and waking early. It was such a joy to be with my Tara and observe her experiencing all that the Disney World had to offer. Tara also made it possible for me to get behind the wheel of a car again. She wanted to go on the bumper cars, but I was reluctant due to my accident and still fearful of driving. But then I decided for the sake of my daughter I would do it, and we had several exciting drives around the course. Due to that experience I lost the fear of being behind the wheel.

On our flight back home, I told Tara I would be selling The Old Farm House, as we didn't need two homes. At first she was upset and especially wanted to know what would happen to Romulus. That question was a heavy weight in my heart too, but I felt as we had a few years before the sale of the house and Romulus was getting old, I would have some time to face the awful prospect of what I was to do with my precious dog. I told Tara we were not in any hurry to leave The Old Farm House—until it was time for her to attend her new school in London—so for now while she finished at Pinewood Nursery school, we would enjoy our beautiful home and our Romulus.

We had a perfect summer and the garden of The Old Farm House was breathtaking. Vanessa came to stay and Grandpa was frequently with us. Tara was anxious to learn how to ride her two-wheel bicycle. I spent a few days running beside her. Finally, after showing impatience and frustration towards herself and her mother, she was able to ride her bike, such jubilation for us both.

During the first week of July, we had a gentleman, Bob and his lady friend, prospect the house; they both loved it. They were getting ready to leave when Tara ran into a piece of furniture, which encased the radiator, and the top of a nail went into her knee. Well, panic stations. I had to ask them to find their way out and was on the telephone to our wonderful doctor. Tara was incredibly brave. I made her lie down on the chesterfield and told her not to move her leg. I knew that the nail had not entered her knee, but the top had torn her skin. Dr. Richard was with us within twenty minutes, and within another twenty minutes, Tara's knee was all stitched up.

Tara insisted on returning to school the next day, as there was only a short time before the end of term. Naturally, she received much attention, not only from the teachers, but all of her little friends—especially her three boyfriends, which she referred to as number one husband, number two and number three—very funny! A special chair was provided for her, as she was not allowed to walk too much, so Miss Tara was in her element. Sadly, on July eighteenth, 1980, Miss

Duggan and her brilliant Pinewood Nursery School closed. I was so grateful that Tara's first schooling had been at that special school.

By the end of July, we continued to enjoy our country home with blissful summer weather. Tara's knee was almost mended, and then she had chicken pox. When Tara was all better, Catherine, Tara's best friend, who lived in the next village from us, often came over to play. A few of her boyfriends also visited. The more we all enjoyed the summer, the more difficult it was for me to realise that our beautiful home would belong to someone else.

On August twenty-first, I thought it would be a nice treat for Tara to invite Catherine and her parents to Battersea Park to see David Smarts Circus. I reserved a box and of course, our Nan was with us. What a success. Tara and Catherine were in awe—their first circus. There were only a few weeks left before we had to return to London, so we filled in the warm summer days with many friends and family.

We returned to London in early September, as I had to prepare for Tara to start at St. Mary's Convent. Tara was excited that she had to wear a uniform, and she looked adorable in it. I travelled back and forth to the country, and Tara and Nan came down for the weekends, as Tara attended her new school during the week. Hans was visiting England and spent a weekend with us. He enjoyed being with Tara and Catherine, as he loved children and felt very much at home. Again he asked me to bring Tara and live with him in Manila, but I told him that I just couldn't do that and we would always remain good friends. After Hans's departure my mother came to visit, and Vanessa came with her. We were all excited, as Vanessa was five months pregnant.

50

Tara celebrated her sixth birthday in London with her new friends from St. Mary's Convent. The show "Annie" was playing in the theatre, and I thought the girls would enjoy going to the matinee, so Tara had eleven friends join her for the show. Shortly thereafter, the autumn term was at an end, and Tara did not have to return until early in January.

Our dear friend Tania, who was now divorced from her husband, suggested the three of us spend Christmas in St. Moritz. Well, I am not one for the cold, but I thought it would be a good idea to introduce Tara to skiing. My first responsibility was to see that our beloved nanny was comfortable. We had been working on trying to find her a council flat in London, and to our delight, we were told she had a sweet little flat allotted to her just off Baker Street. So I made sure Nan had everything she required to furnish her new home and that she would spend Christmas with her sister. Having given instructions to Bill and Ivy not to let anyone look around The Old Farm House during my absence, and to take special care of Romulus, I reserved our rooms at the Badrutt's Palace Hotel in St. Moritz. I would never have dreamed of going there by myself, but Tania knew her way around, having been to St. Moritz many times in the past.

We had a magical Christmas and New Year's Eve party. Tara loved ice-skating with Tania, but didn't do very well with her skiing lessons. The large indoor swimming pool was a great favourite with us, as were the elegant evenings we had in the dining room. The three of us were most glamorous! As we entered the dining room one evening, I was dumbfounded to see my Arab friend, who had been so kind to me and my family, and who had given me the trip of a lifetime to Beirut and the Holy Land when I was nineteen years old. He was dining with his two brothers. We went over to say hello, but he wasn't enthusiastic to see me, and I didn't see him again. However, the meeting brought back a flood of happy memories.

We enjoyed the rest of the evening and had the pleasure of a little boy called Anthony Ali Aziz, a special friend of Tara's who joined us for dinner most evenings. Those little six year olds were out of Vogue, so gorgeous. Many fun activities were organised for the children. In fact, our vacation was most memorable. Needless to say, my thoughts were often with Patrick and in gratitude to him and Jesus for all my blessings.

When we returned to London, we went to visit Nan in her new flat, which was cosy and she appeared very content. Tara had to return to school on January ninth. I didn't want Nan to feel neglected, so I would ask her to come over and help with little jobs in the apartment. I also suggested that she might like to help Vanessa with her new baby when it arrived. On Valentine's Day, Tara and I went over to Vanessa's and spent the afternoon with her and Mother and the next day my sister gave birth to her little boy, Marc Dexter. A beautiful little boy. Vanessa was over the moon with happiness. My gift to her was a two-week holiday at the Lyford Cay Club in Nassau for her and baby Marc.

I returned to The Old Farm House while Nan took care of Tara in London. It was a traumatic time for me. Bob was unable to buy our home, but he brought a couple with him who said they would purchase the house. I am not a good businesswoman and virtually gave away our home, together with almost all the furniture. I liked the potential owners but was sad to hear the buyer was suffering from cancer.

I stayed alone in my country home with Romulus, making lists, packing personal belongings, writing letters and attending to many other things. So many memories, so many happy times. How much we had all loved The Old Farm House. I had Ivy and Bill come each day to look after the house and garden. I made the lists of all the things I would personally take from our home and prepared everything else for the removal firm.

The awful time had now come for me to move out, but before I could, I had to say good-bye to my beloved Romulus. I couldn't take him to the apartment in London; he wouldn't have been happy cooped up, and I knew I would be travelling. I also knew Romulus had a severe ear infection that was bothering him for a while, and the vet told me if I were to stay on at The Old Farm House, he may live for another few years, but would need constant medical attention for his ears. So the vet advised me that as I was thinking of leaving the country and as Romulus was almost thirteen years old, the best and kindest thing would be to have him put down. I knew she would never have suggested me to do that if there wasn't a good reason. In fact, I believe she would have offered to look after Romulus herself.

The day came when I had to say good-bye to my adored Romulus, and I held him tight, telling him how much I loved him. He looked at me as if to say: "What are you doing to me?"

I was sick; my heart ached so much. How painful it is to lose such a loved and devoted friend who gave so much unconditional love. I felt so terribly sad and wished I had Patrick to console me. I had lost my Patrick, now my dearest Romulus, and was saying good-bye to The Old Farm House. After the vet left, I went to the bathroom and threw up. I was trembling, but had to get myself together as Michael our chauffeur was on his way to collect me to take me to London. On my drive to London, I was relieved to have such a compassionate chauffeur who just let me weep.

I regained my composure as I arrived at the flat and was glad to be back with Tara and Nan. It was difficult to think about the pain in my heart when I saw their happy faces, but we did have a tearful session later in remembrance of Romulus. It took me more than two weeks to regain some peace in my heart. I felt really terrible about saying good-bye to Romulus in that way, but I hoped that despite his incarceration in the kennels, that we had given him all the love and devotion he deserved in his life.

Tara and I flew to Nassau for the Easter holidays on March thirtieth, 1981. In many ways it was like returning to our home in the sun. All the staff made us very welcome, and as always I had many beautiful memories of being at Lyford Cay and knowing that Patrick went to heaven while he was staying at that earthly paradise.

The Lyford Cay Club was a happy place, and as usual, Tara made lots of new friends and caught up with her old buddies, enjoying a very social life. Tara had recently learned how to play backgammon and was extremely good, so much so that a couple of the adults we met asked her to teach them; she was taking after her father, who was a terrific backgammon player.

Our beautiful holiday was soon over, and we were back in London for Tara to attend the summer term at St. Mary's Convent.

Although Bob didn't buy The Old Farm House, we became close friends. His friendship helped me get through the sale of the house, and it made the whole departure so much easier, as Bob's friends did buy the house. Bob and I spent some happy times together. We travelled on the first passenger trip to Venice on the romantic Orient Express, and stayed for a few days at the resplendent Hotel Danieli. When we returned to London, he invited me to join his friends to ladies' day at Ascot, and I won seventy pounds! Bob was generous and full of fun. Tara loved him and through him I became close friends with Dawn, the wife of the new owner. Dawn's husband died of cancer shortly after moving into The Old Farm House.

Dawn often invited Tara and me back to our old home. I am not one for remorse or regret. Once I had decided to do something, I believed in my heart that, with God's grace, it was the right thing and did not dwell on my decision; but I retained beautiful memories. I was therefore grateful to revisit my old abode on many occasions.

51

End of term arrived and with it parents' day. Both Nan and Bob accompanied me to St. Mary's Convent to see Tara's work and say hello to the nuns. I knew Tara was progressing beautifully with her education. St Mary's, Hampstead, was the sister convent to St. Mary's that I had attended in Gillingham, Dorset. I was content that Tara was receiving a high degree of education combined with the discipline she required and all of it in a Catholic school.

For the long summer holidays I arranged for us to go to the British seaside, Knoll House at Studland Bay, which was famous for catering to families. I invited both Dad and Mother to join us and Vanessa and Marc too, and Nan, of course. As Dad and Mother lived separate lives, they were able to be civil when they were together and really enjoyed being by the seaside, especially with their grandchildren. Mother had decided she no longer wished to live in Palma, so I found her a little bed-sitter in a perfect location in the centre of London, where she was comfortable and had everything she required. Dad was also happy in his accommodations, which were not too far from me.

When Tara returned to school for the autumn term, I decided to accept an invitation from Peter and Jan to visit them in Toronto. Peter was the managing director of the King Edward Hotel. I asked Nan to take care of Tara while I was away, and I knew that Vanessa would be only too happy to give her a hand with her homework from time to time. I had always wanted to be a passenger on the liner the QE2 and booked myself a cabin to New York; I would then fly from there to Toronto. I was nervous about travelling on my own, but realised that was my life now.

When I embarked on the ocean liner, I was asked if I wished to sit alone in the Queen's dining room or join a table with other passengers. That was a difficult decision for me to make, as I wasn't used to being with people I didn't know. I had been secluded from any sort of public life for a long time. I finally summoned up the courage to say I would sit at a table with eight other passengers.

The crossing from Southampton to New York was fabulous, and I met some interesting people. I mostly enjoyed the delicious food and wine, and the abundant servings of beluga caviar at dinner were almost decadent. It was fun exchanging conversation with the other people at the dinner table. The only problem was that two of the married men were attracted to me and would come knocking on my cabin door in the middle of the night. I was glad for them that they didn't do it at the same time. I told them separately the following day not to disturb me anymore. I had no interest in either of them.

I met a handsome young man who was travelling in the cheapest accommodations way down below, and I asked him if he would kindly accompany me to the Captain's cocktail party. During the evening he told me that he was on his way to New York to meet his girlfriend. I was comforted by his presence, as I was invited to the large suite of one of the couples I sat with at dinner. They had asked me to join them for cocktails before the Captain's party, and I was happy to take my new young friend with me. The best champagne was being served, and then we were both invited to partake of what looked to me like a bowl of salt. I had no idea what it was. My escort whispered to me that it was cocaine. Cocaine? I'd never heard of it. He told me that he "didn't do it." We both declined the offer. I did notice that our hosts were becoming rather intoxicated. I learned that Charles was not married but had been with his woman friend for many years.

The Captain's party was just another cocktail party, which I really didn't enjoy much, but I did enjoy the company of my attractive escort. It was a shame that he was in love. I thanked him for his company and proceeded to the Queen's dining room for dinner. I took my seat at our table and made no reference to the cocaine.

Cruising gently into New York harbour was exciting. I was up early as we entered on a cool and misty dawn, just as the sun was rising, and through my window I could see the Statue of Liberty. I had told the couple who had offered me the cocaine that I had a few hours to kill before my flight to Toronto, and they insisted I join them for lunch. After we had secured our luggage, they escorted me to the longest limousine I had ever seen. We did some sightseeing of New York, had a good lunch, and then I was taken to the airport. Shortly after takeoff, I received a note from the flight attendant. It was from Charles wishing me a happy time in Toronto and he hoped to see me again.

Being in Toronto with Peter and Jan was marvelous. I felt then and feel now, how fortunate I am to have such lovely friends. While I was there, knowing Jan and Peter were busy, I decided to take an excursion to the Niagara Falls. With my old fear of waterfalls I had to know if I would be able to see that amazing sight up close. It was an experience and I have to admit I wouldn't really want to do it again. I was in awe of the majesty of the cascading water. It was frightening and yet mesmerising. I left feeling happy that I had had the courage to witness the incredible sight all by myself.

I flew back to London from Toronto and checked in with my parents, who were both okay, as was Vanessa and Marc, who were now living in London. For Tara's seventh birthday I decided to hire a room at the Lancaster Hotel and invite all her class from the convent. I thought a disco party would be fun, and by the time Tara had counted all her friends, we had invited thirty little people to dance away the evening. Mother and Dad, Canon O'Leary and Tara's godfather, Paul, not to mention our dear Nan, were all in the party spirit.

St. Mary's Convent had invited the parents to the end-of-term Christmas Nativity play. It was a lovely performance, and Tara was a shepherd. I was happy with Tara's report, which arrived before we left London for the Christmas holidays.

We were on our way to Los Angeles to stay with our friend Basil, who was now divorced. Basil's daughter, Heather, the same age as Tara, was with us while we were there, and the big excitement was to visit Disneyland. The girls had a marvelous time, and being near

Christmas, there were many additional processions and other exciting things to see.

After a long and rather exhausting day, we said good-bye to Heather, who returned to stay with her mother over Christmas, and prepared to leave with Basil for Palm Springs the next day. After what seemed like a long and uneventful drive in his Rolls Royce, we arrived at the house Basil shared with some close friends. As Basil and his friends didn't celebrate Christmas, I had to do some hasty shopping for a tree and other essentials to make sure Tara had a Christmas and that Santa Claus had not forgotten her. Basil was most kind helping to make it festive for us and even took me to midnight Mass, which wouldn't have been Christmas had I not attended the birth of Jesus.

Our stay in Palm Springs was different, as sharing a house with other people who were not close friends was a little strange; despite that we had a fun stay with lots of good food and wine, and Tara excelled at beating everyone at backgammon. The weather was lovely, as were the surroundings. The house was big, and for the first time I saw a real walk-in closet, which was huge. It was clear to me that Basil was in love with me and wanted the two of us to live with him, which was very flattering, but I wasn't ready to accept his proposal.

Tara and I returned to London in time for her to resume her studies at St. Mary's and prepare for her First Holy Communion. Neither of my sisters could attend Tara's First Communion, but I was delighted that Mum and Dad, together with Nan and Tara's godmother, Christine, and godfather, Paul, were able to witness the holy and important occasion. It was moving and beautiful to see the gorgeous seven year olds receive the body and blood of Jesus Christ.

After Mass we went to have a celebration lunch at the Ritz Hotel, and our friend Bob joined us. I had also invited Tara's best friend, Catherine, so that she had a pal of her own age with her. In a way it seemed fitting that we were in the ornate dining room of the Ritz to continue to celebrate such a special day. Tara looked lovely in her beautiful white dress, and as it was a balmy, sunny day, I was able to take lots of photographs in the garden. It was a happy day, especially for me, as I remembered with such clarity the day of my First Communion. I was also thrilled that Mother and Dad were with us, and everything went so smoothly.

A few weeks later, I had to face the fact Tara needed her tonsils and

Tara at the Ritz Hotel in her First Communion dress

adenoids removed. Tara had also inherited Patrick's cauliflower ears, so our doctor suggested that while she was in the hospital, she should also have a cosmetic operation to bring her ears closer to her head. Of course I agreed, as my beautiful daughter would not want her father's ears later in her life. We checked in to the London Clinic, and I stayed in the room with Tara for the duration. She was a little surprised to find she had a bandage around her head, having thought that she was only going to suffer a bit with a sore throat.

My friend Dawn wanted to know the name of the plastic surgeon who performed Tara's cosmetic operation, and my introduction was the start of a beautiful love affair for Dawn.

It wasn't long before Tara's social life returned. Occasionally we would go back to The Old Farm House at Dawn's invitation. I was grateful to her that we could still enjoy a visit to the country house. It felt familiar to return to our old home, especially as I had left almost all of our furniture. Dawn had changed some of the interior of the house to suit her requirements. The exquisite indoor swimming pool was now a billiard room. I had no remorse. To me The Old Farm House was now Dawn's home, and I was a visitor. Dawn not only had myself and Tara as guests, but invited Dad and little Tania, who was staying with us, and also invited Tara's friend Catherine to come over for the day. Catherine's home was near The Old Farm House, so whenever we visited, Dawn arranged that she should spend the day with Tara. It was lovely to see the children enjoy themselves so much. As I watched Dawn's corgi Vladimir, I thought of my Romulus and knew he was safely with Patrick and Remus.

52

For the summer holidays I decided it would be nice for us to visit Sylvan, Tania and Kenia in Palma. I invited Mother and Dad to join us. We had those family reunions fairly frequently during the holidays. I felt I was in a position to give a little happiness to my family. Sylvan, alas, was now divorced from her husband, and she needed love and assistance to take care of her beautiful little girls. We would spend a wonderful couple of weeks in a hotel and have lots of fun swimming during the day and dancing during the night.

Back in London, Tara celebrated her eighth birthday and asked five of her closest friends from school to join her for the afternoon matinee show of "The American Dream Machine," and afterwards to the apartment for a super tea party where Nan, Vanessa, and Marc, Mother and Dad, Godfather Paul, and our dear friend Tania joined us. Tara was so delighted to be eight years old. She had always wanted to be eight and that day decided she wanted to be an actress.

For Christmas I invited the whole family to our apartment to celebrate. Apart from my parents and sisters, together with Tania and Kenia, Marc's nanny was there and my friend Tania. Tara and I started off the day by going to Mass at our Church of the Immaculate Conception. We left Nan busy in the kitchen with the turkey. I had decorated the tree and it did look fabulous and heavy with gifts for everyone. I never forgot to thank my husband and Jesus. That would be our last family Christmas together.

My friend Alistair, the owner of the famous Guinea Pub and Restaurant, and boxing companion of Patrick's, whose wife had died a few years earlier, invited Tania and me to bring in the New Year at Annabel's Club. Alistair asked me to marry him. Alistair was a good friend for many years, and he thought, as we were both bereft of our spouses, we should try to make a life together. I declined his offer, but we continued to remain close friends.

As time went on, I was trying to decide what would be best for Tara and me. I knew Tara would soon have to leave St. Mary's Convent and move to a senior school. I applied to St. Mary's Convent, Ascot, but Tara became so ill at the thought of going to a boarding school that I didn't pursue the matter further. As for me, life in London was just not the same. My life revolved around Tara, but the light had left my London town. Wondering and praying about the future, I became ill with rubella—of all things. My lovely London doctor told me that, despite my outward happiness, I was suffering inside. I really wasn't aware of it, but I suppose I was anxious about Tara's and my future.

I had promised Tara to take her to the Lyford Cay Club for the Easter holidays, but due to my illness, we couldn't leave on the arranged date. As we had lost about three days, my friend Robert at British Airways suggested we travel on Concorde to New York and connect with a plane to Nassau, which would save us a day. It was very exciting, especially for Tara to travel on Concorde and, as always, we were thoroughly spoiled.

53

After a few days at the Lyford Cay Club, some friends of mine invited us to dinner and introduced us to Ken, who was in the process of getting a divorce. We were attracted to one another, and the meeting turned out to be the answer as to where we were to go next. Ken was a good looking man and my age. He had attended Brown University, and during our time together, we enjoyed an alumni visit. Tara and I had a happy holiday, and Ken returned with us to London and met Mother, Dad, Nan, and some of the O'Leary family. While Ken was in London, I went to see my obstetrician and asked him if there was a possibility of me becoming pregnant again. Admittedly I was now in my early forties, and felt sure that the answer would be negative. I wasn't really prepared for Mr. de Vere to tell me that I was now a big girl and that due to my celibate years with Patrick, I had already experienced menopause, so no more babies.

The rest of Ken's stay in London was successful. I introduced him to my friends and had a great day in the country with Patrick's niece, the daughter of Dolly and George. Tara had her first experience riding a horse and sure enough fell off, but got right back on. Ken's parents came to London, and I was happy to entertain them and show them a little of my London. Ken returned to Nassau for the summer, and I kept in touch with him while I went with my parents, Nan and Tara to Studland Bay. I had a lot of thinking to do. Vanessa and Marc joined us; it was certainly the perfect English holiday resort for families.

Dawn was very much in my life now, and it was lovely to visit her at The Old Farm House where we always enjoyed Vladimir and Dawn's hospitality. We were also able to have delightful visits to Robert and Carmen, our good friends from British Airways, and their three children all about Tara's age, so there was plenty to do and places to go. Before I knew it, Tara was going to be nine years old. Dawn invited Tara to celebrate her birthday at The Old Farm House. I hired a mini bus and seven of Tara's close friends, together with Vanessa, Marc, Nan and Grandpa, drove to Borden. Mother was also invited, but she decided not to join us. Tara and her friends had a great party.

For Christmas of 1983 we flew to Nassau and stayed in Ken's apartment, which was just outside the gates of the Lyford Cay property and close to St. Paul's Catholic Church. I had decided to move in with him. Tara and I enjoyed the special events at the Lyford Cay Club, but other than that, we were meeting Ken's friends and experiencing a different lifestyle in Nassau, which was really warm and welcoming. I brought Nan out with us, and she was in her element being back there and partaking of the children's Christmas party at Lyford Cay Club. Tara made friends with Ken's neighbours who lived next door and had three children; so Nan and Tara spent many happy days with them in their apartment, at the club, and on the beach.

Alistair came to spend Christmas and stayed in a hotel nearby, and we saw him every day. Tara and I flew back to London for Tara to attend school, and we returned again to Nassau for the Easter holidays, bringing Grandpa with us. I thought while we were in Nassau it would be nice to fly over to Delray Beach in Florida to see Ken's parents; I rented an apartment, and as we all enjoyed our visit so much, I reserved the same apartment for the following year and invited Nan to join Grandpa and us. Both Grandpa and Nan had lots to tell their friends when they returned to England.

My thoughts were now on moving out of London to the Bahamas. Tara was still attending St. Mary's Convent and having a wonderful education. I was delighted with her progress in every way. I knew, however, the day had to come when she would have to leave, and I thought that if I found a comfortable house in Nassau and a good school, it would be a perfect life for a growing girl. Needless to say, I was sure Patrick had wanted us to move to Nassau and felt that was indeed, the answer to my prayers to be close to his spirit and where we had started our love affair.

In the meantime, Tara had now reached her tenth birthday. How the years were flying by. The big day arrived, and Tara wanted to have her ears pierced. We visited the chemist in South Audley Street, and the deed was done. The two of us went on to Harrods to buy her first earrings and to have lunch before going to the portrait gallery. I had made an appointment for Tara to have her photograph taken, and it was beautiful. For her party I rented a riverboat, and Tara invited her class, and I invited my parents and Tara's godparents, Nan, of course, and Vanessa and Marc.

While we floated along the river Thames, the disco music blared, the children danced, and the food was devoured. It was another successful party. As we were saying good-bye to Tara's friends, one of them, Luz, presented her with her gift, a little black-and-white rabbit, which we named Viceroy after the boat. Oh my goodness, did we really want a rabbit in the apartment in Grosvenor Square? Oh, the pleas from Tara and her promises of, "I'll look after it!" Well, being me, I succumbed.

I bought the rabbit its home and placed it in the pantry, making sure there were newspapers everywhere. I quickly learned what a rabbit needed to eat and drink, but Viceroy, being an O'Leary, wasn't happy being cooped up and wanted to enjoy the apartment, which he did. He would even sit on the sofa and watch television with us. Of course, we all loved him, but when the time came to pack up, I gave Viceroy to our British Airways friends in the hope that their children would enjoy the adorable little rabbit, but alas, he didn't last long in their country home. We guess he made a nice lunch for a hungry fox. It was a lovely experience to have Viceroy as part of the family, despite him trying to eat the furniture and leaving his mess around, though I almost had him house trained. He was very smart, and we did miss him.

A few weeks later I thought it would be fun for Tara to spend some time with my sister Sylvan and her cousins in Palma, Majorca, but I hadn't reckoned on my sister upsetting Tara by serving her rabbit stew for dinner! While Tara was with Sylvan, I suggested to Ken that it would be a good idea for me to meet his two daughters, so I invited them to Alicante. We had a few really happy days together, and of course, it was exciting for them to be in Spain.

While we were in Alicante I asked them if they would like to see a bullfight. I decided that although I never wished to see another bullfight it would be an experience the girls wouldn't forget. The toreadors happened to be staying in the same hotel as us, so the interest was more on them then the poor bulls. It was nice for Ken to spend quality time with his daughters before returning them to his ex-wife in England.

The school term was coming to an end, and the children at St. Mary's Convent produced a musical. It was a lively end-of-term performance, and Tara had some lead parts. We said good-bye and a big thank you to the nuns who had taught Tara. Tara had done so well at St. Mary's and was advanced in her education. I had to inform the nuns that Tara would not be returning for the following term after the summer holidays. Anyway, it was nearing the time when she would have to attend senior school.

For the summer holidays of 1984, Tara and I went to meet Ken in Boston. We spent a few days there and then drove to New York, where we stayed at the Plaza Hotel, and I introduced Tara to the book "Eloise at the Plaza". It was during that time I made my final decision to leave London and try to make a life with Ken. Once I was back in Nassau, I would look for a house, as Ken's small apartment would not suffice. Tara needed a home, a garden, and dogs, as did I. We returned to London after the summer holidays and celebrated Tara's eleventh birthday with family and special friends at a pleasant restaurant; it was also our farewell party. That would be Tara's last birthday in London for a very long time.

I was busy packing up the apartment in Grosvenor Square and had become quite an expert, having moved a few times. I assured my father I would continue to take care of him. He now lived in a comfortable boarding house in Epsom, and as long as he was able, would arrange for him to visit us in Nassau. I had every intention, however, for us to travel back and forth to see Mother and Dad.

My mother wasn't happy I was leaving and going so far away, but she too would be financially taken care of, and she did have Vanessa, who was living in London. Mother and Father would be all right and Nan too. I continued to financially take care of Sylvan and her daughters; I wanted them to enjoy their apartment and for both girls to have a good education in Palma.

It was strange to be leaving my life in London, but I truly felt in my heart I was doing the right thing for Tara. I had lost interest in my beloved London since Patrick's death. I couldn't help but reflect that I was closing an amazing phase of my life and was leaving England with a lot of nostalgia, but Tara was now my focal point, and with Patrick always in my heart, we were about to experience a new adventure. My friends Robert and Carmen collected us from our empty apartment and drove us to their home where we stayed the night before leaving on British Airways for Nassau, Bahamas, the next morning.

54

I arranged with the shipping company to hold everything in storage until I had found our home and in the meantime enrolled Tara in the school she would attend. I was pleased there was a school bus, so she could travel with a few of the other children from Lyford Cay. While Tara was at school, Ken drove me around Nassau, house hunting. I told him I was a little hesitant to drive again, so he made me drive, as he said that living on the island, I had to drive. I did begin to regain a little belief in myself after Tara insisted we went in the bumper cars in Disney World. So with Ken beside me, I drove, and it wasn't long before I felt comfortable behind the wheel.

In February of 1986, having seen about one hundred houses, I saw a miniature of Ionia House. The house was not in Lyford Cay. Had I not been a romantic, it would have been worth my while to have bought a small house in the Cay, but I did not like the idea of living in a closed community where everyone would eventually know everything about me. My privacy was paramount, but it cost me.

The house I did buy had recently been bought by an American, and he had started to work on the property when he decided he did not want to continue. The potential of the property was fantastic, and when I saw it in its neglected state, I knew I could make a beautiful home. The view overlooked the ocean and was spectacular. The house was situated in a quiet, residential area. I decided to call our new home "Devon House", Tara's second name.

There was a tremendous amount of work to do, but with my faith in Jesus, I knew I could make a dream home. I felt Patrick was with me. It was déjà vu in a way, but Devon House was much smaller than Ionia House, and there was no language problem and no Mafia. Before moving into the house, I had it tented for termites. The swimming pool had to be rebuilt, as did the tennis court, and I wanted a pagoda at the entrance to the tennis court. I arranged to have a pond built so I could have oriental carp and a small red Japanese bridge, which would cross the pond. The oriental area would be located outside the guest room where my guests could sit and enjoy the tranquility of the sound of water, the rustle of the palm trees, be mesmerised by the luminous carp, and pick a mango from the nearby tree.

I was pleased that the whole property was surrounded by a high wall, as I intended to have four dogs. I had solar panels installed to cut the cost of my electric bills and, being in hurricane country, we needed a large generator. It was suggested that I had bars on the windows, which I thought would distract from the overall effect of the house, but then I remembered the attractive window bars Patrick and I had seen in Tunis, so I had them made and installed. As I looked at the windows after the installation, it certainly didn't seem as if they were safety bars but just an ornamental accessory.

I finally felt I could have my crates shipped, and in amongst electricians, painters, carpenters, landscapers and Ken's two young daughters, who were staying with us and sharing Tara's unfinished bedroom, the three hundred and eighty boxes arrived. I was fortunate that the American who had owned the house for a short period had hired a Haitian caretaker, whom he left with the property. I found him very useful, and he became my man Friday. Of course, I paid him a lot and looked after him exceedingly well. His name was Innocent, but due to his Haitian pronunciation, I understood him to be Nusome, and Nusome he stayed. Ken was never around during the day, as he had to attend to his own work, so I was happy to have Nusome at my beck and call.

I thought it best to have an overseer; I hired a company to make sure all the work was done properly in the house and gardens. By Tara's twelfth birthday, I was able to hold a pool party at Devon House around our redesigned pool, where she entertained all her friends from her new school. We also had three additions to our family, Duke, our Rottweiler, and Duchess and Windsor, our two Golden

Retrievers. Our second female Rottweiler puppy was stolen within a few days of her being with us, which prompted me to immediately fence the property wall with barbed wire. Rottweilers were much in demand, as they were trained as guard dogs by the local Bahamians, and the puppies would sell for a high price.

We spent Christmas Day in Nassau with friends and left the next day for Palma where we visited Sylvan and the girls for a few days, before going to London to welcome in the New Year with the rest of the family, then returned back to Nassau in time for Tara to start her school term.

I was anxious to have Devon House free of all the workmen. It didn't take too long before everything was falling into place, and our new home started to look beautiful. All the English furniture from Grosvenor Square fit perfectly into its new surroundings. The landscaped gardens with romantic lighting at night was a dream. I was happy with all that I had achieved, and I knew Patrick would have been proud of me. I wasn't a good cook, but I wanted to entertain the new friends we had made, so somehow Ken and I managed to hold some lovely dinner parties. Devon House was situated in a piece of heaven with the ocean in front and the stars above, so I suppose it wasn't surprising everyone who was entertained in that venue had beautiful memories.

Shortly after Tara had her twelfth birthday, I made the decision to send her to a well-known school in Fort Lauderdale, Florida, as a boarder. It was extremely difficult for me, and I lamented about it, but I was not happy with the education she was receiving at her current school. To send my beloved daughter away from me was a big sacrifice, but I felt strongly I was doing the right thing. Fort Lauderdale from Nassau was only an hour's flight, and I would make sure I would be there for every school play and at every occasion that required my presence, and that Tara would be home for half-term and all holidays. Leaving Tara at Pine Crest School was very emotional for both of us, but soon, Tara was making close friends and began to really enjoy her life; to this day she thanks me for having sent her there where she received a great education.

Before Tara started at her new school in Fort Lauderdale, I thought I would honour Patrick's memory by taking her to Ireland to introduce her to the home of the O'Leary's. I invited Canon Maurice O'Leary, Patrick's cousin who had not been well, to join us. I thought he would benefit by being in Ireland as my guest, and he would be our guide, showing us the footsteps of our O'Leary clan. Canon O'Leary also knew all the hierarchy in the Catholic Church, plus several friends he had made over the years.

I hired a chauffeur-driven limousine. Canon O'Leary had mapped out our route, starting with our arrival at Shannon Airport and finishing two weeks later in Dublin. We really had a wonderful vacation, visiting all the interesting sights. As we entered Piltown where Patrick's father was born, I felt a little emotional, wishing Patrick could have been with us. Piltown had a field with a couple of cows, a pub where we stopped for a light libation, and opposite the pub was a line of small houses. That was Piltown! Canon O'Leary showed us the house where Patrick's father was born and lived with his nine siblings. It was tiny and humble. Although it was my intention that Tara see as much as possible of her Irish heritage, the motion of the car put her to sleep, so she missed seeing a lot of the beautiful terrain.

The biggest excitement for Tara came when Canon O'Leary had arranged with the Bishop of Cork that we stay at his house. During the course of an early supper, the Bishop mentioned that Michael Jackson was giving a concert that evening. Tara knew about it and wished she was going. Her wish was granted then and there. The Bishop knew a family in the parish who would be attending; he called them and asked them to take Tara. Needless to say, that was the highlight of Tara's visit to Ireland. Tara was the biggest fan of Michael Jackson, and all the boring days for my twelve-year-old daughter travelling around Eire were worth it just to be at the concert.

Canon O'Leary had to return to London, so Tara and I spent a few days in Dublin. I had arranged to meet a friend of my mother's from Ceylon, together with her children, who were my age. We had a lovely reunion, and I wished Mother could have been with us. Tara and I had a fun time in Dublin with our new Irish friends, and when the time came to leave the Sherbourne Hotel, I was presented with a hefty bill. I asked the cashier to please check it, as I knew it was incorrect. She apologised as she presented me with a new bill, which was considerably less, and said that by mistake Luciano Pavarotti's expenses had been added to my bill. He was staying at the hotel and the previous evening had entertained in the Pavarotti manner. Well, the inconvenience was worth the tale.

55

In April of 1987 Vanessa and Marc came to stay at Devon House. I made sure their visit was filled with excitement, especially for my six-year-old nephew, and to give Vanessa a really relaxing holiday. With Nassau's beautiful waters and virgin beaches, how could one not enjoy that paradise? As Tara had her first friend Catherine staying with us too, I thought that after having a wonderful time in Nassau, it would be a good idea to take the two girls, Vanessa and Marc to Disney World. I was becoming familiar with the routine with regard to the hotel we should stay in and our itinerary each day, as Ken, Tara and I had made several visits before. I loved seeing the children so happy and loved every minute of it myself.

As Vanessa and Marc had been to stay with us, I thought it only fair that Sylvan, Tania and Kenia should visit too. During their three-week holiday and after having a fun time in Nassau, the five of us went to the Mickey Mouse Kingdom, where the three little girls and the two big girls had a marvelous time, and en route back to Nassau, we stopped in Miami, as Sylvan wanted to see the city, and again we had a successful visit. My sister and her children were so excited to be in America. The summer holidays were soon over, and Sylvan and her girls returned to Palma, and Tara back to Pine Crest School. In November as a birthday gift to Nan, I had the great pleasure of having her to stay with us. It was the first time I really saw her relaxing, and made sure she had nothing to do except be spoiled at Devon House.

Running a large home kept me busy during the day, and in the evenings Ken and I would relax with friends or familiarise ourselves with what Nassau had to offer. Ken told me he had to take pills for epilepsy, and at the beginning of our relationship, I thought nothing of it, as he seemed totally fine. However, after a while he omitted to tell me he had stopped taking his pills, as he thought he did not need them anymore. Unfortunately, I had to see several grand mal seizures, and while we were in Captiva Island for a visit, he had such a severe one that he was airlifted to a hospital in Fort Myers. I hadn't forgotten the fear I felt seeing the epileptic seizure that Patrick had suffered. Ken's seizures really upset me, as I never knew when those horrible convulsions would attack him. I made him promise me he would take his medication on a permanent basis.

Ken and I visited Peter and Jan in Barbados, as once more Peter was in a new venue as the managing director of a beautiful hotel complex. Our friends always made us very welcome, and we had so much fun together. Ken and I saw a lot of the island I had not seen before.

We often visited Fort Lauderdale to see Tara, and many times I went over on my own. I wanted to make sure Tara knew I would be with her as much as was possible, and we loved our weekends together. Tara also knew I would be with her for every important moment in her life. It was a promise I had made to myself when Tara was born, as I remembered the disappointment and hurt I felt when my parents, due to one thing or another, were never there for me.

After Tara's first couple of terms, I relaxed a little, as she told me she was really enjoying being a boarder at Pine Crest School and was making lots of friends. Back in Nassau, I was invited to many charity balls, and Ken and I attended them all. I asked the new friends that we had made through their work on Devon House, whether they would like to join us, which they did. It was fun to dress formally and dance to the big bands. Later in the year, I received a telephone call from a friend who suggested I might be interested in joining a food and wine society called La Chaîne des Rôtisseurs. I thought it was an excellent idea, as it was also a way to meet new people.

In the meantime, Christmas was almost with us, and we agreed that we would like to take a Christmas cruise with Royal Caribbean. I left the three dogs in Nusome's care, I knew he was fond of them and would look after them well. The idea of taking a cruise was wonderful for me. I didn't have anything to think about for the two weeks except to make sure the three of us had a good time; we all had fun. It was also interesting to visit some of the other islands in the Caribbean, which included Martinique, Dominica, St. Martin, St. Kitts and Puerto Rico, before sailing on to Jamaica.

Arriving back from our cruise, I returned Tara to school, and life continued to be busy in Nassau. In March some friends of ours invited us to a special, fancy dress party, where we had to arrive in an innovative costume. With the help of a dear Bahamian fashion stylist, I went as Nefertiti, the great royal wife of the Egyptian Pharaoh Akhenaten, and Ken as Howard Carter, who led the excavation of Egyptian nobles' tombs. We won first prize! A few months later we were invited to our friends' island home on Long Island, Bahamas, where we spent an idyllic week, enjoying the best of what the Bahamas had to offer—the white beaches, and aquamarine ocean.

For Tara's half-term, Ken and I flew over to Fort Lauderdale and hired a car to drive to Key West. Jan and Peter Rickard were now living there, as Peter was managing director of one of the big hotels. Once again it was great to spend time with our friends and to visit Key West.

I invited Patrick's niece, Maureen, to Devon House. I knew it was going to be her sixtieth birthday, so unless she had made other plans, I enticed her with a two-week holiday in Nassau. I had remembered the lovely day she gave us at her home in Cambridge so was happy I could now reciprocate. In order to thank me for her vacation, Maureen, who is a talented artist, drew some spectacular scenes of Devon House, for which I shall always be most grateful.

After Maureen returned to England while Tara was at school, Ken suggested we visit San Francisco for five days. We managed to see as much of that exciting and beautiful city as we could. Although I am nervous of heights and closed spaces, Ken and I went on a sightseeing helicopter; despite my fears, I did manage to see the bay, the Golden Gate Bridge and Alcatraz Prison from the sky. We ate delicious food and danced in one of the clubs in Union Square. We visited China

Town, rode on the famous trams and tasted abalone at Fisherman's Wharf. After five days we felt we had done justice to that eclectic city.

In August during Tara's summer holidays, she and I travelled to Palma, Majorca, to be present for Kenia's First Communion. I had arranged with Vanessa for Mother and Dad to be with us, and we had a happy family time together. Palma was like a second home, as we had spent so much time going back and forth when Vanessa and Mother lived there, but now, it was to visit Sylvan and the girls. Ken went to England to visit his two daughters. On our return to Nassau, and having taken Tara back to school, I thought that it would be interesting for Ken and I to accept the invitation to join other members of La Chaîne des Rôtisseurs for a visit to the Dominican Republic.

We were excited to travel with La Chaîne in order to see that dramatic island. The itinerary, which had been arranged for the members, was excellent, extremely interesting and most enjoyable. Apart from the chaos at the airport on our arrival, the old Spanish colonial capital was intriguing with beautiful medieval and historic buildings. We visited the Castle of Columbus and the oldest cathedral in the Americas, built around 1540, where we were told that Christopher Columbus's remains were purported to be buried; later they were moved to the Columbus Lighthouse in the early nineties. We walked through a few museums, and I especially liked the amber museum—fascinating and so tempting. There were a few shops where one could buy a piece of the fossilised tree resin, but I didn't. We drove out through the lush countryside, and at the end of our short visit were pleased to have had the opportunity to see that compelling country.

Tara was busy at Pine Crest and apart from all her other activities, she had a part in every theatre production. The plays were extremely professional, and Tara's desire to become an actress—since she was eight years old—became stronger. It made me think of what she would want to do when she left Pine Crest. It was the Christmas holidays again, and at the last minute we decided to take a Christmas cruise to Cancun, Cozumel and the Cayman Islands, where Tara met up with a school friend and we enjoyed a pleasant day at his home with his family.

56

I was happy to be home at Devon House, to have my dogs and enjoy entertaining friends. Tara had some of her school friends visit us, which gave me the opportunity to show them the fun parts of Nassau. Life was tranquil, but I had a black cloud hanging over my head. Although Ken had asked me to marry him on numerous occasions, I realised our relationship was beginning to wane. After six years of walking around the tennis court for an hour each day, which I did as a daily exercise when I was home, and where I did a lot of thinking, I knew it was time for Ken and me to part, as I felt we did not have a future together.

It was with the utmost difficulty and trepidation that I summoned up the courage and asked him to leave Devon House. It was time for us to go our separate ways, as I was tired of paying for everything. My generosity had afforded him a fabulous life, and of course, I benefited by his companionship, but I began to feel, after those many years together, that he had become complacent and was taking advantage of me; it was time for me to be alone.

With Tara away at school, I became used to my own company and had help from reading Robert Schuller's books and watching his television shows. I also became a big fan of Deepak Chopra; I read many of his books, and they proved very helpful and moved me further into meditation. Jesus was always with me, and my weekly visits to Mass and receiving Holy Communion gave me the strength I required to embrace each day. I missed Tara so much, but I knew she was happy and having a great education.

Through being a member of La Chaîne des Rôtisseurs, I started to meet people and make friends and began to have a social life, but I found it rather difficult, as being on my own was not easy when I attended dinner parties and other events. I was nervous, but I knew I had to make the effort. Life was different without Ken, though we remained friendly and saw each other fairly frequently.

After the Christmas holidays, which Tara and I spent in London with the family, I returned Tara to school and flew back to Nassau. I kept busy, and the months were filled with travelling back and forth to Tara, and generally keeping occupied. I am very self-sufficient, therefore being on my own was no problem.

In April my friend Petra, who visited Devon House annually during her holidays, had suggested I visit her in Australia. I, therefore, made my travel arrangements and did everything to make sure Devon House, and more importantly, Duke, Duchess and Windsor would be taken care of by Nusome and my two maids. Tara was at school and would know where I was at every minute, so I flew to Los Angeles and connected with Qantas to Sydney, arriving on May fourth. Petra had arranged that we fly straight to Port Douglas, where we stayed at the beautiful Sheraton Mirage Hotel. Our rooms overlooked the saltwater lagoons embraced by the tropical landscape, and if we wished, we could swim to the Ocean Breeze Bar from them. Every day we walked the magnificent four-mile beach. I felt far away from everything, immersed in the surrounding beauty. The hotel had a golf course, and club house which we visited and I was amused to see the golfers on the practice range hitting their balls into a lake; the balls were collected by a man in a little boat.

Sunday Mass was celebrated in the small Catholic Church of St. Augustine in Mossman, another precious memory for me. Of course, we had to experience the Great Barrier Reef, the largest coral reef system in the world and one of the seven wonders. Petra and I took the ferry out to an island where we would join a tour submarine from which we proceeded to view the magnificent coral, the myriad colours and shapes of the fish, and generally the breathtaking beauty of the Barrier Reef—due to all of those incredible sights, it made me forget I was confined in a small space and underwater. Visiting the

Great Barrier Reef left an indelible impression, and I was grateful for the experience.

A few days later, we boarded the colourful Karunda train. It was a joy for me to be travelling in that quaint little train where we crossed bridges, went through tunnels and experienced fantastic views of the Blue Mountains, while traversing the rainforest of the Barron Gorge National Park. Alighting at the charming little Karunda rail station, Petra and I wandered through the village, looking at the many stalls selling handcrafted goods and various other interesting bric-a-brac. We paid a visit to the famous Butterfly Sanctuary and were overawed by the more than fifteen hundred butterflies of different colours and varieties. We later embarked on the amphibious open riverboat, the Army Duck, and felt as if we were deep in the jungle of the rainforest, as we glided along the murky river. When our boat ride ended, we stopped to have boomerang lessons. I did not do so well, but bought one as a souvenir.

The amazing day was almost at an end, but not without a visit to an Aboriginal Dance Show, and I sat enthralled as we saw an evocative glimpse into the real life of the Aborigine and his masterful use of the didgeridoo. We returned to Sydney via a rainy day in Cairns, and together with Petra's friend Pam, were lucky enough to have seats to a concert to see Shirley Bassey perform. While I was in Sydney, I made arrangements to see my dear friend Anna, who is the sister of my friend, Pina, from Taormina, Sicily.

I was invited to stay the night with her and her husband, and needless to say, Anna and I had much to reminisce about—beautiful memories of Ionia House and my Patrick. Anna had made a wonderful timpano pie for dinner, one of my favourite Sicilian meals, which Angelina used to cook for me. The following day I accompanied Anna to Mass at St. Mary's Cathedral. After Mass we walked around the Rocks, the historic area of Sydney's city centre on the southern shore of Sydney Harbour, and visited some of the tempting little shops. We later joined Petra and Pam for lunch, and alas, didn't see Anna again during my visit.

While I was in Sydney, Petra, Pam and I went to the Opera House. It was such a thrill to visit that iconic building and see Joan Collins in Noel Coward's "Private Lives", which was most entertaining.

Before leaving Australia, I had promised Mother to see a couple of old friends of hers. Petra and I flew to the lovely city of Melbourne, where Mother was born, and we took the bus to visit Mother's dear elderly friend. It was hard for me to believe I was actually in the city where my Mother was born and lived for the first part of her life, and that we were able to have tea with one of her closest friends. After returning to Sydney, I had to say hello to Mother's other friend who lived in Manley, so I took the ferry over the sparkling waters of Sydney Harbour to meet and enjoy another nostalgic visit.

I knew when I left Nassau that Mother hadn't been feeling too well. I had spoken to her on the telephone, and she mentioned she was experiencing cardiac asthma. She had suffered with asthma all her life, and as she was getting older, it was bothering her more. I phoned her from Sydney, as I was anxious to know how she was, and she didn't sound too good, but she cheered up when I told her I had seen both her old friends. However, I was concerned for her health. I told Petra about my conversation, and she said that perhaps a few weeks in the Yugoslav sunshine might be what Mother needed. I contacted Mother as soon as I returned to Nassau and said that I would arrange for her to stay with Petra's relations at the seaside resort of Igrane. I wanted Mother to have something to look forward to, and she did have a lovely two-week visit in July, enjoying swimming in the Adriatic and generally relaxing with Petra's aunt and uncle, who were so kind to her.

My stay in Australia would soon be over, but a few days before I was to depart, Petra thought I might like a short visit to Auckland, New Zealand, to meet her brother and a couple of members of her family. Petra is of Yugoslavian (now Croatian) origin and a citizen of New Zealand. I decided it would be all right to extend my trip in order to take the opportunity of a visit to New Zealand.

When we arrived at Petra's brother's house, we were hungry, but when Petra opened the fridge, it was completely empty. Dick's wife wasn't there, and there was no food in the house; we had to go out to a bar to find something to eat. We returned home and finished a bottle of Port, and none of us felt too good the following day; though Dick, Petra's brother, had delicious lamb cutlets cooking on the barbeque for breakfast, and those were eaten in no time. Petra wanted me to see Rotorua, the town of the hot springs, so borrowing Dick's car, we drove through the countryside, which reminded me of Ireland with the green hills and many sheep.

Arriving at Rotorua, we saw the big sign Kia Ora—welcome! We booked into a lovely hotel, and despite our rather long drive, were eager to explore and to enjoy a really good dinner. Just over a third of Rotorua's population is Maori. We visited the historic villages, the bubbling mud pools, and the world famous Pohutu Geyser. The Maori dance was unusual but a lot of fun, and of course, I had to have a Piupio skirt, which is made from flax. Normally those skirts have to be ordered in advance, but I had my skirt made for me in a day, and I loved it. Rotorua was certainly an experience; however, neither Petra nor I were sorry to leave the thermal springs and the smell of sulfur. It was raining heavily when we left, and Petra insisted I drive Dick's car, as she was having difficulty with her eyes. It was a gripping drive back, but we made it, and Dick was relieved to see his car was returned safely. We had a fun couple of days in Auckland where I bought two large sheepskin rugs before returning to Sydney to say farewell to Petra and Pam and board Qantas to return to Los Angeles.

Basil was at the airport to meet me, and I spent a few days with him, trying to recover from jetlag. Tara and I returned to stay with Basil in August at his gorgeous home in Beverly Hills on Sunset Boulevard. Heather was able to be with us, and during that time Basil drove us to visit Venice Beach, an amusing experience. One evening as Basil was busy, Tara and I decided to go out on the town alone. Basil had already taken us to Spago's restaurant, so that particular evening we visited some other well-known restaurants and ran into Tom Selleck at Trader's Vic. He was very nice to us and only too happy to sign his name for Tara. We said hello to Phil Morris, Rob Lowe and Billy

Crystal, amongst a few other celebrities at other venues, and stopped in at Dudley Moore's restaurant; he too was very charming and funny as he signed his card for Tara. We ended up dancing at Tramp. Wow, what an exciting night. Basil was amazed that we had such an adventure. The next day I had to show Tara the Beverly Hill's Hotel, and Basil was kind to take us there and to all the other important spots in Hollywood. Heather returned with us to Nassau, where we tried to give her an equally fun time, Nassau style!

57

Tara was back at school early in September. A friend talked me into learning golf, which I took seriously, and although I had bought golf clubs earlier in the year, I hadn't used them. I tried to find time to have lessons, as I played badly, but managed to persevere at the game. I enjoyed playing on the lovely course of Lyford Cay. On October fifteenth I travelled to London to be with Mother for her eightieth birthday, which was on the eighteenth. Vanessa and Sylvan were also there, and we gave Mother a really wonderful celebration. She was thrilled to have her "three graces" with her. Mother had mellowed a lot, and I was finally feeling much closer to her and really did everything I could to make her feel wanted and happy.

While in London I took the opportunity to see Dad, Nan and my other dear friends. Returning to Nassau on the twenty-eighth, I only had time to unpack and repack to go over to Fort Lauderdale to be with Tara to celebrate her sixteenth birthday on Halloween. I had reserved a private room in a lovely restaurant where Tara invited her five special friends for a birthday dinner.

Back in Nassau, Petra arrived, and during her stay, we flew up to New York for a few days, as Petra had to visit the firm she worked for in Manhattan, and I took the opportunity to do some Christmas shopping.

Tara and I spent Christmas at Devon House with our dogs and gave a party for our friends. Attending Christmas Mass was the highlight of my festivities. On January sixth Tara returned to school.

La Chaîne des Rôtisseurs was holding the 1991 Grand Chapître at The Cloisters in Sea Island, Georgia, and I decided I would really like to visit that venue. I always remembered Patrick's beautiful shirts were made out of the finest Sea Island cotton. The weekend turned out to be so much fun. The food was delicious, as were the wines, and I was impressed with the enormous bowl of beluga caviar, which was such a treat and devoured in no time. I was happy that a friend of mine, Henry from Nassau, had also attended the event, as did a couple of other friends.

At our first cocktail party hosted in a delightful old private house, I met a judge from North Carolina and found him totally fascinating. We stayed up all night drinking champagne, talking and walking the beach. He told me he had experienced the Korean War and had received a medal for bravery, and he was in the middle of divorce proceedings. I fell totally in love with him. We spent most of that weekend together, walking the tree-lined lanes and having flirtatious repartee.

The weekend was over and I flew back to Nassau, but before my departure, my judge told me he would meet me in Fort Lauderdale, as he would like to be introduced to Tara. His visit to Fort Lauderdale was wonderful, and the three of us had so many laughs. He also helped me choose Tara's seventeenth birthday present, a Jeep. My judge invited me to North Carolina, where we spoke about our future. He was ten years my senior and a Pisces. I was so happy. I was in love again!

When I returned to Nassau, Vanessa called to say she and her boyfriend had decided to marry and she would have a big church wedding the following year on May twenty-fourth in London. I was excited for her, but deep in my heart wondered if she was doing the right thing. Anyway, it was time for the family to celebrate. I knew Dad hadn't been too well and suggested to him he need only attend the reception, and could be accompanied by a lady from the home to assist him. I told him not to worry about what he was going to wear, as I would send him all his clothes, except his suit which he had already. Tara was a little unhappy as she would be missing her school prom. However, arriving in London, I had arranged for Catherine to stay with us at the Grosvenor House Hotel and attend the wedding; both girls were delighted by the arrangements.

It was a beautiful nuptial Mass at the lovely old Catholic Church in Spanish Place in London. My friend Tania was there, Nan, of course, Sylvan and her girls, and Mother, who looked wonderful. Vanessa had a magnificent reception, and I was amazed at how many people she knew. It made me happy to see Vanessa, her new husband with his little boy from a previous marriage, and little Marc so united. I was especially delighted that we were all gathered for the celebration, and had a family photograph taken. It was the last time we would all be together.

Family group photograph at the wedding reception of Vanessa and Bernard

Diana

Tara and I had to be back in Fort Lauderdale, as Tara still had to finish her term at school. For the summer holidays, she returned to London to stay with Catherine and her family in the English countryside, before staying with Vanessa for a few days in London. En route back to Nassau, she visited her friend from school who lived in Bermuda. After Tara's super summer holidays, she was back to finish her last term at Pine Crest School.

Tara receiving her graduation certificate from Pine Crest School

I went over to the school and sat in the auditorium with the rest of the proud parents and applauded as Tara received her graduation certificate. We flew back to Nassau and enjoyed just being together at home. The Christmas celebrations were spent at Devon House, and in January, I celebrated my fiftieth birthday. I was very happy that Tara would be home for the occasion. As it was a special birthday, I decided to give a black tie dinner party and invited thirty-six of my friends. The party was elegant and the evening was just beautiful. We ate suckling pig, drank perfumed wines and danced under the stars. I felt elated and grateful that I was able to give myself a birthday party, and to this day friends remember it with nostalgia.

I was sad when Dad said he was no longer able to travel to Nassau, but Mother came to stay for a few weeks. In February of 1992, Vanessa called to say Dad wasn't well and that he was in hospital. He died within a couple of days of Vanessa's call to me. I was upset I didn't know earlier and, therefore, wasn't able to be with him to say good-bye. Vanessa said Dad had been cremated, and she gave him a fitting farewell, having invited several friends. I told Vanessa I wished to pay for his wake, which I did.

It was astounding that Dad had lived until the age of eighty-four, as due to his delinquent lifestyle and having suffered seriously with malaria in the early days of his arrival in Ceylon, his doctors had informed him in his forties that he would die young. My father was a very stubborn man! I thought about him and knew that I would miss him. Despite his proclivity to alcohol, he was a good and gentle man, and did what he was told by Mother. His life with us three girls growing up wasn't much fun, and he knew he was despised by Mother, but somehow he made us laugh and was always around to give us our wake-up call in the mornings; and apart from everything else, I loved him just because he was my dad, and I will always miss the aroma of his St. Bruno rough-cut tobacco.

58

As Tara had wanted to be an actress from the age of eight years old, she decided that she would like to attend the Tisch School of the Arts at New York University and submitted the necessary applications, together with my financial assistance. I was apprehensive to leave her in New York, and wanted to make sure that she would be in a comfortable and safe dorm. I didn't like that she was in a room with one bed, which a precocious Venezuelan had taken, and Tara, who was twice as tall, had to sleep on a bunk bed. So I proceeded to remove one of the beds and eventually won my case with the dorm mothers that my daughter sleep on a regular bed.

It didn't take Tara long to make friends, but she was homesick. I found myself visiting New York regularly. We celebrated her eighteenth birthday at a restaurant of her choice, and she also had a celebration with her new friends. Tara was so happy to have me with her when I visited, and sometimes she would ask her teachers if I could accompany her to some of her classes, which I did and was interested to see what she was learning and how she was progressing. I was proud that Tara was making an effort to like her new life, but it wasn't at all easy for her.

In March I flew up to North Carolina to surprise my judge for his sixtieth birthday—I arrived in a long limo, having bought sixty balloons! Unfortunately, the greeting I expected wasn't forthcoming, and my heart sank. Though my judge was courteous and always the gentleman, he had omitted to tell me that his wife would not give him a divorce, and perhaps all the decisions he had made to be with me, were just figments of his imagination. I returned to Nassau feeling desolate, but at the same time I had no regrets, as our brief time together was enlightening, fun and very special.

During the summer I received a letter from my mother telling me that Vanessa was moving to Malta. Bernard had found a house for them, and there was a small guest room with a bathroom on the property where Mother could live. I was concerned about Mother, knowing her health had not been good, and she had had to spend time in hospital in London; plus there was always her big problem with asthma. As I was busy with Tara being at school in New York, I was unable to fly to London to help Mother pack up her small apartment.

A few weeks later, I received a little note from her dated September second and posted from Malta saying that the move had been terrible, so exhausting. Mother also told me that she felt her days were numbered; she didn't feel well, and was going through a slow strangulation, finding it difficult to breathe. Her health had deteriorated since her arrival in Malta, and said she was near the end. I realised the move had been much too much for her. I also knew that Vanessa, together with her new husband, were trying to find a school for Marc and what with settling into a strange house, didn't have too much time to attend to Mother. I was very worried, especially as Mother had said she had an awful experience in the hospital in Malta.

Mother's letter of September second had arrived in Nassau on the twelfth, and I made plans immediately to fly over to be with her. The same day I received Mother's letter, Vanessa called to say that Mother was very ill and in a hospice. I told Vanessa I was leaving the next day for Malta, which wasn't the easiest of places to travel to from Nassau. I had to fly to Rome, spend the night there, which I did, and while I had an evening to spend on my own, I took an excursion bus around the familiar city. I flew out the following morning, and on my arrival to Malta, Vanessa said Mother had died the previous day.

It was six months after Dad's demise and on what would have been his eighty-fifth birthday. I was heartbroken, but there it was. I just didn't have enough time to get to her. However, had I known how sick she was, I would have been there earlier. I was also sad that none of us three daughters were with her when she died. The hospice was run by a mother and her daughters, who were wonderfully compassionate and kind. Mother died of pulmonary edema.

Mother had wanted to be cremated and her ashes scattered on the waters of the Mediterranean, but she died in Malta, which didn't recognise cremation. Vanessa told me she would consult with the Maltese Navy to bring the coffin on one of their boats, and we would sail out of the harbour and the coffin would be dropped into the Mediterranean Sea. Sylvan had flown in from Majorca, so the three of us, together with Vanessa's husband and young Marc, gave Mother a beautiful burial at sea. While I watched Mother's coffin bobbing about in the deep blue ocean surrounded by the many colourful bouquets of flowers, I couldn't help but think that although she didn't achieve fame as an actress or as a writer, she did have three wonderful girls who did everything to make some of her smaller dreams come true. For my part I have to include Patrick, who helped me make many of them possible.

As I grow older, I miss Mother and Dad and wish they were still around, as I now want to hear more about their lives, their thoughts, their experiences. I can't have that, but I know they aren't far from me, and Patrick too is with me daily. That evening we invited the ladies of the hospice to dinner. Those Maltese ladies were so kind, and I felt deeply grateful that one of them was holding Mother's hand as she slipped away and into heaven.

Tara came home to Nassau for Christmas, and as usual we had a happy time at Devon House. Christmas time in Nassau was always busy with lots of parties and, of course, the famous junkanoo, which we tried to attend most years, as it was a special celebration in Nassau. In the New Year I accompanied Tara to New York; she had decided to move to a different room in a different building, therefore I had much to do to make her as comfortable as possible in the space of a postage stamp. I was constantly freezing in New York. For me it wasn't any fun being there, but one makes sacrifices for one's children. After I had settled Tara, I went to visit my dear friend Dawn.

It had been some years since she had sold The Old Farm House and moved to live in London. The plastic surgeon I had introduced to her and whom she loved passionately was walking in Harley Street one day when he had heart attack and died on the road. Dawn moved to the remote island of Montserrat, where she and Michael had vacationed together. Dawn was going to celebrate being sixty years young on March first, and I knew she wasn't doing anything special for her birthday, so I told her I wanted to be with her.

It was a rather long journey from Nassau. I flew to Puerto Rico from Miami and then to Antigua, and from there on a small plane to Plymouth, Montserrat. I decided to take my golf clubs with me, as Dawn had said there was a nine-hole golf course, and she too had recently started playing golf. Dawn was at the tiny airport to meet me, and we drove along the winding roads through the thick vegetation on either side to her attractive home in the hills.

Montserrat is a British overseas territory in the Leeward Islands, which is part of the chain of the Lesser Antilles. It is known as the Emerald Isle of the Caribbean, due to the Irish descent of its inhabitants. The Bahamas, and Nassau in particular, seemed to me to be so sophisticated compared to Plymouth and that humble, virgin island. I was aware of the dormant Soufrière Hills volcano, which loomed overhead, and although it was almost always covered by clouds, when it did make an appearance, it looked daunting.

Due to Montserrat being a volcanic island, the beaches were black. It was strange for me to see the black beaches after the pristine beaches in the Bahamas, but they reminded me of those in Sicily. Dawn seemed happy and had made a few friends, but I sensed she was running away from her deep hurt, having lost Michael. We spent two memorable weeks together visiting the town of Plymouth, the markets, the grocery store, playing bad golf, going to Mass in the tiny Catholic church, and avoiding the goats as they crossed the roads from the hilly terrain. We ate simple dinners in simple restaurants with beautiful views, and languished on the terrace of Dawn's home. She was an excellent cook, and it was fun to sit out under the stars and eat a delicious dinner, listening to the sounds of the earth while indulging in many diverse and deep conversations. Once in a while one of Dawn's precious cats would bring her a prize of a snake, a bird or a rat—none of which were graciously received. I wasn't happy to say good-bye to my friend; she was in too remote a part of the world, and who knew what the volcano would do.

Tara was unhappy in New York; she told me she was homesick and didn't want to continue at NYU. She also told me she had decided that she wasn't cut out to be an actress and wanted to come home. I flew to New York and helped her pack up, and we returned to Nassau. I did feel sad that she had given up on her life-long desire and wondered what she would want to do next. Tara really didn't have anything she wanted to do. She was a beautiful girl who would shortly be nineteen years old.

In order to make some pocket money, she decided to work as a waitress in some of the restaurants in Nassau, and was much in demand at the top restaurants and nightclubs. One of the clubs she worked at was The Drop-Off, and while she was there, the organisers of the Miss Commonwealth of the Bahamas Beauty Pageant approached her and asked her to participate. I didn't have any objection and thought the whole experience would be beneficial.

The season lasted for a few months and was lots of fun. It was competitive, but Tara, despite being the only non-Bahamian, was very popular. It was all most exciting, and Tara looked gorgeous. The night of the big contest arrived, and there was no doubt that Tara should have won the title, but she hadn't been told that as she wasn't a Bahamian citizen, she would not be able to win. Nevertheless, she was second runner-up, and it was a good experience, which Tara will remember with pride.

59

We spent the rest of the year in Nassau, and I was happy when Dawn said she would spend the Christmas holidays with us. Unfortunately, Dawn didn't feel too well during her visit, but she did join Tara and me for Christmas Day at the family home of one of Tara's school friends. Over forty family members congregated at the home of Tara's friend, Lisa, who had shared the dorm with her at Pine Crest. The atmosphere was warm and welcoming. When the family got together to sing Christmas carols before the feast, it was fantastic and emotional.

After the reception we were shown to our tables, and as there were so many of us, each table took it in turns to help themselves at the many buffet tables. While we were dining, we were introduced to the chef, who had cooked the abundant and delicious spread. He was Lisa's cousin. I took one look at him, and he took my breath away; he was gorgeous. I whispered to Dawn that I would like to meet him, and as he was a member of the family, we were introduced, and I thanked him for the appetising meal that he had cooked for all of us.

Tara was living at home, which made me happy, but had a boyfriend, who was divorced with a child. I did, however, have a really difficult time with Tara during that period, but was grateful that she lived at home, though I didn't see much of her. I spent a lot of time on my own at Devon House and was fortunate to have such a beautiful home, but it now seemed too big for me. From time to time I had houseguests and special friends like Peter and Jan. Even though I was without an escort, I made myself attend the dinners arranged by La Chaîne des Rôtisseurs.

At one of those dinners I was seated next to the Taiwanese Ambassador to Nassau, who became a great friend, as did his lovely wife. During that period Tara surprised me when she said she wished to move out of Devon House into an apartment, and asked me if I would help her find one. I was deeply unhappy about the arrangement, but there was little I could do. I did find her an apartment not too far from me, but was constantly worried about her safety.

I spent a lot of time reading and meditating. I would try not to think about my daughter in a rented second-rate flat, but that is what her boyfriend wanted. Needless to say, I did not like him. However, in order to keep as close as I could to Tara, I had to bend to her requests and pray that the nightmare would soon be over. I had to tread carefully and be extremely diplomatic, because if I had told her what I thought about her situation, it wouldn't have solved anything at that juncture. I knew she had to pass through the phase and had to work the man out of her system, but until then, Mother was not the most popular person to have around. All I asked from her was that she would call me once a day to let me know that she was all right, which she did. In the meantime, I knew she was in Jesus's protection.

Petra made her usual annual visit to stay with me. During her stay I suggested that we make a trip to Cuba. I didn't really know much about life in Havana, but it soon became apparent how hard it was for the Cuban people. As we drove from the airport to our hotel, we could see what would have been beautiful large homes, which had just been left to decay. The streets were almost bare of any traffic, and we couldn't help but smile when we saw a bride, obviously in a hurry to get to the church, riding side-saddle on the back of a motorbike with her veil blowing in the breeze. The shelves in the supermarkets were empty, and if there was a chicken for sale, it cost twenty-five American dollars.

We paid a visit to the famous old restaurant La Bodequita del Medio, a haunt of Ernest Hemingway's, where they introduced us to the cocktail Mojito, which is immortalised by Hemingway and it is said that he would drink several of those after a day of fishing. The atmosphere at that restaurant was exciting, filled with people and noise, and it was where we had the best meal of our stay. The restaurant was situated in the old part of Havana, but the other restaurants we visited, although they offered a menu, had virtually nothing to serve us to eat.

We walked around Havana and could see how resplendent it must have been before Castro; the architecture of the old buildings was impressive. I made sure to bring chewing gum and pencils, so when the children almost suffocated me, as we walked through the streets, I had those to give to them. Patrick had told me a lot about his visits to Havana in the 1950s. Those indeed were the days! I suggested to Petra we go to see a show at the Tropicana. The showgirls were lovely, but it was a shadow of what it must have been in the days gone by.

After the show we returned to our hotel in one of the few taxis; they were fairly scarce, as was any form of transport on the road. Driving back along the waterfront, I noticed the street was without any form of lighting, I asked the driver to explain, and he said electricity was not provided. What astonished me was the fact that people were running across the road to the waterfront where they socialised, and as it was dark, the driver told us that there had been many accidents with people being hit by cars. The young people had no place to enjoy each other's company, so they would meet by the sea wall to cuddle and converse.

Our hotel was rather rundown, but it was luxurious compared to a lot of what we had seen. In the hotel lobby we observed the making of the Cuban cigars, and I bought a few to take back to Nassau to enhance my humidor! Petra and I left Havana with sadness in our hearts for the plight of the Cuban people.

60

One day a friend called and invited me to dinner. She and her husband owned one of the best restaurants in Nassau, but the invitation was to her home. It was a nice summer evening, and we sat out on their patio. We were seven seated at the table, and I was enjoying meeting a few new people, and then he arrived and took the seat opposite me. He was the handsome young chef from the Christmas dinner. He had a job working for my friends at their restaurant as a sous chef. We were both attracted to one another and playfully flirted during the evening.

As I was leaving, I mentioned to the guests who perhaps were driving home in my direction if they would like to stop and have a nightcap at Devon House. Only one car stopped by my gate, and that was Dean. I directed him to the top gate, not wanting him to enter the bottom gates as Duke, my Rottweiler, would not give him a proper welcome, being very jealous of any male friends. I tripped and fell face down in a ditch—talk about falling for someone! How embarrassing! I quickly got to my feet and went to meet Dean at the top gate, and when he saw me after we had entered the house, he said my cuts must be cleaned. I didn't realise it at the time, but I had a deep cut over my lip and several other smaller ones. We went to the medicine cabinet and Dean proceeded to clean my face. I should have had a few stitches the following day but really didn't think about that.

After he cleaned my face, we went out to the terrace and talked way into the early hours of the morning. I found out he was twenty years my junior and his birthday was the same date as the judge. I wasn't sure if that was a good omen, but another Pisces.

Dean never left Devon House, though he returned to his parents home to bring a few articles of clothing, which consisted of a couple of shirts and shorts, and very little else. I introduced him to Tara, who was now back living at home, but her boyfriend was still an item. Dean told me he had been working with the US Coast Guard for a few years and had recently arrived back in Nassau and worked with our mutual friends.

I found Dean's company wonderful; he appeared much older than his thirty-two years and was very knowledgeable. I never felt any age difference and was delighted we had a lot in common to talk about. While he was working at the restaurant for my friends, as he didn't have transport, I would drive him to work and had to drive late at night to collect him. Dean never ate at the restaurant, though he could have, so I always had a small feast waiting for him when he arrived home.

For the first little while he told me that he did not drink alcohol, but as time went on, I discovered he had a penchant for it. I was happy that he and Tara got along well, and we both felt lucky when Dean started cooking dinners for us, when he wasn't working. He told me stories of when he was in the Coast Guard and that he had starved for fifty-seven days, which surprised me, and I didn't really understand the reason for that dire act. He continued to baffle me about certain incidents of his life, which I did find a little bizarre, but attributed it to the fact he admitted that he had been using heavy drugs for some time. Tara told me his cousin, her school friend, wanted to warn me he was heavily into drugs. However, Dean had told me about the matter, and he was now clean and had no intention of returning to his old ways. Dean had promised me that was all behind him.

After a few months I knew Dean and I were meant to be together. We made several visits to the shops in Fort Lauderdale, and it wasn't long before Dean had a wardrobe filled with new clothes. I couldn't wait to introduce him to my friends at La Chaîne des Rôtisseurs. Naturally, I was teased that I had a toy boy, but that didn't bother me, as I think my lady friends were quite envious of me having such a gorgeous man as my escort. Dean fitted into my life as if we had been together forever. He had told me he had been married and had a daughter and that we should visit New Orleans for her birthday.

I made the necessary arrangements, and we stayed in the house with his ex-wife and energetic five-year-old daughter. We spent a lot of time with both of them, but managed also to spend time by ourselves in the evenings, visiting restaurants and nightclubs. Dean showed me around all the places of interest in New Orleans. We were in love and the city embraced us. One night after dinner Dean, with a red rose between his teeth in the middle of traffic and people, went down on his knee to profess his love to me; it was beautiful!

As Dean's ex-wife drove me around New Orleans so that Dean and his daughter could have some quality time together, she told me she had had a difficult life with him, and warned me to be careful. In fact, she warned me not to continue with our relationship. I was a little taken aback by her honesty, but I loved him, and thought perhaps it was a bit of bitterness on her part.

Returning to Nassau, I suggested to Dean he didn't really have to work so hard at the restaurant; he therefore quit his job. Consequently, Tara and I were spoiled by delicious meals and we had epicurean dinner parties at home. We were invited to many dinners hosted by my friends, who were intrigued with my beau. We didn't see much of Tara, as she spent time with her boyfriend, but when she was at home, the three of us would have a lot of fun playing trivial pursuit and scrabble, and just being together as a little family.

I visited Dean's home and his parents were cordial. Dean didn't care for his parents and reminisced about his difficult childhood. His tales brought tears to my eyes and made me love him more. We spent beautiful days in Nassau, and he showed me 'his' Nassau, places I hadn't seen before. Dean was not only an excellent chef, he was good at everything; anything that needed doing in the house, he was able to fix. He was a man of many talents. Unfortunately, my adorable Duke didn't care for him as he knew someone else had taken his place. So I didn't let them get together, which was difficult and sad for me. Duke considered himself to be the only male in my life. I was his girl!

Before I met Dean, I went to a New Year's Eve party with our dear family friend Henry, who liked to be referred to as number one pot-cake (the name for a stray dog in Nassau). In the wee hours of the morning, Henry dropped me home, and as I opened the gate, I didn't know that Duke was right there. He flew out of the gate after Henry, who was running to his car, and caught him in the rear and tore the pants of his tuxedo and his underpants. Fortunately, he did not bite into his flesh. Henry later told me that while he was dropping off another friend at her block of apartments, the doorman was smiling at him, and then made a remark and asked what had happened. It was only at that moment when Henry realised he was walking around with a bare backside! To this day Henry recounts the story with much hilarity and has kept the spoils as a memento to Duke.

As Dean wasn't working, some mornings he would suggest we go to one of the hotels on Cable Beach for breakfast; we would run along the beach and enjoy a big buffet breakfast. Dean made me feel young and even introduced me to the songs of Tom Petty. On our first Valentine's Day, he wanted us to go to the botanical gardens. I was unaware he had prepared a delicious picnic, and as I had never been to the gardens, it was an adventure for me. Dean found a private spot and laid a rug for us to sit on; he poured the champagne and proceeded to read me poetry. I really appreciated every special moment and felt enormously fortunate to be with such a fabulous young man.

Tara wanted to go to London with her boyfriend for her twenty-first birthday, so that was my gift to her. When she returned to Nassau, she told me that she and her friend had split. I was tremendously relieved! Tara continued to work at the various clubs in Nassau as the head hostess, but became bored with her life and wanted to move to the States. We discussed the matter, and I started preparing myself for the time when Tara would be leaving home. I was happy that Dean was with me; I wouldn't be alone in Devon House.

That summer I wanted Dean to meet Peter and Jan Rickard, so we flew to Toronto and visited them at their lovely new home in Bracebridge. We had such a fabulously happy time together and they were delighted to meet Dean. We then visited Los Angeles to stay with Basil and spent a wonderful week with him in his beautiful home off Sunset Boulevard. He and Dean got along very well, and one evening

Dean cooked a sumptuous dinner for all of us. After dinner Dean and I would go dancing at the nightclubs along Sunset Boulevard. I felt I had returned to my twenties! I started noticing that after Dean had had a lot to drink and when we returned to our room, he would become quiet and not talk to me at all, just go straight to sleep.

As Basil had to leave on a trip, we moved into a nearby hotel. Dean had a cousin who was from an Indian tribe, and Dean's mother had made us promise to see him. We had arranged that he would collect us from our hotel and drive to an Indian reservation, as he had wanted us to meet some of his relatives. The trip was a revelation to me. First of all, it was a very hot August day. The little car didn't have air-conditioning, and we seemed to drive for miles, finally arriving at the reservation. I was frankly appalled at the poverty and the way those poor families lived. We then drove into the remote countryside to a nearby casino and were told that the money from the casino would help the American/Indian families. I really hoped that was the case.

I didn't enjoy casinos, and just having seen the poor families living in such squalid conditions in America bothered me, and that together with the dry heat with temperatures over a hundred degrees Fahrenheit, made me want to be back on the road to our hotel before I fainted. It was not one of the most enjoyable days, but in retrospect, it was a learning experience.

Dean and I had a few more days in Los Angeles and decided to visit Santa Monica. We had been to a few nightclubs the previous evening, and I noticed Dean's charming, attentive mood was changing. The following day we drove to Santa Monica and there seemed to be an atmosphere, which was upsetting to me. I loved Dean and just couldn't understand why he had those moods.

We walked around the pier and had lunch in a delightful fish restaurant, but I was so sad. He wouldn't talk to me and seemed unfriendly. After some hours, his mood lifted and although I felt like a wet rag, I noticed a merry-go-around, one of my all-time favourite things in life. I hoped that by riding it we would be happy again, and fortunately it seemed to work. Dean apologised for upsetting me by his moody behaviour. There just didn't appear any reason why he would want to change towards me, as basically we were happy together.

We had enjoyed our visit to Los Angeles and left with fond memories of Basil, his warm hospitality, and our own fun on Sunset Boulevard.

Petra had decided she wanted to be with me for Christmas rather than earlier in the year. She had always got on well with Ken, so much so that they became close friends. As Dean was still fairly new on the scene, they were respectful to one another. Both felt a little possessive of me, which was rather difficult. However, we had a lovely Christmas and a delicious dinner, which Dean cooked. He and I both declined to go to junkanoo, but Petra had never been, so Tara asked her ex-boyfriend to join them as protection.

Junkanoo is a Bahamian festival that occurs in the early hours of December twenty-sixth and again in the morning of January first welcoming in the New Year. Thousands of Bahamians dressed in a multitude of colourful cardboard outfits, which are truly magnificent, parade and dance through Bay Street, as if entranced and possessed, gyrating to the drums, whistles, cowbells and brass horns. I had been a spectator for many years and didn't feel like joining them that year, neither did Dean, but I knew that Petra would really enjoy the experience, and I suggested to Tara that they may like to stop at a local restaurant and eat boiled fish and grits for breakfast before returning home at sunrise.

In the New Year Tara moved to Fort Lauderdale. Dean and I went over to help her find an apartment and furnish it. She seemed happy to be in familiar territory and soon found work in a restaurant. So long as my daughter was happy, I could not say anything.

Dean and I were getting along well, and were happy. He made it clear he wanted to spend the rest of his life with me, even if I ended up in a wheel chair. So we decided to get married. He told me he wished to change his name to O'Leary by deed poll, as he wanted to disassociate himself from his family. Under the circumstances I thought it was an excellent idea, as it was far too complicated for me to change my name to his, and that way it was easier for us to have the same name.

It was difficult for me to accept he wanted nothing much to do with his family, however, that was his decision. Tara was delighted with our news. She liked Dean, and both of them got along well. I asked my lawyer, who was also a justice of the peace, to conduct the civil ceremony. I spoke to my priest who said that before we could have a church wedding, Dean would have to have his marriage annulled. Dean not only agreed to that, but also wanted to become a Catholic. We scheduled our wedding for June the following year, which gave us time to be sure of our intentions.

I had a telephone call from Hans in the summer of 1995, who said he would be visiting friends in Long Island New York to recuperate after his knee-replacement operation and would love for me to spend the weekend with them and meet his Philippina wife and twin daughters. Old friends are few and far between, and although Dean wasn't happy at me going to see him, I wasn't going to lose the opportunity. I was delighted to see Hans and meet his wife and adorable girls. His friends were hospitable, and I had a really lovely weekend. Hans had brought me a gift of a dress that he had made for me in Manila, and he didn't know it at the time—neither did I—but it would be my wedding dress!

61

For Dean's thirty-fourth birthday, I surprised him with tickets to Cairo and for us to cruise the Nile. He was very excited, as was I. Although I had been to Cairo a few times in the past, I had not been on the Nile cruise. I had booked for us to join an inclusive tour, and from start to finish the arrangements proved to be fantastic.

Our arrival at Cairo airport was an experience. We had to go through immigration and customs, where all cameras and video cameras had to be examined. Finally, after what seemed like hours, our group was through, and we boarded the bus, which was waiting to take us to the Mena House Hotel at Giza. Dean and I made the mistake of sitting in the front seat. I had been in crazy traffic many times before, but the journey from the airport to Giza was like riding a roller coaster, a nail-biting experience. Our driver was quite amazing, and we had to applaud him on our arrival. Although worn out, we had made it safely to our destination.

Both Dean and I were so excited to be in Egypt, and the hotel, Mena House, was lovely. As we waited for our room allocation, we enjoyed a glass of Omar Khayyam wine at the attractive bar. We had requested a room in the old part of the hotel and were pleased with our spacious mini suite. The squeaky floorboards were covered with well-worn carpets and the whole atmosphere was delightfully ethnic. Having unpacked and refreshed ourselves, we went to the dining room where we had reservations for dinner. It was all so romantic, especially as we could see the moon over the lighted pyramids.

The following morning we were up early and eager to see and taste our Egyptian breakfast, which was brought to our room. It was delicious and very healthy. We then joined our guide, Sami, and our group to visit the pyramids. We had the choice of going in the bus or riding on a camel, which we both decided to do. Despite the stench of halitosis from both the camel and its owner, I climbed on the camel but nearly fell off, as it got to its feet; no one had warned me that when the camel raised itself, one could almost fly over its neck. I loved being in the desert on my camel with the mighty pyramids in the foreground. I thought of being a female Lawrence and riding my camel through the hot, vast Sahara.

Sami said we could enter one of the pyramids, and I joined Dean, but within two minutes of entering I couldn't breathe. I had to leave. The feeling of claustrophobia was overpowering. I sat outside on a rock chatting with the souvenir vendors, while I waited for Dean and the rest of the party. We then boarded our coach to visit the Great Sphinx and afterwards drove to the pyramids at Sakkara and then on to Memphis.

We made a stop at a carpet weaving school and were a little disturbed as we watched very young children weaving the carpets. I love oriental carpets, and to see the work that went into them was fascinating. I bought a couple of small rugs, as I knew we couldn't carry much more back to Nassau. The owner told us the children worked for him for half a day and were paid, and the other half he would pay for them to go to school. That information made us feel a little easier about the situation.

I loved the drive into the countryside to see the date trees, the fields, and just getting a glimpse into the everyday life of the people. We stopped at a picturesque tavern where we saw our naan bread being made, which made us hungry and ready to enjoy the simple lunch accompanied by a good Stella beer.

A side trip of our tour was to travel by air to the Abu Simbel Temple, which is in Nubia on the western side of Lake Nasser. Two massive rock temples were carved out of the mountainside during Pharaoh Ramses II reign, as a monument to himself and Queen Nefertari. Dean and I were thrilled to be actually viewing the famous and incredible temple complex.

Our visit to Aswan to see the High Dam, which was built by the Soviet Union, was awesome, and we learned that the dam waters from the Nile formed the artificial Lake Nasser. We drove on to the temple of Philae, which was beautiful, and while there we bought a few of the djellabahs that Dean would wear for the whole time we were in Egypt. As we were now in Aswan for our overnight stay, we took a water taxi across to our hotel on Elephantine Island, before embarking on our Nile cruise the following day. The hotel was large and comfortable.

On our arrival, we were offered a drink of the hibiscus flowers. At dinner I saw that Sami was sitting by himself, and I said to Dean we should join him. Well, Dean did so reluctantly. We had interesting conversation and left the dining room fairly late. We should have retired to our room, but Dean wanted to go to the bar upstairs, which was also a games room, where he proceeded to play billiards.

The night was moving into the early hours of the morning, and we had imbibed a lot, including a very expensive bottle of champagne. I was really tired, and eventually made it to our room. Dean's mood had changed and he didn't say a word to me. In fact, he was hostile. I hoped that by the time we had to leave the hotel in the morning things would be different, but nothing had changed. I was in tears as I looked out over the beautiful gardens, the desert hills in the distance and the happy feluccas on the Nile. I was distressed and couldn't understand what had happened. We had to pack and be ready to leave the hotel, and in my anguished state, I left my precious address book in the room. I didn't realise until I was halfway through the trip and asked Sami to please post it to me to Nassau. Amazingly, after almost two months of arriving back in Nassau, I received it and was so grateful, rewarding Sami with multiple thanks and small gifts.

Before we boarded our cruise ship, Dean apologised for upsetting me. I was relieved, as I really wanted us to enjoy our cruise. The Nile was so perfect, so beautiful; it was another world. As we glided along the water, we watched the fishermen, the farmers, the water buffalos and the children waving to us. It was mystical, marvelous Egypt, and

I was grateful and excited to be on that wondrous journey; my deep gratitude was always to Jesus.

We visited the temples of Kom Ombo and Edfu, before arriving at the temples of Luxor and Karnak and home to the Valley of the Kings. The ship docked in Luxor overnight, and Dean said he would like to go ashore and have a few drinks in the bar at the renowned St. George Hotel. It was dark as we walked to the hotel. I wasn't afraid, as I was with my six-foot-six-inch pharaoh, who was wearing his djellabah— and to everyone who saw him, he was an Egyptian. Ever since we had arrived in Egypt, Dean was taken for an Egyptian, which made him very happy.

The hotel was impressive, as was the bar, which was busy with many well-dressed Europeans and ex-pats. We enjoyed our libation and were aware of causing a stir, an attractive redhead and a tall, handsome Egyptian. No one knew any differently. We found a horse and cart to return us to our ship.

The temples of Luxor and especially Karnak were stupendous. We were fortunate enough to see a Son et Lumière production at the temple of Karnak. I was in my element; perhaps I had been an Egyptian queen in one of my previous lives. Our tour continued with a visit to the Valley of the Kings, Hatshepsut's Temple, the Colossi of Memnon and the tomb of King Tutankhamen. I was determined to see that famous tomb and managed to breathe without discomfort, as the path to the tomb was not so claustrophobic. Both Dean and I were in love with Egypt, and as we returned to Cairo, it was difficult to imagine being in any world other than that of the Pharaohs.

Back in Cairo, we visited the famous Egyptian museum with all the spectacular artifacts, especially those of King Tutankhamen. The following day we drove to see the Hanging Church, which was named for its location, being above a gatehouse of a Babylon Fortress in Coptic Cairo, known as Old Cairo. I thought the church was gently ethereal. The central sanctuary was made of ebony and ivory, and surmounted by icons of the Virgin Mary and the Twelve Apostles which were breathtaking. It is said this was the site where Mary and Joseph stayed while in Egypt.

Our tour took us next to the Walled Old City, which looked dark and dismal, more so when we were told that people were living there. We were both in awe of Saladine's Citadel and the incredible Alabaster Mosque, which was magnificent. After washing our hands and removing our shoes, we were allowed to enter the impressive Mosque. The tour was fabulous, and the more we saw, the more we loved Cairo and Egypt. Our trip was coming to an end, but we wanted to see the Khan el Khalili souk.

The entrance to the bazaar was bustling with people, and many Egyptian men were taking a great interest in my handsome Bahamian, wanting to talk to him first in Arabic but then in English. We were back in modern day Cairo with its never-ending activity; it was like going from the sublime to the ridiculous.

We strolled through the lanes of the Khan el Khalili, looking at the merchandise in all the numerous stalls and loving every aroma and every sound that emanated from the busy marketplace. On our way back to the Mena House, we decided we would not join our travel companions to dine there that night, but would hire a taxi to return to the souk. The concierge of the hotel had mentioned there was an authentic little Egyptian restaurant deep in the Khan el Khalili market and called a taxi for us. Our driver told us his profession was that of a lawyer, but as there was so little crime in Cairo, he had to have the job as a taxi driver to make ends meet. He was a very educated young man who spoke excellent English. I would have liked to have invited him to dine with us, but I knew Dean never enjoyed the company of anyone other than mine for most of the time.

We had a wonderful evening eating exotic Egyptian fare in the exclusive little restaurant. After dinner we sat in the alleyway outside the restaurant with a group of Egyptians smoking the hookah, and hoping that the evening would never end. However, our magical visit to that enchanting land was almost over.

As we left Cairo airport on our way back to Miami and then to Nassau, Dean told me that he had left his heart in Egypt—everything he had seen and heard was recorded in his memory forever—and having been taken for an Egyptian on numerous occasions made him more resolved to return. Shortly after we were back at Devon House, we gave an Egyptian dinner party for a couple of close friends and asked them to arrive in djellabahs. Dean cooked many Egyptian delicacies, and we enjoyed a hilariously happy evening as we shared our memories and photographs of glorious Egypt. We had tried to make a drink out of all the hibiscus flowers we had in our garden, but without success.

62

Our civil marriage would be on June twenty-second, 1996. We invited eight special friends to witness our vows. My Bahamian friend and lawyer conducted the ceremony, which we had at Devon House. I was nervous, but having lived with Dean for two years, I knew the union would work. He loved me and wanted to spend the rest of his life with me. I wore the pretty dress that Hans had brought from Manila for the brief ceremony; it was perfect, and when I told Hans some years later that his gift was my civil wedding dress, he was amused.

After the ceremony we drove over to Paradise Island and to the Atlantis Hotel, where we had a wedding supper in one of the restaurants. Robert and Carmen had flown in from London to be with us and joined our small group of friends for a lovely evening.

I was happy as I looked at my handsome husband and my precious Tara, and took the opportunity to thank her for the beautiful poem she had written for us as her wedding gift.

The following evening we had thirty-six friends join us for a romantic evening at Devon House. Basil and his future wife came in from California. Dean and I organised everything ourselves, and we provided a delicious sit-down buffet dinner around the pool, which Tara and I enhanced with floating candles. The terrace of Devon House was made for romance, and after dinner we danced under the stars. I remembered my lucky birthmark, and as I thought of Selina, I knew she would approve of me wearing a sari for that auspicious occasion. The evening was filled with laughter, and everyone enjoyed our celebration. My thoughts also went to Patrick, and I prayed he would agree with my decision, but I wasn't sure. Patrick was the kindest man in the world and would never have criticised me. However, he would have gently given me a few words of wisdom.

After three days of celebration, I was grateful I had arranged for the two of us to attend the 1996 Grand Chapître in Boston; it would be good to just relax and enjoy the excellent arrangements made for us by La Chaîne des Rôtisseurs. Although I had been to Boston with Tara and Ken many years earlier, I didn't really remember much of the city, so was pleased to have had another opportunity to be there together with Dean on our honeymoon. We had a lot of fun and met engaging people from all over the world. One of the many highlights of our four-day visit was to meet Julia Child and watch her receive a commendation from La Chaîne at the famous Fanueil Hall.

At the end of July, the Reverend Patrick Pinder conducted our church wedding ceremony at St. Francis Cathedral. Before the nuptial Mass, he baptised and confirmed Dean into the Catholic Church. Our dear friends Becky and Heinz offered to be our witnesses. Tara was not in Nassau. It was a simple ceremony and I prayed Jesus would watch over us and keep our union happy forever. Our friends then kindly took us for a pub lunch.

We stayed in Nassau enjoying Devon House and a rather good social life, as by now we had made lots of friends from La Chaîne. As Dean was such an excellent cook and I was a perfect front-of-house hostess, our dinner parties were spectacular.

In September my beautiful Rottweiler Duke became ill. I was so sad and felt incapable of taking him to the vet myself. I knew he was close to death, so I asked Mac (who adored Duke), whom I employed to take care of the dogs' baths and walks, to go in my place and stay with him; he was there when Duke died of cancer. In my opinion I had the best vet in Nassau, Dr. Basil Sands, and I knew he did everything for Duke to die as peacefully and painlessly as possible.

The following year while I was away, Mac took Windsor to the vet, who also had cancer, and Mac was by his side when he died at Dr. Sands' clinic. They had both lived for a little over ten years, which Dr. Sands said was good considering the climate in Nassau. I felt guilty I hadn't given my dogs a better life; they needed me, and I should have been with them more often. Now I just had little Duchess, who felt lonely without the boys. I had her with me as much as possible until she started to lose control of her bowels and became disorientated. I spoke to Dr. Sands, and he came to Devon House to give Duchess her injection to doggy heaven. I was so miserable and for a fortnight afterwards kept thinking about my sweet babies. Dean was comforting and dug a grave in the garden for Duchess. I think of Duke, Duchess and Windsor joining Rocky and my beloved Romulus and Remus, and all of them with Patrick.

One day I received a call from Petra saying she was coming to Nassau just as she had done for years. I knew Dean would not be happy to hear that and would not want her to stay. I was a little surprised Petra had wanted to come and visit again, knowing she didn't like him. They hadn't got along well when she was there at Christmas the previous year. As Dean was now my husband, and in order to keep the peace, I had to let Petra know I would prefer she didn't come to stay with us at that time. I was aware she did not care for Dean, and the feeling was mutual.

To tell her it was not a good idea was extremely difficult for me and it upset her. She didn't understand why I couldn't have said to Dean that she could visit me, as she felt she should take precedence over him, having known me for much longer, but I knew my terrain and didn't want to make potholes.

For many years, therefore, Petra did not make her annual visit to Devon House, but she did visit Nassau and stayed with Ken while visiting the friends I had introduced her to. She also made it known to them what she thought of me. Dean was my husband, and I knew if I had insisted Petra stayed with us, her visit would bring unwanted difficulties and contentious fireworks. Dean and I were still getting used to one another, and we didn't need any outside influences to put a strain on a sometimes tenuous relationship. Dean's moods would often upset me, so although for the most part life was happy, there were times when I felt uncertain and couldn't really understand the reason.

In October, Dean and I went to San Jose, Costa Rica. We had been invited by a couple from Nassau to stay with them. Our friend was at the airport to meet us. The drive to her home was uncomfortable, as the roads were awful. We finally arrived at the plantation, a large property with a large house. The house was really impressive and had great potential. As we were shown to our room, our hostess explained that the room was not finished and the bathroom hadn't been built. There were no closets to hang our clothes, no curtains. Why we had been invited, goodness only knows. Dean and I tried to make light of it, but walking through a strange house in the middle of the night looking for a toilet was not my idea of comfort.

We both dressed for dinner and joined a couple of friends that had dropped by. Dean and I were really hungry and looked forward to a good meal. We were offered wine and more wine, and some nuts were on the table. Although our host was trying to keep us amused, there was no sign of our hostess, and by ten o'clock no sign of any food. The other guests had left, and we were ushered into the kitchen, where our hostess had apparently forgotten all about us. Some frozen food was heated up, and we were grateful not to have gone to bed hungry. As the house was deep in the country, there were no restaurants in the vicinity.

Neither Dean nor I slept well, and in the morning I needed to shower. Dean managed to find a portable shower he was able to work. Our hostess said I could use her shower, which was just off her large bedroom. I was repulsed. I didn't know when that shower had been cleaned, but our hostess didn't seem to notice or care. Their eldest son asked us if we would like to go sightseeing and look at one of the many volcanoes. We enjoyed our drive and were especially happy to stop at a delightful roadside restaurant to have a good lunch.

Our host was from a prominent German family. He tried to do the best he could to make our stay interesting by showing us around his vast property. I think his wife was having problems and wasn't about to apologise or put herself out for us in any way. The second night we were all invited to a party of some friends of our hosts; it was a super party, and we saw a glimpse of how the ex-pats lived. Everyone loved living in Costa Rica; life was inexpensive, and there was much to be said for the lush vegetation. After the second night Dean and I agreed we had had enough discomfort and would move to a hotel—especially as Tara was due to arrive to celebrate her twenty-second birthday.

When she arrived we told her of our experiences and that we were still incredulous of the way we had been treated by our hostess. However, we invited them to dinner at the hotel, and after dinner Dean and Tara asked me to leave, as they wished to confront the people we had come to see in Costa Rica. I understand that my two Tigers, Chinese horoscope, really told them how despicable they were, especially our hostess. We spent a couple more days visiting the city of San Jose and taking a tour around the environs, but we were all happy to be back on the plane and to say good-bye to Costa Rica. Under different circumstances we may have had a more enjoyable visit.

For many years I had contributed to the welfare of Sylvan and her two girls, and thought it would be nice for Dean to meet them. So we flew to Palma, Majorca, where they lived. We had a happy dinner together, and were enjoying our days in Palma. The next dinner we had with Sylvan and her eldest daughter was anything but pleasant. Sylvan said they had moved out of the flat I had loaned her for many years, which came as a surprise to me, as did the rest of the conversation, which became contentious, especially with the remarks made by her eldest daughter. I really thought my financial assistance had helped my sister and her two children—to provide a simple way of life for them and to give the girls the chance to attend school.

When they were little I was told they would be put in foster homes, so I was determined that shouldn't happen. I was shocked and hurt to hear that my "charity" had not been appreciated, and I was considered arrogant and mean. Since that time they chose not to communicate with me at all. I remain confused as to where I went wrong. Vanessa kindly told me that when Patrick died, I could have left with Tara and not given any thought to helping the family, but I didn't choose that path and did my best to be there for everyone.

When Dean and I went to the flat in Palma, which Sylvan and the girls had vacated, we saw there was an awful lot of work to be done to make it presentable for sale. We went there every day for ten days cleaning, scrubbing, and painting. Despite not speaking Spanish, we managed to buy all the necessary items for the major undertaking, and eventually it was done. Dean was absolutely wonderful and did such a professional job that we were able to sell the apartment before departing. We spent our last days discovering the lovely city of Palma and were sad that our visit had an unhappy ending with regard to Sylvan.

Dawn had now moved from Montserrat to Southern Spain and invited us to visit her. While I chatted to Dean about our proposed visit to Dawn, I said as we would be so close to Morocco, we should take the advantage of exploring that country. I laughed when he said that he could be an Arab again and wear his djellabah.

We decided to spend three days in Barcelona, before travelling on to Malaga. Our days in Barcelona were glorious; we stayed at the Ritz Hotel and walked the Ramblas, where we stopped at many of the bars for a glass of rustic wine and the delicious tapas. We were enthralled and delighted by La Boqueria, the large fish and produce market just off Las Ramblas, and found a tiny restaurant at the back where we had a marvelous meal. We saw most of the splendour of the city, including the architectural works of Antoni Gaudi, and were in awe of his unfinished iconic Cathedral, La Sagrada Familia, which Pope Benedict XVI consecrated as a Basilica in November of 2010.

Dawn was at Malaga airport to meet us and drove to Sotogrande, where she lived in an attractive little hacienda. I didn't think Dawn looked well, but she never complained and was happy to show us around. We dined in atmospheric restaurants and during the day lunched in little taverns with spectacular views. We also had lunch at the famous Valderrmera Golf Club, which was very exciting. Dawn and I went for walks, and during that time she told me that she was having health problems, but wasn't sure the cause of her discomfort.

She was happy to meet Dean, and although she had seen him at the family Christmas party in Nassau, hadn't actually met him. They both got along well and would sit up into the wee hours talking and drinking brandy. Dean was a night owl, and once he had a glass of something alcoholic and his cigarettes, he became alive. I knew those two Pisces would get along very well.

As we weren't too far from Gibraltar, Dawn drove us there, and we had a pleasant visit to the Rock. It was years since Vanessa and I had been there for our exciting adventure. We didn't spend too much time wandering around, as there wasn't much to see, but it was well worth a visit.

63

After our fabulous three-day stay with my dear friend, we were headed for Morocco. Dawn put together a hamper for us, saying the food on the ferry would not be up to our standards. She drove us to Algerciras, where we boarded the ferry to Tangier. Before we left I hugged Dawn and wished she was coming too. I knew she enjoyed having us to stay, and I loved every minute of being with her.

Once on the ferry, we settled ourselves at a table and opened the hamper—there were two bottles of wine, one chilled white and one red, two wine glasses, and lots of yummy food. Dean had changed into his djellabah, and I knew he was ready to be an Arab again! As we crossed the Straits of Gibraltar, we happily ate the contents of our hamper and enjoyed the wine although neither of us ever drank much during the day. I was really looking forward to our time in Morocco and especially to discover it with my handsome husband. The hotel car with driver was awaiting our arrival from the ferry, and we were soon in our attractive room at the El-Minzah hotel in Tangier, which overlooked the Straits of Gibraltar. After unpacking we set out to explore the souk. Dean bought a fez and a couple more djellabahs, and then we looked at some exquisite carpets and rugs. We should have left the purchase of a carpet to the following day, but we didn't and ended up buying a highly overpriced rug, having been tempted by the mint tea and the magic of Tangier.

We made our way back to the hotel with our new purchases to have a little rest before dining at the famed el-Korsan restaurant in the hotel. Dean suddenly went very quiet, and his mood changed. He became distant and unfriendly, so much so it brought me to tears. After a few hours he seemed to pull himself together, and we made our way to dinner. I tried to make the most of the evening, but I was hurt and confused. It was a shame, as the restaurant was stunning, and I wished I could have done it more justice.

The next morning Dean was himself, and we decided to explore Tangier. We walked through the Souk Dakhli, a square in the Medina, which took us into the really old part of Tangier, where we watched the Riffsan women selling their fruit and vegetables. There was much activity with many street vendors trying to sell their wares. I didn't let go of Dean's hand for fear of getting lost. The new city was so different to the old part, which we both preferred. That evening we dined at the Marhaba Palace, which was situated within the old Medina. The ambiance in that restaurant was sensuous and captivating, as we sat at low tables on red, cushioned seats, ate the delicious and varied ethnic food, and had the accompaniment of three turbaned musicians playing an assortment of Arabic music.

The following day Dean had to arrange to hire a car for our adventure to Fes, Rabat and Marrakech. While he was at the car rental office, I sat in the Café de Paris, a familiar coffee establishment, observing the myriad people of different nationalities who frequented the popular water hole. As we had to leave early the next day, we decided to have a less formal dinner and just enjoy the wine and mezze at Caid's Bar. The next morning we said good-bye to the el-Minzah and fitted our luggage into Spot, our mini two-door hatch car. Dean told me they only had gearshift cars, and thank goodness he was familiar with driving it.

Trying to navigate our way out of Tangier was tricky, especially as we drove through the Grand Socco. Anyway, somehow we made it to the outskirts of the city and were soon driving along the coast road. Remembering Patrick, I had ordered a picnic basket to be made up for us and delivered with our breakfast, as I wasn't sure where we would have our next meal. Our drive through the countryside, the villages and the Rif Mountains was a kaleidoscope of colour and diverse scenes. The roads were good, but had no highways; so if one happened to be behind a donkey and cart, there was no use trying to be in a hurry.

I noticed a picnic site in a bucolic pasture. It was good to stretch our legs, and then sit on the wooden bench, while we opened our picnic basket. Everything seemed more delicious being in the middle of nowhere. We felt content with the open sky and the silent mountains around us. Our only other stops were to fill Spot with petrol and make use of the conveniences, which were not at all pleasant. However, I became well acquainted with squatting and aiming into a hole in the ground, and despite the discomfort, I have to admit the relief was worth it.

The single-traffic road to Fes was attractive but slow, and when Dean said we were getting low on petrol, I was concerned, as we still had about an hour before we reached the city. We hadn't seen a petrol station in hours and dusk was falling. I was praying hard that Jesus would soon show us where we could fill Spot, as neither of us wished to be stuck on a lonely and dark road at night. We were becoming rather nervous, but I knew Jesus would take care of us, and just as we were entering Fes, there it was—a happy miracle, as the tank was on empty.

We drove into the city and despite looking at the signs, were completely lost and had no idea how to get to our hotel. At a traffic light I leaned out of the window to man on a motorcycle and asked him if he would direct us to the Palais Jamai Hotel.

Thank goodness he spoke English and said: "Follow me." At that time in the evening, especially as it was rush hour and night had fallen, we would never have found our hotel without the help of our good Samaritan. Once we arrived at the hotel, he waved to us, "enjoy your stay," and was gone. Naturally, we felt most grateful for such kindness.

It was good to be able to unwind in our room after driving over two hundred miles. We were hungry and ready for a glass of wine. We found our way to the Moroccan Al Fassia restaurant in the hotel. As we sank into the inviting cushions, we felt we were dining in an old Moorish Palace. The surroundings were exotic and lustrous with painted ceilings and walls covered with a myriad of colourful mosaics. Dean, wearing his elaborate djellabah, was in his element and loved being taken for an Arab. We feasted while the musicians played and the belly dancer entertained. I fell asleep with gratitude to Jesus for having guided us safely to Fes and for such a memorable evening.

The next morning our guide was there to take us through the ancient souk. We entered the medina of Fes, a walled city with madrasas, mosques and palaces dating back to the thirteenth and fourteenth centuries. We had entered another world, a labyrinth of many alleyways, which housed merchants and craftsmen, stalls selling dates, food, spices, copper and carpets. It seemed spiritual to me, as I observed an almost mystical world. No cars were allowed in the area, but there were the sweet mules moving goods from place to place.

Our guide suggested that we should see the oldest tannery in the world and handed us perfumed jasmine flowers. As we followed him through the winding, narrow streets and up some steps, we began to understand why we had the flowers. We reached the balcony overlooking the tannery, which hadn't changed since the eleventh century, and it was an awesome sight, despite the terrible stench. After that we continued our walk amidst the constant flow of people, stopping from time to time to look at the exquisite carpets and rugs, the little shops selling many diverse merchandise and were especially fascinated by the pharmacies, which sold all sorts of unusual and exotic potions. As we left the maze of alleys, I thought to myself that was the most intriguing souk I had ever visited.

In the afternoon we explored more of our old Moorish hotel and walked through the manicured terraced gardens. I found a little shop on the property and bought a pretty djellabah, which I wore that evening for dinner at Al Fassia restaurant—we didn't want to dine anywhere else! We loaded up Spot the next morning and were on our way through the Atlas Mountains to Rabat. We decided to leave early and stop for a late lunch. Our drive from Fes to Rabat was like a dream, as if we were motoring through a watercolour painting. Beneath us were the arable fields and the little farmhouses, and embracing us were the magnificent slumbering mountains. The roads were wonderful, and as there were such few vehicles, we had the strange feeling of just being alone in Spot in that ethereal world.

After driving for approximately one hundred and thirty miles, we entered the city and capital of Morocco, Rabat. We were given the name of the Hotel Rabat, Jardin des Roses, which we found without too much difficulty and were happy to partake of the buffet lunch at the coffee bar restaurant. The hotel was modern, and what we saw of Rabat was a sophisticated city with beautiful homes, wide boulevards–and very clean—it was most impressive.

We left Rabat around two in the afternoon feeling refreshed, and as we drove once more on the breathtaking Atlas mountain road, we noticed the road seemed even more remote. We had hoped to arrive in Marrakech before darkness surrounded us, but despite Dean's amazing driving and my navigator skills, we reached the city around eight o'clock. Fortunately, Marrakech was a little easier to enter than Fes, and I did manage to read the signposts, which eventually brought us to La Mamounia Hotel.

Dean and I felt somewhat disheveled after travelling in little Spot over three hundred miles and arriving at the grand hotel. Nevertheless, we were happy to have arrived safely. I immediately fell in love with the hotel and looked forward to exploring it the following day. We didn't feel like dressing for dinner so decided to have room service. I opened the window to see the night and was greeted by the seductive scent of jasmine wafting upward. Apart from being absolutely thrilled to be a guest of that splendiferous hotel and knowing I would have a few days to enjoy all the amenities, my big delight that evening was to see rose petals in the toilet. Dean and I ate a superb supper accompanied by a welcome bottle of fine wine, but there was little conversation, and I imagined Dean was tired after the long drive.

The following morning while having breakfast, we looked out at the gardens framed by the regal Atlas Mountains in the background and relished the beauty. We took our time to familiarise ourselves with the palatial hotel, which was situated at the edge of the terracotta walls of the old city, and walked through some of the twenty acres of magnificent gardens. I understood why Sir Winston Churchill said it was, "the most lovely spot in the whole world."

After we both indulged in a much needed massage, we wandered into the town and to the Djemma El Fna Square, where we spent most of the afternoon. The square was buzzing with people and stalls selling every conceivable item. There were the snake charmers, the magic men and so many other entertainers. We stopped at several of the food stalls to sample the delicacies that were for sale. It was another world, and we were thrilled to be part of the effervescent market place; most exhilarating. Walking back through the neighbourhood, we were tranquil, as no one bothered us; though a couple of men called out to Dean, saying that they thought he was gorgeous! Whenever we passed any women, there were many admiring glances towards my husband. I knew how handsome he was and was proud I was on his arm.

For dinner we had made reservations at La Marocain, the Moroccan restaurant in the hotel, and wore our djellabahs which brought many admiring comments from the staff. After a perfect Moroccan meal, we went to have a nightcap in the famous Churchill Bar. I really didn't know what to drink but thought as I was in that very exotic hotel, I would have Pernod, the anise flavoured liqueur on the rocks. I whispered to Dean as we sipped our nightcaps that I was thinking of all the illustrious guests who had sat in the bar before us and couldn't help but wonder if there were any intriguing people mingling that night. Later as I was preparing for bed, recounting our perfect day, I had a nosebleed, which was strange, but I thought nothing of it.

The following day we took a horse and buggy to explore the Old Medina, which was most interesting. Returning to the hotel, we walked in the gardens and had a light alfresco lunch. That evening Dean and I dined at a dazzling restaurant called Azur. It was like a mini palace with radiant mosaics and candles everywhere. Our dinner started with about ten different dishes called the mezze, both hot and cold. It was followed by the famous lamb tajine. The aromatic Moroccan dish is named after the earthenware pot in which the lamb is slowly cooked until it falls off the bone—very delicious.

We felt replete after our romantic dinner and arrived back to the hotel, where we went to the Churchill Bar for our nightcap. As we approached the bar, we found our drinks were already waiting for us. I was most impressed, and of course the bar man was tipped well. We loved soaking up the atmosphere in the bar, so many people from different countries.

On reaching our room, my nosebleed started and was quite bad. I realised it must have been caused by drinking Pernod. I never touched that liqueur again and didn't suffer any more nosebleeds.

Dean and I bid farewell to La Mamounia Hotel and were on our way to Casablanca. We had a chauffeur-driven car for the journey. Spot had been wonderful, but I felt that after driving over five hundred miles, Dean had had enough. Therefore, we were both able to relax and enjoy the scenery on our last leg in Morocco. We had reservations at the Hyatt Regency Hotel in Casablanca, which was in the centre of the city.

The next day we went to see the Hassan II Mosque, and as we crossed the great square, were excited to be visiting the seemingly iridescent and celestial mosque, which overlooked the Atlantic Ocean and which has the tallest minaret in the world. It is the largest mosque in the country and second only to the one at Mecca. It is said that it was inspired by the verse in the Koran, which says, "the throne of Allah was built on water." On entering the mosque, we were overawed by its majesty, which bore a strong Moorish resemblance to the Alhambra in Granada, Spain. The interior of the mosque was impressive, and we were shown around by the resident Imam, who pointed out the automated sliding roof, which, opened up to the heavens; the spectacular women's gallery with the intricately carved wooden ceiling; and beneath the glass floor were the Turkish baths and fountains for washing. The mosque was certainly a resplendent monument and was in stark contrast to the rest of Casablanca. As

Dean and I left the mosque, we both felt serene and grateful for our visit.

On our way back to the hotel, we stopped at a small medina and bought a few souvenirs. Departing from Morocco the next day we were filled with many wonderful memories of a beautiful country and a courteous and friendly people.

64

On our way back to Miami, we stopped overnight in Madrid at the Ritz Hotel and had a delightful dinner in a rustic restaurant and then went on to see a flamenco show, which was thrilling. I loved to travel, involving myself in the different customs, sampling ethnic foods and making friends with the inhabitants of the country. My only regret when travelling was not to be able to attend Mass; it was very difficult. I spoke to Jesus about it and was sure He would understand that circumstances were my only reason for not visiting Him. Shortly after arriving back to Devon House, we gave a Moroccan dinner party, and our friends arrived wearing their djellabahs; it was a memorable evening. Dean cooked an aromatic tagine, and I did not forget to have rose petals in the guest toilets.

Life was good. Dean and I were happy and enjoyed each other's company, and we were popular with our friends. However, I became rather unsettled when I discovered that many a night Dean was not in our bed. I would find him downstairs in the study lying on the floor wrapped in one of the oriental rugs. The strange occurrences upset me, as we hadn't had any disagreements. We had a seven-foot square bed, so there was plenty of room for him. I was totally bewildered. I would ask him to come back to bed. Sometimes he did, but sometimes he didn't.

I wondered why he did that, and he didn't really have an answer for me. During the day Dean was quiet, always finding things to do around the house, which I appreciated, and it was only in the evenings that we would converse properly while having dinner with wine. I had noticed after a few years that his consumption of alcohol had increased, but it never seemed to affect him outwardly.

On our trips I observed he showed little affection towards me, especially at night after he had consumed much wine and brandy. Dean's strange behaviour was making me feel unhappy, so I had to talk to him. I told him that his remoteness was making me so sad that I would even consider divorce if he wanted out of our marriage. I thought we were happy, and he often told me as much. After our conversation I noticed he really tried to be more attentive, but deep in my heart I had fear. I had to act normally, and to all our friends we had the perfect marriage. I knew Dean loved me, but there were many times when I felt estranged from him.

For Christmas I decided it would be nice for Tara to join us in London, and that we would spend the holidays at the Marriott Hotel in Grosvenor Square, attend Mass at the Church of the Immaculate Conception in Farm Street, where Tara was baptised, and go to Annabel's to bring in the New Year. Unfortunately, the holiday wasn't as joyful as I had hoped. Tara felt left out at times, and my two tigers didn't always see eye to eye. Nevertheless, on the whole, it was great for the three of us to be together, and for most of the time we had a really good holiday. Tara and I walked across Grosvenor Square and looked up at our old apartment. Living there seemed like a lifetime ago.

The following year Dean and I went back and forth to Florida to see Tara, whom we had helped over the years move from place to place, until she found an apartment in Kendall. I was so happy that she had decided to go back to her studies and knew she found life at the University of Miami very stimulating. I told her that Dean and I were going to the international event of La Chaîne des Rôtisseurs in Paris and would be away for a little while. Our friends Heinz and Becky had also decided to attend, and we met up in Paris.

The four of us had a lovely time walking around the city sightseeing and eating delicious meals. We joined the members of La Chaîne on a river cruise on the Seine, and spent a delightful evening at the Moulin Rouge. It was such fun to watch the Can-Can.

Dean and I stayed at the Intercontinental Grande Hotel where the Chaîne held their Gala evening in the brilliant ballroom. It was a glittering affair, and we were happy to be there.

In Nassau I had made friends with a German girl, who now lived in Paris with her lover. I had written to tell her Dean and I would be in Paris, and she invited us to their country home, and the invitation included Heinz and Becky. Herta came to the hotel to collect us. The drive through the countryside was lovely. We eventually arrived at an old farmhouse and were shown to our bedrooms. The house reminded me a little of my Old Farm House with the narrow passages and creaking floorboards. The walls were decorated with the heads of deer and all sorts of other animals. Herta's fiancé, Pierre, was a hunter and a taxidermist, which was a little unnerving as we made our way to bed later in the night.

We freshened up and went into the charming dining room for a most luscious dinner with delectable wines. Apart from the human company, there were nine gorgeous well-behaved Jack Russell Terriers who sat on their sofa in the dining room, while we indulged in gourmet courses and convivial conversation. After dinner we adjourned to the cosy living room where a glowing fire added charisma to the ambiance and where we partook of more wine.

The next morning we returned to the dining room for brunch, and what a feast it was. Pierre kept ostriches, and the six of us, together with four friends from nearby homes, ate an omelet, a savoury made from one egg. After our brunch we walked across the road to the many acres of land owned by Pierre and were accompanied by the little Jack Russell Terriers. Dean and I fell in love with those dogs and wanted to take one back with us. Our stay in the French countryside was so memorable. We shall never forget our visit to Herta's and Pierre's home and their warm and generous hospitality.

We returned to Paris, and having said adieu to Heinz and Becky, boarded the train to Monte Carlo. I thought, as we were in that part of the world, I would introduce Dean to some of my memories, and had reserved a room in the Hotel de Paris. We enjoyed our days roaming around the principality, eating well at the little restaurants, and always ending up at the famous bar in the hotel.

Dean wanted to gamble, so we went to Le Grand Casino only to realise we were far too poor to enter those elaborate rooms, and walked over to the little casino in the Café de Paris, where Dean was in his element. He was lucky to start, but when I returned to him after playing the slot machines, Dean's winnings were back with the house. Nevertheless, it was a fun experience. The bar in the hotel was closed when we returned, so we had a nightcap in our room.

While I was in the bathroom getting ready for bed, I wasn't aware Dean had left the room, but when I did, I discovered him wandering the corridors wearing only his shirt and underpants. I was terrified that someone would see him. Dean was extremely inebriated, and I kept saying to him, "please don't make any noise." I finally managed to get him back into our room; he was happy and laughed a lot about his little escapade. He was just such a loveable and charming young man that I too had to smile at his daring.

It was soon time for us to leave Monaco. As we both loved to travel by train, I had booked a sleeper cabin on the Blue Train to Paris. Dean had been to the market earlier, so we could enjoy a picnic dinner on our journey. We had fun as we sat on our beds eating and drinking into the early hours of the morning, and our arrival into Paris came far too quickly. We were soon on our way to Orly airport and back to Miami. Tara was at the airport to meet us, and we spent a couple of days with her in Kendall, enjoying her company and telling her about our adventures.

Despite Dean's strange behaviour at times, we were happy together. There was much that we had in common. He always made me feel that I was the only person that existed for him, and he was also very funny; he made me laugh. At the same time he was a bit of an enigma, one that I tried not to worry about too much. I just wanted him to be happy, and he assured me he was.

In December we went to the University of Miami to be with Tara for her graduation and were very proud to see her accept her certificate as Bachelor of Science in Communications. Tara was the first in our family who had ever been to college. We went back to Nassau to spend a beautiful Christmas together. Tara told us she wanted to move to live in Los Angeles and had arranged to have a job with Warner Brothers. In the New Year we returned to Tara's flat in Kendall and helped her pack up her furniture and possessions to have shipped to Los Angeles, where she, together with Basil's daughter, Heather, and another girl, Nichole, would share a comfortable apartment. Tara loved Los Angeles and found her job interesting and sometimes exciting, especially when she was invited to attend the Oscars.

In June, Dean and I joined the National Chapître of La Chaîne des Rôtisseurs in San Antonio. We felt it was an excuse to see another city in America and to meet Chaîne members we had seen at other events. We were also pleased that some friends from Nassau were visiting and that we were able to invite them to the gala dinner. Tara flew over to be with us for the weekend, and we all had a relaxed and interesting time, especially enjoying the riverside area of San Antonio. Our friend Henry from Nassau was also there, and as always, he was the life and soul of all the parties; everyone had a lot of fun.

65

Tara returned to Los Angeles and Dean and I to Nassau. Dean busied himself with painting the house. I was always amazed by his talents. There was nothing he couldn't do, and everything he did, he did so well. There were times when I used to tease him, saying he loved the house more than me, as during those work sessions, it was if he was in another world. There was no communication between us for many hours. He would unwind during dinner. Dean was a cigarette smoker, which I didn't mind, as he was thoughtful and considerate of me, but it upset me that he would go outside every time he needed to smoke, and eventually I told him to smoke in the house, and, with one thing and another, I started to smoke too.

Every year between the months of June and end of November we would prepare ourselves for hurricane season. I had experienced several hurricanes living in Nassau. Tara, I and the dogs used to listen to the howling winds and hug together as we came through the storms.

We were advised that September would bring a big hurricane by the name of "Floyd". Dean, together with extra help, installed our wooden shutters. We made sure the generator was working and that it had enough fuel. One gets used to living in hurricane country, and we all knew what to do. As Floyd approached, I just had a feeling it would be bad. Dean went to bed and to sleep, and I stayed awake and peered through the cracks of the shutters.

I could hear the wind and the rain, but when I saw the storm surge, the enormous waves coming over the road and the wall into our garden, it was really frightening. The lower garden looked like a lake, and the waves kept pounding. I couldn't really see everything, but I wondered why the waves were cascading into the garden, as I had an eight-foot high, one hundred and sixteen foot long wall in front of the property. Our generator died during the storm, and in the morning we looked out over the devastation. I then knew why the waves had come into the garden; the sea wall was gone, totally destroyed. Dean was very upset. The terrible destruction really unnerved him. We had no electricity and no water.

He told me he needed to leave the house and have breakfast at a hotel on the beach. Grabbing my hand, we tread our way through the trees and branches littered on our now exposed property. As we approached the road, it looked as if all of Nassau was out on a sightseeing tour to see the damage that Floyd had left, and Devon House was one of the main attractions. We crossed the road and were just about to arrive at the beach when Dean's mother called out; she was in her car bumper to bumper with all the other people who were driving around to see the damage left by Floyd. We were both surprised to see her and gave her a wave.

Despite our sombre mood, we managed to eat a good breakfast and walked slowly back to Devon House. For many years no one could see behind the big wall of the property, so the people in the traffic were curious and took a good look at the garden. Amazingly, the tennis court was intact, as was the pagoda, but many of the trees had been uprooted, and the swimming pool was filled with debris. There wasn't anything we could do when we arrived back to the house; we sat out on the little breakfast terrace, and Dean opened a bottle of champagne, lamenting what Floyd had left us. As we were discussing how we had to get things back to normal, a friend of ours appeared with lots of drinking water and offered to help in any way. I was very grateful to our dear friend Carol, who thought of us and drove over to make sure we were all right.

I wanted to get the property cleaned up as quickly as possible and was lucky enough to have some Haitians stop by to ask if we could use their help. Of course, we said yes, and by the end of the day, the property looked a good deal better.

I had to get estimates to have the wall rebuilt, and despite having insurance on the property, there was one reason after another why the claim could not be honoured. We were anxious to have our wall back, and within a few months, the wall was built, but it came at a high price. I didn't fully understand what an impact Floyd had made on Dean; it troubled him for some time.

After everything we had been through with Hurricane Floyd, I thought it would be nice to spend Christmas in England at a members club I belonged to. The club, situated about twenty minutes outside of Windsor, Stoke Park, did us proud and gave us an enormous suite. It was all so festive and had the perfect atmosphere for Christmas. Tara flew in from California to join us for the holidays. Our friends Robert and Carmen, who lived nearby, invited us to a fabulous family dinner at their home, and on Christmas Eve came to visit us at Stoke Park. We sat and chatted in front of a glowing fire in the living room of our suite.

The previous day we had joined other guests around the Christmas tree to sing carols. The old English mansion was the perfect setting for a beautiful, warm yuletide Christmas. The only thing that worried me was that I couldn't go to midnight Mass or any Mass, as I had to consider Dean and Tara, so I sacrificed my Mass.

Opening the curtains on Christmas morning, I was dazzled by the iridescent snow that carpeted the vast property; it was awesome to behold. The three of us had a relaxed day and in the evening dressed for a black tie dinner followed by dancing; it was a memorable evening and alas the last Christmas we would share together.

On Boxing Day I had booked for us to go to a pantomime in Windsor. I knew Dean had never been to one, and it was many years since Tara and I had, so I thought it would be fun. Prior to us leaving the club I started to feel an uneasy current between my two tigers but managed to keep the waters still. We had a drink in a pub in Windsor before going to the theatre. The tiny, intimate theatre was quaint, and the pantomime was delightful.

Before leaving the club that evening I had arranged for a light supper to be served to our suite on our return. After we had finished and Tara was about to return to her room, she mentioned to Dean that it was about time he found a job when he was back in Nassau. Well, that was like waving a red flag in front of a bull. Tara was just at the door to leave when she made the remark, and in a flash Dean was on his feet and at Tara. He threw her against the wall and held her neck in his hand. I was terrified that he was going to kill her. I pressed the service bell in case the situation became worse, and then I pleaded with Dean to let her go. A maid came to the room, but the situation was in control, and Tara left.

I followed her to her room to make sure she would be all right. Tara wasn't afraid, but from that moment she hated Dean. We were leaving Stoke Park the following day, and the atmosphere between Dean and Tara was icy. The incident that occurred really upset me, as I had not seen that side of Dean and it frightened me. However, I was not going to change our plans.

We left Stoke Park for a lovely hotel near Gatwick airport. The hotel was different and homey, but with neither Tara nor Dean talking to one another, it wasn't easy for me. Anyway, we got through it and managed by dinnertime to be civil. The next day we left for Nassau.

We were invited by friends to be their guests at their New Year's Eve party to welcome in the year 2000. Our hostess, whose father had been a friend of Patrick's, gave an amazing party, so generous to so many friends. Dean wanted to leave immediately after we welcomed in the year 2000, but Tara didn't; already the omen was dark. The three of us left the party in silence.

The following day was very tense. I wanted to spend time with Tara, as I knew she was soon headed back to Los Angeles. I drove her to the airport and was relieved that she would be away from Dean. I would miss her terribly, but her safety was paramount.

Dean and I continued to keep our social engagements, but I began to feel I was stepping on eggshells. I noticed he was drinking more in the evenings and would find fault with me, which invariably ended in him choosing to fight me verbally. I really didn't know what was going on, as his persona was changing daily. Despite the disruptions, we were entertained by our friends and had our dinner parties. I wanted so much to believe it was just a phase and would pass, as I knew that Dean loved me. I was smoking more, thinking that if I joined him in the habit it would bring us closer. It was fortunate that Devon House was spacious and I could spend time in our bedroom, and Dean could enjoy watching the television downstairs and busy himself with things around the house.

Dean wanted a dog, a Jack Russell Terrier like those we had seen in France. I was elated, as not having a dog around was strange for me, so I was excited. On Monday April tenth, we drove to see a woman who was selling her Jack Russell puppies, and we chose a little female, who was as big as my hand. I was scared in case I may hurt her, as I had never held such a tiny puppy.

66

The next few days we spent trying to name our little puppy. As Dean still felt a strong affiliation to the Arabs, he wanted to give her an Arabic name, and finally decided on Alil Baraka, which meant little blessing, and deep in my heart I prayed she would be just that and help me through what was developing into a perplexing period.

For weeks we enjoyed our little Baraka. She was mischievous, energetic and just adorable. Since her arrival Dean seemed more relaxed, and the three of us would spend hours happily playing with our puppy in the garden.

At the beginning of 2000, I was informed that I should seriously consider selling Devon House, as my money was rapidly being depleted. I took the advice and started talking to estate agents. On May twenty-third, an auspicious day, as we should have been celebrating six years of being together, Dean started as the executive chef at a hotel on Paradise Island. His hours were long, and he had an enormous amount of work before the hotel officially opened. We only had the one car, and usually Dean drove himself to work and kept the car, but occasionally I would drive over with him in the morning and collect him after work. One morning I put Baraka in her cage, as she was too young to leave alone and too small to sit on my lap. So she and I accompanied Dean as he drove to work from Devon House on Cable Beach. I held my breath all the way, as he made it to the hotel on Paradise Island in seven minutes; the drive usually takes fifteen minutes or longer. I've never been driven so fast. Fortunately it was early in the morning, but I knew better than to say anything. I just prayed. After Dean left us for work, I checked on our puppy, and poor little thing had dirtied her cage. I knew exactly how she felt and proceeded to clean up, reassuring her she was okay, and we drove home quietly and calmly.

Life was very busy. I made numerous lists of what I had to do to close Devon House. I needed to arrange for a firm to pack up the house, find somewhere to live, and apart from everything else, I had to come to terms with the fact that I had to leave my beautiful home. Dean communicated with me sometimes, but he spent hours working at the hotel and continued his work when he came home. He slept for a few hours at night, and much to my amazement, started to speak with a Bahamian accent, which he had never done before. I tried to take it all in my stride, as I had the onus of selling Devon House and was careful not to irate Dean. I refused to be scared of him, though he would constantly fight verbally. I kept quiet rather than respond to what he said to me. I was beginning to think he could be mentally sick, and therefore I must show deep compassion. I tried to defuse the situation by being amused when he talked with a pronounced Bahamian accent, but I was concerned. Dean was losing a lot of weight so quickly. I just did not recognise what was happening to him. My handsome gentle giant was turning into a monster.

I prayed to Jesus to help me, to give me strength during that strenuous time. I had married Dean for better and for worse, and I wanted to help him in every way I could. None of our friends knew what was going on, and we still appeared at social functions. It would interest me to see how graciously Dean would behave in company and showed no indications whatsoever that there was fire burning inside him.

As the days went on, Dean's demeanour worsened. He left his job and behaved in a way that scared me; he was like a Jekyll and Hyde. I didn't know what was happening, and I really didn't have time to delve deeper to find out, as I now had a buyer for the house and was busy sorting out what had to be packed and stored, what had to be given away, and what had to go with us to our rented accommodations. I had to close down Devon House and be out by August thirty-first.

On August the second, Dean went berserk. That time I was terrified; he smashed my cell phone and was drinking so much, saying he was going to smash everything in the house, including me and Baraka. Before he ripped the telephone out of the wall in the bedroom, I had called the police and told them to come and that they would have to climb over the wall and enter the house by clambering up to the bedroom balcony. I held Baraka tightly as we hid in my clothes closet, and she kept very still, as if she understood my fear.

The police found their way up to the bedroom and checked on me, asking me what had happened. I told them that Dean had threatened to kill me and Baraka and was generally terrifying us. They then went downstairs to where Dean was sitting on the floor in front of the bar. When the police talked to him, it was as if butter wouldn't melt in his mouth; his whole persona had changed to charming and totally sane. To see Dean like that brought back memories of my Dad. I remembered Mother calling the police to say that Dad was in a terrible alcoholic state, and when they arrived, he would appear completely lucid.

The Bahamian police were bewildered as to why I had called them, telling them that my life was in danger, as they were amused by Dean and didn't see him as any threat. I asked them to stay while I called Dean's doctor. His doctor was with us in a few minutes and handled the situation brilliantly. He knew how dangerous Dean could be, especially having imbibed a lot of alcohol. He told me to bring Baraka and that the two of us could spend the night at his house. His wife was the daughter of friends of Patrick's of years gone by, and it was at their house that we had celebrated bringing in the New Year. I was very grateful not to spend that night with Dean. A few minutes after arriving at the doctor's home, Dean called and said he wanted to have Baraka returned, that she was his dog. I was reluctant to let her go, but my friends felt it would be better if they returned Baraka to him.

The next day, much to the concern of my friends, I returned to Devon House and to Dean and Baraka. I felt I could manage. I had to. I had the packers coming and so much to do; I had to keep my sanity.

When I went upstairs to my closet, I found Dean had completely destroyed the door; it wasn't there anymore. During one of his less emotive moods, I asked him to please replace it with a new one before we left.

Knowing we had to find somewhere to live by the end of August, I anxiously looked at possible rentals and finally found a small house on the waterfront. The rent was high, but I didn't have time to look further. On August the fifteenth, I signed the lease and was able to move some of my furniture to our new rental. The packers were in Devon House for five days. Dean's mood was up and down, and he talked non-stop in the Bahamian dialect. He was angry with everyone, yelling at the staff and anyone who came in contact with him. I was concerned about his language, which was often blue, and had to apologise to the packers, who were very good-natured about everything. I was spreading myself thin, trying to keep an eye on the six men packing all my china, glass, ornaments and furniture. As I had done at The Old Farm House, I left the majority of my big furniture with the house and only chose pieces that were special to me to keep.

Dean was very vociferous, I had to make sure he didn't keep the men from doing their job by distracting them with his absurd stories. There were times when I wondered if I would make the deadline, as Dean's aggressive behaviour towards me and his racing speech and impulsiveness was exhausting; not to mention his decreased need for sleep. I was so relieved when he had to leave me to go diving, which he loved and would attend two to three times a week.

I didn't want Tara worrying about me, but I had to let her know that life was rather difficult, and although I was having all those problems with Dean, I didn't know what was wrong with him; I innocently went along and just accepted the turbulent situation. Tara had been invited to stay for a month with my Sicilian friend Anna and her husband in Sydney, Australia, and left for her trip on August thirtieth.

At midnight on August thirty-first, together with Dean's lawyer, who had brought us a sandwich, as we hadn't eaten since early morning, we sat on the terrace, and my heart was sad for many obvious reasons, but mainly for the last eight months. I had been living a nightmare and had to say good-bye to my home in such a sorrowful manner. I took one last look at the beautiful property that I had created and knew it was only through the grace of God I had made it by the stroke of midnight.

I tried to make the rental house as comfortable as possible, and we were soon settled into our new environment, but nothing had changed; our relationship was very strained. Dean had started a new business with a friend, which didn't last long, as no one could comprehend his moods. He continued to fight with me for no reason, constantly reminding me that he was a military man and a warrior, but he was not physically abusive, though he often told me how easy it would be for him to kill me with his bare hands by just snapping my neck. I was sad, as I knew he loved me, and I loved him and couldn't understand why he had changed so much; I didn't recognise the man I had married. I would talk to him and tell him I couldn't live like that, and he would assure me of his love and that things would improve. As I watched him speak, he would froth at the mouth, which was disconcerting and scary.

I wasn't au fait with the computer, but one night when Dean was out, I wrote an email to Tara, and in it I wrote how sorry I was that she had to share those past turbulent months with me—even if it was from a distance—and felt it was selfish of me to worry her. I had called Tara a couple of times while she was in Sydney, and now I decided to send her an email instead. I told her it even hurt to recount the trials I had endured, as the whole scenario seemed so fruitless, but I could only conclude that the intensity of Dean's job, the enormous weight loss, lack of sleep, the frustrations to do with the sale of the house and trying to form his own company, plus his ingestion of much alcohol, had caused him to combust.

As I was the closest to him, I received the brunt of his demonic demeanour, but I never felt any anger, just enormous sadness for both of us; though the cruel words that emanated from his anger crushed me. I told her as we were now out of Devon House, I had to try to rebuild trust, and due to my love for him as his wife, I would do everything possible to get our life back to what it used to be. I said I wasn't unhappy, as when things were calm, life was okay. I just wanted Tara to know what was going on and that despite everything I was all right.

The following day Dean saw the letter I had written to Tara and flew into a furious rage. I wasn't aware that he could read it, but being a novice at the computer, I obviously hadn't deleted it. He called me a whore, shouting and cursing at me. I tried to tell him to please read the email before accusing me of being disloyal, but I realised that any communication with Tara, whom he hated, was a mistake on my part. That night he locked me downstairs, telling me that that is where the help and whores should stay. I wasn't able to prepare myself for bed—no cleansing cream, no toothbrush, no nightclothes, but I did have the guest toilet and a basin, which I could use. I hoped I would be able to sleep on the sofa, but the hurt I was suffering in my heart was intolerable.

I had arranged for our masseuse to give Dean frequent massages to help soothe him, and amazingly enough, she never noticed any significant change in him; he was clever to hide his persona to those friends he liked. Dean was no longer interested in cooking, so we ate out at a small local restaurant many a night and managed to have reasonable conversations, but I was careful as to what I said. I knew how he behaved with me at the house, but would be totally charming in the company of others, so I did not say anything to anyone, not that anyone would really be able to understand our predicament.

One afternoon he returned to the house from being out somewhere and told me he had invited some friends, people I didn't know, for dinner. Dean cooked the meal, and I was pleased that he wanted to entertain despite not knowing the guests. I did my best to be attentive, and although the evening was a little strained, it was successful. When the four people had left, Dean screamed at me and told me that he and Baraka were going upstairs, and that as I was the maid, I should have all the washing up done and cleared away by morning. He took Baraka and locked the gate at the bottom of the stairs, saying that I was a bitch, and he didn't want me sleeping near him. I cleaned up everything and once again spent the night on the sofa. I was so exhausted the following day and was deeply saddened by what was happening in my life, that I decided to go to see my doctor.

I told my doctor my heart didn't feel too good, and then I dissolved into tears, telling my wonderful GP everything that was going on with Dean. As he tried to console me, he said the symptoms sounded like bipolar, mania to be exact, and explained to me what that was. In a way I was relieved to hear that Dean was ill. At least I could now read about the illness and try to understand what was going on.

I had to tell Dean's doctor that life was becoming almost unbearable, and I was now a little apprehensive for my safety. I told him Dean kept threatening to take possession of all my things and threatened to have Baraka euthanised and would make me watch as she died, and that he would do everything in his power to ruin me. Dean's doctor decided to see him almost every day, trying unsuccessfully to put him on medication. His patience with Dean was admirable, as he was treated almost as badly as I was.

Dean would spend hours on the computer during the day, and after we had something to eat in the evening, usually at the little restaurant close to us, he would go downtown late at night and return in the small hours of the morning, frightening Baraka and myself. Baraka would hide under the bed when she heard him coming up the stairs, and I would lie at the edge of the bed trying not to breathe until I knew he was asleep. Dean had no income, which meant I was paying for everything, and I thought it rather ironic that I was paying to be in hell! Even Baraka, who as a Jack Russell Terrier was described by a Bahamian as, "a dog with its head wrapped up crazy," became worse by having to live such an unsettled life; at times I thought she too had mania.

In October of 1999, I had made arrangements for us to go with La Chaîne des Rôtisseurs to Italy on October twenty-fifth, 2000. Now with life being so unsure, there was no way I would consider

394 | DIANA O'LEARY

Dean going on the trip and thought of cancelling it. When Dean was out diving one day, I called Tara and told her things were getting progressively worse and that I had been advised by Dean's doctor to leave Nassau. As I had paid for the trip to Italy, I asked Tara to come with me.

On October the nineteenth, Dean and I went to see a psychoanalyst at Doctors Hospital, who confirmed that Dean was manic, and at the same time considered that I was suffering from a depressive illness as a result of the emotional abuse, and he prescribed anti-depressant medication for me. In order to appease Dean, I went to the pharmacy and bought the pills. I never ever opened the bottle. In fact, I wouldn't take any prescription pills without first consulting my own doctor. However, Dean told me he knew I was on drugs and was mentally sick.

The following night he came up to the bedroom and stood at the doorway, telling me he had called Sandilands, the hospital for the mentally ill, and that they were on their way to take me there and if I objected, they would tie me down on the stretcher and forcibly take me out; and while I was there, he would bring Baraka and have her killed in front of me. He looked really evil as he spoke. I remained calm and quietly dialed Dean's doctor and asked him to please hurry. He was with us in a few minutes and managed to convince Dean that as I was sick he had to take me to his home for the night and in the morning he would have me admitted to the hospital.

67

Anxiously, I followed Dean's doctor to the car and wanted to take my little Baraka with me and not leave her with that maniac. Dean accepted what his doctor said, and he seemed happy as I left. Tara flew into Nassau, unbeknownst to Dean. I was at the home of Dean's doctor and his wife, and Tara was invited to stay there too. When Tara saw me, she burst into tears, as she had never seen me look so thin and so very sad. From weighing one hundred and twenty seven pounds, I had lost ten pounds and was smoking. I wasn't a heavy smoker, but for some reason it seemed to pacify me a little during my nightmarish ordeal. Dean's doctor and his wife were very kind. Tara and I stayed with them in their beautiful home, and Dean's doctor informed him that on the pretense of clinical observation, I had to stay longer.

I phoned Dean and said I wished to collect some clothes from the house. He was there when I was going through my clothes and fortunately didn't notice I was taking some warm clothes, which I needed for my trip to Italy. He was affable, as he thought I was now the one suffering from a mental illness and under his doctor's care. I had managed previously to contact my maid, Tanie, who had been with me since 1986 and whom Dean fired in a fit of rage. I wanted her to be around in case of any unpleasantness, but fortunately there was none. It was really difficult for me to leave Baraka, and of course, I was sad to leave Dean. For all of the heartache, I was most upset that my gorgeous husband had been reduced to a shadow of himself; he looked gaunt and old. There was no alternative. I had to leave Nassau for my own safety.

Dean's doctor's wife drove us to the airport the next day, and it was with some relief when the plane was airborne to Miami. As I relaxed with Tara on Alitalia, I couldn't help but have many mixed feelings. What had happened to my life? Why was I running away? What did the future hold? Tara was so happy to have me away from Dean and also excited to be going to Italy. Her love had sustained me, and I didn't want to disappoint her by showing any evidence of my heavy heart.

After a relaxing flight, we arrived at Rome's Leonardo da Vinci airport and hired a taxi to take us to the Sheraton Golf Hotel, which was situated on the outskirts of Rome. This was the hotel arranged for us by La Chaîne des Rôtisseurs, and in the evening at dinner, we met the three other couples from the Bahamas, who were also on the tour.

The next morning we joined our confrères from the United States and our Bahamian friends, and boarded the coach for a visit to the wondrous Sistine Chapel and Vatican Museum, where in the evening, a lavish dinner had been arranged for us, together with the members of the Rome Bailliage.

On Saturday we visited St. Peter's Square and attended an audience given by Pope John Paul II. We had all anticipated a private audience, but instead stood with the many hundreds of other visitors and saw the Pope on large television screens. It was, nevertheless, a joyous occasion. That evening a gala dinner was held at the stunning Palace of Doria Phamphilj where we were enraptured by the breathtaking ambience. We dined beneath the shimmering chandeliers and surrounded by magnificent paintings and burnished mirrors. Most unfortunately, Tara did not feel well and left before the dinner. I stayed on and after dinner was unable to find any transport back to the hotel so, although dressed in my formal attire, I managed to navigate my way across the Piazza del Collegio Romano to a taxi rank, where I stood in the long queue, and eventually it was my turn to have a taxi take me back to the Sheraton Golf Hotel.

The following day we left the hotel and were on our way to Orvieto. We stopped en route at the Villa D'Este in Tivoli, where we walked through the old palace and enjoyed the beautiful sixteenth century gardens with the magnificent fountains, nymphs and grottoes, and afterwards had lunch at the Restaurant di Diana. I was so happy to have Tara with me to share all the beauty. Tara did everything in her power to keep me amused and interested. I told her the last time I was at the Villa d'Este, I was her age and with her father.

After lunch we boarded our coach and drove on to Orvieto, where we spent the night at the delightful little Hotel Maitani. As dusk was falling, we walked through the town to the restaurant Grotte del Funaro, and had a fun rustic dinner with our group. On October thirtieth, we visited the city centre of Orvieto and the interesting cathedral (duomo), an example of the Italian Romanesque gothic architecture, before going on to Siena. Stopping for lunch in Montalcino, I think we all bought a bottle or two of the Brunello di Montalcino wine and then drove on to the Park Hotel Villa Gori in Siena, where we had a sumptuous dinner and spent the night. The wonderful trip was keeping us busy, and I tried not to think of Dean and Baraka too much.

The next day was October thirty-first and was Tara's twenty-sixth birthday. I wanted it to be memorable. We were with our friends from Nassau as we explored the medieval city of Siena, and all of us had a happy birthday lunch in the famous shell-shaped Piazza del Campo, which hosts the Palio horse races twice a year. After our visit to Siena, a brief stop was made in the divine old town of San Gimignano where we both felt a million miles away from any unpleasantness.

I had whispered to our tour guide that it was Tara's birthday and wondered if he could arrange something special for her that evening. While walking through the streets of Siena to the restaurant Grotta del Gallo Nero for dinner, I hoped our guide had remembered my request. We sat at a long table with our friends from the Bahamas, and while enjoying our dinner, our guide brought in a huge flower arrangement for Tara and a cake, together with some small souvenirs of Siena, and soon word went around that it was Tara's birthday. The restaurant suddenly became alive; it was party time! The German group of our tour, who was sitting upstairs, came down to our part of the restaurant and started entertaining us with singing, dancing and performing. What a night! It certainly was a birthday that Tara will not forget.

The following morning we were all a little tired, so it was lovely to relax in our comfortable coach and drive through the tranquil countryside of Tuscany. Our stop for lunch was in the town of Greve in Chianti and the Castello Vicchiomaggio, where we tasted some fabulous wines in the cellars. It was a perfect day, and as Tara and I wandered around the gardens of the castle with a glass of refreshing wine in our hands, overlooking the magnificent vineyards and rolling hills, I had to admit that my thoughts were far from Nassau. I did remember that it was All Saint's Day, but there was no chance to attend Mass. Lunch was soon announced, and we took our seats in the Salone Lorenzo di Magnifico for a superb meal and lots more wine. Back on our coach we tried to observe the quiescent landscape, but our eyes were heavy, and most of us indulged in a wee siesta, while the coach bounded along the Tuscan roads into Florence.

Ah, Firenze! One of the most beautiful cities in the world noted for its history, culture and the cradle of renaissance. We left the coach and walked through the city and the shopping centre, stopping at all the important monuments and churches, until we came to the breathtaking Basilica di S. Croce. Tara and I spent some time there just enraptured in the aura that surrounded us. I was enormously grateful, as I prayed to Jesus and thanked Him that I had booked that wonderful trip way before I knew of what I had ahead of me, and how important it was that I was out of Nassau and with my precious daughter.

Walking beside the River Arno, I shared with Tara that her father had told me that many of the antiques from Florence were dropped in the river before being sold as antiques! Naturally we had to take a look at the little shops on the Ponte Vecchio, which were so tempting. As the sun set, we relished the amazing view of Florence from our vantage point, before going to dinner.

Our group was ready for a glass of wine as we entered the welcoming restaurant La Certosa. After we had partaken of a good Tuscan meal and were entertained with Tuscan folklore music and dancing, we were glad to head back to the Park Hotel in Siena. It had been a long day, and we were happy to see our beds, but not too pleased to have an early start for our trip to Assisi the next morning.

I was excited to be visiting Assisi, St. Francis being one of my favourite saints, the patron saint of Italy and of animals. The Basilica of S. Fransesco was amazing. As it was All Soul's Day, I was thrilled that a Mass was being offered in the little lower church, where Tara and I were able to receive Holy Communion. Although we had visited many churches, this was the first opportunity we had to go to Mass. The lower church was surrounded by beautiful frescoes of the simple and humble life of St. Francis. The upper Basilica was the first gothic church in Italy and also displayed scenes of the life of St. Francis painted by Giotto. I would have liked to have spent more time in Assisi, but it was the last day of our tour, and we had to leave for our final lunch at a typical Perugian restaurant before returning to Rome. We said farewell to our fellow travellers and thanked our hosts, the Grand Chapître International d'Italy, for their organisation of such a fabulous and memorable trip through Rome and Tuscany.

After leaving the tour, Tara and I checked in to the Excelsior Hotel on the Via Veneto in Rome. It was where Patrick and I stayed many times while in Rome, and I wanted Tara to experience the hotel while I recounted to her some of my memories of being with her father. I was also anxious to know what was happening in Nassau, so as the hotel had Internet, I sent Dean an email asking how he was, and of course, Baraka. At first Dean's emails were full of love and concern for me, as he believed I was getting the treatment he thought I needed at the mental hospital in Nassau.

I had to find out from his doctor exactly what was going on and if it would be all right for me to return to Nassau. Tara sent an email to Dean's doctor's wife, and she replied, telling her I must not return until Dean had accepted to take medication, as life would not be safe for me. She also mentioned that he was seen spending a lot of money and not taking any advice from his doctor. Every day during our sightseeing through Rome, we would stop at an Internet café to receive emails from Dean. Tara was wonderful, and because of her, I tried not to impose the anxiety I was suffering.

We had arranged with two of our friends from Nassau, who had been on our trip through Tuscany, to meet them for lunch at a restaurant near the Spanish Steps. It was such a delightful lunch, but difficult for me, as I didn't want to mention anything about Dean, which our friends found rather confusing. The next day I arranged with the hotel to have a private car and chauffeur, who was also our guide, as I wanted Tara to see as much as possible of Rome. We had an extensive visit to the renowned Colosseum and then visited the Fontana di Trevi, where we threw in our coins and hoped to return one day.

We hadn't entered St. Peter's when we were with the group, so I asked our guide to take us to the Vatican, where we had an extraordinarily interesting visit, spending a leisurely time in the glorious ambiance of St. Pietro's. That evening I decided we should have dinner at one of the restaurants in the Piazza Navona, enjoy the activity in the square, and have our portraits sketched by a local artist.

After beautiful days exploring the eternal city and eating lots of pasta, I decided to telephone Dean before departing for Malta. Hearing his voice, his hatred of both me and Tara was very upsetting, especially when he told me he had Baraka euthanised. I was so upset that I had to run to the bathroom where I was sick. I couldn't go out to dinner, so we had room service. As the time difference was still within working hours for my vet in Nassau, I called him that night from Rome and asked if Dean had brought Baraka to him and had her put down. He was bemused and said that if ever Dean brought Baraka to him he would never, ever do what he wanted. I was comforted. My vet was a marvelous human being and had looked after Duke, Duchess and Windsor, and was very fond of little Baraka.

As Dean's doctor's wife had said in her email to Tara that I shouldn't return to Nassau, I phoned Vanessa, who was in Malta with her husband, and said we would like to pay her a visit, and would she reserve us a room at a hotel close to where they lived. On our flight to Valletta, I told Tara how great it was that she was able to take a month's vacation from Warner Bros. so she could be with me. I was also happy she was able to experience travelling in Italy and now to see my sister and her husband in Malta.

Vanessa's husband, Bernard, was at the airport to meet us and drove us to our hotel, which wasn't too far from where they lived. My sister was unable to invite us to stay, as they didn't have the room. However, they were extremely hospitable, showing us around the island and giving us a good time. Vanessa was a wonderful cook, so we ate very well in their home. I had cut down on my smoking, just having the occasional cigarette, but even that really upset not only Tara, but also my sister and Bernard. I would go outside the house and probably didn't smoke more than five a day; it somehow prevented me from being tearful.

When I spoke to Dean early in November, he told me he had received the supplementary American Express card, and I asked him not to abuse it. I had tried to cancel the card but was unable to do so. I wanted him to know I had transferred money to our joint account so he could pay the rent and all the relevant bills. I also tried to make him understand that I was heartbroken, that I missed being with him and my home for what it was. I told him I had the greatest respect for him and his abilities, but since his personality had changed, I didn't feel safe in his company.

I asked him to please receive treatment from his doctors; otherwise I would not be able to live with him. I wrote that Tara had never been anything but totally happy for us and that I loved him and wanted to be back with him soon. I didn't mention Baraka, as he told me he had had her put down. Deep in my heart I prayed that was not the truth. I was, however, badly shaken by his verbal abuse and his awful words of cruelty with regard to Baraka. He also told me he had destroyed Tara's four baby books that I had carefully put together in the small hours of the morning while Patrick had slept. I found it difficult to believe that Dean, who was so gentle, loving and attentive, could be the same man I married. I kept reminding myself that his persona was not my Dean, but was the sickness that had taken control.

I did my best to try to keep my emotions in check, as my sister and brother-in-law were both most gracious to Tara and myself. Every so often I had to go outside and have a cigarette, which really upset everyone, but their cat, Stimpey, would join me, and I felt he understood my sadness. If anyone was addicted to good health, it was me, so I knew what I was doing and kept my smoking to a minimum.

I told Vanessa and Bernard that while we were in Egypt, Dean had fallen in love with the country and wanted us to move to Alexandria after the sale of Devon House. I had actually obtained our Egyptian visas and booked our flights, so we could visit Alexandria and look for accommodation and enquire into work requirements for Dean. When I learned Dean was suffering from a mental illness, I cancelled all our arrangements.

Vanessa and Bernard were appalled by the thought of the possibility of us moving to Egypt that they made me watch the terrifying movie, "Not Without My Daughter," which told the story of an American Christian woman married to a Moslem Iranian and her life in Iran with his family and her eventual escape. It did make me think and thank Jesus for everything that had happened to prevent me from going to Egypt. The thought of being over there with Dean suffering from mania made me shiver.

The next news from Nassau wasn't good. Dean was seen around town spending lots of money, fighting with the caretaker of the apartments, whom he apparently almost killed, and generally being a threat to himself and to anyone who came in his way. I knew that I could not return. I was concerned, however, not only for Dean's health, but wondering if all the bills had been paid and how much money he was spending. I was advised to sell Devon House early in April of 2000, as my income was being badly depleted, so all of the extra expense was worrying.

As I still couldn't return to Nassau, I decided we would fly over to Sicily and visit my friends in Taormina. It was wonderful to see my dear friends Pina and her husband, Peppino, and Franco and his wife, Nora, and to introduce Patrick's daughter to them. We were made very welcome and wined and dined everywhere. It was a thrill for me to show Tara my Taormina, and we even looked over the wall into the property of Ionia House—the garden looked beautiful, but the trees and vegetation had grown so much that we couldn't see the house properly. It all seemed like a lifetime away. Did I really live in that magnificent dream house?

Pina and her husband invited us to their grand villa and introduced us to their handsome and talented son, Arturo. Tara and Arturo made a striking couple, and there was an instant bonding. I felt revitalised as I was embraced by my friends and reminisced of Patrick, Romulus and Remus, Ionia House and our lives in Taormina. I didn't have time to think about Dean.

During those revivifying days, walking through the cobbled streets of ancient villages with Franco and Nora as our guides, and Tara being introduced to the environs of Taormina and enjoying the warmest hospitality, I thought about what Vanessa and Bernard had said to me, and it seemed that my Sicilian friends, who were like family, echoed the same sentiments, trying to help me to understand my predicament more clearly and said I had to return to Nassau.

On November sixteenth, Tara and I flew to Miami. Tara's great friend Michael met us at the airport and made us welcome in his picturesque home in Fort Lauderdale. Michael was a gem of a friend, and we would sit on his gorgeous little wooden patio, which overlooked the canal at the bottom of his tropical garden, while we sipped wine. Michael and Tara patiently watched and listened to me as I went in and out of tears, trying to understand the horror of what I was experiencing. Finally, after a few days of Michael's gracious hospitality, I knew I had to return to Nassau to see if I could talk to Dean and try to find out what was going on.

68

I had phoned the Lyford Cay Club and reserved a room, but on the morning of my departure from Miami, Tara checked the emails, and there was one from Dean telling me he knew I would be arriving in Nassau and staying at the club. As far as we knew no one had mentioned anything to him, so it was a big surprise that he knew about my plans. Unfortunately, the rest of his email was distressing.

While Tara and I were sitting in the bar at Miami airport, I wondered whom I could call to ask if I could stay for a week while I sorted out a few things and spoke to a lawyer. Due to Dean knowing I was going to stay at the club, I had to cancel that reservation. Dean had already informed me he was going to divorce me and had hired a lawyer and that it was going to be ugly.

I called my friends Heinz and Becky, who were the witnesses at our church wedding, and without hesitation they said I could stay with them and that Heinz would be at Nassau airport to meet me. My cheeks were moist with tears. I was so relieved and so was Tara. Tara took the red-eye flight back to Los Angeles, and I would join her once I had sorted out what was going on with Dean. My friends lent me their car in order that I could keep the appointment with the lawyer, but I was terrified I would meet Dean by chance somewhere in Nassau.

I was anxious to receive the restraining order from the psychologist who had seen Dean, and it was waiting for me at the lawyer's office. I called Dean to make an appointment to meet him and knew I was taking a chance. However, it didn't transpire. While on the phone to him, he kept on ranting and raving at me. His words were so painful and left me numb. I couldn't believe I was experiencing such excruciating pain, and it was hard for me to believe his apparent hatred for me. I had to remind myself that he was sick. Of course, he was making out that I was sick and that, in fact both, Tara and I were suffering from bipolar. During one of my phone calls, I told him if he hadn't had Baraka put down that he must give her the heartworm pill. No one seemed to think that he had her put down, which was a relief to me.

My friends were very kind and caring. I knew it wasn't easy for them to see me in that situation, but they were always around to console me during the difficult and sad time, and made me feel I was part of the family. I sent Dean an email telling him our last phone call had resolved nothing, and I wanted to talk to him in the presence of our lawyers to discuss what we must do. All of that was costing me a fortune, as I was not just paying for the rental house, all the bills and the psychologist, but also paying for all of Dean's legal fees and pocket money. I felt no animosity, just terrible sadness that Dean was so afflicted.

No one seemed able to help him with his terrible mental illness, despite every effort by his doctor. Dean was the only one who thought that he was perfectly sane, and the rest of us were crazy. Every day I tried to make contact in the hope I might get through to him. I was naïve as to what the illness entailed, and therefore, each time we spoke, I was abused and again was told that Baraka was dead and that Tara's baby books had been destroyed, and that he was going to have my residency in the Bahamas yanked, and he would do everything in his power to destroy me and take all my possessions. According to the sums of money that were being spent, he was on his way to destroying me financially.

On December the second, I sent another email directly to him. He had requested that I send any communication to him through his lawyer, but I had not been able to reach her for three days, so wrote to him directly. As Dean was under the impression it was I who was sick, I told him I had now finished my medication and was fully recovered. I wrote that what happened to him before he met me, when he fasted for fifty-seven days while he was with the Coast Guard, when he ran from Fort Lauderdale to the Keys in his underwear before he was picked up by the police, that the same illness he had then had returned, and that if he allowed himself to be treated, he would return to be the loving man I had married.

I begged him to talk to his doctor and ask to have medication so that our lives could return to normal. I continued to tell him I would have to stop his credit card, as I was aware that spending large sums of money was part of the manic behaviour. However, I assured him there was sufficient money to pay the rent, his food, all the bills, play golf, go diving and eat out. I told him it wasn't fair that he was keeping me hostage, had to live out of two suitcases, and I had to pay for his selfishness. I also told him how cruel he was to have had Baraka put down when he could have left her with the vet or at Animal House, the boarding kennels, which were like Baraka's second home. I wanted him to know he had put me through so much sadness and misery, due to the fact that he would not take medication. My kindness in supporting him, though I was going through hell, would have to stop in February the following year, when the lease of the rented house came to an end and at which time he would have to fend for himself.

Dean replied to me with a long email, telling me he still loved me and that Baraka was alive and well. He proceeded to blame me for all of the upset and claimed I had retained hurt and anger (of what I wondered) and that I was travelling and enjoying myself and not attending to my responsibilities. He said I should not cancel his credit card, as there were certain things that needed attention and that they could not be done if I stopped the card. It was sad to read his email. I knew deep down he still loved me and really began to think it was I who was sick, who was selfish and uncaring. By now his hatred of Tara was so apparent in every email and phone conversation. He blamed her for our problems and was going to cite her as co-respondent in the divorce.

My stay in Nassau had served its purpose. It was time for me to leave to be with Tara in Los Angeles, but before I left, I spoke to Dean's doctor again, and he told me he was concerned for Dean, and if he didn't receive medication soon, his state of health would progressively become worse. He told me there was no use in me seeing him on that visit, not until he accepted medication. There was nothing further to do, but hope and pray that somehow I was able to think of a way in the not-too-distant future to inveigle him to listen to his doctor. I left feeling deep gratitude to my friends who had been so supportive during those trying days, and as always, my deepest thanks to Dean's doctor, who never charged a cent for all the tedious work, and of course, to his wife. I checked in to my flight with my same two suitcases and a heavy heart, wondering what the future held. I knew that during that horrendous time in my life, I would not have survived without my faith in Jesus. He was with me throughout, and due to Him I was able to keep my composure and integrity. For all that my world was in turmoil and turned upside down, I experienced His peace throughout.

I moved into Tara's bedroom in the flat she shared with two other girls in Los Angeles. Fortunately, Tara had a queen-size bed, and the bathroom was en suite. We managed well in tight quarters and had the spacious living room and nice kitchen at our disposal. Tara included me in everything, introducing me to her friends and making me feel wanted. We arranged to see Basil and his wife for dinner, and I realised how difficult it was for them to understand what it was like to have a spouse who was suffering from manic bipolar. They couldn't comprehend what I had been going through, and I think they thought I was being a little dramatic. I was pleased I hadn't told anyone apart from the two couples in Nassau; therefore, no one knew of my sad plight.

I was on the phone most days to Nassau, communicating with my lawyer, trying to find out what was going on. I also called Dean frequently, but nothing had changed. When Tara's flat was empty, as the girls were all working, I would go out to the landing and stand on a little balcony to smoke my cigarette, asking Jesus why was I there. I didn't feel sorry for myself. I just found myself asking why.

Tara knew one of my wishes was to visit the famous Crystal Cathedral at Garden Grove in Orange County; as a Christmas present she told me that we had seats for the nativity play. Robert Schuller's books and television sermons had helped me a lot during the years when I was alone, and I really wanted to see his cathedral. On December seventeenth, as I sat with Tara in the glass cathedral, I was thrilled to be in that unique building and able to watch the wonderful performance. I felt quite emotional, and considering that my life seemed torn apart, I knew I was so blessed.

As the Christmas holidays drew nearer, I called my lawyer in Nassau, trying to establish the most recent occurrences. She was unable to tell me much except that Dean had instructed his lawyer to continue with divorce proceedings and make it ugly for me. I wished her a happy Christmas and said that we would talk again in the New Year.

Tara and I enjoyed going around the shops and looking at all the beautiful Christmas decorations, especially in the Century City shopping centre. We attended the first Mass of Christmas on Christmas Eve at the Good Shepherd Catholic Church, which had now become familiar to me, as it was the church where Basil had always brought me on my numerous visits to Los Angeles. On Christmas Eve after Mass, we visited Basil and his wife and stayed for a light supper, which Basil cooked himself. He apologised for not including us on Christmas Day, saying that the day was for the family, which we understood. I wasn't in the mood to socialise anyway, and Tara was concentrating on her forthcoming return trip to Sicily.

On Christmas Day we went to a take-out restaurant that served a Christmas lunch, turkey, and all the trimmings. It was different to the past lavish Christmas dinners, but it was all that we wanted. The restaurant was inexpensive and patronised by people who had no family to go to. Tara and I joined the queue carrying our individual trays and went down the line together with all those who wanted a warm turkey dinner. The meal was really tasty, and we were happy we had had the opportunity to eat turkey for Christmas! Returning to the apartment, I called my friend Dawn, who was now living in Atlanta, and asked her if I could visit her from December twenty-seventh to January fifth. As Tara was going to be in Sicily, I didn't want to be alone in Los Angeles. I just wanted to be with Dawn at that time.

Tara and I were busy deciding what she should pack for her trip, and choosing a few gifts to take with her. I was excited for Tara, as I knew she would have a great visit and see a little more of our friends and the country. Tara drove me to the airport on the twenty-seventh and left the following day for Catania, Sicily.

Dawn was at the airport to meet me, and I was so happy to see her again. She was the only person who seemed to understand the horror of what I had been going through, with the exception of Tara, and was also able to comprehend my concern and love for Dean and my desire for everything to return to normal. We conversed long and deep, trying to elucidate on life. Dawn had had her troubles and heartaches, and had just been told that she was in remission from colon cancer, for which I was most grateful. Our friendship was truly real. She and I could talk to each other about everything with love and respect. As the weather was cold, we were happy to remain in her warm home for the majority of my visit, but we did venture out on occasions to grocery shop and to go to Mass.

We greeted the New Year with a bottle of champagne and many hopes and wishes that 2001 would be a great improvement on the year 2000. I returned to Los Angeles on January fifth and spent many hours in meditation and prayer. As I reflected on the past year, I attempted to understand what it was that Jesus wanted of me. I knew I had to help my husband. Contrary to what Dean said to me and to his doctor—that as his wife I should have stayed with him during that period and not left—I knew I was helping him by not being with him, as by now he might have killed me! I wanted so much to help him and hoped by leaving he would decide to receive the medication.

I found my way to a local bookshop and bought three books on mania. "The Unquiet Mind" by the psychiatrist Kay Redfield Jamieson was a revelation, as I did not have a complete picture as to what was involved with that mental illness. I knew Dean did not know he had suffered from mania in the past. He told me he had been heavily into drugs and hadn't taken any since leaving rehabilitation in South Florida. He said he was advised to keep away from alcohol. His family didn't tell him that his illness was genetic and that several members of his extended family had bipolar. Had we had that knowledge ahead of time, much of the distress to both of us and Tara, not to mention our friends, could have been avoided, and I would have known alcohol was the demon that attributed to reigniting the manic flame.

69

I tried to speak to Dean often from Los Angeles. I wanted him to really want me back, but I would not return until he promised me he would start his medication and that I would hear from his doctor that was indeed the case. Our phone calls were not pleasant. In between telling me how awful I was, he said he had used the American Express card, which I had thought I had finally managed to cancel, and had flown to London, business class, for the Christmas holidays. He said he had stayed in a great hotel where he had his own butler, who, apart from taking care of him, went shopping to purchase an overcoat, as the weather was very cold. He then went on to the Stoke Park club in Berkshire, where he spent the New Year. I wasn't angry, though I could have done without the extra expense, and in a strange way I was happy for him, as I felt that he too must be suffering in some way from his illness.

I spent my fifty-ninth birthday alone with a call from Tara, saying that she was returning on January fifteenth. On the day after my birthday, Dean called and once more raved and ranted at me and asked me to return. I said I would, once I heard from his doctor that he had started his medication. Amazingly he said he would, and I received confirmation to that effect the next day.

Tara had a wonderful visit to Sicily, but was unsure when she heard of my decision to return to Nassau; it was time, and I trusted Dean's doctor. So on January nineteenth I flew into Nassau and stayed with my friends again. I had agreed to meet Dean at the outdoor restaurant of a hotel, so that there would be people around. I wanted us to talk and make sure all would be well, and we would try to remake our lives. When I saw him, I found it difficult to realise he was the same man I had married. He was very thin and his demeanour was different;

he looked strange. He had been such a handsome man when we first met, and I hoped with us being back together that his looks and health would return.

With help from Heinz, we found a cottage on the property of a German couple. Funnily enough, it was the same property my Taiwanese friends had lived in while they were in Nassau. The cottage was semi-furnished, so the majority of the furniture I had in the last rented accommodations I packed and stored. There were just a couple of pieces of furniture that I wanted with me. I asked my faithful maid Tanie to come and give me a hand in moving out of the old place and into the new.

Dean said he had met someone who was doing business in Cuba and he wanted to go, as he thought it would be a good business deal for him. I took an interest in everything he did, and of course, financed all his whims. I wanted him to feel secure and have things to do.

Moving into the cottage together was a little awkward to start with, but as Dean was on medication, I could at least converse with him, and although our spark had died, we were friends. I was very careful with what I said and careful too with our consumption of wine. We went to the grocery store, watched television and ate together, and went to Mass. We even travelled to Fort Lauderdale on a couple of occasions but didn't socialise at all, though we invited Heinz and Becky over for dinner one night. Only they and Dean's doctor and wife knew what we had been through. Neither Dean nor I were ready to see the friends that we had associated with before.

I busied myself keeping in touch with my friends abroad, never letting on that our lives were anything other than great. I kept the cottage clean, as Dean didn't want Tanie around. Baraka and I went for several walks a day, and generally did my best to keep occupied. Of course, I read many books. I saw little of Dean, as he spent hours on the computer. At suppertime he would cook, and we would eat together and watch the news on television before he would retire to his room. That was our life, but we had promised each other we would give it a year to see how things worked out.

Our new way of life was a big strain on me. So much damage had been done to our relationship, and although I tried hard for normalcy, it really wasn't there. One night as I was reading in bed, I had an asthma attack and found it difficult to breathe. I asked Dean to take me to the hospital, where I went on the ventolin machine for an hour. The attack was attributed to stress.

Dean had to go to court for almost killing the caretaker of the rented properties where we had stayed. The caretaker had seen Dean go to the garbage dump where he proceeded to destroy all my photographs that were in two suitcases. He then emptied two of my portable filing cabinets, where I had many precious papers, including the receipts of all the purchases that had been made around the world; he destroyed those, and the last correspondence from my parents. I was very relieved that he had not destroyed Tara's four baby albums.

The caretaker tried to intercept, as he knew that those things belonged to me, but Dean was so furious that he was interfering that he hit the poor man, who was taken to hospital, and Dean was placed in police custody, spending the night in jail. Baraka obviously survived the night alone. Dean had to appear in court, but his case was dropped on payment of the funds, which I gave him.

We led a quiet and somewhat peaceful life, and he helped me to try to become acquainted with the computer, so I could write a few lines to Tara. He was always respectful towards me, always the gentleman.

The highlight of my week was to attend Mass, which I did at a church near to us and where no one knew me. Dean would accompany me sometimes, but that became less and less. We had problems in the cottage. The kitchen ceiling fell in, and that had to be attended to, but our German landlords were far from friendly. However, we made the most of living in the cottage and were content to be together, if apart.

Tara had moved back to Fort Lauderdale and had been living there for a while, so I went over for a few days to see her. She was having a tough time deciding what to do and really wanted to be back in California. I suggested she check the Internet. There was a writer of a travel magazine in Santa Barbara, and I told Tara to write to him and find out if he required an assistant, and she did. Incredibly, his assistant had left a few days earlier, and the job was open. The following day Tara flew out to Santa Barbara for an interview and was accepted. Her job would commence the following month.

When I returned to Nassau, I mentioned to Dean we should have a change of scene. Leaving little Baraka with the girls at Animal House, Dean and I flew to the Turks and Caicos Islands. We had considered leaving Nassau and moving there. After looking at various homes, realised the prices were out of our reach and that we really preferred being in Nassau.

We stayed at the Ocean Club Resort in Providenciales, relaxing on the fabulous Grace Bay beach and swimming in the tranquil aquamarine ocean. In fact, we spent a happy time together. We played golf and ate at super little restaurants. Everyone who saw us thought we were an attractive and engaging couple. We were both comfortable sharing a room and knew that intimacy was a thing of the past. Dean did not speak much during the day, but he was attentive at dinner, so I took the opportunity to tell him that I wished to accompany Tara on her drive to California and that I would return in ten days.

Under our present circumstances, he was happy for me to do what I had to do. He was comfortable in the cottage; he had his computer and Baraka. He would see his doctor from time to time, and the pills were certainly working, thank goodness; for if he had gone on much longer without medication, I was told that he could have become completely brainsick.

I arrived in Fort Lauderdale and spent the day with Tara, packing up her furniture for storage and what we were taking in the car with us. We had AAA plan our route to Los Angeles and where we should stop overnight. Having those maps was an enormous help. We left Fort Lauderdale on July fifth. Tara drove, and I was the navigator. I was excited about the trip and especially to be with my girl.

Our first day took us to Pensacola. It hadn't occurred to me that driving from one end of Florida to the other would take a day, and how happy we were to stop at the Ramada Inn to have dinner and a couple of glasses of wine.

The next day on our drive through Texas we felt totally isolated, and to our horror, we were running short of gas. We were in the middle of nowhere on a beautiful Saturday, not a car to be seen as we drove through the Texan countryside. I knew we had to see a gas station soon and prayed we would make it in time. I recounted to Tara about the similar situation that Dean and I had on our drive to Fes in Morocco. Silence fell between us, and Jesus was bombarded with prayers and thanks to Him, we did make it with the needle on red. Phew, very tense. We spent that night at the Hilton in San Antonio and enjoyed a good dinner and a comfortable sleep.

The following day our drive was to Tucson, where we stayed at the Holiday Inn. Once more our desire was to have a good dinner; we were so hungry and ready for a glass of wine. After a good night's sleep, we were up early in order to arrive to Los Angeles that evening, where we stayed at the Beverly Plaza Hotel, a favourite little hotel of ours. Tara suggested we go to dinner down the road to a popular restaurant, The Little Door.

We drove to Santa Barbara the next day and checked into a hotel on the beach, and on the following morning started flat hunting. I wanted to see Tara settled before returning to Nassau. We met Tara's new boss and his wife for dinner, and they suggested that Tara stay with them until she found her own flat. They were a lovely couple, and I felt relieved I could leave her safely in Santa Barbara, knowing she would be happy. I took the bus back to Los Angeles on July fourteenth and had dinner with Basil and his wife after attending Mass at the Good Shepherd Church, and the following day returned to Nassau.

70

Life with Dean continued in a peaceful manner, and gradually we allowed ourselves to get back in touch with a couple of friends. It was like old times, as Dean was always so charming, and no one suspected anything had been wrong. We played golf on occasions and started to remake a life for ourselves. In August we decided to pay a visit to Freeport, as La Chaîne des Rôtisseurs was having an event; it was a nice excuse for us to have a change of scenery. We enjoyed ourselves with our confrères from Grand Bahama and appeared to everyone as a loving couple. However, there was an incident. When walking from the hotel, someone accidentally bumped into me, and immediately Dean flew into a terrible rage. I was quick to calm him, but realised that a little of the manic Dean still existed.

Back at the cottage, in Nassau, on the morning of September eleventh, we sat on the floor in front of the television and watched in horror at the unfolding scene in New York, putting us in a reflective and sombre mood for the rest of the day.

Towards the end of September, I wanted to pay a visit to Tara, and it caused us to have a big fight, which lasted a couple of days. Dean really hated Tara, and the thought of me visiting her made him angry. I did go over for a quick visit; she needed me, and I had to be there for her. When I returned Dean said he wanted to talk to me. He told me he didn't want to continue to live with me and said he wanted to travel to Russia. Russia?

That really did surprise me. I knew he always wanted to live away from the Bahamas one day, but Russia was far away and cold. I told him whatever he wanted to do he could, and I wouldn't give him any problems. I knew our marriage was over, but hoped we would remain friends. In the meantime we had a hurricane approaching, Hurricane

Michelle, and were in a rented cottage, and nothing was being done to protect it or us. Finally, the landlords did pay attention to protecting the cottage, and we survived the hurricane.

Dean and I talked further about his intentions, and he said that all the months we had been together and the hours he had spent on the computer were to decide his future; to that end he was in touch with a marriage agency in Russia and had chosen a bride. I caught my breath, as that came as another big surprise. He was excited and said she was a beautiful blonde and a Taurus, and would be compatible with his Pisces sign. Well, I knew the pain I had suffered in 2000 had emptied my heart of the deep love I had for Dean; I now had the love for him as a friend and knew he would need me to help him with his future plans.

Early in December he had to attend court again, and once more I was there to bail him out. After I heard what Dean intended to do, I started looking for somewhere to live once our lease expired at the end of January. In the meantime, we went over to Fort Lauderdale, as he wanted to live there for a while before moving to Russia. We found an apartment, which he would move into at the latter part of February.

Tara was really enjoying her job writing for the travel paper. Her boss had sent her to Ireland and to South Africa. I was pleased she sounded well and happy. However, we both realised that as Christmas and the New Year approached we hadn't made any plans. I communicated to her that due to the tenuous situation, I would stay in Nassau with Dean. It would be the first time ever we wouldn't be able to celebrate together. I told Dean I would spend the holidays with him, but I wanted to be with Tara to celebrate my sixtieth birthday.

Now I knew our life together was nearing the end, he made no objection. Dean and I had a pleasant and delicious Christmas dinner, which he cooked. Of course, my thoughts were with Tara, wondering how she would spend the holidays. It was difficult not having her with me, but she had found an evening job where she helped out at a restaurant and had met some nice young people who were also away from home. I sent her lots of little Christmas gifts; she knew my heart was with her.

For New Year's Eve, which would be the last one Dean and I would spend together, I reserved a table at the famous Ocean Club on Paradise Island. It was a black tie affair, and after our champagne dinner as I watched the flamboyant fireworks, standing close to Dean, my heart was sad as I thought about early times where life was exciting and filled with promise of many happy years ahead. We would shortly be closing our chapter, and I hoped that 2002 would be kinder to both of us. On January ninth I left for California.

Tara and I stayed in Los Angeles that night and drove to Santa Barbara the following day. As always I was introduced to all of Tara's friends with whom she worked, and we had fun eating at her special restaurants. On the eve of my birthday, Tara told me we must be ready to leave the apartment by eleven thirty the next morning. The day was clear, crisp and just beautiful. Tara said that our limo was waiting, and when we entered inside, it was decorated with balloons and there was a lovely bottle of champagne on ice. I felt very spoiled, and as I settled back with my glass of champers looking out at the magnificent Pacific Coast, I thanked Jesus for all of my blessings, especially my Tara.

Tara had arranged for us to visit three vineyards where we would taste the aromatic wines of Santa Barbara. The countryside was spectacular, and I felt very happy, although I wished in a way, had things been different, Dean would have been with us. Our last stop was at the Firestone Vineyard, which was interesting, as I had met Brooks Firestone at a Chaîne event. We were shown around the vineyard and invited to taste some of the fine wines. Tara mentioned it was my birthday, and I was given a bottle of wine and two glasses and was told there was no way I could be sixty; I think I preferred the compliment to the wine!

After a light lunch, we returned to Tara's flat, where I received a few phone calls from my friends around the world, as Tara had told them where I would be. In the evening we relaxed at another delightful restaurant in Santa Barbara for a birthday dinner. Naturally, Tara wanted to know what was happening with Dean, and I told her that he would be leaving for Russia later on in the year and that through a Russian marriage agency had found a potential wife, but in the meantime he wanted to move to Fort Lauderdale, after he helped me settle into my rented house.

I arrived back in Nassau on January seventeenth and two days later found the house I wanted to rent. It was perfect for Baraka and me. Dean and I, together with Tanie, started to pack up the cottage and move things to the house on Lakeview Drive. On January thirty-first, we rode in the front seat of a lorry with the last of my things and happily waved good-bye to the German cottage. For the few days while I moved into my new accommodations, I boarded Baraka at Animal House for her own safety and my peace of mind. On February fourth I introduced her to her new home, and she liked it.

Baraka had to go back to Animal House on February twenty-sixth, six days after her second birthday, as it was time for Dean to move to Fort Lauderdale. He had stayed with me in the guest room of my new home and had been a great help, attending to odd jobs around the house, for which I was most grateful.

On arrival at Fort Lauderdale, we decided to stay at the Holiday Inn for a few days until Dean moved into his apartment. The day before we left Nassau, I agreed to give him a large sum of money, which was painful, and he in return told me to go ahead with filing for divorce. He asked for various things, including some of the antique carpets and rugs. I packed up his large golf bag, and at his request, included a photo album with some photos of our happy years together.

On February twenty-eighth, I said good-bye to Dean at his apartment, after helping him buy a car. I knew he didn't have any furniture, but it didn't seem to bother him. He would attend to buying what he needed in the days to come. While sitting in the plane on my way back to Nassau, I couldn't help but reflect over the last years and felt sad that the awful mental illness had come between us; for if it had not, I knew that despite our ages, we would have been happy together.

I thought about what he had told me of his life with the Coast Guard, his refusal to eat for fifty-seven days, and his run from Fort

Lauderdale to the Keys, amongst other strange occurrences. He said he didn't know anything about suffering from a mental illness. I had taken him at his word that his weird behaviour must have been due to his heavy addiction to drugs which of course, exacerbate mania.

Arriving in Nassau, I needed to have Baraka with me and went to collect her. On March first, I called Dawn; it was her birthday. After we had finished talking, I prayed to Jesus Dawn's cancer wouldn't return. She was so brave, and selfishly I wanted her to live for a very long time.

71

A few days after my return to Nassau, it would be Dean's fortieth birthday. I knew he still didn't have his furniture and hadn't arranged to do anything to celebrate; I telephoned a seafood restaurant in Fort Lauderdale, which we used to frequent, and ordered a feast of all his favourite shellfish to be delivered, at least I knew he would have a delicious dinner to enjoy. He called me later that evening saying he was very appreciative.

Tara was enthusiastic about her job with Entrée, writing for the travel newsletter and doing more travelling. She was off to London and then a visit to her school friend in Bermuda. In May she visited Malta, but my sister and her husband had already left.

In July I heard from Dean that he would be going to Russia; I wished him well. He seemed happy. A few days later the terrible pain I had been experiencing around my chest, on and off, over the previous year had returned. I went to have X-rays and was told I was suffering from gall stones.

When Dean returned from Russia at the end of July, he called me and I said I was going to go ahead with the divorce and reminded him that he had promised to agree to see my lawyer. I didn't have a lawyer at that time. A few days later, my friend Father Patrick Pinder, who had been my Parish priest for years, came for dinner, and I told him about the whole sorry saga. He was compassionate and informed me that his niece was a lawyer and that he would call her. Mrs. Stewart was a lovely lady, and I felt comfortable with her; needless to say, we both thought the world of Father Pat.

In August Dean called and said he had second thoughts about us getting a divorce; he wanted me to spend a weekend with him, and we chose the Mandarin Hotel in Miami. We spent a pleasant time together always as friends. The love we had as a married couple had long since died. Nothing had changed the fact we had to lead separate lives, and it was necessary for Dean to be served with the divorce papers. After our weekend in Miami, Dean returned with me to Nassau and went to see my lawyer and admitted he had committed adultery.

Mrs. Stewart was now able to go ahead with the divorce proceedings. Dean left Nassau back for Fort Lauderdale, and he also left his wedding ring. As he was leaving, he gave me a hug and thanked me for teaching him how to love saying that until he had met me, he never experienced that emotion. After he left, I felt totally worn out. I poured myself a glass of wine, and with Baraka snuggled up to me, I wondered how I had managed to live through those last few years—but of course, I knew the answer—it was the love of Jesus that had kept me going.

I called Tara and told her that the divorce proceedings could now continue and that the pain I had been suffering was due to gall stones, and was advised to have my gall bladder removed. I would be going into the Princess Margaret Hospital to be operated on September fourth.

Tara flew into Nassau on the third, and how grateful I was to have her with me and take care of Baraka. We were asked to arrive at the hospital before seven thirty in the morning for admission and sat in the waiting room, but no one came to us. So after an hour, we finally found someone who motioned us where to go. We took the elevator to the floor with the private rooms, and on trying to check in, was told that there was no reservation for me. Fortunately, my surgeon appeared at that moment, and I was shown to my room. It was a relief to have my own bathroom, but had not been advised to bring towels.

My next surprise was a nurse informing me it would not be possible for me to have my blood tests, EKG, and chest X-ray in time for my operation, and that the operation would have to be postponed to the following day. I remained calm, as I knew all would be well when I saw my surgeon again at nine twenty-five that morning. Dr.

Munroe assured me my operation was on schedule and I would be having laparoscopic surgery.

A very young and efficient female doctor stuck some needles in my hand and took my blood. I was then handed a gown, asked to sit in a wheelchair and was pushed off to have my chest X-ray and EKG. I was wheeled through the busy corridors with many patients everywhere. I felt that half of Nassau was standing around waiting to be seen by a doctor.

We finally stopped at a room which looked to me like a large linen closet. It turned out I was right. The young Bahamian male technician asked me to expose my chest, and he performed the EKG. During that process there were two interruptions of orderlies entering to collect clean linen.

I was then whisked off to the radiology for my X-ray, and while I waited, I heard someone say the machine was broken, so after sitting there for more than twenty minutes and no one informing me of what was going on, I asked to be returned to my room. My surgeon's assistant came to see me and asked me further questions as to my health. I had stopped smoking a few months earlier, but I did use the ventolin a couple of times during the day to help me breathe, as I suffered mildly from asthma. He told me I should prepare for surgery and on the way would stop again for an X-ray, as the machine was now working.

Tara waited with me until I was on my way to the theatre. I told her to go home and check with me later. I climbed on to the hospital bed and covered my head, mentally preparing myself for what was ahead of me. I didn't want to be seen by all the people that lined the corridors.

As I lay in the waiting room theatre, listening to the strange clicking and ticking noises, my thoughts and mind were with Jesus. I knew He was with me. My solitude was interrupted by a doctor with an Indian accent. He told me he was my anesthetist and asked further about my problem with asthma. I was then wheeled into the operating theatre and lifted onto the bed. I had about five faces peering down at me, and then my surgeon appeared, who sweetly took hold of my left hand, and immediately I felt reassured and comforted. The Indian anesthetist put his needle into the top of my right hand, and within seconds my head was spinning. I felt very strange, and saw my surgeon look at the Indian doctor and say something to him, and I was given a further dose of anesthetic.

The next thing I knew I was coming around after surgery. I heard myself breathing loudly, conscious of gasping, coughing and commanding my lungs to work, fighting to breathe.

I heard someone say, "Give her oxygen. Give her ventolin."

And someone tried to place something over my nose, but I needed my nose to help me breathe. I finally managed, with the help of the medical team, to regulate my breathing. My surgeon told me later he was worried about me, so much so he had a bed ready in the intensive care unit.

When I reached my room, I was happy to see Tara. The three doctors came to see me, and I think they, like me, were relieved that I had survived and the operation had been a success. Tara went home, and I had a good night with nurses in and out giving me painkillers and changing my intravenous bag. I felt no discomfort and credit that to my excellent surgeon.

In the morning, Dr. Munroe came to see me and asked if I had had breakfast. The nurses didn't want to give me any solid food until they had the okay from the doctor. I wasn't given any water. Dr. Munroe said I must have water and avoid any greasy foods. I had to laugh when breakfast arrived with a large plate of grits covered with chunks of sausage in greasy gravy. I did eat a small bunch of grapes and a couple of slices of melon that were also on my tray. As I was allowed lunch and dinner, my plates were filled with macaroni cheese, peas and rice, and fried chicken. Needless to say, I ate nothing.

I was told I could leave that evening after the doctor had seen me. Tara came to collect me, but by eight forty-five the doctor hadn't arrived, and she was making her way to the elevator to return home. Just as she approached the elevator, the door opened, and Dr. Munroe walked out and said he was on his way to me and was holding a small glass bottle. I was very pleased to see him and Tara, and with a smile Dr. Munroe showed me the bottle with over fifty tiny grey stones. I declined his offer to keep them! At nine thirty that night we left the hospital. It was an experience, but I was so grateful to have had such a super surgeon.

Tara and I started talking about having a small wine bar in Sandy Port, a fairly new area in Nassau, with many homes and a shopping centre, but the more involved we became, we knew we were completely out of our depth and shelved the idea. During the following days while Tara was with me, she said she wanted to leave Santa Barbara and return to Fort Lauderdale. Of course, I was very happy with the idea. We decided that when she was ready, I would fly out to help her pack up and we would drive back together.

In the meantime, Dean called me and told me he had married the Russian girl, who was a Muslim, and that he would be leaving Fort Lauderdale to live permanently in Russia. I gulped gently and said that legally we were still married and wondered if he had heard of bigamy. He said he would sell his car, but asked if I would buy his furniture and the contents of his apartment for the price he had paid. I knew Tara would require a place to live when she returned to Fort Lauderdale; I agreed to his request.

72

I left for Los Angeles on October fifteenth. Tara was at the airport and we drove straight to Santa Barbara. We spent two days packing up and cleaning the flat, and late on the evening of the seventeenth, feeling rather exhausted, relaxed in our quaint little suite in a delightful hotel Tara had found enjoying a delicious 'take-out' dinner and a couple of well-deserved glasses of wine. As we had a long day ahead of us, we slept early.

Tara and I always travelled well together. She loved to drive, just like her Dad, and I loved to be the passenger. Lala, the name we had given the car, was ready to perform again and carry us safely back to Fort Lauderdale. Lala was packed to capacity with Tara's personal possessions. We had given away the small items of furniture that had been purchased for her flat.

Our first day on the road brought us to Tucson and the next to Sonora in Texas. On Sunday we drove to Baton Rouge, Louisiana, and late on Monday evening arrived in Fort Lauderdale and stayed with our dear friend Michael. When I think back to both this and our first cross-country adventure, I realised how fortunate we were to have had no mishaps along the way. I knew we were being protected on that long and in many parts, isolated terrain. The following day we returned to Nassau and celebrated Tara's birthday with Baraka.

On November twenty-second, I was really pleased Tara flew back from Fort Lauderdale to Nassau to be with me, as we attended court where I was granted a Decree Nisi, the waiting period of ninety days to six months before the divorce becomes final; this is known as the Decree Absolute. I invited Father Patrick Pinder and Diane Stewart, my lawyer, to join us afterwards for lunch at Café Matisse.

What had started out beautifully six years ago with every desire to be together forever, was now over; our vows had been dashed. Therefore, it was with mixed feelings, but also relief as I thanked both my priest and lawyer, and my beloved daughter, who had been with me on the arduous and frightening journey. During lunch I mentioned to Father Patrick that I knew the church did not accept a civil divorce, so if I was to have another relationship I would be committing adultery, and unable to receive Holy Communion. I had to have my marriage annulled.

Tara and I spent Christmas and the New Year in Nassau. It was lovely to socialise with her and we both looked forward to a peaceful and happy 2003. On January seventh, Tara departed for Fort Lauderdale, and I was looking forward to Dawn's visit on the tenth. I really wanted to see her and for us to do as much as possible while she was in Nassau, but she was suffering from ill health. Dawn was always so brave. I knew her cancer was in remission, but she had other complications; anyway, we managed to have a beautiful time together and I was sad to see her leave.

On January twenty-first, I celebrated one year of being in my little rented house at Lakeview Drive. I was serene in my new life and felt blessed that I had survived the tempest unscathed. It was all due to my faith and deep love of Jesus. I was also very grateful to my daughter and the friends who had discreetly come to my rescue.

In February I went over to Fort Lauderdale to stay with Tara and was delighted to see how happy she was. Her apartment was within walking distance of Las Olas Boulevard, and she was making contact with her old friends.

Thank goodness for Animal House, which over the years had become Baraka's second home. She was well looked after and enjoyed the change of scenery; it was run by two amazing ladies who adored animals. When I returned to collect Baraka, one of the owners had the most precious little puppy in her hands; he was only a baby. I thought Baraka had made friends with the little chap, but no, Baraka wasn't interested. The owner said she thought Baraka needed company and asked if I would like to hold the bundle of fluff. It was love at first sight. Oh, my goodness! He was seven weeks old.

I told her I would return the following day to collect and pay for my new addition to the family. He was half Shih Tzu and half Jack Russell Terrier, and was absolutely gorgeous. The following day before I returned to Animal House, I went to a baby shop and bought a playpen. I knew my little one would be safe in there where he had his newspapers and his little bed. I had to watch out for Baraka, who had a jealous streak and was not the motherly type. It was such a joy to have my little puppy and I called him Babu. I remembered as a child that sometimes a Hindu servant at one of the private clubs would call my dad Babu. It seemed fitting that my little boy should be called Sir!

As Babu grew, he wanted to play with Baraka, but Baraka didn't want to be bothered with him. I asked my lovely vet to come for dinner and help me with Baraka to accept her little brother. Eventually Babu won over Baraka's affection, and the fun they had together was most gratifying to me. I was in heaven with my Baraka and Babu.

Babu as a puppy

73

At the beginning of May, Tara came for the weekend, and apart from spending most of the time playing with Baraka and Babu, she told me the building where she was living had informed the occupants they had to vacate by a certain date, as it was being sold. Tara thought it would be the perfect opportunity, rather than rent another apartment, to look for a house instead.

As Tara was working, I decided to fly over to Fort Lauderdale and had previously arranged to meet with an estate agent, who showed me a few homes. On the Saturday of my three-day visit, I saw a delightful little house, which was only a five minute drive from Tara's alma mater. I knew immediately that was the one. I wasn't able to see Tara, as I had to leave the next morning. I left a message on her phone and told her she must see the house on Sunday with the agent. She called me later in the day and was so excited; she loved the house and would start working with the estate agent on the Monday.

Tara moved all her furniture and belongings from the apartment into her new home. On July first, she called to tell me she had been to the humane society and had a mate in the form of a nine-month-old black Labrador, and she would name her Keona, which is Hawaiian for "God's gracious gift". I travelled back and forth to Fort Lauderdale often to help Tara settle in.

Returning to Nassau, my life kept busy seeing old friends, playing golf and also entertaining at home. As Christmas was approaching, I wanted to be with Tara in Fort Lauderdale. I arranged all the necessary papers with the Ministry of Agriculture for the dogs and found a charter flight that accepted Baraka and Babu as passengers— and they didn't have to pay! We had the plane to ourselves, and my babies were amazing as they sat in their seats taking an interest in everything. I was so proud of my travelling companions.

Tara met us at the airport, and the next hurdle we had to overcome was to introduce Baraka to Keona. Keona was the sweetest and most loving dog, and she was excited to see Baraka and Babu. Of course, Babu had no problems at all, but it took a little while to coax Baraka to be friends with Keona. By the end of day, all was well, and we were one wonderfully happy family of five. We had such a lovely Christmas, and having the three dogs made it all the more special. Being in Tara's sweet home with a large garden, a swimming pool, a mango tree and lots of squirrels and birds, my heart was filled with gratitude.

I returned to Nassau with my two precious dogs. Dean continued to email me and tell me about his new life and he was in desperate need of money. He asked if I would help him through Western Union. I couldn't understand why he hadn't approached his wealthy relatives, but he promised he would make sure they would repay me. Although I sent him money on many occasions, I was not repaid, and eventually I had to tell Dean, I did not wish him to contact me anymore, nor to ask for money.

In May I heard that my sister, Vanessa, was having a rough time with her husband and was leaving him. I sent her the airfare for a ticket to Fort Lauderdale to stay with Tara for a month, and then come on to me in the hope that during the two months, she could formulate her ideas as to where her future lay. Vanessa had a good time with Tara and Keona, enjoying a daily swim in the pool and having dinner ready for Tara each evening, when she arrived back from work.

After a month Vanessa flew over to Nassau. She was in a bad state, but as I had bought her a laptop computer, she felt that by working with it she would be able to get her life back to a position where she could develop her ideas for the future. Vanessa is a very good cook, and her curries are especially delicious; so I took the opportunity to share her talents with my friends in Nassau and invited them to curry dinner parties, which we enjoyed on two different nights. Vanessa had had a relaxed and happy time in Nassau and benefited a lot from being away from life in England. She felt renewed as she returned to stay with close friends and see her son, Marc.

A few weeks later, Baraka, Babu and I went to see Tara. I left the dogs with her, while I flew to Toronto to attend the wedding of Peter and Jan's daughter. It was supposed to be a happy occasion, but on the day of the wedding, Peter was rushed to hospital, where he had to remain for a few days. Despite Jan's concern for Peter, she was determined nothing would further upset the wedding, and as she walked Stephanie down the aisle, there were many damp eyes and prayers not only for the new young couple, but also for Peter's quick recovery. The rest of the joyful wedding festivities went off without more surprises, and a super time was had by all. However, it was obvious we all missed the father of the bride and were consoled that he was going to be all right, and able to join in the rest of the fun celebrations which continued for several days.

When I returned to Fort Lauderdale, I decided to delay going to Nassau, as Hurricane Frances was approaching the Bahamas and was scheduled to travel to South Florida. I was pleased that Baraka, Babu, and I were with Tara during the storm, especially as the electricity was off for four days.

When my babes and I did return to Nassau, I had to leave them at Animal House, as I was going to join Tara in Santiago, Chile, for the wedding of Blake, the eldest son of Heinz and Becky. I met Tara at the airport in Santiago, and we had six beautiful days. The city was lovely and very interesting. Heinz and Becky had arranged for their wedding guests to be thoroughly spoilt.

As many friends had travelled to Santiago, a couple of small buses were hired to take everyone out of the city to a well-known vineyard, where we were all invited to see the process of winemaking, and this was followed by a luscious lunch with copious amounts of excellent wine. A fun dinner had been organised for the next evening when we became acquainted with the bride and her family.

The special day arrived and we attended the enchanting wedding and Nuptial Mass, which was held in an impressive old Catholic church. After the service, we returned to the Ritz Carlton Hotel to join Blake and his beautiful bride, Paula, to a sumptuous feast and dancing in the banqueting rooms. It was a memorable celebration.

Tara and I stayed on for a few days and stopped at the Veramonte Winery en route to Valparaiso, where we did a little sightseeing and had lunch overlooking the Pacific Ocean. On our last day we hired a car to take us up to see a ski-resort in the Andes; the drive through the mountains was most dramatic. We departed Santiago very grateful to Heinz and Becky for their expansive and generous hospitality and for having introduced us to the capital of Chile. Tara returned to Fort Lauderdale, but I stopped in Atlanta to spend a few days with Dawn. I was happy that Dawn seemed to be her old self again, and we spent quality time together. It was almost five years since Dawn's cancer had been in remission.

Baraka, Babu and I flew back to Fort Lauderdale to be with Tara and Keona for Christmas. We stayed for a month, during which time I had to have a cataract operation on both my eyes. Fortunately, everything went well, and when I was back in Nassau, my faithful Haitian maid, Tanie, mother of five children, told me she had finally decided to get married and invited me to the wedding. The church service was interesting and filled with lots of Haitian families dressed in their best attire. Tanie looked great and was so happy to be marrying her man, the father of her youngest daughter. I felt extremely honoured to have been invited to share her special day.

I started thinking that it didn't make sense for me to be living in a rented house in Nassau, when the dogs and I could be with Tara and Keona in Fort Lauderdale. We seemed to be spending more and more time over there. I therefore decided to pack up Lakeview Drive and move in the hope of finding a home near Tara.

Before my departure, I wanted to start proceedings for the annulment of my marriage to Dean. The Reverend Father Patrick Pinder was now the Catholic Archbishop of the Bahamas, and he kindly invited me to have dinner with him at Archbishop's house and introduced me to Father Kendrick Forbes, who was the Judicial Vicar and the priest who would help me with my annulment. It was difficult, as I had to answer many personal questions in order for my petition to proceed. It was also tough to relive many hurtful memories, but I knew I had to persevere.

In July I had a busy time packing all my belongings and furniture once again and had them shipped over to Fort Lauderdale for storage. As Tara's home was now furnished, alas, none of my furniture could be of use. The last three days in Nassau were spent with two special girl friends, who gave me a lovely farewell. Sitting in the little aeroplane on my way to Fort Lauderdale, I looked down at the shimmering aquamarine waters and felt grateful and blessed for the twenty-two years I had lived in the beautiful islands of the Bahamas.

As I wasn't a resident of the United States and was only allowed a visitor's visa, I had to plan to be away. After settling in with Tara and leaving Baraka and Babu in her care, I decided to visit Vanessa in Dorset, England, and to continue on to Sicily to spend a few weeks with my friends. I was away for six weeks and had a super visit with my sister, who now lived in the same village, Gillingham, where I lived with Auntie Elfrieda and Uncle Charles—and we even paid a visit to Wyke House, which evoked so many memories. I also had the pleasure of seeing Robert and Carmen and was their guest in their lovely home. My two weeks with my dear friends in Sicily were sublime. I treasured being with Pina and Peppino, two wonderful people, with whom I discovered exciting new experiences of that intriguing island.

Shortly after arriving back to Fort Lauderdale, Tara and I were expecting our friends from New Zealand. It had been ten years since I had heard from Petra, as she had taken umbrage to the fact that Dean hadn't wanted her to pay her annual visit to Devon House. She had found out I had moved to Fort Lauderdale, and as I was no longer with Dean, decided to make contact and pay a visit. Our meeting was a little strained at first, as she told me she thought as we had known each other for such a long time, I would put her before Dean. Anyway, we chose to make peace, and Tara and I did our best to give our Kiwi friends a happy and fun visit.

A few days after their departure, Hurricane Wilma came roaring into South Florida. It turned out to be a ferocious storm, and within a short time our wooden shutters had blown away. We thought we would lose the French doors, as now they had no protection. The wind was so strong and blew violently at the doors, but due to our tenacity by holding on to them for two and a half hours—Tara in the living room and I in the main bedroom—while Wilma raged and the doors pulsed, we prevented them from blowing in and saved the interior of the house from being destroyed.

Wilma arrived a few days before Tara's thirty-first birthday, and she was miserable. I think it was the worst birthday she has ever experienced! For eight days we had no power. The garden was a mess and the neighbourhood more of a mess, with many fallen trees. We felt blessed, however, that our house was intact and that the menacing coconut tree hadn't fallen on the roof. Some friends of ours in the neighbourhood invited us to dinner and to shower with warm water, for which we were deeply grateful. We were fortunate enough to have cold water, which was better than no water. When Wilma left, we knew we had to install permanent shutters and buy a small generator.

74

In August of 2006 it would be my old friend Hans' ninetieth birthday; I decided to fly out to Manila to help celebrate the occasion. I would then travel on to Taiwan and see my friends, Peter, who was the Taiwanese Ambassador to the Bahamas and his wife, Susanna, who were now living in Taipei.

Leaving Tara with her three charges, I flew to London and stayed with Robert and Carmen for a couple of nights, and to my surprise, they had also invited Vanessa to stay, we had a fun time all together. Robert kindly drove me to London airport to connect with my Virgin Atlantic flight to Hong Kong, as I wanted to break my journey in order that I wouldn't arrive in Manila totally jet lagged. At the duty-free shops I bought two bottles of good red wine and some other little souvenirs of London to give to my friends. I then made my way to the Virgin Atlantic lounge, where I had breakfast of smoked salmon, scrambled eggs and a glass of champagne.

On board I changed into the Virgin pajamas and settled into my welcome upper-class seat, which I had bought with reward points. As always, the Virgin Atlantic flight was wonderful and extremely comfortable.

After going through customs and immigration at Hong Kong airport, I met the chauffeur who had been sent from the Peninsula Hotel, and who would drive me there in one of their fleet of Rolls Royce cars. A lot had changed since my last visit in the 1980s, especially the airport. The Peninsula Hotel was enchanting. I was excited to be staying in the world renowned hotel where I spent the rest of the day and night in my mini suite. I hadn't realised how tired I would be, so it was extremely gratifying to be able to enjoy my comfortable accommodations and soak in the large bath, which had a small television at the end of it—luxury personified, I thought.

The following day feeling much better I made my way up to the fabulous spa where I had an appointment for a massage. After the excellent and invigorating massage with hot stones, and surrounded by tranquil music and candles, I felt renewed. I then wandered around the shopping arcades, looking at their tempting merchandise, and stopped for afternoon tea in the romantic Lobby. Sitting there beneath the neo-classical arches, listening to the muted sounds of the string orchestra while sipping my tea, my thoughts were with the ghosts of all the famous people who had been guests in that exciting venue.

In the evening I ventured up to the bar Felix with its panoramic view of Victoria harbour. I ordered a glass of champagne and looked out at the glittering scene in front of me, and my memories went back to Patrick, to the awesome time we had spent together in one of my favourite places and how I wished I was sharing those moments with my daughter.

The next morning I said good-bye to the Peninsula Hotel, and as I was departing, was given a little silver box from the management, together with some kind words, which momentarily choked me. As I thanked the lady, I told her that for many years it had been a dream of mine to stay at that fabled hotel, and was so happy that my wish had been granted. Sitting back in the Rolls while it made its way to the airport, I was pleased to have stopped in Hong Kong and felt much better for the visit. As Cathay Pacific took off for Manila, I bid farewell to Hong Kong and hoped I would return again one day.

The Cathay Pacific in-flight service was as good as I heard it would be. Manila airport seemed a little less chaotic compared to my last visit. Hans's home had not changed since I had first been there with Patrick in 1968. It was still filled with beautiful and exotic antiques from India and the Far East, but it did have more statues of the Buddha. For this visit I had been invited to stay as a house guest. I had not stayed in the house before and was rather surprised at the simplicity of the guest room, plus the fact that I had to share the bathroom across the way with a male guest of theirs. Anyway, I tried to make myself as comfortable as possible. I was happy to be with Hans and his family. In some ways it was strange to be back in such familiar surroundings with Florinda, his wife, and twin teenage daughters.

For Hans's birthday, he and Florinda gave a resplendent birthday dinner party for their influential friends, most of whom were ex-pats. The dining room table was decorated with small flower arrangements placed on an antique white tablecloth. The gold cutlery, silver wine goblets encrusted with semi-precious stones and the magnificent bone china plates were a joy to behold. Sitting in the ambient dining room surrounded by so many breathtaking antiques made for a dazzling birthday dinner.

Two days later there was the big birthday party. Over a hundred guests had been invited to the Polo Club to give greetings to Hans on his ninetieth birthday. Many diplomats and the cream of Manila society were in attendance at the big buffet luncheon. Hans was enjoying every moment of his special day, which also happened to be the birthday of his wife, Florinda. I stayed on for a couple more days, and when the day of my departure arrived, Hans insisted on accompanying me to the airport. As I hugged him good-bye, I said I would be back to celebrate his one-hundredth birthday. Hans died shortly before his ninety-first birthday a year later. I was very grateful I had been with my long-time friend and able to reminisce over our many years of friendship.

Having said good-bye to Hans, I walked through the airport to security. I had forgotten I was not allowed to carry liquids on the plane, and before I knew it, my two bottles of red wine were going to be confiscated. I had bought them at the duty free in London and wanted to share them with my friends in Taiwan. I was determined not to leave the wine in Manila! Fortunately, I had the assistance of a kind Cathay Pacific employee, who said the only way I could take them with me was to send them through as baggage. I had no room in my suitcases, which had already gone through, so my wine was packed like a parcel, complete with baggage tag.

After an excellent flight on Cathay Pacific, and arriving at the clean and efficient airport in Taipei, I wondered whether my wine had made it. I was thrilled when I saw the package proudly arrive on the carousel, together with all the suitcases. The gentle persuasion at Manila airport had worked.

My friends Peter and Susanna were at the airport to greet me. I hadn't seen them since they left Nassau. Driving from the airport, Peter said we would be making a stop at an orchid farm in order for me to choose the orchid I would like to have in my room for the duration of my stay; what a thoughtful and lovely idea. When we arrived at the orchid farm, I was speechless, I had never seen so many gorgeous colours or varieties of orchids, which made it extremely difficult to decide which one I wanted. I finally made my decision, and we were on our way to where I would be staying. Peter told me as their apartment was too small, they had reserved a room at the Shih Hsin University Club House, which was within walking distance of their block of apartments. The accommodations were perfect, and the price was very reasonable. The three of us had a simple dinner and I retired to my room.

The following morning Peter informed me we would be joining another couple I had met in Nassau at a favourite restaurant of theirs. On our way to lunch, I asked Peter if he knew of an acupuncturist, as my knees were rather painful, due to lifting my heavy luggage. I was taken around the back roads to a doctor he knew. The entrance didn't look much, but walking through the house into the room where I was to receive the acupuncture treatment, I thought of Hans, as the house was filled with antiques.

I liked the doctor, who didn't speak any English, so Peter translated. In a few minutes both my legs were covered with the smallest needles, which were twisted from time to time. I have to say it wasn't painless; I think I felt every needle and was very relieved when it was time to have them removed. In the meantime, while my needles were doing their work, several other patients arrived and their treatments caused much noise –so don't believe it when you are told that you don't feel any pain. My knees and legs felt wonderful afterwards and made all the difference to my travels.

We then drove to the Tang Kung Mongolian barbecue restaurant, which was large and filled with families, businessmen and office employees, among others. It was noisy and the aroma was wonderful. It was obviously a popular luncheon venue. Our lunch lasted almost three hours. We had numerous courses, each one more delicious than the previous. I thought I would feel heavy after eating so much, but strangely enough, I felt extremely comfortable and replete.

After our superb lunch, Peter took me to the National Museum of History. The museum had a collection of around sixty thousand artifacts, which were all beautifully displayed. The main emphasis was on the Chinese folk culture in relation to the Taiwanese. It was a lovely museum and overlooked the palace grounds. Unfortunately, it was a damp, rainy afternoon, but didn't let that deter us, as we continued on with our sightseeing through the rain hoping our umbrellas would give us a little protection.

Our next stop was at Chiang Kai-Shek's Memorial Hall, which looked rather gloomy in the cloudy, wet afternoon. The memorial of Generalissimo Chiang Kai-Shek, president of the Republic of China, was erected in 1975. I didn't really know anything about that charismatic man, but by the time I had been through the library and the museum, which had documented his life and career, I was a fan and understood the reverence the Taiwanese people had for their former president. The museum also had a few little shops, a post office and a coffee bar, where we were happy to relax, as I digested my introduction to the famous Chiang Kai-Shek.

After our exciting visit to the museums, I wanted to buy a digital camera for Tara. We drove to a Costco. I found the camera I wanted, which was reasonably priced. The only problem was the instructions were in Chinese; nevertheless, I bought it.

We all decided we were hungry and ready for dinner. Peter took us to the food court, where there was a variety of mouthwatering dishes at all the little stalls. I said to Peter I would like a glass of wine, and he told me that alcohol was not sold in the food court. As was my luck, I saw a shop from where I was sitting and a bottle in the window that looked distinctly like a wine bottle. I excused myself, and with a big grin on my face, returned with a bottle of French red and three paper cups!

Vanessa had asked me to contact two girlfriends of hers in Taipei, which I did, and arranged to meet at the Sheraton Hotel for lunch the following day—Peter, Susanna, their grandson, the two friends of Vanessa's and I enjoyed a marvelous buffet luncheon. Vanessa's friends were most interesting, and I was happy to have had the opportunity to meet them.

After lunch Peter took me to the National Palace Museum. It was an impressive building and busy with many visitors. There were over six hundred and seventy-seven thousand pieces of ancient Chinese artifacts and artworks to view. The museum was one of a kind and is the largest in the world. It contained the history from the Neolithic Age to the late Qing Dynasty. There was lots to see, but Peter directed me to the most important pieces, the famous Jadeite Cabbage, which was carved in the shape of a cabbage head with a large and small grasshopper hidden in the leaves; it was perfect. Peter had my camera and took a photo, though no photos were allowed. I was thrilled he had taken the chance. It was such an amazing museum with many treasured items.

We left the museum to meet up with Susanna and made our way to the train station. I didn't really know what had been planned for the day, but as I found out, it was going to be a long one. The train station was spotless, and purchasing a ticket was easy. As our train sped along, it was a thrill for me to see so much of the countryside. I was the only non-Taiwanese passenger, but no one took any notice of me or certainly didn't show it.

We arrived at our destination called Danshui, a popular seaside resort. The friends from Nassau were waiting to receive us, and it was good to see them again. We strolled along the promenade, with lots of stalls, lots of eateries, a McDonald's, which was crowded, and many families taking their evening stroll, or just people watching and enjoying the fresh air.

It was soon time to go for dinner and we walked up to a beautiful restaurant with a spectacular view. The River Restaurant and Café was small and perfect; we could have been sitting in a restaurant in the hills above Cannes on the French Riviera. The only difference, was the ladies room. There was no sit-down toilet but a hole in the ground. However, it was more refined than many I had met before!

After a super dinner we wandered back to the train station and I thought we were headed home, but no, we were on our way to visit the Shilin, the oldest all-night street market. The street was fairly narrow, and on either side were hundreds of little stalls selling everything and anything one would ever want. It was exciting and packed with people, emitting a carnival-like atmosphere. I had read much about the all-night markets and had to pinch myself to realise I was actually experiencing a visit. I have to admit, however, being pleased when Peter said we would be headed home.

Peter told me the following day we were going for a long car ride to the mountain village of Jiu Fen, and would leave at ten in the morning. Susanna drove and I sat beside her. Peter and their grandson were in the back. Our drive through the beautiful countryside along the excellent roads was enhanced by Peter's tales of mysterious folklore fables.

We finally arrived at the small village of Jiu Fen, which used to be the centre of gold mining and was now a famous tourist attraction, with the hills of northeast Taiwan behind it and the ocean view of the Keeling Sea below. Susanna parked the car and we entered the street that ran through most of the village, where we headed straight to a tiny restaurant for a late breakfast and early lunch, and were served the specialty of the house, meat balls in a thick soup—very different for me, but very good too.

Having left the little restaurant, we strolled along the busy, colourful alleyways. There was no space between each small shop, and each one was more enthralling than the other – I felt I was in a Taiwanese wonderland! I stopped at a cobbler's shop and watched some shoes being made; I had to buy a cool pair of red wooden clogs for Tara. Before returning to the car, we proceeded for light refreshments where we were able to look out over the spectacular panorama.

It had been another wondrous day. I was so grateful to Peter and Susanna for showing me as much of their captivating country in such a short space of time. When we arrived back, Peter said I must hurry, as we had dinner reservations at a popular Taiwanese restaurant, and then tickets to the Taipei Eye Chinese Opera and Performing Arts.

Our ethnic dinner in the bustling restaurant was delicious, after which we hurried to the theatre. The show was wonderfully entertaining. There were several scenes of young school children performing joyful folk games, which included the Tai Pin drum, Diabolo spinning and Top Twirling. The performers were very skillful and created incredible visual entertainment. There was a short intermission followed by the Joys of Peking Opera with "The Legend of Eight Celestials Crossing the Sea". I was totally immersed in the story and the elegance and beauty of the performers and performance. It was another magical evening. As I knelt to say my prayers, I felt blessed to have such great friends who had put enormous thought into giving me a memorable visit.

The following morning Susanna drove me to her beauty salon. In all my travels, I have to say that small and simple salon gave me the best wash and blow dry I have ever experienced. I was there less than half an hour, and the price was negligible, but I felt a million dollars and was told I looked pretty terrific too.

I returned to the club house to finish packing and then spent a little time with Peter in the gardens of his apartment block. He told me he had been suffering from colon cancer and had been in remission for a while, but on the whole felt pretty good. He made me think of Dawn and I wondered how she was doing. Our final meal all together was at the Skylark Café—Californian cuisine. During lunch I was beginning to feel sad that I was leaving Peter and Susanna, especially knowing about Peter's illness. Although I had only been with my friends for four days, I felt I had been with them much longer and that I was very much part of the family.

Peter and Susanna drove me to the airport. As I hugged my friends, I really hoped we would see each other again and that Peter's health would improve. While I waited in the departure lounge, I recalled all the memories of my wonderful visit and being with two special people. Peter died a few years later in California surrounded by his family. Susanna and I stay in touch and keep Peter's memory alive.

Cathay Pacific made a smooth landing at Hong Kong International Airport. The airport was huge and I was grateful to have some exercise by walking from one end to the other. I knew I had plenty of time before the departure of the Virgin Atlantic flight to London, and therefore took advantage of the comfortable lounge, which offered delicious little canapés and a good selection of fine wines.

75

My flight into London arrived early in the morning, so early that I had to wait before the Virgin Atlantic lounge opened. Once there, I was able to freshen up, have a neck and shoulder massage, and a delicious breakfast while catching up with the world news. It wasn't long before I was back on the plane headed for Miami.

Arriving at Miami Airport, I was one of the many passengers but the only Caucasian, segregated to go through immigration in a different section of the airport. It was explained to me that as I was born in Sri Lanka, I was suspect. Of what, I never did find out. Fortunately, I wasn't kept cooped up for too long and was advised by the officer who interrogated me that I should become a permanent resident, as I had informed him that my daughter was an American citizen.

Tara was at the airport to meet me and said there was the possibility of a hurricane headed our way. When we reached home, I was so excited to see Baraka, Babu and Keona, and received a joyous welcome from them. The next morning we started putting up the shutters expecting Hurricane Debby to cause a problem. However, Debby soon turned into a tropical storm and faded away.

I called Dawn to find out how she was, and she told me the cancer had returned and spread to her liver. She said she didn't have much longer and that she had her beloved cat put down—as her departure from this earth was imminent—and her cat, who was getting on in age, would never survive being with anyone else, nor did Dawn want her to be with anyone else. Dawn told me she would soon be moving into the hospice.

I wanted to fly up to be with her, but she declined my offer, so instead I thanked her for her friendship over the years and told her I loved her very much, and we sadly said good-bye. On September eighth, Dawn's son, Marc, called to say his mother had quietly slipped away. I felt crushed. I knew I would miss my friend tremendously. Ten days later, I flew to Atlanta just for the day to be at the All Saints' Episcopal Church to say my final farewell to a wonderful lady and a great friend. As I wiped my tears, I knew Dawn was where she had wanted to be for a long time.

Our friends from New Zealand informed me they would be visiting us for eight days, but as Tara was here, I said they would have to stay at a hotel, which was within walking distance from us. They only spent the nights there, and during the days were with us sunbathing by the pool and enjoying the gorgeous Florida weather.

Tara had found a job working with a couple who were in the wine business and were opening a new company. Tara loved learning about wine, and after she had been with them for a little over a year, her former boss from Santa Barbara told her that the Chesterfield Hotel in Mayfair, London, was looking for a sommelier, and on October sixteenth, Tara was offered the job. She was excited, and it was impossible for me not to be thrilled for the opportunity.

Tara was not due in London until later in November, so we had enough time for me to apply for my residency, obtain my driver's licence, familiarise myself with living full-time in the area. I would stay in the house, and together with my two babies, would take care of Keona.

We celebrated Tara's thirty-second birthday at her favourite sushi-bar with the friends she had made in Fort Lauderdale. On November twenty-second a friend of Tara's drove us to Miami, where we had lunch before taking her to the airport. Little did I realise, when saying goodbye to my daughter, that Tara would make her life in London, and in retrospect, I understood why I had left Nassau for Fort Lauderdale. As usual, Jesus had it all planned for me to give Tara the opportunity to live her new adventure.

It didn't take me long to feel totally at home in the friendly residential area where the supermarket, the church and the vet were all nearby. I wasn't bothered I had moved into a new way of life where

I knew no one, as I have always been a loner, totally happy with my own company. And of course, I had Baraka, Keona and precious little Babu, who gave me so much love; but I missed not having Tara with us for Christmas and the New Year celebrations. For my sixty-fifth birthday, I was delighted to receive my green card and became a bona fide resident of the United States.

In August of 2007, I decided to visit Tara in London, and she arranged for me to stay at the Chesterfield Hotel where she was working. The weather in London was sunny and warm, and Tara re-introduced me to London. I felt like a tourist when visiting the Oxo Tower and the London Eye. Despite new restaurants and changes, there remained places that reminded me so much of my London.

For years while I lived in London, I had always wanted to attend the open-air theatre at Regent's Park, and was lucky enough to accomplish that wish. The colourful evening was divinely entertaining and so much fun. Watching George Gershwin's "Lady be Good" on a glorious summer evening in the middle of Regent's Park was memorable.

I have been an overseas member of Annabel's private club and Harry's Bar, a member's only restaurant, for years, but living abroad, I did not have much opportunity to visit them. I therefore decided that Tara and I would go to Harry's Bar for dinner, an extravagant treat for us. We had a most delicious dinner, and added to the excitement of being in that refined restaurant was Prince Andrew, who sat opposite with a couple of friends. Seated at the next table were two gentlemen, and Tara remarked to me that she recognised the wines they were drinking, which were worth at least five hundred pounds sterling a bottle—we both also found that exciting!

I invited Vanessa to stay with us for a few days in London and organised a dinner for her and our family friends, Julia and her husband, Mike, Tania, Robert and Carmen and Gerry from Nassau, who just happened to be in London at the time. I was delighted she could be with us, together with her son, Philip Jr. Tara arranged an inviting menu with delectable wines and we all had a really enjoyable evening.

My days in London were fast coming to an end, but I wanted to see "The Last Confession" by Roger Crane with the British actor David Suchet at the Theatre Royal Haymarket. It was the story from the Vatican in 1978 when the Smiling Pope, John Paul I succeeded Pope Paul VI and quickly showed himself to be a liberal, which the Catholic Church feared. Anyway, Pope John Paul I only lasted thirty-three days before he was found dead. The play was fascinating and complex, and a true story of intrigue at the Vatican with the mystery of the death of the Pope never solved. It was a brilliant production.

Walking back to the hotel at around ten thirty at night was exhilarating; Piccadilly Circus was filled with people, and we felt safe as we walked down Piccadilly into Berkeley Square, enjoying the warm August night.

For the last evening of my visit, Tara wanted the two of us to have a special dinner at the restaurant in the Chesterfield with epicurean food and delicious wines; it was a perfect evening. I returned to Fort Lauderdale on August fourteenth, having had a wonderful time with my Tara and sad that we lived so far apart.

76

Returning home, my first commitment was to collect my babies from the vet where they were boarding. I don't know who was happier to see whom, so many hugs and kisses. During my walks with the dogs around the neighbourhood, I often saw an attractive mature lady walking her dog, and one day she spoke to me and invited me to have a drink with her. I liked her immediately and her gorgeous four-legged companion, Dandie. Alla was a widow in her late seventies. As we became friends, I learned she came from Polish/Russian parents and moved from Poland to live in Germany during the war. At the age of eighteen, she met a dashing young American GI, whom she married a year later in a Russian church and who brought her to America. I felt blessed, as Alla became a special friend and was extremely kind to show me around, helping me to become better acquainted with the area in which I lived.

In August of 2008, I flew to Nassau to celebrate my friend Gerry's seventieth birthday. I stayed for two nights at the Lyford Cay Club where Gerry's celebration party was held, and the room that had been allocated to me was room eleven, which was the same room where Patrick and I had spent our first time together at the club. How I wished he were with me.

Tara went to stay for a few days with Petra and Pam in Igrane, Croatia, and in September they came on to see me. Much to my delight, Tara came home for her birthday, and we invited a few friends for a fancy dress evening. Before Tara returned to London, our dear friends Peter and Jan were in Fort Lauderdale, and we were delighted to invite them for dinner at home with us. The hours flew by as we reminisced.

I was beginning to worry about Babu, as he had had a couple of epileptic attacks. He always came through those wagging his tail. Oh, how I loved my Babu. Dr. Thieme, our wonderful vet, gave me the grave news that Babu probably had a heart problem. There were many tests and much medication. It was important for Babu not to get excited, which was difficult, especially on our walks, as he would bark and become excited at seeing another dog. Babu was my baby; he was the most affectionate, sweet and fun-loving dog, and I don't know whether he loved me more than I loved him.

We were thrilled when Tara told us she would be able to be with us for Christmas, and the five of us had such a wonderfully happy time. Tara and I went to Mass in the morning, and the rest of the day was devoted to playing with our babies; though we did manage to put together a turkey and plum pudding.

Tara had to return to London after Christmas, and I watched television as the ball dropped in Time Square to welcome in 2009. On January ninth, I was going over to Nassau to receive a badge stating I had been a member of La Chaîne des Rôtisseurs for twenty years. I had reserved the large kennel at the vet's for my three babes. The morning of my departure to Nassau, I awoke early and had walked Keona and Baraka, and now it was Babu's turn. As we trotted along in the fresh air of the early morning, we saw a beautiful big dog being walked by his owner. I quickly guided Babu to the opposite side of the road, but Babu was excited at seeing that lovely dog. The owner and his dog walked passed and Babu fell to the ground.

My instinct told me Babu was having a heart attack. I tried to give him mouth-to-mouth resuscitation and to pump his little heart, but I knew Jesus had taken my beloved Babu. The owner of the dog happened to look back and saw us on the ground and rushed back, put his dog into his house and drove us to our vet. My adorable little Babu lay quietly on my lap, and as I cradled him, my heart was broken. I had lost my little love. He would have been six on the thirteenth; as I didn't know exactly when he was born in January, I said we would share our birthdays. I was very grateful to the kind neighbour who drove us to the vet in the hope that Babu could be resuscitated, but I knew he was already in doggy heaven.

Dr. Thieme and everyone at the animal hospital shared my sadness. I had to rush back to collect Baraka and Keona—who had seen the whole sad scene from the window—and take them to the vet's for boarding. My vet subsequently told me that for the first few days of their stay, they both seemed upset and suffered from diarrhea.

Alla drove to the executive airport as I wept quietly, she knew little Babu and shared my loss. When I arrived in Nassau, I didn't know how I was going to make the elegant evening. Tears were close. I had lost my beloved Babu. I knew I had to make a big effort to look good and to try to control my emotions. Fortunately, the champagne helped, and although my heart was heavy, I managed to survive the evening; my friends were very kind.

Returning home to Fort Lauderdale it was strange not to have Babu greet me, but the girls were excited and happy. Babu was the one who played with both Baraka and Keona, and life wasn't the same without him.

77

It had been several years since I had applied for my annulment on grounds of mental cruelty, and had almost given up hope, when I received a letter from the Archdiocese of Nassau, informing me my petition for the annulment of my marriage to Dean had been granted. I knew Dean and I, had in all good faith married because we loved each other and had fully intended to be together for the rest of our lives, but as the will of God knows no why, we both had to endure the hurt and sadness of a horrible mental illness, which tore us apart. The first few years we spent together before the illness reared its ugly head were very happy, and I shall always treasure those memories. I am most grateful to Archbishop Patrick Pinder and the Reverend Kendrick J Forbes, Judicial Vicar, who helped me during that difficult time and were able to assist in having my petition granted.

The rest of 2009 went by with life going on quietly. Tara was busy and became more involved in carving out her profession in wine; she had finally found her niche and passion. She had worked hard to pass all the exams that would qualify her to write about wines, to teach, to talk, and to introduce her website www.winepassionista.com.

On January thirteenth 2010, having left my babies with our vet, I flew on Virgin Atlantic to London to spend a week with Tara. I wanted to be with her when she received her diploma from the WSET, the Wine and Spirit Education Trust. Tara met me at the airport. I hadn't seen her in a while and noticed that my girl was now a beautiful lady. I was so proud of her. We spent my first evening sipping champagne at the Dorchester Hotel as the guest of the manager, who had asked Tara to talk about wines at a dinner for visiting South Africans. The two of us then walked to Shepherd's Market and had a cosy dinner at the delightful little Le Boudin Blanc restaurant. It was a very cold evening, but the warmth of that tiny restaurant was embracing.

The next day we enjoyed having lunch with our friends, Robert and Carmen, and in the evening Tara had tickets for the two of us to see the deliciously witty musical "Priscilla, Queen of the Desert"– and what a laugh it was, such a great show. On Saturday evening, we went to Mass at our old church in Mayfair, the Church of the Immaculate Conception, where Tara had been baptised. I was at home in that lovely church where so many memories returned to me. After Mass we walked over to the Connaught Hotel in Mount Street. Tara knew the head barman, who was pleased to see her and spoiled us with several glasses of delectable champagne.

While relishing the excellent champagne, I mentioned to Tara it was there that her father and I had our first date. I had met him in the old bar, and we dined there that night. I told her how Mother had insisted he send a car to Richmond to collect me, and while dressing for the evening, I felt like Cinderella on her way to the ball! A few years later we stayed at the Connaught Hotel for a month, before departing on our world tour. Some parts of the interior of the Connaught Hotel had changed, but the name would always remain a special memory of my Patrick.

After we left the Connaught, Tara introduced me to one of her favourite restaurants, Hush. As she was known there, we received much attention and had a sumptuous dinner. I raved about the mini Yorkshire puddings stuffed with roast beef and horseradish; just divine!

On that visit to London, I was introduced to Tara's boyfriend. Tara and Chris were flat-mates, but now were bonding as boyfriend and girlfriend. Chris, together with their other flat-mate Tania, who was Australian, joined us at the restaurant, and afterwards I treated us all to a visit to Annabel's. It was a thrill for me to have the opportunity to enjoy my old club again. We had an amusing evening with too much champagne.

The following day Vanessa, Julia, Mike, Tania Hirsch and a couple of Tara's friends joined us for curry tiffin. We ordered the aromatic curries from a nearby Indian restaurant, and the luncheon was a great success. It was good to see my sister and my old friends, but I have to admit I felt a little fragile after too much of the grape the previous night.

Monday was the day of Tara's graduation. Chris together with Tara and I took a taxi to the Guildhall. I was impressed by the imposing building and by the many people attending the graduation. The WSET ceremony was hosted by the honourary president Hugh Johnson of wine acclaim. Chris and I watched with pride as our Tara received her accolade.

We then went to dinner at a wonderful Michelin starred Chinese restaurant, Hakkasan, where we had asked Tania, Tara's Australian flat-mate, to join us, and where she encouraged me to continue to write my book. The next day I departed the cold weather in London and returned to the warmth of Fort Lauderdale and the excited welcome of Baraka and Keona.

In October, as a present to Tara for her birthday, I took the opportunity to treat us to a cruise on the "Silver Wind". I had seen the itinerary, and although had visited all the ports of call, with the exception of Alexandria, this cruise was really for Tara to experience a little of what each country had to offer; it also gave us ten days of quality time together. Our cruise, which commenced in the mesmeric city of Istanbul and started with a big celebration dinner for Tara's birthday, sailed on to the port of Kusadasi in Turkey, and to the islands of Rhodes and Cyprus and the memorable city of Haifa in Israel, where Tara was invited to tour the Carmel Winery.

The next port of call was Alexandria in Egypt, which was fascinating, but not how I had imagined it, and my thoughts returned to Dean. I have to admit I was relieved that Jesus had other plans that prevented us from moving there, despite those plans being traumatic. However, the alternative could have been disastrous for me. Tara spent a glorious day at the pyramids before we sailed for our journey's end to the port of Piraeus. We stayed a couple of days in Athens and then parted company. In a way it was like a last hurrah for me, as I knew that it was time to seclude myself and concentrate on finalising my book.

On January thirteenth of 2012, I celebrated my seventieth birthday. Tara and Chris were with me. I received greetings from my sisters and friends; it was good to hear from all of them. Tara arranged for Philip and Gerry, my friends from Nassau, to join us for a special dinner in the private wine room at the Ritz Carlton Hotel in Fort Lauderdale. I had a beautiful birthday, but couldn't help feeling I was far too young to be seventy years old! Earlier that day I checked on my birthmark; it was still there, though faded. I wondered what that meant and what the future held.

For many years I had thought about my extraordinary life and considered I should write about it, but wondered if it would be of interest to anyone else other than Tara. However, with my constant prayers, a small seed was sown. Jesus was talking to me. He made me decide that the path He had given me was worth writing about, and I humbly came to the conclusion that I should share my experiences in the hope they would bring courage to those who were suffering similar trials to the ones I had endured, and give hope to those who believe in miracles. Therefore, during my reclusive life in Fort Lauderdale with Baraka and Keona as my only companions, and with the grace and inspiration from Jesus, I was given the opportunity to open up my life and heart in order to let you into the secrets that were held by my birthmark.

The deeper sorrow carves into your being, the more joy you can contain.

Kahlil Gibran

Keona

Baraka

Tara Devon